Portraits of Battle

Studies in Canadian Military History
Series editor: Andrew Burtch, Canadian War Museum

The Canadian War Museum, Canada's national museum of military history, has a threefold mandate: to remember, to preserve, and to educate. Studies in Canadian Military History, published by UBC Press in association with the Museum, extends this mandate by presenting the best of contemporary scholarship to provide new insights into all aspects of Canadian military history, from earliest times to recent events. The work of a new generation of scholars is especially encouraged, and the books employ a variety of approaches – cultural, social, intellectual, economic, political, and comparative – to investigate gaps in the existing historiography. The books in the series feed immediately into future exhibitions, programs, and outreach efforts by the Canadian War Museum. A list of the titles in the series appears at the end of the book.

CANADIAN WAR MUSEUM
MUSÉE CANADIEN DE LA GUERRE

Portraits of Battle
Courage, Grief, and Strength in Canada's Great War

Edited by Peter Farrugia and Evan J. Habkirk

UBCPress · Vancouver · Toronto

30 29 28 27 26 25 24 23 22 21   5 4 3 2 1

Printed in Canada on FSC-certified ancient-forest-free paper
(100% post-consumer recycled) that is processed chlorine- and acid-free.

Library and Archives Canada Cataloguing in Publication

Title: Portraits of battle : courage, grief, and strength in Canada's Great War /
    edited by Peter Farrugia and Evan J. Habkirk.
Names: Farrugia, Peter, 1965- editor. | Habkirk, Evan J., 1983- editor.
Series: Studies in Canadian military history.
Description: Series statement: Studies in Canadian military history |
    Includes bibliographical references and index.
Identifiers: Canadiana (print) 20200400509 | Canadiana (ebook) 20200400541 |
    ISBN 9780774864916 (hardcover) | ISBN 9780774864923 (paperback) |
    ISBN 9780774864930 (PDF) | ISBN 9780774864947 (EPUB)
Subjects: LCSH: World War, 1914–1918—Canada.
Classification: LCC D547.C2 P67 2021 | DDC 940.4/1271—dc23

Canadä

UBC Press gratefully acknowledges the financial support for our publishing program of the Government of Canada (through the Canada Book Fund), the Canada Council for the Arts, and the British Columbia Arts Council.

This book has been published with the help of a grant from the Canadian Federation for the Humanities and Social Sciences, through the Awards to Scholarly Publications Program, using funds provided by the Social Sciences and Humanities Research Council of Canada.

Publication of this book has been financially supported by the Canadian War Museum.

Printed and bound in Canada by Friesens
Set in Helvetica Condensed and Minion by Artegraphica Design Co. Ltd.
Copy editor: Deborah Kerr
Proofreader: Alison Strobel
Indexer: Cheryl Lemmens
Cartographer: Mike Bechthold
Cover designer: Alexa Love

UBC Press
The University of British Columbia
2029 West Mall
Vancouver, BC V6T 1Z2
www.ubcpress.ca

This book is dedicated to all the courageous
men and women who served in the CEF in the Great War
and to their families who still bear the wounds
as well as the pride.

Contents

Figures and Tables

Figures

Tables

Acknowledgments

IN ANY COLLABORATIVE PROJECT of this kind, many people need to be recognized for their contributions. Matt Symes, late of the Laurier Centre for Military, Strategic and Disarmament Studies (LCMSDS), was the person who came up with the original concept for this collection and who did much of the foundational research. Additional data and documents were provided by Geoffrey Hayes and by the Great War Centenary Association, Brantford, Brant County, Six Nations. Emily Andrew, of Cornell University Press, was the first editor who supported this project and provided wise counsel. Randy Schmidt at UBC Press offered further encouragement and timely advice. Heidi Northwood, the senior executive officer at the Brantford Campus of Wilfrid Laurier University, secured funding that brought together many of the authors at the annual LCMSDS colloquium, allowing us to hear one another's work and draw connections between chapters. We were also the beneficiaries of an internal Wilfrid Laurier University grant for knowledge mobilization purposes. Sam Cronk provided valuable editing assistance at a critical juncture, and Graham Broad also did considerable work throughout the editing process. Meanwhile, contributing authors brought their wealth of knowledge to this collection and stayed with us on the long journey to completion.

Along that road, both of us have been fortunate to have wonderful companions. For Peter, Liisa and Michael provided invaluable support, knowing when to draw him out of his writing lair and when to bar the door! Evan, who was also in the process of completing a doctoral thesis while finishing this volume, could not have succeeded without the support of the family of Private Wilfred Lickers and especially his new wife, Vanessa, who allowed him time and space to work on both projects simultaneously, while reminding him to leave some energy for home life.

Portraits of Battle

Introduction

Peter Farrugia

Every soldier must know, before he goes into battle, how the little battle he is to fight fits into the larger picture, and how the success of his fighting will influence the battle as a whole.

– BERNARD LAW MONTGOMERY, *THE MEMOIRS OF FIELD-MARSHAL THE VISCOUNT MONTGOMERY OF ALAMEIN*

THIS COLLECTION BEGINS WITH a simple, if startling, fact about the Great War. Approximately 13 percent of all Canadian casualties between 1914 and 1918 were incurred on ten specific days in the conflict. To put it another way, about one in eight of the dead and wounded fell during ten battles. Of course, the mere recitation of statistics, no matter how arresting, would be of limited historical value without additional detail and context. By fusing the story of these battles with the lived experiences of some of the men and women who died in the fighting (or those who were otherwise affected by it), this volume mines a rich vein of historical material.

The aim of this collection is to bring together the life stories of a cross-section of Canadians who served in the war, including Maritimers, Westerners, Québécois, First Nations people and recent immigrants, infantrymen, officers, nurses, and airmen, those injured in body or mind, decorated veterans, and those who were court-martialled, and to fit them into the larger social and military picture, in order to understand the profound impacts that the Great War has had on Canada. In applying this approach, the book poses fundamental questions about the nature of the Great War and the ways in which it has been remembered since 1918. By accentuating the individual among larger social and military concerns, we can convey some sense, however partial, of Monty's "little battles" and what they tell us about the war itself.

There are a number of advantages to this approach. First, we can offer a glimpse, however momentary, of battle – not to satisfy some sort of voyeuristic urge but rather to communicate a sense of the confusion, fear, elation, and pain that intermingle in war. For the present-day Canadian reader, generally living in peace and comfort and spared the sensations and moral quandaries of the battlefield, this establishes important context. In addition, the focus on individuals provides a snapshot of flesh-and-blood men and women who waged war or were caught up in its currents. Given recent post-modernist suspicion about the trustworthiness of grand historical narratives, history has seen a "biographical turn" that some historians have welcomed. For example, Barbara Caine suggests,

> At a time when historians want to stress the need to encompass the many different historical narratives which could be produced at any one time, all of which are contingent on particular situations and locations, individual lives have come to appear more and more important because of the many ways in which they can illustrate how differences of wealth and power, of class and gender and of ethnicity and religion affected historical experiences and understanding. Within this framework, biography can be seen as the archetypal "contingent narrative" and the one best able to show the great importance of particular locations and circumstances and the multiple layers of historical change and experience.[1]

This biographical turn has been in evidence in both the professional and popular realms of history. During the last two decades, academic examples, such as *Paddling Her Own Canoe*, by Veronica Strong-Boag and Carole Gerson, or *Thomas Cromwell: A Life*, by Diarmaid MacCulloch, have won plaudits from peers.[2] Meanwhile, popular versions of history, from the television adaptation of Daisy Goodwin's *Victoria* and Lin-Manuel Miranda's smash Broadway hit *Hamilton* to the television adaptation of Jennifer Worth's memoirs, *Call the Midwife*, have attracted large followings.[3]

Call the Midwife is an example of collective biography. An important variation on biography, this has a long lineage that can be traced back to Plutarch. "Often built around the interlinked stories of members of a single family or small group," it allows the practitioner to avoid artificially isolating the protagonist from other figures, who can become little more than props.[4] *Portraits of Battle* contains a number of noteworthy exemplars of this type of history. Cynthia Comacchio, Sarah Glassford, and Teresa Iacobelli, in their explorations of twin brother infantrymen, nursing sisters, and court-martialled soldiers, all allow room for probing of the interactions that occurred between the people presented.

The perspective of an individual or of an intimate group can contribute to our understanding of the Great War. Nevertheless, it is important to recognize limits. None of the people who are at the centre of the following chapters are *typical.* They are meant to be *suggestive* rather than *definitive.* There was no single experience of the First World War; that immediately becomes clear upon reading the stories in this collection. It is in reflecting on points of similarity and points of contrast that a fuller and more variegated image of the impact of this conflict emerges.

In the same way, the authors' exploration of the bloodiest days for the Canadian Expeditionary Force (CEF) is not meant to suggest that these specific dates are the most significant ones between 1914 and 1918. The battles may not even be the most important ones. We should keep in mind that those who were charged with commemorating the conflict deliberated long and hard before selecting Vimy as the site of Walter Allward's impressive monument. The Battles of Second Ypres (22 April–25 May 1915) and Mont Sorrel (2–13 June 1916) – one a victory marked by the use of a new and terrible weapon, the other a catastrophic defeat – were among the engagements that were considered for the honour.[5] Some of the battles discussed in this collection are etched on national consciousness, and others rest in obscurity; this in itself offers insight into the ways in which history and memory function. And nobody would deny that the implications of some moments – far removed from the battlefield – outstripped those of many a bloody assault. Examples here include Prime Minister Robert Borden's speech in January 1916, promising to maintain a force of 500,000 men, or the Easter 1918 riots in Quebec City. The eleven encounters that have been chosen for exploration in this book serve primarily as portals into the examination of critical questions: How were technological advances integrated into operations, and how powerful and immediate was their impact? Were men in the CEF immersed in a culture of war that slowly brutalized them and made them impervious to the horror around them? What role did First Nations soldiers play in the conflict, and how did their service affect their standing in the eyes of non-Indigenous Canadians? Does the way that we choose to remember the Great War say more about contemporary Canada than it does about the conflict itself?

We have endeavoured to connect individual, battle, and theme in our chapters. In some cases, this has been easier to accomplish than others.[6] Vimy, Canada's most recognized battle, lends itself easily to a discussion of the interplay of history and memory. At Hill 70, the 107th Timber Wolf Battalion – an infantry unit half of whose soldiers were Indigenous men that was later converted into a pioneer battalion – played a significant role in the assault, which provides an excellent opportunity to consider the experiences of Indigenous soldiers during the war and upon their return home. Battles drawn from the Hundred Days – Amiens, the D-Q Line, and Bourlon Wood – offer fertile ground for the examination of themes such as the coping mechanisms of troops at the front, strategies for replacing officers due to high casualties, and the motives for and reaction to desertion among Canadian units.

In other instances, the individuals selected linked well with specific historiographic themes. Talbot Papineau's extraordinary trajectory and his preoccupation with manliness, loyalty, and duty suited a discussion of shifting gender expectations during the war. Similarly, the intense emotional bond between the Westcott twins and the enduring grief of the surviving brother, Arnold, provided the perfect platform for a treatment of mourning in the Great War. The themes that the authors have chosen to investigate are intended to fill out our picture of the war and to sharpen our image of this country during the most significant test in its young life.

IN CREATING THIS COLLECTION, the editors wanted to ensure that the individual soldiers and nurses chosen represented a cross-section of Canada socially and geographically. We also wanted the social and military history surrounding these individuals to be as strongly represented as possible. We approached this through a twofold process. First, during the initial stages of this project, we identified potential themes and dominant questions about the First World War and gathered the names of scholars whom we could approach to write on these subjects. The team then began to identify soldiers from across Canada who were connected to the ten costliest battles for the Canadian Expeditionary Force. During this process, we also discovered that Canadian nursing sisters

Table 1.1

The costliest days for the CEF in the Great War

Battle	Date	Number killed
Vimy Ridge	9 April 1917	2,398
Flers-Courcelette	15 September 1916	1,064
Hill 70	15 August 1917	976
D-Q Line	2 September 1918	956
Amiens	8 August 1918	934
Passchendaele	30 October 1917	849
Canal du Nord	27 September 1918	843
Regina Trench	8 October 1916	792
Thiepval Ridge/Mouquet Farm	26 September 1916	742
Bourlon Wood	28 September 1918	719

Note: These figures are courtesy of Geoffrey Hayes, from his presentation "Vimy by the Numbers," 28 January 2013, which was in turn based on the casualty figures at the Commonwealth War Graves Commission website. Sarah Glassford's contribution to this collection (Chapter 7) does not deal with one of the ten costliest engagements for the CEF.

had their own costliest day – 19 May 1918, when German aircraft bombed No. 1 Canadian General Hospital at Étaples. This compelled us to include that episode in our analysis, in the form of Chapter 7, by Sarah Glassford.

As we began contacting authors for the project, we found that some were unable to participate or wanted to shift their contribution to better reflect their current research. This affected the alignment of the themes we wanted to explore. Some authors wished to bring certain servicemen and -women into the project, necessitating further shifts. Although this created a predominance of Ontarians among our veterans, we were still able to include soldiers and nurses from seven of the nine provinces at the time of the Great War. These individuals are split evenly between officers and other ranks. Further, these selections continued to represent a cross-section of experiences, including those of recent immigrants, women, Indigenous people, bachelors, married men with families, working-class Canadians and individuals from prominent families, and those with differing levels of education. In addition, their battlefield experiences varied: some survived, whereas others were killed; three were court-martialled, and two were decorated for bravery. Even their ages varied, ranging from twenty to thirty-seven.

Although the adjustments described above were time consuming, they furthered the overall goal of exploring the war as a multi-faceted event that affected the experiences of Canadians, allowing us to examine many seemingly discordant themes, using a battle, personal narrative, and exploration of key historiographical debates. These chapters talk to each other, sometimes agreeing and sometimes differing. This underscores the fact that the debates we have scrutinized are ongoing and that no single experience of the war was universal. These examinations, like the war itself, can be messy and controversial, but they enabled us to provide a balanced treatment of Canadians' experiences in the First World War.

As MENTIONED ABOVE, Canada's introduction to the ferocity of the Great War came in early encounters such as Second Ypres in April–May 1915 and Mont Sorrel in June 1916. However, the moment imprinted in public consciousness when Canada was thrown into the cauldron of war remains the Somme offensive, launched on 1 July 1916. This collection begins with Graham Broad's examination of the experiences of Eddie McKay in the fledgling Royal Flying Corps around the Battle of Flers-Courcelette. The role of new technologies in the combat on the Western Front has long been of interest for scholars.[7] Broad focuses on the impact of the airplane, both as a novel piece of technology that promised to help unlock the front and as a vehicle that enabled young men like McKay to break free of class bonds. He also explores the enduring myth of "lions led by donkeys" (or as Broad puts it, "eagles led by ostriches"). This interpretation insists that the military leaders of the Allies (the donkeys) – especially Field Marshal Douglas Haig, commander of the British Expeditionary Force – were callous to the suffering of their men (the lions) and squandered lives in futile attempts to break through enemy lines.[8] Broad's analysis is at loggerheads with this view. He finds evidence that commanders used aircraft reasonably well, even if casualty rates remained high among pilots.

The airplane was but one technological innovation that had an impact on the Great War. The manner in which new developments were quickly adapted to the battlefield has been linked to the larger militarization of culture that some historians have seen as operating between 1914 and 1918. In Chapter 2, Jonathan Vance examines the war experience of Robert Buchan, from the rural Ontario community of Waterdown, and tackles the notion of war culture. This term, coined by Stéphane Audoin-Rouzeau and Annette Becker, refers to the network of beliefs, artifacts, and practices that were shaped by the war and that manifested in trends such as the appropriation of military images and names for commercial products, the development of militaristic games for children, and the tightening of military justice at the front.[9] Could the penetration of the war into all facets of life and the mounting violence on the battlefield transform citizens – especially the citizen-soldiers at the front – as some have suggested? Reminding the reader that his soldier hailed from the village of Waterdown near Hamilton, Ontario, Vance argues "it is unwise to minimize the isolation of a village, even one that was just a few miles from a major city" (page 51), Vance dismisses the notion of an all-powerful and all-permeating set of associations. He suggests that Buchan remained a small-town lad, motivated by and drawing support from his bonds with friends and family rather than any smouldering hatred of the enemy stoked by elites or some process of brutalization that was operative at the front. He concludes, "Nothing in Rob's life before 1914 suggests that he was an inherently violent man, but he seems to have assimilated well into a world of violence. He saw his friends killed, and he almost certainly killed men on the other side, and yet toward the end of it all, he insisted that he was essentially unchanged by the experience" (page 60).

As Vance is quick to note, though talk of a pervasive war culture might be exaggerated, there is no question that the experience of 1914–18 profoundly affected those who served at the front. In Chapter 3, Kyle Falcon looks at the various elements of trench life that helped soldiers cope with what they were seeing. He follows Francis Jenkins, a Scottish-born carpenter who attested in Manitoba, into the Battle of Regina Trench. Using the experience of Jenkins and other combatants, Falcon shows that the troops "developed a unique culture, one in which large, impersonal forces were acknowledged, but meaning and agency were bolstered" (page 66). He underlines the fact that the men in the firing line were not above a certain ecumenism, willing to embrace a variety of spiritual practices and beliefs that may have conflicted with their stated religious faith. Like Vance, Falcon sees a great deal of home paradoxically surviving in Flanders and France, with music, trench journals, and concert parties all playing their part in helping the men adjust to their circumstances. These were the means by which they asserted their individual agency, all the while taking out insurance policies such as charms and rabbits' feet to guard against capricious fate.

. If it was impossible for the men and women of the CEF to predict whether they would survive the war, it was equally improbable that they could predict how their exploits on the battlefield would be portrayed in years to come. The interplay of history and memory in the remembrance and commemoration of the Great War has spawned a vibrant literature.[10] In Chapter 4, my own contribution to this collection, I focus on the assault on Vimy Ridge, beginning with the role of Samuel Bothwell of the 1st Canadian Mounted Rifles and widening the scope to understand the ways in which Vimy has been deployed by various elites for their own purposes since 1917. A survey of how the battle was regarded over time reveals that the meaning of Vimy has been anything but stable and uncontested. The empty combat boots that were arranged around the Vimy monument for the 100th anniversary ceremony in 2017 act as a metaphor for the disembodied soldiers, remobilized all too often for contemporary political or commercial purposes. For its part, the life of Bothwell argues against a simple, monochromatic, and heroic interpretation of the battle in April 1917.

Chapter 5, by Evan J. Habkirk, could also be said to touch on the elusiveness of memory. It delves into what has often been labelled the forgotten engagement: the Battle of Hill 70.[11] It is fitting that Habkirk examines this particular battle, as a central theme of his work is the frequently overlooked contribution of First Nations soldiers to the CEF between 1914 and 1918. A stubborn fallacy endures among some Canadians that Indigenous communities did little to support the war. Habkirk demonstrates that, on the Six Nations of the Grand Territory at least, this was not the case. He argues that Six Nations men enlisted "as a natural extension of their traditional military support of the British Crown" (page 110).[12] He further notes the irony of the fact that Indigenous warriors were integral to Canadian success on the battlefield and yet failed to attain full humanity in the eyes of their European overseers. Focusing on federal government intrusion into the life of First Nations soldier Wilfred Lickers, Habkirk demonstrates that "surveillance and interference in the lives of Indigenous soldiers began well before they were discharged from service" (page 110). The poignant story of Lickers's personal losses, coupled with his inability to exercise full control over his affairs upon his return to Canada, makes it clear that the Great War did not have the desired emancipatory effect for First Nations people.

Ostensibly, a more striking contrast to Lickers's powerlessness could not have been found than the subject of Chapter 6, by Geoffrey Hayes, which looks at the bloody battle of Passchendaele and explores the twofold struggle of Major Talbot Papineau. Descendant of the Lower Canada radical Louis-Joseph Papineau, he became a key Quebec voice in favour of the policy of conscription,[13] which was introduced by the Borden government. Born into wealth and influence, and with dreams of a post-war career in politics, he grappled with his own choices on and off the battlefield in light of the strict gender expectations operating at this time.[14] Like Samuel Bothwell, who died at Vimy, Papineau had many reasons not to place himself in harm's way. Hayes argues that his actions – most notably his decision to return to the front lines after having served in relative comfort as a staff officer – were largely determined by prevailing gender norms, which emphasized duty, manliness, and loyalty. In the final analysis, the well-connected and politically ambitious Papineau may not have enjoyed the unencumbered agency that a cursory glance at his case might suggest.

Gender roles during the Great War are central to Chapter 7, written by Sarah Glassford.[15] She delves into the experiences of three Canadian nursing sisters who were killed in a German air raid of May 1918. This is the only chapter that does not concentrate on a specific battle. Because the nurses in the Canadian Army Medical Corps were non-combatants, they suffered comparatively few casualties; nevertheless, their wartime experiences are definitely worth examining. Glassford looks at their motivations for enlisting, the numerous gendered expectations that confronted them, and the ways in which their service was understood by others, both during the war and in the decades that followed. She contends that "acknowledging the gendered ways in which early-twentieth-century military service was perceived encourages a rereading of nursing memoirs, one that looks past the stereotypes of caring mothers and angels of mercy to recognize the labour, skill, and professional competence they demonstrate, as well as how nurses themselves understood their service" (page 169). She shows that the women whom she selected – Katherine Maud Macdonald, Margaret Lowe, and Gladys Wake – encountered the common stereotypes of the day and overcame them, kindling a spirit among themselves and their peers that would equip those who did return for the battles they would fight for equality back in Canada.

Stereotypes have also recently been challenged when it comes to the Great War's impact on faith.[16] In Chapter 8, Gordon L. Heath tells the story of Solon Albright, who went to war and died in the Battle of Amiens at the outset of the Hundred Days. Heath looks at the role that religious belief played among Canadians at the time of the First World War and also touches on the tensions that confronted a young man such as Albright, who was of German descent and who lived in Kitchener (formerly Berlin), Ontario. To what extent might ethnicity fuel or extinguish the urge to fight on behalf of Canada in the Great War? The author rightly acknowledges that the war acted as a crucible, testing individuals' identity, both in terms of ethnicity and religious observances.[17] He also points out, much like Vance in Chapter 2, that "there was no radical post-war decline in religion, but neither was there a widespread revival. People returned to life as best they could and, in many cases, sought solace in religion and religious communities" (page 192). At both the front and at home, they were forced to learn how to accommodate to the new normal, even though the war challenged many individuals' theology, most notably on the issue of the propriety of war.

Learning has proven a contentious theme in the historiography of the Great War. The theory of the "learning curve" has gained considerable support, particularly in the United Kingdom over the last twenty years.[18] This interpretive approach holds that the British High Command – far from being the callous donkeys of popular imagination – worked assiduously to implement hard-won lessons during the war. In Chapter 9, Lee Windsor examines one important way in which the Canadian Army learned its own lessons on the job. He draws on the life of New Brunswicker Roy Duplissie to emphasize the value of the emerging system of Canadian officer replacement and argues that, in the system that finally developed, "it was up to battalion and company commanders at the front to observe the performance of their soldiers and to flag the ones that had officer potential" (pages 203–4). Duplissie fully justified the faith of his superiors, fighting with courage and initiative through the Battle of the Drocourt-Quéant Line and deeper into the Hundred Days until his death on 28 September 1918. The recognition that the Canadian military developed an effective officer replacement system under considerable duress would go some way to counteracting the "lions led by donkeys" understanding of the Great War and would, instead, bolster the notion of a learning curve.

The final two contributions in this collection return us to the central fact of the Western Front between 1914 and 1918: death and its impact on both those in the midst of the carnage and those who anxiously awaited word of loved ones.[19] In Chapter 10, Cynthia Comacchio tells the story of Arnold and

Clarence Westcott, twin brothers from Seaforth, Ontario, who served with the CEF. Clarence was killed in the Battle of the Canal du Nord, but his brother survived the war. Comacchio conveys both the personal and the societal impact of loss during the conflict. On the one hand, she underlines the ways in which traditional grieving rituals were challenged as a result of the pervasiveness of death at the time. She concludes that "the Great War's unrelenting death count ... pre-empted some of the public signifiers of loss" (page 228). The enormity of the cost incurred in France and Belgium was bound to act as a catalyst for change. At the same time, grief on a more intimate level was also leading to profound consequences. The author traces the echoes of Arnold Westcott's aching loss down through the generations, painting a picture of a man who was, in many respects, seeking to justify his own survival in the wake of his brother's death.

In Chapter 11, Teresa Iacobelli also treats the impact of death. The unremitting drumbeat of suffering marked the men and women at the front. Most managed to keep going, to perform their duties with resolve if not relish. However, others could not maintain their balance and sought to escape the fighting. Iacobelli explores the phenomenon of desertion and courts martial in the CEF.[20] She examines the cases of John Wellman Campbell, George Murree, and Edward Dean, three friends from the same unit who fled the battlefield prior to the assault on Bourlon Wood, immediately after the taking of the Canal du Nord. Iacobelli notes that "in comparison to other forces, the CEF was relatively stable" (page 254); that is to say, the indiscipline that characterized some armies during the war was largely absent. However, she also remarks on the inconsistency in official response to cases of desertion. The previous disciplinary records of offenders counted for less than the current state of unit morale or the likelihood of a major attack in the near future. Thus, the stories of Campbell, Murree, and Dean illustrate the precarious balance between individual agency and chance that operated on the Western Front.

WHAT MIGHT AN EXPLORATION of the ten costliest days for the CEF in the Great War yield? Why is this approach worth taking? The cumulative impact of the chapters in this book – at once balancing personal narratives, battle accounts, and the examination of key historiographical debates – is threefold. First, by focusing on individuals – regardless of the wealth or dearth of material – the authors underline the obvious (though sometimes overlooked) fact that the war was fought by flesh-and-blood men and women. Just as Abel Herzberg could write of the Shoah in the Second World War that "there were not six million Jews murdered; there was one murder, six million times,"[21] it is equally true that knowing the sum total of killed and wounded between 1914 and 1918 does not necessarily help us to understand the meaning of the Great War. Being able to quote statistics conveys neither the enormity of the grief occasioned by these losses nor the ways in which Canadian thinking about and modes of waging war shifted in the course of the conflict. Rather, the personal is the gateway into the general, with individual veterans providing suggestive commonalities, despite their differences in age, gender, region, and a host of other markers. Who would have imagined that Talbot Papineau, the scion of a wealthy Quebec family, and Wilfred Lickers, a simple farmer from Six Nations, were both constrained by external pressures in their choices in the field? The son of German immigrants and the middle-aged family man with military honours earned in the Boer War – Solon Albright and Samuel Bothwell – both felt duty bound to enlist despite currents that could easily have dissuaded them from participating. And the twin whose brother never returned, as much as the three men who deserted when they were pushed past their limits, were indelibly marked by the trauma of the war in which they fought.

This last comparison raises a second important theme that emerges from these collected stories. The American historian Thomas Laqueur was among the first to articulate the ways in which the Great War fostered a sense of the "democracy of death."[22] Certainly, particularly as the war dragged on and the casualties mounted, some Canadians would have agreed with Erich Maria Remarque's wily veteran, Kat, who asks, "Now just why would a French blacksmith or a French shoemaker want to attack us?" and answers his own question with, "No, it is merely the rulers. I had never seen a Frenchman before I came here, and it will be just the same with the majority of Frenchmen as regards us. They weren't asked about it any more than we were."[23] Some critiques of the Great War suggested that certain sectors were profiting while others were suffering disproportionately. Still, even as ardent an anti-war campaigner as E.D. Morel of the Union of Democratic Control could write, "Death is in the very air we breathe ... Its outstretched wings beat against the mansion of the rich and the cottage of the lowly."[24]

Was this merely a literary flourish on Morel's part? The evidence would suggest otherwise. Some forty years ago, in 1977, Jay Winter tackled the myth of the "Lost Generation" and found that it was not without some validity. Whereas casualties among the elites represented a fraction of those suffered by the working class in sheer numbers, a different story emerged when it came to percentages, leading Winter to conclude that "the demographic consequences of male mortality during the Great War varied by class. The most severely depleted social groups were the most privileged."[25]

Certainly, this imbalance seems to have operated in the industrial hub of Brantford, Ontario. There, the Cockshutt family – which had established a leading farm implements manufacturing company in 1877 and which continued to have a profound effect on economic, political, social, and cultural matters in the city – saw five of its privileged sons serve overseas. Of them, Harvey Watt Cockshutt, only son of the late founder of the Cockshutt Plow Company, died in the debacle at Mont Sorrel in June 1916.[26] Similarly, the future Group of Seven painter, Lawren Harris, and his younger brother Howard – born into another influential manufacturing family – both volunteered for combat. After being deemed medically unfit for overseas action, Lawren worked at Camp Borden and later Hart House as a musketry instructor. Howard enlisted in the British Expeditionary Force and served with the 3rd Battalion Essex Regiment, where he earned a Military Cross before being killed in action on 22 February 1918.[27] If the sons of two wealthy families in one of Canada's most productive industrial towns were vulnerable, who was safe?[28]

Many of the privileged ranks, who might reasonably have escaped death in earlier conflicts, perished in the Great War. There was not only a democratization of suffering but also a democratization of recognition. This is clearly demonstrated in the insistence of Fabian Ware of the Imperial (later Commonwealth) War Graves Commission on uniformity of gravesites and prohibition of distinction by rank.[29] So, too, do the many monuments that record the names of the local dead, major next to private, lawyer beside farrier, old stock English teen next to middle-aged Hungarian immigrant. Finally, there was a lively discussion throughout the empire about the relative merits of artistic versus utilitarian monuments, with populations in some locales insisting that memorials should serve a useful contemporary purpose for the common people.[30] Thus, a thirty-seven-year-old Brantford dentist named Panayoty Percy Ballachey, who had ten years' experience on the Brantford School Board and who was killed in action near Ypres, was recognized by having a local elementary school named in his honour.[31]

Despite all of this, it is equally important to remember that democratization had limits. The faithful service of those who belonged to the "other ranks" was not universally rewarded with democratic reform upon their return. Likewise, the women who served so capably in Europe were largely expected to revert to their pre-war roles in Canadian society, and the First Nations men who fought in the CEF saw, if anything, further government intrusion into their lives after the conflict ended.[32] In this, they were much like the African Americans who served with distinction in the American Army.[33] Nevertheless, the experience was formative for many Canadians. This is captured movingly in "My Company," a poem by Herbert Read:

You became
In many acts and quiet observances
A body and soul, entire.

I cannot tell
What time your life became mine:
Perhaps when one summer night
We halted on the roadside
In the starlight only,
And you sang your sad home-songs,
Dirges which I standing outside you
Coldly condemned.

Perhaps, one night, descending cold,
When rum was mighty acceptable,
And my doling gave birth to sensual gratitude.

And then our fights: we've fought together
Compact, unanimous;
And I have felt the pride of leadership.[34]

Labourers, women, First Nations people, and visible minorities all bled the same way. They laughed, cried, and died just like those who were perceived as their superiors. And that recognition was pregnant with the possibility of change.

Finally, these portraits of men and women who lived through (and, in many cases) died during the ten costliest days for the CEF help to present a more nuanced picture of Canada in wartime. The notion of "costliest battles" can be extended (metaphorically) well beyond the cessation of hostilities into our own era. All too often, the Great War has been refought in the pages of magazines, newspapers, and learned journals. For some, it was an amalgam of mud, blood, and ineptitude.[35] It was irredeemable, and only armchair generals and nationalists would dare seek to resuscitate notions of honour and glory.[36] For others, this response epitomized precisely the sort of left liberal bias that has ruined the field of Canadian history. This position was famously articulated by J.L. Granatstein in his bestseller *Who Killed Canadian History?* Granatstein summed up his argument thus:

My point is, or should be, simple: history happened. The object is not to undo it, distort it, or to make it fit our present political attitudes. The object of history, which each generation properly interprets anew, is to understand what happened and why. A multicultural Canada can and should look at its past with fresh eyes.

It should, for example, study how the Ukrainians came to Canada, how they were treated, how they lived, sometimes suffered, ultimately prospered, and became Canadians. What historians should not do is to *recreate history to make it serve present purposes.* They should not obscure or reshape events to make them fit political agendas.[37]

Whatever the objections to Granatstein's larger thesis – and there have been many – we must, at least, take seriously the charge that we have often reinterpreted the First World War through the lens of the present and even, sometimes, with specific contemporary agendas, whether political, cultural, or commercial, in mind.[38]

A more nuanced approach would allow us to integrate seemingly discordant themes, to bring together ostensibly contradictory facts. Undeniably, the Western Front between 1914 and 1918 was replete with horrific scenes, with shattered bodies, chest-deep mud, and desecrated landscapes. But it was also home to acts of bravery, bonds of camaraderie, and even, on occasion, revelry and joy. The women who enlisted may have been infuriated when they were expected to return to their subordinate position in Canadian society. However, their experiences had confirmed their belief in their abilities and opened the eyes of many others who had doubted their qualities. Returning Indigenous soldiers like Wilfred Lickers were no doubt frustrated by the persistence of paternalism that marked settler-Indigenous relations in Canada. But the knowledge of the strength of their Great War contribution, coupled with the passion aroused by continual injustice, fuelled the efforts of people such as Frederick Loft (who founded the League of Indians of Canada, forerunner of today's Assembly of First Nations) or Levi General (who attempted to address the League of Nations regarding Canadian mistreatment of First Nations people).[39] Their activism helped to launch a new period in the long fight for First Nations rights that persists to this day.

A similarly lengthy struggle continues over the meaning of the Great War. What were its cascading effects on Canadians at the front and back home? How has it been remembered and commemorated? Have we flattened out the narrative in an effort to simplify its significance or to deploy it for contemporary ends? The contributors to this volume asked themselves these questions as they applied the novel approach favoured here – bringing together biography, battle accounts, and historiographical discussion. This new approach enables us to work from the personal to the general, to contextualize the losses that made these moments in the Great War so costly, and to bring a fresh perspective to some of the key historiographical issues that have long been controversial in the study of the First World War in Canada.

Notes

1 Barbara Caine, *Biography and History*, 2nd ed. (London: Red Globe Press, 2019), 2.
2 Veronica Strong-Boag and Carole Gerson, *Paddling Her Own Canoe: The Times and Texts of E. Pauline Johnson (Tekahionwake)* (Toronto: University of Toronto Press, 2000); Diarmaid MacCulloch, *Thomas Cromwell: A Life* (London: Allen Lane, 2018).
3 The debut of ITV's *Victoria* was viewed by an estimated 5.4 million people. BBC Reel, "ITV's Victoria Reigns over BBC's Are You Being Served? and Porridge Revivals," *BBC News*, 5 September 2016, https://www.bbc.com/news/entertainment-arts-37213042. A December 2018 article announcing that Lin-Manuel Miranda and three key collaborators had been awarded Kennedy Center honours reminded readers that the play *Hamilton* had won several Tony Awards in 2016 for "Best Musical," "Best Score," and "Best Choreography," and added that its creator had received the 2016 Pulitzer Prize for drama as well. Gwen Aviles, "Lin Manuel Miranda, Hamilton Creators Awarded First-of-Its-Kind Kennedy Center Honor," *NBC News*, 3 December 2018, https://www.nbcnews.com/news/latino/lin-manuel-miranda-hamilton-creators-awarded-first-its-kind-kennedy-n943171. The February 2012 launch of the BBC drama *Call the Midwife* attracted a viewership of 11.4 million people, helping make it the "highest-rated BBC new drama launch on record." PBS, "BBC Worldwide and PBS Sign Deal to Bring Critically Acclaimed 'Call the Midwife' to the US," Press release, 14 May 2012, https://www.pbs.org/about/blogs/news/bbc-worldwide-and-pbs-sign-deal-to-bring-critically-acclaimed-call-the-midwife-to-the-us/.
4 Jeremy Popkin, "Review of *Biography and History*," *Biography* 34, 2 (2011): 331.
5 John Pierce, "Constructing Memory: The Vimy Memorial," *Canadian Military History* 1, 1 (1992): 5.
6 Inevitably in a collection of this kind, scholars whom we originally approached were not always able to participate. Themes sometimes shifted in alignment with the research interests and expertise of contributors.
7 See, for example, Guy Hartcup, *The War of Invention: Scientific Developments, 1914–1918* (London: Brassey's Defense, 1988).
8 This theory was first articulated in Alan Clark, *The Donkeys* (London: Hutchinson, 1961). A strong overview of the theory's continued relevance is provided in Dan Todman, *The Great War: Myth and Memory* (London: Continuum, 2005), 199–203.
9 Stéphane Audoin-Rouzeau, *Men at War, 1914–1918: National Sentiment and Trench Journalism in France during the First World War* (Washington, DC: Berg, 1995), 164. For an early foundational work on this theme, see Stéphane Audoin-Rouzeau and Annette Becker, *14–18: Understanding the Great War*, trans. C. Temerson (New York: Hill and Wang, 2002). For a work bringing together younger and more established scholars, see Pierre Purseigle, ed., *Warfare and Belligerence: Perspectives in First World War Studies* (Boston: Brill, 2005). For an excellent overview of the debate surrounding "war culture," see Leonard V. Smith, "The 'Culture de guerre' and French Historiography of the Great War of 1914–1918," *History Compass* 5, 6 (2007): 1967–79.
10 The discussion begins with Paul Fussell, *The Great War and Modern Memory* (New York: Oxford University Press, 1975), and continues with Jay Winter, *Sites of Memory, Sites of Mourning: The Great War in European Cultural History* (New York: Cambridge University Press, 1996), and Todman, *The Great War*.
11 An excellent recent volume on this engagement makes the link to forgetting explicit. See Douglas E. Delaney and Serge Marc Durflinger, eds., *Capturing Hill 70: Canada's Forgotten Battle of the First World War* (Vancouver: UBC Press, 2016).
12 Here, Habkirk cites Janice Summerby, *Native Soldiers – Foreign Battlefields* (Ottawa: Veterans Affairs Canada, 2005), 8. It is critical to understand that First Nations communities

saw themselves and Britain as allied nations, equal in dignity and rights. There was no conception of a ward-protector relationship.

13 Papineau's heightened notoriety was achieved largely as a result of his conversation with Henri Bourassa on the issue of Quebec's contribution to the war effort. Although this is not the main focus of his chapter, Hayes does provide insight into it. An early study of conscription was J.L. Granatstein's *Broken Promises*, which was reprinted in 2016 with a revised analysis of the question. J.L. Granatstein, *Broken Promises: A History of Conscription in Canada* (Oakville, ON: Rock's Mills Press, 2016). For the mechanics of conscription, see Richard Holt, *Filling the Ranks: Manpower in the Canadian Expeditionary Force, 1914–1918* (Montreal and Kingston: McGill-Queen's University Press, 2017). For an important reassessment of the impact of conscription on Canada's effectiveness, see Patrick Dennis, *Reluctant Warriors: Canadian Conscripts and the Great War* (Vancouver: UBC Press, 2017).

14 Masculinity and the war is a relatively new area of historical interest. Important texts include Mike O'Brien, "Manhood and the Militia Myth: Masculinity, Class, and Militarism in Ontario, 1902–1914," *Labour/Le travail* 42 (Fall 1998): 115–41; Mark Moss, *Manliness and Militarism: Educating Young Boys in Ontario for War* (Don Mills: Oxford University Press, 2001); Jessica Meyer, *Men of War: Masculinity and the First World War in Britain* (Basingstoke, UK: Palgrave Macmillan, 2009); Allison Fell, "Gendering the War Story," *Journal of War and Culture Studies* 1, 1 (August 2007): 53–58; and John Horne, "Masculinity in Politics and War in the Age of Nation-States and World Wars, 1850–1950," in *Masculinities in Politics and War: Gendering Modern History,* ed. Stefan Dudink, Karen Hagemann, and John Tosh (New York: Manchester University Press, 2004), 22–40.

15 A strong overview of issues regarding women in the Great War is provided by Susan R. Grayzel and Tammy Proctor, eds., *Gender and the Great War* (New York: Oxford University Press, 2017). An indispensable volume for the Canadian perspective is Sarah Glassford and Amy Shaw, eds., *A Sisterhood of Suffering and Service: Women and Girls of Canada and Newfoundland during the First World War* (Vancouver: UBC Press, 2012).

16 For this subject, see Michael Snape and Edward Madigan, *The Clergy in Khaki: New Perspectives on British Army Chaplaincy in the First World War* (Burlington, VT: Ashgate, 2013); Jonathan H. Ebel, *Faith in the Fight: Religion and the American Soldier in the Great War* (Princeton: Princeton University Press, 2010); Jonathan F. Vance, *Death So Noble: Memory, Meaning, and the First World War* (Vancouver: UBC Press, 1997); Duff Crerar, *Padres in No Man's Land: Canadian Chaplains and the Great War,* 2nd ed. (Montreal and Kingston: McGill-Queen's University Press, 2014); and Gordon L. Heath, ed., *Canadian Churches and the First World War* (Eugene: Pickwick, 2014).

17 Recent scholarship has made it clear that reflection, experimentation, and re-evaluation in the spiritual realm were definitely operative at this time. For example, Kyle Falcon demonstrates that, in the wider British context, acts of syncretism that grafted superstition or belief in the supernatural onto orthodox Christianity were commonplace. See Kyle Falcon, "The Ghost Story of the Great War: Spiritualism, Psychical Research and the British War Experience, 1914–1939" (PhD diss., Wilfrid Laurier University, 2018).

18 Countless treatises have been written on this subject. Among the best are Gary Sheffield, *Forgotten Victory – The First World War: Myths and Realities* (London: Review, 2002); Geoffrey Jukes, Peter Simkins, and Michael Hickey, *The First World War* (New York: Routledge, 2003); and I.F.W. Beckett, Timothy Bowman, and Mark Connelly, *The British Army and the First World War* (Cambridge: Cambridge University Press, 2017).

19 For death and bereavement in the Great War, see David Cannadine, "War and Death, Grief and Mourning in Modern Britain," in *Mirrors of Mortality: Studies in the Social History of Death,* ed. Joachim Whaley (New York: St. Martin's Press, 1981), 187–242; Adrian Gregory, *The Last Great War: British Society and the First World War* (New York: Cambridge

University Press, 2008); Pat Jalland, *Death in War and Peace: A History of Loss and Grief in England, 1914–1970* (Oxford: Oxford University Press, 2010); and Winter, *Sites of Memory, Sites of Mourning.*

20 For the British situation, see Cathryn Corns and John Hughes-Wilson, *Blindfolded and Alone: British Military Executions in the Great War* (London: Cassell, 2001). For the Canadian case, see Teresa Iacobelli, *Death or Deliverance: Canadian Courts Martial in the Great War* (Vancouver: UBC Press, 2013).

21 Abel Herzberg, quoted in "The Holocaust: Crimes, Heroes and Villains," http://www. auschwitz.dk/. This sentiment underpins the remark allegedly made by Josef Stalin to US ambassador Averell Harriman, to the effect that "the death of one man is a tragedy. The death of millions is a statistic."

22 Thomas W. Laqueur, "Memory and Naming in the Great War," in *Commemorations: The Politics of National Identity*, ed. John R. Gillis (Princeton: Princeton University Press, 1994), 151.

23 Erich Maria Remarque, *All Quiet on the Western Front*, trans. A.W. Wheen (New York: Random House, 2013), 151.

24 E.D. Morel, *Truth and the War* (London: National Labour Press, 1916), 114. Formed in 1914, the Union of Democratic Control was tinged with isolationism. Between 1914 and 1924, it was one of the most authoritative anti-war voices in Britain, largely as a result of its influence among unions. Martin Ceadel, *Pacifism in Britain, 1914–1945: The Defining of a Faith* (Oxford: Clarendon Press, 1980), 319.

25 J.M. Winter, "Britain's 'Lost Generation' of the First World War," *Population Studies* 31, 3 (November 1977): 465.

26 The other four sons included Captain C. Gordon Cockshutt (son of Frank Cockshutt), as well as Lieutenant Eric Morton Cockshutt, Captain George Turner Cockshutt, and Lieutenant William Ashton Cockshutt (all sons of William F. Cockshutt). These soldiers are among the more than five thousand individuals from Brantford, Brant County, and Six Nations who are chronicled on the website of the Great War Centenary Association at http://www.doingourbit.ca.

27 "Lawren and Howard Harris," Great War Centenary Association, https://doingourbit.ca/ blog/9494.

28 Kyle Falcon attributes the rise of spiritualism in part to the dramatic casualty numbers, which were especially bad for junior officers, who were drawn from the higher ranks of society. See Falcon, "The Ghost Story," especially 19–21.

29 "About Us," Commonwealth War Graves Commission, https://www.cwgc.org/about-us. A 1918 report to the Imperial War Graves Commission by Lieutenant-Colonel Sir Frederic Kenyon, Director of the British Museum laid out many of the principles that were to inform the process of interment (see Frederic Kenyon, *War Graves: How the Cemeteries Abroad Will Be Designed* (London: His Majesty's Stationery Office, 1918), 8, which is available through a link at the Commonwealth War Graves Commission webpage above).

30 Nowhere was this more apparent than in Australia. See K.S. Inglis, *Sacred Places: War Memorials in the Australian Landscape*, 3rd ed. (Melbourne: Melbourne University Press, 2008), 131–38.

31 "Panayoty Percy Ballachey," Great War Centenary Association, https://doingourbit.ca/ profile/panayoty-ballachey.

32 This was most clearly evident in October 1924, when elections were ordered by the federal government to replace the deposed hereditary council of Six Nations. See Tom Hill and Joanna Bedard, *Council Fire: A Resource Guide* (Brantford: Woodland Cultural Centre, 1989), 25–26; E. Brian Titley, *A Narrow Vision: Duncan Campbell Scott and the Administration of Indian Affairs in Canada* (Vancouver: UBC Press, 1986), 126; and Susan M.

Hill, *The Clay We Are Made Of: Haudenosaunee Land Tenure of the Grand River* (Winnipeg: University of Manitoba Press, 2017), 234–36.

33 See, for example, Arthur E. Barbeau, Bernard C. Nalty, and Florette Henri, *The Unknown Soldiers: African-American Troops in World War I* (Philadelphia: Temple University Press, 1974).

34 Herbert Read, "My Company," available at https://allpoetry.com/My-Company.

35 Todman, *The Great War,* especially xi–xii, where the dominant myth of the war as futile is laid out in detail.

36 This is in large measure the approach taken by Ian McKay and Jamie Swift in *The Vimy Trap: Or, How We Learned to Stop Worrying and Love the Great War* (Toronto: Between the Lines, 2016).

37 J.L. Granatstein, *Who Killed Canadian History?* (Toronto: HarperCollins, 1998), 105 (emphasis added). Granatstein's statement is particularly relevant in view of the contemporary purposes for which the war was mobilized during the centenary commemorations, nowhere more than in the 100th anniversary of the Battle of Vimy Ridge.

38 For responses to Granatstein, see, for example, Ken Osborne, "Who Killed Canadian History?" *Canadian Historical Review* 80, 1 (March 1999): 114–18; and Veronica Strong-Boag, "Who Killed Canadian History?" *Historical Studies in Education* 11, 2 (October 1999): 283–85.

39 For Loft, see Timothy C. Winegard, *For King and Kanata: Canadian Indians and the First World War* (Winnipeg: University of Manitoba Press, 2012), 164; and Peter Kulchyski, "'A Considerable Unrest': F.O. Loft and the League of Indians," *Native Studies Review* 4, 1–2 (1988): 95–117. For General, see Laurence Hauptman, *Seven Generations of Iroquois Leadership: The Six Nations since 1800* (Syracuse: Syracuse University Press, 2008), 137–38; and Grace Li Xiu Woo, "Canada's Forgotten Founders: The Modern Significance of the Haudenosaunee (Iroquois) Application for Membership in the League of Nations," *Law, Social Justice and Global Development Journal* 1 (2003), https://warwick.ac.uk/fac/soc/law/elj/lgd/2003_1/woo/.

1

The View from Above: A Canadian Pilot in the Battle of Flers-Courcelette

Graham Broad

WHEN THE FIRST WORLD WAR erupted in August 1914, the airplane was still an experimental technology, not yet eleven years old. This is the essential fact about airpower in the war, one that must underpin any assessment of its role in that conflict. But apart from the official histories, including Syd Wise's superb *Canadian Airmen and the First World War*,[1] literature in the field of First World War aviation until very recently has been dominated by memoirs (some of dubious veracity and authorship), biographies of aces, and popular histories whose authors have often succumbed to the irresistible temptation of hindsight.

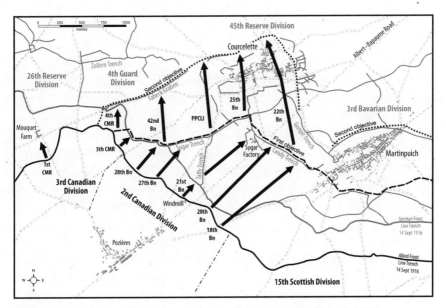

Figure 1.1 The Battle of Flers-Courcelette, 15 September 1916. | Map by Mike Bechthold.

Many of these works are highly sensationalist, written as if to appall readers with accounts of slipshod flight training, the brief, frenetic lives of pilots, and their gruesome, fiery deaths. Senior British military commanders are lambasted for their timidity in failing to recognize airpower's potential sooner, for their ham-fisted use of it when they finally did, and for their bloody-minded offensive tactics and cold-hearted refusal to issue parachutes.[2] These claims and others like them constitute the air service's equivalent of the "lions led by donkeys" myth, wherein the resolute rank-and-file lions of the British Army were hurled to their deaths in one futile trench battle after another by the incompetent and reactionary donkeys of the officer class.[3] I have ventured to call the air war's parallel myth "eagles led by ostriches," and though it has not yet been subjected to the full weight of scholarly analysis, it might most charitably be described as an incomplete and frequently inaccurate assessment of a complex topic. Some of the oft-repeated claims about the British air services – that half of pilots were killed in training, for example – are simply false.[4] Others are misunderstandings and exaggerations resulting from a failure to appreciate the novelty of airpower in August 1914.

The Royal Flying Corps (RFC), comprising a "military" (army) wing, a naval wing, a flight school, and an aircraft factory, was established in April 1912, barely two years before the war began.[5] This was a trifling four years after the first flight of an airplane in the United Kingdom and just under three since Louis Blériot became the first pilot to cross the English Channel. When the British Expeditionary Force (BEF) embarked for France in late August 1914, it was accompanied by some sixty airplanes of the RFC, making the same perilous flight. Even to one contemporary observer, the early RFC's French-built Maurice Farman machines looked like "an assemblage of bird cages."[6] Their top speeds were comparable to what a modern racing bicycle might achieve on a steep downward slope. Pilots sat in open cockpits, without oxygen equipment or parachutes, navigating by rudimentary instruments or dead reckoning. None of the planes were armed. In 1914, only a handful of pilots had ever fired a gun or dropped a bomb from the air. Aerial photography, which rapidly became the RFC's raison d'être, remained an immense technical challenge.[7] Interpreting reconnaissance photographs posed tremendous challenges of its own. Even certain elementary principles of aeronautics remained poorly understood, such as the physics of the spin and how – or even whether – pilots could recover from one.[8] Historians have debated the extent to which the British and dominion armies ascended a "learning curve" during the war, but where the air war is concerned the picture seems unequivocal. In August 1914, there was simply no precedent for the large-scale deployment of military aviation. Despite the existence of the RFC's promising pre-war *Training Manual*, nearly everything about the practical use of the airplane in wartime had to be learned through a dangerous process of trial and error.[9]

Given the persistence of the lions and donkeys myth throughout the recent centennial commemoration of the war, it seems likely that the "eagles led by ostriches" trope will prove equally stubborn. Nonetheless, it is my purpose in this chapter to challenge some widely held myths regarding the RFC while considering its role in the Battle of Flers-Courcelette (15–22 September 1916), in which the Canadian Corps debuted on the Somme battlefield. The focal point of my discussion will be the career of a single pilot, Alfred Edwin "Eddie" McKay, a Canadian who served with No. 24 Squadron, RFC, over the Somme and about whom I have previously written.[10] McKay never achieved the fame or reputation of the leading aces, but it is for precisely this reason that his career is more representative of the average pilot's.[11] He left no diary and few letters; moreover, RFC records have suffered through misadventure and archival malpractice over the years, with one author estimating that 90 percent of them are now lost.[12] Nonetheless, the almost miraculous survival of McKay's personal logbook and the squadron's complete record book, in addition to the availability of RFC war diaries from 1916, gives us a view from above as the Canadian Corps suffered one of its bloodiest days of the war, 15 September 1916.[13]

Born two days after Christmas in 1892, Eddie McKay grew up in Harrington, Ontario, a tiny farm community in the province's southwest. In his early teens, McKay moved to nearby London, where he emerged as a prominent local athlete, dominant in every sport he played, especially rugby and hockey. In August 1914, just as the war broke out, he enrolled as a student in the faculty of arts at Western University, then a fledgling institution of about two hundred students in London.[14] His decision to go to school rather than enlist is an important reminder that, for many Canadians, the war seemed somewhat remote in August 1914, and that great numbers of young Canadian-born men did not rush to sign up. Nonetheless, McKay declared an interest in serving as a pilot if the war lasted long enough.[15] This was no meagre ambition. Canada had no air service of its own, and most Canadians had never seen a plane, let alone flown in one. Those who wanted to be military pilots were typically advised to join the Canadian Expeditionary Force (CEF) and then apply for a transfer to the RFC once overseas, but there was no guarantee that a transfer would be approved. In early 1915, the RFC and Royal Naval Air Service established tiny recruiting missions in Canada, but the officers who commanded them established a set of requirements, two of which disqualified many candidates: a recruit had to be both an officer in some branch of the Canadian military and a licensed aviator.[16]

These two stipulations, which were dropped as large-scale pilot training began in Canada during late 1916, were partly a reflection of the cultural and class biases of British recruiters. With rare exceptions, British pilots were officers, and officers were expected to be gentlemen, albeit, in the specific case of pilots, gentlemen with certain permissible eccentricities. They were, moreover, expected to be glowing exemplars of the sort of "strong, physically able, loyal, morally upright, and dutiful" manhood whom Sarah Glassford describes in Chapter 7 of this volume (page 162). Propaganda may have styled the officers of the early RFC as "knights of the air," but they preferred to think of themselves as a more modern equivalent: flying "cavalrymen and fox-hunting country gentlemen," as Edward Bujak put it in a recent cultural study of the RFC.[17] British recruiters apparently hoped that the dual requirement of an officer's commission and the financial wherewithal to pursue a pilot's licence might deter colonial riff-raff from enlisting. Captain C.J. Burke, who led British recruiting efforts in Canada in late 1915 and early 1916, boasted in one letter to his superiors that he had "saved" them from a "farm labourer" and a man who "ran a newspaper stand in Regina"![18] In the same way, as Evan J. Habkirk and Sarah Glassford illustrate in Chapters 5 and 7, stereotypes about Indigenous peoples and women influenced the experiences of First Nations soldiers and nursing sisters in the Great War.

Though rooted in class consciousness, the requirements for admission into the RFC also reflected the pragmatic need to recruit men who already possessed the necessary knowledge and skills to become both a soldier and an aviator, lest the RFC go to the expense of paying for the crossing of Canadians who were liable to wash out of military flight training. McKay was undeterred by these barriers. He was a farmer's son but, with a year of university and respectable grades, highly educated by the standards of his day. Unwilling to navigate the shoals of transferring from the CEF, McKay took a commission in the 33rd Huron Regiment, Canadian militia, shortly after completing his final exams at Western in May 1915.[19] The more challenging requirement was to earn a civilian aviator's certificate. These were overseen by the Fédération Aéronautique Internationale (FAI) and its affiliate branches in various countries, including the Aero Club of America. The cost of flight training was exorbitant, typically $500. This was the better part of a year's wages for a common labourer, all for a brief course involving perhaps four or five hours of actual flying. To ease the burden, the RFC offered a stipend of £75, or $375, but only after the licence was secured, meaning that the money would have to be raised in the first place.[20] There was, moreover, only one flight school in Canada: the fledgling Curtiss School of Aviation at Long Branch, near Toronto. In the summer of 1915, the school was overwhelmed by demand and by rainy weather that had turned its airfield into a bog. It graduated only a handful of pilots during that year.[21] McKay therefore chose to pursue his training at the Wright School of Aviation, located just outside

Dayton, Ohio. Not only did the name "Wright" still carry a certain cachet, but the surviving Wright brother, Orville, had shrewdly cut his prices in half that year, anticipating a flood of Canadian applicants.[22]

McKay arrived in Dayton, with his tuition and money to spare, on Halloween, 1915. He may have been surprised to discover that more than two dozen other Canadians had preceded him and that only one Wright Flyer was operational. The other had been damaged in a failed FAI test flown by a fellow student, Roy Brown, who would later be credited – probably erroneously – with downing Manfred von Richthofen, the German ace known as the Red Baron.[23] With the fall weather turning rainy and cold, flying days were few and far between, and in December the school moved to its winter campus in Augusta, Georgia. The promised eight- to ten-day course of instruction ended up taking twelve weeks. Finally, on 27 January 1916, McKay took his FAI test: a series of figure eights, two "distance" flights of about three kilometres, and an "altitude" test in which the pilot had to reach 100 metres without touching down.[24] McKay passed, receiving Aero Club of America certificate 401. The certificates were numbered sequentially, meaning that he was almost certainly among the first hundred Canadians to learn to fly.[25] With a year of university, an officer's commission in the Canadian militia, and a pilot's licence, he had proven himself worthy, at the very least, of securing the status of a "temporary" gentleman. Two weeks later, he was seconded to the RFC as a probationary second lieutenant and ordered to Halifax to embark for England.[26]

Obviously, McKay's flight instruction to date constituted no more than a very rudimentary introduction to piloting, and he, like most FAI-certified applicants to the RFC, required a great deal more training. His RFC training commenced in mid-March 1916, with No. 3 Reserve Squadron at Shoreham.[27] Over the next three months, he rotated through four squadrons – two reserve and two service squadrons, working up for deployment to France – as he progressed through the syllabus of instruction. RFC pilot training has not enjoyed a good reputation, with one historian referring to it as "culpable, if not criminal negligence."[28] But we must be wary of hindsight bias and also of pilots' own tendencies to engage in sensationalist storytelling in their memoirs. There is every indication that the training authorities made continual efforts to improve the quality of instruction, based on feedback from the front. As early as December 1915, the RFC had opened the School of Military Aeronautics, a ground school for men without previous flight training, located at Reading University. A second school opened at Oxford in July 1916. Contrary to the assertion that RFC trainees received no instruction in such matters, the course at Reading taught theory of flight and navigation, as well as aircraft and engine maintenance, wireless telegraphy for observers, and so forth.[29]

Undeniably, the rapid expansion of the RFC put enormous pressure on the training establishment, which struggled to keep up with demands from the front. In particular, there was a notable shortage of qualified instructors, who tended to be pilots rotated home from France – experienced aviators but not necessarily good teachers. So, though rationalizing the training system and applying uniform standards was challenging, it is not true that the system lacked a syllabus or tests. And though minor accidents were routine (McKay twice tore the landing gear off a plane in hard landings during his training), some of the extreme claims about the mortality rate in training are not to be taken seriously.[30] In his bestselling and influential popular history, Denis Winter claimed that eight thousand pilots, or over half of all those killed, died in training, a figure subsequently repeated in several popular works, by the BBC, and even in scholarly studies.[31] In addition, in line with a number of earlier works, Winter stated that pilots were routinely dispatched to the front with an average of seventeen hours flying time as late as 1917.[32] Both claims might be called zombie myths: lifeless but shambling on, unkillable. Winter's eight thousand pilots killed in training roughly equals *total* pilot deaths in all theatres and is quadruple the number suffered in the Home Establishment forces from all causes.[33] It is notable that, of the thirty-six pilots on the roster of No. 3 Reserve Squadron during the week McKay commenced instruction, not one was killed in training.[34]

Regarding the assertion that pilots were posted to France with as little as twelve to seventeen hours' flight time, writers may be assuming that the training hours of 1914–15 remained consistent throughout the war. In fact, McKay arrived in England at a fortuitous moment, just as the training establishment and the RFC in the field were about to undergo a major reorganization. In March 1916, the War Office issued a directive based on "serious complaints" emanating from France "concerning the insufficient training of some of the pilots sent out as reinforcements."[35] Under new regulations, pilots would be required to have experience on a service machine (that is, a model of aircraft they would actually fly in France, as opposed to trainers), to complete a cross-country flight of at least sixty miles, to remain at an altitude of six thousand feet for fifteen minutes, and to complete two landings at night, in addition to training in formation flying and aerial combat. By contemporary standards – indeed, even by the standards of pilot training by the end of the war – these stipulations may seem trifling, but they were a great deal more stringent than what was required to receive the FAI certificate. The new regulations also compelled pilots to have at least fifteen (shortly changed to twenty) hours of solo flight experience; in practice, it would have been virtually impossible for a pilot to complete his training and meet these requirements in under twenty hours anyway.[36] An examination of three logbooks I have located for pilots who flew in No. 24 Squadron over the Somme illustrates the point. Harry Wood, posted in mid-June 1916, arrived in France with fifty-two hours. McKay followed him two weeks later with forty-six, not counting his hours at the Wright School. Robert Saundby, who survived the war to rise to the rank of air marshal and deputy air officer in charge of Bomber Command in the Second World War, arrived in July with about sixty.[37]

None of this is to suggest that the training system in the first two years of the war was immune to the pressure of rapid expansion or the inexorable demand for new pilots. McKay, for instance, soloed for the first time in the RFC after the shocking total of about 1.5 hours dual instruction.[38] Moreover, like most pilots at that point in the war, he had taken a machine-gun course but probably had never fired one in the air before going to France. The assumption was that pilots would complete their training at the front, but McKay was posted to No. 24 Squadron just two days after the Battle of the Somme began. The need being urgent, he was pressed into action very quickly, making his first patrol to the line only three days after arrival.[39] In hindsight, even the improved training of mid-1916 might appear dangerously slapdash, but there are grounds for believing that it was better and more responsive than is often claimed. Certainly, it is overdue for a major reassessment, one based on the surviving records from the time and less reliant on anecdotal evidence gleaned from memoirs often written – or ghostwritten – years or even decades after the fact.

In early 1916, the RFC in France underwent a major reorganization under its commanding officer, Major General Hugh Trenchard.[40] Each of the BEF's field armies would be supported by a correspondingly numbered RFC brigade. The brigades, in turn, were subdivided into "corps" or "army" wings, indicating their various tasks. As they were organized in mid-1916, corps wings assigned one squadron to each of the field army's corps formations for photographic reconnaissance, artillery observation, and light bombing, whereas the army wings typically deployed a squadron of multi-purpose two-seaters and one squadron of single-seat fighters ("scouts" in the nomenclature of the time) to patrol the army front as a whole. In addition, shortly before the Battle of the Somme began, the RFC raised the establishment strength of a squadron from twelve to eighteen machines, divided into three "flights" of six machines each.[41]

Nonetheless, as the war entered its third year, the RFC remained a minuscule appendage of the BEF. On the eve of battle, Henry Rawlinson's Fourth Army, which delivered the blow on 1 July, comprised half a million officers and men, of whom roughly 150 were pilots. Commanded by Brigadier General E.B. "Splash" Ashmore, the 4th Brigade consisted of a balloon squadron and seven airplane squadrons, organized into two wings. In addition to No. 1 Kite Balloon

Figure 1.2   Lieutenant A.E. McKay, RFC
Special Reserve, c. June 1916. | Author's
collection, courtesy Eugene Kittmer.

Figure 1.3   The De Havilland Scout, or DH-2, the backbone of British fighters on the
Somme, ca. summer 1916. Outclassed by new German scouts after September 1916, it
continued to serve until spring 1917. | Author's collection, courtesy Barrington Gray.

Squadron, the Third (Corps) Wing comprised Nos. 3, 4, 9, and 15 Squadrons. The latter three squadrons used the two-seat BE2C, a slow but stable plane that was the backbone of the RFC observation aircraft, whereas No. 3 flew a mixed force of mostly obsolete French-built Morane monoplanes. The Fourteen (Army) Wing comprised two squadrons, flying out of the Bertangles aerodrome a short distance north of Amiens: No. 22 Squadron, flying the two-seat FE-2B, and No. 24 Squadron, which flew the De Havilland Scout, or DH-2, the mainstay of the RFC fighter force in 1916. RFC Headquarters at Fienvillers, twenty kilometres north of Bertangles, also had at its disposal several squadrons designated Nine Wing, operating as a reserve and performing long-range bombing missions.[42]

Only the most promising pilots, such as McKay, were selected to fly scouts. These were thought to be the most difficult machines to handle, as aerial combat involved the most challenging and dangerous manoeuvres. And though the exploits of the "knights of the air" would capture the public imagination, scout pilots understood that theirs was a supporting role. The RFC's main duties were photographic reconnaissance, artillery spotting, and contact patrolling, where the position of attacking forces was communicated to headquarters (most commonly by dropping or hand delivering notes). When the Battle of the Somme began, the task of ensuring that Third Wing squadrons could carry out these duties fell principally on the shoulders of the eighteen pilots of No. 24. Its DH-2s were pushers, with the engine and propeller located behind the pilot. This was already known to be a less efficient layout than the forward engine "tractor" configuration, but it had the advantage of offering pilots an unobstructed field of fire. This was a crucial counter to the German Fokker monoplanes, which were fitted with an invention that British engineers were still struggling to develop: reliable synchronization gear that allowed a machine gun to fire safely through a propeller arc. The DH-2 was never more than a middling performer and one plagued by mechanical unreliability at that. McKay reported serious engine troubles on a third of his patrols in 1916. Moreover, the DH-2 was armed only with a single Lewis gun that had an alarming tendency to jam in the extreme cold of high-altitude combat. Nonetheless, the plane turned tightly and proved in most respects to be superior to the Fokker monoplanes that had terrorized British aviators in 1915.[43] Even before the battle began, No. 24 Squadron, with important assistance rendered from 22 Squadron's two-seat FE pushers, had attained air supremacy over the Fourth Army front.[44]

Major Lanoe Hawker, formerly of the Royal Engineers, was No. 24 Squadron's commanding officer. At only twenty-five years of age, he was already a legend in the RFC. He was its first "ace" and the first pilot to be awarded the Victoria Cross for combat in the air. His "chickens," as he called his hand-picked pilots, were in awe of him but also cheered by his antics. He encouraged roughhousing and was not averse to "binges" when flying ended for the day.[45] Evening sojourns to nearby Amiens and its fine restaurants, including the famous Godbert's, were frequent.[46]

It is some indication of the calibre of McKay's potential that he was posted to Hawker's squadron. McKay arrived on 3 July 1916, two days after the offensive began. Three other Canadians were already serving with the squadron. Twenty-year-old Arthur "Gerry" Knight was a former student of Ontario's prestigious Upper Canada College who was awarded the Distinguished Service Order later that year. Harry Wood, the only one of the four to survive the war, was a graduate engineer of the University of Toronto, and he became McKay's closest friend in the squadron.[47] The last of the quartet was Boer War veteran and range-rider Henry Cope Evans, formerly of the Alberta Dragoons. At six foot three, Evans was one of the tallest pilots in the RFC; at age thirty-six, he was almost certainly its oldest. Despite his age, he had somehow finagled a transfer from the CEF in late 1915. In July and August, his total of five victories over German machines earned him the Distinguished Service Order.[48] In the years to come, the top aces would tally up extraordinary – it is tempting to say "unbelievable" – numbers of victories, far surpassing such totals, but in these early days of aerial combat, and especially in the somewhat plodding and under-armed DH-2, bringing down even a single German aircraft was considered a heroic achievement.[49]

Debate over the Battle of the Somme began even before it ended and continues to rage a century later. Whatever else might be said about the first two months of battle on the ground, there can be little doubt that they were a period of victory for the RFC in the air. It is too glib to credit the RFC dominance to the superior performance of its pushers, as they had only a slight edge over German machines. Nor can numerical superiority be the primary issue, as German aerial reinforcements from the Verdun front began to arrive on the Somme as early as mid-July, and the balance of fighters was roughly equal.[50] Rather, British ascendancy in this period was a product of leadership, doctrine, pilot training (for all its flaws), and logistics.[51] It is beyond the scope of this discussion to give full consideration to each of these factors, but the doctrine of continual offensive endorsed by Hugh Trenchard requires some analysis. Trenchard was convinced that, given the width of front involved, there was no means of preventing German planes from crossing British lines, attacking his corps machines, and conducting their own reconnaissance, if they chose to do so. The best defence, Trenchard concluded, was offensive patrolling by scout squadrons. They would attack German planes deep on their own side of the line, near their own aerodromes, throwing them onto the defensive. These raids would be reinforced by regular bombing of German aerodromes and other important targets in rear areas – an aspect of the air war that awaits serious consideration.[52]

The policy of offensive patrolling has been the subject of acrimonious debate ever since. Critics have alleged that like the donkeys on the ground, Trenchard possessed a singular, bloody-minded zeal for the offensive.[53] Undeniably, his policy gave the German air service a home-field advantage: a wounded German pilot or one flying a damaged aircraft had a better of chance of making it home safely – or of crash landing in friendly territory – than his RFC counterpart. Nonetheless, though it is difficult to construct a counterfactual analysis in which a different policy was pursued, there are good grounds for arguing that the policy ultimately succeeded. As in operations on the ground, success or failure was not simply a question of lives lost. It bears repeating that the raison d'être of the RFC was reconnaissance in various forms. During the Battle of the Somme, a period in which very few corps machines were lost to German fighters, the RFC was eminently successful in this task. With the pusher pilots of the Fourteen Wing ascendant (and reinforced by the arrival of 32 Squadron in late July), the 4th Brigade's corps squadrons were able to carry out and refine their techniques of photography, artillery cooperation, and contact patrolling with a minimum of enemy interference, at least when weather permitted. Moreover, the growing efficiency of RFC photographic reconnaissance was demonstrated in a series of timed tests in July, in which photographs of the German line were taken, developed, and delivered to headquarters in as little as thirty minutes each.[54]

British squadron-level tactics, too, deserve greater consideration than they have often received. Commander Lanoe Hawker's mantra was "attack everything," and this standing order, which was prominently posted on the 24 Squadron bulletin board, might seem like reckless bravado. But Hawker was also an innovator who encouraged his pilots in the mess to engage in open discussion and debate about tactics.[55] An example of how offensive tactics, coupled with the continual development of pilots, either in the Home Establishment or at the front, could lead to success occurred in the famous action of 20 July 1916, often referred to as the first aerial dogfight. As dusk approached, four pilots of 24's "B" Flight, including McKay, attacked a much larger, mixed formation of eleven German machines near Flers, which was then deep behind German lines. In the ensuing brawl, three German planes, including one claimed by McKay, were downed and the rest dispersed.[56] Dogfights of this size and larger were to become progressively more common as the year went on, as RFC patrols continued to take on larger German formations even when the technological scales began to weigh against them in late September.

McKay's aircraft was badly shot up in this, his first major scrap. He managed to pilot it home nonetheless, through some amalgam of skill and good fortune.[57] Popular literature about the air war often refers to the short lives of pilots and is replete with clichés about "old hands" turning a cold shoulder on replacements, who were sure to die in short order. Life expectancies of fighter pilots were measured in days, not weeks, so the claim goes.[58] Whatever the case may have been in the deadliest periods of the war for the RFC (such as April 1917), the more hyperbolic claims regarding life expectancies are not borne out by an examination of 24 Squadron loss rates in 1916 and early 1917. In the nine months that McKay served with the squadron, approximately seventy pilots passed through it, their average posting lasting 4.5 months. Most survived to rotate to other postings. Nine were killed, four of them in operational flying accidents. This is not to deny that the cumulative losses could be wearing: in all, about thirty of the seventy pilots were killed or died at some point during the war. Of the six members of McKay's "B" Flight on his arrival in June 1916, four were killed (two that year), one seriously wounded, and one shot down and taken prisoner.[59] Still, most pilots agreed that their comfortable and well-paid life behind the lines was preferable to frequent rotations through the desolation and filth of lice- and rat-infested forward trenches.

It is notable that several survivors of 24 Squadron's tour on the Somme, including McKay himself, were tapped to become combat instructors at the elite Central Flying School in early 1917. Much has been written about the laconic eight-point "dicta" produced by the dean of the German fighter force, Oswald Boelcke, who returned to the Western Front after a two-month absence, just as the Battle of Flers-Courcelette began.[60] The Dicta Boelcke, which gave advice such as "always attack from the sun," "fire the machine gun up close," and "in any form of attack, approach the opponent from behind," has been valorized as a foundational treatise in fighter tactics, but surviving reports and subsequently written manuals reveal that British scout pilots had already reached similar conclusions.[61] In the Darwinian environment of aerial combat, only strong tactics survived.

In late August and early September 1916, the Canadian Corps, then three divisions strong, redeployed from the Ypres salient to the Somme. There it took up position on Fourth Army's left flank as part of Lieutenant General Hubert Gough's Reserve Army. On 8 September, Canadian Corps HQ received a preliminary operational order of an imminent major operation against the German third line. But the order noted that "the *exact* objective will be fixed by the Corps after making necessary reconnaissances and studying air photographs" – an important indicator of how indispensable the RFC had already become in the planning of battles.[62] The final plan for what became the Battle of Flers-Courcelette required Fourth Army to seize the German positions be-tween Morval and Le Sars. Reserve Army, spearheaded by two divisions of the Canadian Corps, would secure Fourth Army's left flank by taking Courcelette, a village on the north side of the Albert-Bapaume Road whose most notable feature was a heavily fortified sugar refinery.[63] The plan, as historian William Philpott describes it, was "conceived as the first stage of a broader offensive, the break-in that might be followed by a break through."[64] In his operational orders to the 4th Brigade, Brigadier "Splash" Ashmore noted that "for the last two and half months we have been gradually wearing the enemy down, his moral is shaken, and he has few, if any, fresh reserves available, and there is every prob-ability that a combined determined effort will result in a decisive effort."[65] This was not bravado. Successive localized British and French attacks during the first ten weeks of the Somme campaign had severely weakened the German defend-ers along the entire Somme front.[66] Anticipating a German retreat, Ashmore urged that "every effort will be made to increase the confusion among the enemy by bombing and coming down low and using Machine Guns against the troops on the ground."[67]

In July and August, Reserve Army had been supported solely by a single wing, but at the end of August it was deemed necessary to attach a full RFC brigade to the greatly expanded formation. On the eve of the Battle of Flers-Courcelette, the 5th Brigade RFC's order of battle consisted of roughly one hundred pilots serving in Nos. 4, 7 (tasked to the Canadian Corps), and 15 Squadrons in the Fifteen (Corps) Wing, mostly flying BE2Cs; and 23 and 32 Squadron in the Twenty-Two (Army) Wing, flying FE-2Bs and DH-2s, respectively.[68] Combined, the four wings of the 4th and 5th Brigades constituted what was, by the stan-dards of 1916, a very formidable air armada, and on the basis of their perform-ance since June, the RFC's commanders and pilots had good grounds for optimism. In particular, interrogation of German POWs had revealed immense frustration at the inability of their own air service to prevent British and French planes from reconnoitering their positions and calling down artillery fire upon them. "During the day one hardly dares to be seen in the trench owing to the English aeroplanes ... Nothing is to be seen of our German hero airmen ... One can hardly calculate how much additional loss of life and strain on the nerves this costs us," read an extract from the diary of a German prisoner taken at Delville Wood, one of many such examples quoted in the British official hist-ory.[69] It was a sentiment fully shared by the German First Army's own post-battle assessment of the first two months of the Somme, which noted "the complete inferiority of our own air forces" and the "heavy losses in personnel and ma-teriel inflicted on our artillery by the enemy's own guns, assisted by excellent air observation."[70] These pressures resulted in the further reinforcement and reorganization of the German air service on the Somme front. Oswald Boelcke, who had returned from the east with a hand-picked group of pilots – including the young Manfred von Richthofen – organized new "hunting" squadrons, the Jagdstaffels, also known as Jastas. These would be dedicated fighter squadrons like 24 Squadron, equipped with the new Albatros D1 and D2 scouts, faster than the DH-2 and more formidably armed.[71] The RFC, therefore, began to see both its quantitative and qualitative superiority eroded in the third phase of the Somme battle, but it would be entirely wrong to think that the RFC conceded its aerial supremacy easily, if at all, in 1916.

By the time the Battle of Flers-Courcelette began on 15 September, Eddie McKay was, by the standards of mid-1916, an experienced military pilot. He had over a hundred hours of flying time, had flown more than thirty patrols, fought in half a dozen combats, and had brought down an enemy machine.[72] Within the squadron, he had a reputation as a good pilot and a "very amusing" comrade, although some of his superiors apparently considered him too outspoken to be promoted.[73] The squadron record book indicates that he never shied from action, but neither did he seem to press for it, unlike some of his more aggressive squadron mates such as Arthur Knight and Ireland's Patrick Langan-Byrne. On the other hand, he survived the year and they did not. Moreover, four 24 Squadron pilots had been killed since the beginning of the month, fully a quarter of the squadron in just under two weeks. McKay's compatriot and fellow "B" Flight pilot Henry Evans had been shot down by anti-aircraft fire on the third; Lieutenant A.E. Glew had been killed on the ninth when his engine had thrown a cylinder, severing his plane's tail boom; Philip Manfield, also of "B" Flight, was downed later that day by Boelcke, to whom Lieutenant John Bowring also fell on the fourteenth.[74] These were heavy casualties, the worst the squadron had sustained. Losses were usually replaced immediately by pilots drawn from the reserve pool, but when 24 Squadron went into action on 15 September 1916, in what would prove the heaviest aerial engagement of the war to date, it had nonetheless lost a quarter of its experienced fliers. The frequently cited statistic that pilots had life expectancies of two or three weeks ("about a month," Denis Winter claims) may have been an exaggeration, but casualties such as these were deeply wounding to a pilot's psyche in the tiny, enclosed cosmos of an RFC squadron.

Memoirs frequently describe pilots flying a gruelling schedule of two, three, or even four patrols per day, but 24 Squadron's record book and the surviving logbooks from squadron members suggest a more moderate routine, at least in scout squadrons in 1916. Between duty rotation – Hawker usually held one flight in reserve on any given day – bad weather, leave, and sickness, McKay flew an average of one patrol every three days during the Somme campaign and was active on just four of the seven days of the Battle of Flers-Courcelette. First World War aircraft were always at risk from bad weather, and this was particularly true for pushers such as the DH-2, whose pilots sat exposed in a nacelle, forward of the top wing. Weather that seemed moderate from the ground was often blinding at higher altitudes. Hence on 13 September, two days before the battle began, weather that was described as merely "dull and overcast" severely limited reconnaissance from the air. That day, Jock Andrews of "B" Flight attempted three times before succeeding in reconnoitering the German line from Le Transloy to Sailly-Saillisel, in a rare case of a 24 scout being deployed for this purpose. On the homeward leg, Andrews got lost several times in the clouds and nearly landed on a French airfield. He found his way home by following the Albert-Bapaume Road at a height of eight hundred feet.[75] The fourteenth was windy and cold but clearer. While escorting FEs from 22 Squadron on a reconnaissance, Arthur Knight and Sergeant Cockerell – one of 24's rare NCO pilots – brought down a Fokker in flames over Fremicourt, just east of Bapaume, but that day had also seen Lieutenant Bowring brought down by Oswald Boelcke.[76]

The day of the attack itself, 15 September, dawned misty but the sun soon burned off the haze. The remainder of the day was clear but cool, with a ground temperature of about sixty degrees Fahrenheit and thus ideal for flying – though the temperature would have been well below zero at patrol altitudes over ten thousand feet.[77] This day would see the greatest amount of aerial activity to date, with the pilots of the two brigades flying over six hundred hours total.[78] With the British barrage raining down below – McKay noted it in the squadron record book – "B" Flight embarked on an early morning offensive patrol. These typically followed the Albert-Bapaume Road northeast, and on the fifteenth they probably crossed the German lines at Courcelette before turning southeast around Bapaume. No doubt it cheered McKay to be supporting his fellow Canadians below; 24 was formally attached to Fourth Army, but operational orders indicated that Twenty-Two Wing and Fourteen Wing scout squadrons patrolled the Somme front as a whole.[79] The aerial battlefield was not, of course, hermetically sealed – one could fly the length of the Reserve and Fourth Army fronts in about ten minutes – and the whole doctrinal basis of offensive patrolling was that attacking a German formation in one place protected corps machines in another.

As the RFC rose up in unprecedented numbers, so too did the German air service. McKay later recorded in his logbook that there had been "numerous H.A. (hostile aircraft) about" – a quite typical understatement of the kind expected from the cool, collected gentlemen pilots of the RFC.[80] Around 8:30 a.m., south of the Albert-Bapaume Road, McKay and his comrades – now reduced to three machines because two others had turned back with engine problems – encountered and then dispersed a mixed formation of seventeen German aircraft near Morval, sending one down in flames.[81] A running battle ensued until about 9:15 a.m. Shortly after nine, McKay singly attacked two German planes that were approaching the British line near the Albert-Bapaume Road, on the other side of which the Canadians were in heavy action south and east of Courcelette. McKay drove one down to a thousand feet but was then set upon by a German scout of a type he had never encountered before: "streamlined" and "very fast" was how he described it in the squadron record book.[82] After several inconclusive tilts at McKay, it headed east, faster than he could pursue. Very probably, this was one of the newly arrived Albatros scouts belonging to Jasta 2, perhaps even piloted by Boelcke himself. At about 9:35 a.m., the German formation reassembled for another go but was eventually driven east. Lieutenant Langan-Byrne had gone through seven full drums of .303 ammunition on his Lewis gun – nearly seven hundred rounds in all. Famously aggressive, he replenished his fuel and ammunition at a nearby aerodrome and went out again, hungry for more.[83]

In many respects, this engagement, though longer in duration than most others to date, typified the kinds of aerial combats that 24 Squadron would engage in during the Battle of Flers-Courcelette and over the Somme generally. It had been sharp but indecisive, in the sense that just one of the roughly twenty engaged aircraft had been brought down. Indeed, during the squadron's entire tour on the Somme, February 1916 to March 1917, only about 5 percent of its 774 combats resulted in a decisive victory.[84] This illustrates the futility of counting kills as a means of assessing the outcome of aerial battles. In dispersing the German formation, the three 24 pilots – one of whom, William Nixon, had replaced Henry Evans only five days earlier – had accomplished precisely what Fourteen Wing's scout pilots were supposed to do.[85] They had done vital work, protecting the corps aircraft, including those of 7 Squadron, which directly supported the Canadians at Courcelette, just a few kilometres distant. Moreover, they had prevented German observation aircraft from carrying out their own reconnaissance and artillery cooperation duties.

The 2nd Canadian Division's attack on Courcelette has been expertly described elsewhere and will not be dwelled on here.[86] Supported by an immense concentration of artillery and six tanks that were making their debut on the battlefield, five battalions of the 2nd Division led the assault on Courcelette just after 6:00 a.m. They moved forward behind a creeping barrage but were briefly caught out in the open just short of the German line and had to advance through eviscerating fire. By 8:00 a.m., the sugar refinery was in their hands, as was the rest of Courcelette by 6:00 p.m. The impact of tanks has been much debated.

All six were out of action by day's end (they suffered similar fates on the Fourth Army front), but they had materially assisted in crushing wire and had terrified unsuspecting German troops. Indeed, in an effort to maintain the element of surprise, several RFC planes had been instructed to use the drone of their engines that morning to mask the sounds of the tank engines coming to life.[87] As for the role of the RFC, a close examination of the 5th Brigade RFC and Canadian Corps war diaries reveals just how much the Canadians relied on 7 Squadron to be their eyes and ears during the battle and in the days of consolidation that followed. Weather permitting – it was very poor on the eighteenth, during part of the day on the nineteenth, and for most of the twentieth – 7 Squadron furnished corps headquarters with regular updates about the location of its battalions, the movement of German troops, including reserves, the position of enemy artillery, and photographs of new German lines being dug as the enemy retreated. The observers also paid special attention to the location of the tanks. This was in addition to the artillery observation role played by 7 Squadron's planes and those of other Fifteen Wing squadrons. Typically, a corps squadron would dedicate two flights to counter-battery cooperation with the artillery.[88] These flights were of inestimable value; the RFC official history notes that in the hilly terrain of the Somme, virtually all successful counter-battery work in 1916 required the cooperation of RFC observers.[89] On the day itself, the 5th Brigade reported that twelve enemy batteries were destroyed and fifteen damaged.[90] Late in the day, 7 Squadron reported that a battery of eight guns was being brought to bear on the Canadians, who were then consolidating their position at Courcelette.[91] When a counter-battery strike failed to achieve complete results, the pilot and observer of the 7 Squadron plane took it upon themselves to strafe the battery, putting the rest of it out of action.[92]

For the Canadians, 15 September marked a critical point in the Battle of Flers-Courcelette. Several days of consolidation in the face of German artillery and heavy counterattacks followed; Fourth Army, to the south, also met with strong resistance, but by the end of the day on the eighteenth, most of their objectives were in their hands. The battle had not achieved everything that was hoped for, but it can be judged a remarkable success on the whole, especially in comparison to what had been achieved beforehand. The Canadian success at Courcelette was particularly notable, with William Philpott remarking that the 2nd Canadian Division "had initiated the process that would turn the Canadian Corps into first-class shock troops."[93] But as always, on the Somme, the price for such distinctions was a heavy one: over a thousand Canadians had been killed in the taking of Courcelette. That number would almost certainly have been higher but for the efforts of the two hundred pilots who flew in support of the Fourth and Reserve Armies.

We should therefore reject any inference that, because the air services were small, airpower was somehow inconsequential, a mere sideshow worthy of a few paragraphs in books about the war's great campaigns. The combatant countries invested tremendous economic resources in the development of their air services, resources out of all proportion to the number of personnel the air services deployed, because senior military commanders believed that airpower was a critical adjunct to operations on the ground. Just as the Battle of the Somme has often been misjudged on the basis of its first day, so too has the overall performance of the RFC sometimes been unfairly adjudicated in the light of the calamitous casualties of "Bloody April" 1917, or because the balance of victories in the air favoured the Germans in the third phase of the Somme.[94] But it is too obvious to state that success or failure in military operations cannot be measured solely by the scales of lives lost. This chapter has hinted at avenues for further research but makes no claim for the decisiveness of airpower over the Somme or in the Battle of Flers-Courcelette. Assessments of the importance of the RFC must necessarily be speculative, as there is no way to precisely evaluate the impact of its operations. Arguably, the three hundred tons of bombs that the RFC dropped in September 1916 were mere pinpricks – albeit pinpricks delivered well beyond the range of ordinary artillery – but surely the three thousand photographs taken during the same month were of tremendous value to commanders on the ground, the kind of intelligence that their forebears even a generation earlier could scarcely have imagined.[95] Similarly, it is impossible to quantify precisely the importance of aerial observation work for the British artillery, but the RFC observed thousands of shoots during the Battle of the Somme, and the gunners themselves clearly felt that aerial observation was invaluable. The temptation to discount the importance of all this on the grounds that such efforts did not prevent disastrous attacks is perilous: not all attacks were disasters, and those that were might have been worse without the efforts of the RFC.

The Somme offensive marked an important stage in the development of the RFC. During the Battle of Flers-Courcelette, RFC pilots, including Eddie McKay, were better trained and better led than is often believed, retained air supremacy against an increasingly dangerous German adversary, performed tactical air support in the form of bombing and strafing, carried out bombing raids against distant, strategically important targets, developed further competence in contact patrols, and continued to refine techniques in photographic reconnaissance and artillery spotting. And though the service still faced a steep and very painful learning curve – a phrase that should be understood metaphorically, not literally – there is no doubt that the RFC established itself as an integral formation of the BEF during the Battle of the Somme.

As for those Canadians who served in the RFC, they proved themselves the equal of their British counterparts over the Somme, whatever doubts British recruiters in Canada had harboured during the previous year. For reasons never fully or satisfactorily explained, Canadians went on to account for a disproportionate number of pilots in the British flying services. This was despite the delayed and highly tentative start of pilot recruitment and training in Canada. In part, their enthusiasm for joining the flying services may owe itself to the fame gained by certain aces, including Billy Bishop and Billy Barker, who became heroes and role models during the war itself. In a conflict of titanic armies trapped underground by lethal new technologies, individual soldiers were often rendered anonymous. But in the skies above the trenches, technology had, paradoxically, restored something of the romanticism of an imagined age of chivalric heroes.[96] Pilots captured the imagination of the public, and if British authorities were sometimes reticent in exploiting the propaganda value of the aces, Canadian authorities and the Canadian press had no such hesitation. Well before Billy Bishop became a national hero, to be paraded in recruiting drives across the country, Eddie McKay himself briefly attained national fame when he was erroneously credited in Canadian newspapers with having brought down Oswald Boelcke. In fact, Boelcke had been killed on 28 October 1916 in a collision with a squadron mate while pursuing McKay and Arthur Knight near Bapaume, but neither Canadian pilot had claimed a victory.[97] The story was false and its origins dubious, but one wonders how many young men on the home front were inspired to enlist in the RFC because of it.

Only one of the four Canadians who served in 24 Squadron over the Somme survived the war. The fate of Henry Cope Evans has already been revealed. Arthur Knight, posted to 29 Squadron as a flight leader, was killed in combat against Manfred von Richthofen in December 1916. Eddie McKay and Harry Wood made it through the remaining weeks of the Battle of the Somme and the harsh winter of 1916–17. Some of their squadron mates did not, including Lanoe Hawker, who fell to von Richthofen's guns on 23 November.[98] In March 1917, McKay was promoted and posted to the Home Establishment as an instructor. He seemed to excel in this capacity and was promoted again, to captain and flight leader, at the end of April. He served for a further five months as an instructor in England, then requested a posting at the front. He returned to France at the end of October 1917, two years to the day after he had arrived at the Wright School in Dayton, Ohio. With 425 hours of flying time behind him, he took command of 23 Squadron's "A" Flight just as the Battle of Passchendaele reached its crescendo.[99] On 28 December 1917, he was killed in action while leading his patrol near Ypres.[100] He is commemorated on the Arras Flying Services Memorial, alongside nearly a thousand other fallen fliers who have no known grave, brave men who fought the war from above.

Notes

1 S.F. Wise, *Canadian Airmen and the First World War: The Official History of the Royal Canadian Air Force*, vol. 1 (Toronto: University of Toronto Press in cooperation with the Department of National Defence, 1980). Though part of the Canadian official history, this work is often considered one of the most important studies of British airpower generally in the First World War.

2 Examples include Denis Winter's beautifully written but highly sensationalist *The First of the Few: Fighter Pilots of the First World War* (London: Allen Lane, 1982); Ian Mackersey, *No Empty Chairs* (London: Phoenix, 2013); and the very unreliable "memoirs" of Billy Bishop, *Winged Warfare* (New York: G.H. Doran, 1918), and Manfred von Richthofen, *Der rote Kampfflieger* (1917) published in English as *The Red Baron* in 1918, both of which are still in print but must be understood as wartime propaganda pieces.

3 On the development of the "lions led by donkeys" myth, see Dan Todman, *The Great War: Myth and Memory* (London: Continuum, 2005).

4 The source of the claim seems to be Winter, *The First of the Few*, 36. I discuss it in greater detail below.

5 On the origins of the RFC, see Walter Raleigh, *The War in the Air* (Oxford: Clarendon Press, 1922), 1:198–276. The naval wing, the Royal Naval Air Service (RNAS), operated with growing independence from the RFC and came wholly under the direction of the Admiralty in 1915. In April 1918, it amalgamated with the RFC to form the Royal Air Force.

6 V.M. Yeats, *Winged Victory* (New York: H. Smith and H. Hass, 1934), 65.

7 Raleigh, *The War in the Air*, 1:260.

8 Ibid., 261.

9 The 1914 RFC *Training Manual* has been called the foundation of RFC doctrine throughout the war, but having a doctrine and actually being able to execute it are obviously different things. See James Pugh, *The Royal Flying Corps, the Western Front, and Control of the Air, 1914–1918* (Abingdon, UK: Routledge, 2017).

10 See Graham Broad, *One in a Thousand: The Life and Death of Captain Eddie McKay, Royal Flying Corps* (Toronto: University of Toronto Press, 2017).

11 First used by French journalists in 1915, "ace" came to refer to a pilot who had brought down five or more enemy machines. It had no official standing and its use is probably somewhat anachronistic, as it does not seem to have been widely employed even colloquially in the British flying services until late in the war.

12 Winter, *The First of the Few*, 217. The figure is an exaggeration, but it is likely that something in the range of half of all documents used to write the British official histories in the 1920s are lost to us. Apart from Combat in the Air (CAR) reports, only a handful of squadron-level RFC records survive. Almost all squadron-level operation orders are lost, for example. Fortunately, the redundancy of military reporting and record keeping means that a reasonably complete picture of RFC operations on the Somme can be pieced together from wing, brigade, and RFC HQ war diaries, work summaries, and précis of operations. In addition, valuable information can be gleaned from the RFC communiques, which from July 1915 on were issued daily by RFC headquarters and were intended to keep personnel informed of RFC activities. These have been complied in three volumes by Christopher

Cole, including *Royal Flying Corps Communiques 1915–1916* (London: Tom Donovan, 1969) which was of great use to this chapter.

13 Many thanks to Eugene Kittmer for sharing McKay's logbook with me. The 24 Squadron Record Book is located in the National Archives (NA), United Kingdom (UK), Air 1/169/15/160/5, 24 Squadron RFC and RAF Record Book. A squadron record book is essentially a ledger that served as a collective logbook.

14 Except where otherwise noted, references to McKay's life prior to entering the RFC are from Broad, *One in a Thousand*, 1–14.

15 C.S. Grafton, "The Eddie McKay Memorial Cup," *London Advertiser*, 10 April 1920, 8.

16 Library and Archives Canada (LAC), RG 24, RFC in Canada, vol. 2032; LAC, RG 25, Colonial Office Canada, vol. 151, file C9/91. For an overview of early RFC/RNAS recruiting in Canada, see C.W. Hunt, *Dancing in the Sky: The Royal Flying Corps in Canada* (Toronto: Dundurn Press, 2009), 28–29; and Wise, *Canadian Airmen*, 23–45.

17 Edward Bujak, *Reckless Fellows: The Gentlemen of the Royal Flying Corps* (London: I.B. Tauris, 2015), 1.

18 LAC, MG 40 D1, vol. 35, Air Ministry, Air 2/13/058/4066, C.J. Burke to War Office, 19 December 1915.

19 Canada, Department of Militia and Defense, *Quarterly Militia List of the Dominions of Canada (Corrected to 1 July 1916)* (Ottawa: King's Printer, 1916), 295.

20 LAC, RG 24, vol. 4331, file 34-2-34, Aviators for RFC.

21 LAC, Curtiss School of Aviation fonds, MG 28 III 65, "The Log of the Curtiss Flying School, 1915–1916."

22 Few records of the Wright School survive. The best account of its operations is John Carver Edwards, *Orville's Aviators: Outstanding Alumni of the Wright Flying School, 1910–1916* (Jefferson, NC: McFarland, 2009).

23 On Brown's training as a pilot, see Alan Bennett, *Captain Roy Brown: A True Story of the Great War, 1914–1918* (New York: Brick Tower Press, 2011), 1:57–125.

24 University of Western Ontario, Archives and Regional Collection Centre, Beatrice Hitchins Memorial Collection of Aviation History, box 4647, Aero Club certificates.

25 McKay's Aero Club of America certificate is in the author's possession, courtesy of Robert MacKay, Eddie McKay's great-nephew.

26 LAC, RG 24, vol. 2022, HQ6978-2-92, Director of Supplies and Transport to Lt. A.E. McKay, 17 February 2016. McKay recorded a narrative of his pre-RFC and early RFC flight training on the inside flap of his logbook, under the heading "Reference." A copy of the logbook is in the author's possession via Eugene Kittmer.

27 "Reserve" squadrons were utilized for training. They had no direct relationship to the correspondingly numbered service squadron.

28 Ralph Barker, *A Brief History of the Royal Flying Corps in World War I* (London: Robinson, 2002), 117. .

29 NA (UK), Air Ministry, Air 1/1831/204/204/8, School of Military Aeronautics (Reading and Oxford), Establishment of school and instructors.

30 McKay, Logbook, 23 April 1916 and 22 May 1916.

31 Winter, *The First of the Few*, 36. For two recent works that repeat the claim, see Mackersey, *No Empty Chairs;* and Bujak, *Reckless Fellows*. Writers for the BBC have repeated it in several locations on the BBC web services, including Chris Long, "Flight: Art Journey Remembers World War One's 'Suicide Club,'" 7 July 2016, https://www.bbc.com/news/entertainment-arts-36712829; and "Plaque for WWI Pilot Robert-Smith Barry in Gosport," 9 April 2014, https://www.bbc.com/news/uk-england-hampshire-26952538.

32 Winter, *The First of the Few*, 57.

33   See Wise, *Canadian Airmen*, 645–49; and Chris Dobson, *Airmen Died in the Great War, 1914–1918* (Suffolk: J.B. Hayward and Son, 1995). NA (UK), Air 1/39/15/7, gives total deaths from all causes in the Home Establishment, as roughly two thousand up to the end of October 1918.

34   NA (UK), NA (UK), Air 1/1273/204/9/147, 7 Wing RFC Daily Routine Orders, Officers of No. 3 Reserve Squadron, 22 March 1916 (7 Wing).

35   NA (UK), Air 1/676/21/13/1773, Notes on Flying Training at Home – Part 1.

36   NA (UK), Air Ministry: Air Historical Branch, Air 1/131/15/40/218, "Pilots Sent to Expeditionary Force with Insufficient Training; General Training of Pilots" and "Notes on Flying Training at Home."

37   A partial copy of Harry Wood's logbook is located in the University of Texas at Dallas, Eugene McDermott Library, George H. Williams Jr., World War One Aviation Library, Ola A. Slater collection, box 11. Robert Saundby's logbook is in the RAF Museum, RHMS Saundby Papers, box 1, AC 72-12.

38   McKay, Logbook, "Narrative" and "Time Flown at Shoreham." (Undated entries in McKay's logbook.) McKay's service file begins with his appointment as a flying officer and provides few details of his training. NA (UK), Officers' Service Records, Air 1/76/31/176.

39   McKay, Logbook, 6 July 1916.

40   NA (UK), Air 1/1/4/3, Organization of RFC in the Field 02 February 1916. See also the official history, Raleigh, *The War in the Air*, 2:146–48. Trenchard was promoted to major general in March. On Trenchard, see Andrew Boyle, *Trenchard* (London: Collins, 1962).

41   Raleigh, *The War in the Air*, 2:196.

42   4th Brigade's order of battle from NA (UK), Air 1/1211/204/5/2625, Order of Battle RFC on Somme.

43   On the design and development of the DH-2, see Jon Guttman, *Pusher Aces of World War 1* (Oxford: Osprey, 2009), 30–59.

44   See Raleigh, *The War in the Air*, 2:195–202.

45   On Hawker, see but handle with care the hagiography written by his brother: Tyrrell Mann Hawker, *Hawker, VC: The Biography the Late Major Lanoe George Hawker* (London: Mitres Press, 1965). See also NA (UK), War Office, WO 339/50030, Major Lanoe George Hawker, Royal Engineers.

46   On the squadron's social life, see A.E. Illingworth and V.A.H. Robeson, *History of 24 Squadron* (n.p., 1920); and Selden Long, *In the Blue* (London: John Long, 1920).

47   NA (UK), Air 1/76/279/155, Arthur Gerald Knight service record; NA (UK), Air 1/76/558/124, Harry Allison Wood service record.

48   NA (UK), War Office: Officers' Services, First World War, WO 339/73845, Henry Cope Evans. The word "victory," widely used in First World War aviation literature, is, like "kill," an anachronism. The RFC's peculiar and unique combat reporting system counted enemy planes destroyed, out-of-control, and, until late 1916, "forced to land," including those that landed on their own side of the lines. The "scores" of individual pilots were not kept, although they were often included in citations for medals.

49   Apart from Lanoe Hawker, who had downed seven German planes in 1915, the highest "scoring" pilot in 24 Squadron was Alan Wilkinson, who had brought down five German machines by mid-June 1916.

50   Raleigh, *The War in the Air*, 2:262.

51   On logistics, see Peter Dye, *The Bridge to Airpower: Logistics Support for Royal Flying Corps Operations on the Western Front, 1914–1918* (Annapolis: Naval Institute Press, 2015).

52 On the policy of offensive patrolling, see Raleigh, *The War in the Air,* 2:164–87, 259–71.
53 One severe critic of Trenchard's policy was Arthur Gould Lee, who became an air vice-marshal. See Arthur Gould Lee, *No Parachute* (London: Jarrolds, 1968), Appendix A.
54 NA (UK), Air 1/123/15/40/144, Photography in the RFC: Reports on Progress, Report on Photographic Speed Tests.
55 Hawker, *Hawker, VC,* 180.
56 NA (UK), Air 1/1221/204/5/2634, Combat Reports: 24 Squadron; Combats in the Air (CAR), 20 July 1916, Hughes-Chamberlain, Evans, McKay, Chapman.
57 McKay, Logbook, 20 July 1916.
58 Denis Winter states that pilots in 1916 had a life expectancy of about three weeks. Winter, *The First of the Few,* 153.
59 These figures are based on a roster of 24 Squadron pilots and their fates, which I compiled using the Squadron Record Book and the Commonwealth War Graves Commission "Find War Dead" database at https://www.cwgc.org/find-records/find-war-dead.
60 On Boelcke and the Dicta Boelcke, see R.G. Head, *Oswald Boelcke: Germany's First Fighter Ace and the Father of Air Combat* (London: Grub Street, 2016).
61 For example, see NA (UK), Air 1/129/15/40/191, Formation Flying and Fighting in the Air: Notes Forwarded by the RFC in the Field.
62 LAC, RG 9-III-D-3, vol. 4813, file 6, War Diaries, Canadian Corps, General Staff 1916/07/01-1916/09/30, Reserve Army Preliminary Operation Order, 8 September 1916 (emphasis in original).
63 Tim Cook, *At the Sharp End: Canadians Fighting the Great War, 1914–1916* (Toronto: Viking, 2007), 433, 439.
64 William Philpott, *Three Armies on the Somme: The First Battle of the Twentieth Century* (New York: Alfred A. Knopf, 2010), 329.
65 NA (UK), Air 1/2248/209/432/12, War Diary, 4th Brigade, June–September, Instructions No. 51, 14 September 1916.
66 Philpott, *Three Armies on the Somme,* 317.
67 NA (UK), War Diary, 4th Brigade, Instructions No. 51, 14 September 1916.
68 Raleigh, *The War in the Air,* 2:246.
69 Ibid., 269.
70 Quoted in ibid., 270.
71 On the reorganization of the German air service on the Somme, see Greg VanWyngarden, *Jagdstaffel 2 'Boelcke'* (Oxford: Osprey, 2007), 6–13.
72 McKay, Logbook, entries for July–September 1916.
73 Broad, *One in a Thousand,* 86, 93.
74 Illingworth and Robeson, *History of 24 Squadron,* Table "pro patria," n.p. Bowring survived as a prisoner of war.
75 NA (UK), Air 1/169/15/160/5, Squadron Record Book (SRB), 24 Squadron, vol. 3, 13 September 1916.
76 Ibid., 14 September 1916.
77 McKay, Logbook, 15 September 1916. Temperature from Gerald Gliddon, *Somme 1916: A Battlefield Companion* (Stroud: the Military Press, 2016), 27, and computing for altitude recorded in McKay's logbook.
78 NA (UK), Air 1/762/204/4/164-170, RFC Summary of Work, September 1916.
79 NA (UK), Air 1/2220/209/40/8, War Diary, 5th Brigade, Operation Order, 14 and 15 September 1916.
80 McKay, Logbook, 15 September 1916.

81 McKay records in the SRB that the encounter took place "East of Bapaume," whereas the CAR report specifies Morval, which is roughly eight kilometres south. NA (UK), Air 1/1221/204/5/2634, CAR, 15 September 1916.

82 NA (UK), Air 1/169/15/160/5, SRB, Vol. 5, 15 September 1916.

83 NA (UK), Air 1/1221/204/5/2634, CAR, 15 September 1916, Byrne, McKay, Nixon. The squadron's Lewis guns carried a double-sized pan of ninety-seven rounds.

84 NA (UK), Air 1/169/15/160/5, SRB, vol. 5, Summary Table of Operations.

85 NA (UK), War Office, WO 339/58356, Officers' Service Papers, William Eric Nixon.

86 See, in particular, the analysis in William Stewart, *Canadians on the Somme, 1916* (London: Helion, 2017).

87 Raleigh, *The War in the Air,* 2:272–73.

88 NA (UK), Air 1/2053/204/391/4, Notes on Artillery Co-Operation 1916.

89 Raleigh, *The War in the Air,* 2:172.

90 Communique No. 54, 15 September 1916 in Cole, *RFC Communiques,* 256–63.

91 LAC, RG 9-III-D-3, vol. 4813, file 6, War Diaries, Canadian Corps, General Staff 1916/07/01–1916/09/30, 15 September 1916.

92 NA (UK), Air 1/2220/209/40/8, War Diary, 5th Brigade, Intelligence Summary, 15 September 1916.

93 Philpott, *Three Armies on the Somme,* 337.

94 On the air battle in April 1917, see Peter Hart's balanced perspective in *Bloody April* (London: Cassell, 2007).

95 NA (UK), Air 1/765/204/4/243, RFC Summary of Brigade and Squadron Work.

96 For an exploration of the myth of the knights of the air, see Eric Leed, *No Man's Land: Combat and Identity in World War I* (New York: Cambridge University Press, 1979), 134–35.

97 I describe the Boelcke-McKay engagement and the subsequent newspaper cover in *One in a Thousand,* 77–86. The story was front-page news in Canadian papers in early November 1916 and was even carried by the *New York Times.*

98 Several somewhat dubious retellings of this engagement exist, almost entirely based on von Richthofen's own account in his wartime "autobiography." For the perspective of 24's pilots on the opening phase of the battle, see the 24 SRB, vol. 5, entries for 23 November 1916 and appended material.

99 McKay, Logbook, entries for November 1917.

100 NA (UK), Officers' Service Records, Air 1/76/31/176, A.E. McKay.

2

"When Told to Advance, They Advanced": War Culture and the CEF

Jonathan F. Vance

"Morning broke with a clear and warm day." So begins the war diary of the 15th Battalion (48th Highlanders) for 26 September 1916.[1] How many days on the Western Front opened with such innocent promise, and how many closed in unimaginable pain? The twenty-sixth of September was such a day, and it would be one of the deadliest for the Canadian Corps. The campaign on the Somme produced three of the ten bloodiest days – Flers-Courcelette, Thiepval Ridge, and Regina Trench. All three actions were confined to an area of a few square miles, and they spanned just a few weeks. For the Canadian Corps, the reward for surviving Courcelette was being asked to capture Thiepval Ridge and Regina Trench. On the Somme, as at Passchendaele and during the Hundred

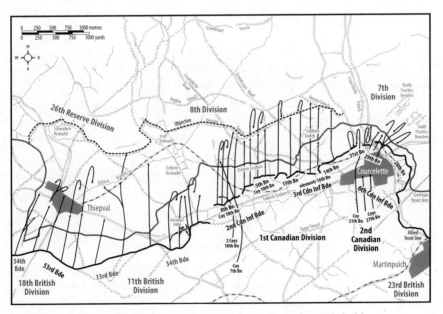

Figure 2.1 Thiepval Ridge, 26 September 1916. | Map by Mike Bechthold.

Days, there was always another attack to launch, always another trench to take; the men at the sharp end must have felt that it would never end. As their ranks were thinned, refilled, and then thinned again, each man must have wondered when he would become a statistic.

And yet, most of them stuck it. Canadian soldiers never downed tools en masse. As Teresa Iacobelli demonstrates in Chapter 11 of this volume, they were certainly prone to indiscipline – from minor disobedience to desertion and everything in between – but at no point did entire units in the front lines break.[2] When told to advance, they obeyed, no matter how dire the conditions or unpromising the plan. Robert Oliver Buchan of the 15th Battalion, raised by the 48th Highlanders, a Toronto militia unit, was one of those soldiers. Thiepval Ridge was far from his first taste of battle. He had joined the 15th Battalion on 1 October 1915, just before it went into divisional reserve near Ploegsteert, in the Ypres salient, and he remained with it through the winter of 1915–16. He fought at Mont Sorrel in June 1916, when the 15th lost over 250 killed, wounded, and missing, and was promoted to corporal on 10 July 1916. He stayed with the 15th for another year until a wound put him out of action for good.[3] Except for those four years in uniform, Rob Buchan lived a most unmilitary life; he was an archetypal citizen-soldier of the kind that became a focal point in Canada's mythology of the Great War. Through him, we can get a sense of that dreadful day at Thiepval Ridge in September 1916 and of how the civilian world that produced him also enabled him to endure in the world of violence to which he had been committed.

THE LONG AGONY THAT was the Battle of the Somme was entering its final stages when the Canadian Corps readied for the assault on Thiepval Ridge. The Somme, as a campaign, always suffered from an identity crisis. Whatever its initial aim had been, it had become hopelessly muddled by September 1916. Was it to draw pressure off the French at Verdun or the Russians in the east? Was it about gaining ground or killing Germans? Indeed, one could argue that, by the fall, there remained only one realistic goal: securing advantageous positions on which to shut down the offensive and dig in for another winter.[4]

The attack on 26 September was one of a sequence intended to push British lines farther north, toward high ground that they could occupy for the winter. Along the line in that sector, the shattered remains of villages slowly and painfully fell to the British armies – Morval, Combles, Martinpuich, Courcelette, Gueudecourt. Now it was time to take Thiepval and the higher ground behind it. On the west, the British 2nd Corps would capture Mouquet Farm, Zollern Redoubt, and Stuff Redoubt. To the east, the Canadian Corps was given the task of taking Zollern Trench, Hessian Trench, and Regina/Kenora Trench. The job fell to the 1st Division, alongside the 2nd Corps, with the widest frontage (the 8th and 5th Battalions on the left, the 15th and 14th Battalions on the right), and the 2nd Division on the right (31st, 29th, and 28th Battalions), which would push north from the ruins of Courcelette.

Almost in the centre of the Canadian front, facing Sudbury Trench, was the 15th Battalion. Immediately north of the unit's first line was an area that the Canadians would know as Death Valley; it sloped toward the German lines, meaning that any advance would have to be uphill. In the distance ahead, beyond an old trench called Fabeck Graben, was the low ridge northwest of the rubble of Courcelette, which had been captured a few weeks earlier; beyond it was the main German position, Regina Trench. Despite the daunting tactical picture, the brigade's operational order for 26 September was deceptively simple:

5. (a) At zero hour, which will be communicated separately the intense shrapnel barrage will begin and the Assaulting Infantry will advance up to it.

(b) On arrival at 1st Objective the waves intended to reach the 2nd and Final Objectives will cross and reform beyond it, leaving in it only the parties detailed to Mop up and consolidate it.

(c) On arrival at 2nd Objective there will be a pause, while patrols will be pushed forward, following up the barrages, to report whether the wire in front of the final Objective is sufficiently cut for an Infantry Assault, and whether the REGINA Trench is occupied by Germans ...

(d) As soon as the final Objective is reached, Patrols will be pushed out as far as the barrage permits.[5]

By the same token, the 15th Battalion war diary's description of the attack is stark and entirely unrevealing, giving little indication of the drama and difficulty of the day.[6] The prose is matter-of-fact and unadorned, as one would expect from a war diary, and the account is a masterpiece of understatement. The adjective used most frequently is "good," which appears eight times in a single page.

For a more detailed, and indeed realistic, account, we must turn to the battalion's official history.[7] Published in 1932, it was written by Kim Beattie, who had lied about his age and joined the 92nd Battalion when he was just fifteen years old. He reached the 15th Battalion in the field on 18 March 1916 (two weeks after his sixteenth birthday) and remained with the unit until July 1917, when a notarized copy of his birth record reached the army. He was soon back in Canada with his discharge. Beattie became a journalist and prolific author after the war, writing a two-volume history of Ridley College in St. Catharines, Ontario, the Second World War history of the 48th Highlanders, and a biography of mining magnate and soldier Joe Boyle – as well as his own Great War novel *"And You!"*

In his preface to the 15th Battalion history, Beattie reflected on what soldiers remembered and how those memories formed the stuff of his historical account:

> Now and then there were stark impressions – little things burned deep where all else was welter. A comrade twisting, shattered and broken, to the shell-spouting earth, was often the one indelible and clear memory of a battle that changed history. Dead-cluttered gully and pummelled ridge, trench angle and road direction, night routes and up-the-line trench-ways, were clouded in the roar and stress and chaos. So the author sorted and discarded from the narratives conjured up for him from the fogs of battle and here are set down those truths and near-truths that could be sifted from the jumbled whole.[8]

These guiding principles are evident in Beattie's portrayal of the fighting on 26 September, which has a ring of authenticity. It is dramatic but not over-dramatized; the horrors are not hidden, but neither are they gratuitous. He begins by describing the pent-up energy of the battalion waiting to attack: "There was restrained excitement but plenty of confidence and if the officers worried, with their added responsibility, the men were surprisingly free from it and none showed it." Then, at 12:34 p.m. precisely, "the machine-guns opened with a storm of fire that utterly smothered a shout at arm's length – and it was on! ... Men moved as they do when facing a hail of fire, like automatons, appearing unafraid but with a white, strained look of waiting for something." The war diary recorded that "casualties [were] apparently light," but Beattie's version is rather different. In fact, the 15th was badly held up by machine-gun nests that had escaped bombardment due to the German tactic of abandoning trenches in favour of advance shell holes when an attack seemed imminent. This meant that the battalion faced stiff enemy fire immediately upon leaving the trenches: "Highlanders fell just after leaping over the parapet, white knees showing and rifles held high ... Fabeck Graben was alive with Germans." The casualties mounted alarmingly, giving the survivors memories that were likely to burn deep: "A sergeant crashed backwards, his hands to his face and blood spurting from between his fingers. Another laughed, then gushing blood choked him as he fell, slowly with unutterable surprise on his face." Cradling helmets full of bombs in the crooks of their arms, two Highlanders cleared a couple of machine-gun nests and allowed the advance to continue but not before heavy losses had been sustained: "The space between the trench and our front-line was dotted with kilted figures ... Over every foot of ground men were twisting suddenly and queerly and going down with a crash of equipment as men do when hit hard."[9] As casualties climbed, the battalion's advance slowed. By 3:00 p.m., the forward platoons were starting to dig in (or, rather, were using German prisoners to do the digging) by connecting shell holes into defensible lines. Dusk saw the 15th settled into positions about 150 yards south of Regina Trench.

Headquarters, showing a fondness for double negatives, judged the outcome of the attack to be "not unsatisfactory."[10] It would be fairer to say that the results were decidedly mixed. The 14th Battalion (Royal Montreal Regiment), advancing on the right shoulder of the Highlanders, did extremely well; within thirty minutes of zero hour, the lead companies had passed Sudbury Trench and were on their way up the slope toward the eastern end of Kenora Trench. But having advanced farther than the two battalions on either side, the Montreal men were at the mercy of solid enfilade fire and eventually had to fall back toward Sudbury Trench. Around Courcelette, the 29th Battalion advanced quickly and was in the enemy trenches within ten minutes; the 31st Battalion alongside encountered stiffer resistance and made only limited gains. The 28th Battalion, which was to push eastward from Courcelette with tank support, had its attack cancelled when 50 percent of its tanks (that is to say, one tank) became bogged down. On the other side of the Canadian front, the 8th and 5th Battalions made good initial progress but were unable to clear Zollern and Hessian Trenches completely. The 1st and 2nd Divisions were therefore instructed to make ready for further operations to close a few worrying gaps in the Allied front line. In the British 2nd Corps sector, results were also mixed. Zollern Redoubt, Mouquet Farm, and most of Thiepval were in British hands by dusk, but it took another four days to clear the village and get a foothold on Stuff Redoubt.

And the day's cost had been terrible. The 1st and 2nd Divisions of the Canadian Corps lost over 700 dead, most from just a handful of battalions. The last line in the 15th Battalion war diary for 26 September, which reads almost like an afterthought, noted that the estimated casualties for the operation were 330. In fact, they were 343. Two officers and 115 other ranks had been killed, 10 officers and 213 other ranks were wounded, 1 man was gassed, and 2 had been captured. One of the wounded was Private Harold Bell, who described the experience in a letter to his mother near Cobourg, Ontario:

> We were in one of the big fights that have come off lately and got what we went after but lost pretty heavily, but nothing to what the Germans did. I got a dose of shrapnel in the face, at least three pieces, just before we reached the front line, but stayed until we had it, and was going on, then I made my way back towards the dressing station taking some prisoners with me.[11]

In his account, Beattie hastened to add that the men got over the losses fairly swiftly: "The old soldier appeared to forget most quickly for he long ago had learned the wisdom of pretending to himself that he had forgotten."[12]

We have no way of knowing if Rob Buchan was one of those who forgot quickly; all we can say is that he got right back to business. He was rewarded with ten days' leave at the beginning of December (his first leave since reaching the 15th Battalion over a year earlier) and was back with the unit for Christmas. He took part in the attack on Vimy Ridge, but on 14 April 1917 was sent to No. 7 Canadian General Hospital with the catch-all diagnosis PUO (pyrexia of unknown origin), a non-specific fever. It kept him away from the 15th for a month.

By 10 June 1917, the battalion had settled into reserve positions northwest of Neuville St-Vaast. The work of an infantry battalion is never done, and the Highlanders were called on to supply drafts for trench repairs. That night, they were detailed to work in Canada Trench, on Vimy Ridge, when they came under a heavy artillery barrage that lasted for hours and killed Captain J.S. Laycock and Private A.J. Riddle of Toronto.[13] The rest of the Highlanders were heading back to their billets when, around 2:30 a.m., a shrapnel shell burst near Rob, depositing a chunk of iron in his left forearm. Medics from the advance dressing station of No. 3 Canadian Field Ambulance dressed the wound and inoculated Rob before sending him back to No. 23 Casualty Clearing Station, where he had surgery just eighteen hours after being hit. He had further treatment at No. 26 General Hospital at Étaples, and on 20 June crossed to England on HMHS *Princess Elizabeth*. Rob Buchan never returned to the front lines. After he was released from hospital, he spent the rest of the war at West Sandling in Kent, with the 5th and 12th Reserve Battalions, taking in drafts of fresh soldiers from Canada and getting them ready to be sent to the trenches. On 10 December 1918, he boarded the SS *Melita*, arriving in Canada nine days later.

WHAT IMPELLED ROB BUCHAN to fight? Why did he enlist in the first place, and what carried him through those terrible days on the Somme, not to mention all the other terrible days of that terrible war? He left only the slimmest of archival records – a handful of letters published in the local newspaper – and I never had the chance to talk to him about his experiences. I knew some of his siblings: his eldest sister, Matilda, known as Mattie, a delightfully garrulous woman of the type that the Victorians might have unkindly called a crone; and his younger brother Stan, a thin, tidy man with a string tie and very little to say. Mattie pronounced her surname with a short U and the first syllable accented; Stan preferred a long U and the accent on the second syllable. I don't know which version Rob adopted.

Modern scholars might suggest that the notion of "war culture" can explain Rob's ability to endure battle. As Henry Giroux writes, "War culture provides the educational platforms that include those cultural apparatuses, institutions, beliefs and policies with the capacity to produce the discourses, spectacles of violence, cultures of fear, military values, hypermasculine ideologies and militarized policies that give war machines their legitimacy, converting them into symbols of national identity, if not honored ideals."[14] In this reasoning, the ability to make war is culturally conditioned by a dense web of practices and ideals that ennoble martial conduct; soldiers are able to survive in that world of violence because their upbringing has persuaded them that violence, apparently in pursuit of nationalist aims, is normal and indeed desirable.[15]

The argument is persuasive for the twenty-first century. One need only turn on the television to see myriad examples of "spectacles of violence, cultures of fear, military values, hypermasculine ideologies and militarized policies that give war machines their legitimacy." But applied to Canadian society as it existed a century ago, the war culture concept makes less sense. Indeed, very little of it can apply to the world that Rob inhabited before 1914.[16]

Rob's life before the war gave little hint of a war culture, or indeed of the qualities that allowed him to rise to a non-commissioned rank in the 15th Battalion. Born in 1890 to a family of market gardeners in the rural Ontario township of East Flamborough, at the western end of Lake Ontario, he was one of eleven siblings born between 1887 and 1909. Waterdown, the township's largest village and Rob Buchan's home, is only six miles from Hamilton, the nearest major urban centre that was large enough to have the kind of platforms, apparatuses, and institutions to which Giroux refers. But it is unwise to minimize the isolation of a village, even one that was just a few miles from a major city. Not until Rob was an adult did Hamilton become easily accessible. There was no train connection until 1912, and automobiles were few and far between in the early twentieth century. Most people owned horses, but the notion of using them for anything other than work was foreign to villagers. Farmers like Rob might take their rigs into Hamilton for market day, but there was hardly time to partake of any "spectacles of violence" when the produce had to be sold – and in any case, taking the harvest to market was typically women's work.

Rob went to school in Waterdown but probably not beyond grade eight – and if the broad statistics can be applied to any one student, his attendance was perhaps spotty at best. In 1895, when he probably started school, fifty-seven students were registered in Waterdown's high school, but the average attendance was only twenty-six (45.6 percent).[17] Through the 1880s and 1890s, when Waterdown's future members of the Canadian Expeditionary Force (CEF) were being educated, average attendance hovered between 45 percent and 55 percent, rarely surpassing 60 percent. Canada's schools certainly tried to be agents of patriotic instruction, as many scholars have shown, but on any given day, only half of the registered students showed up to be culturally conditioned by their teachers and textbooks.[18]

The church is another institution that is implicated in a war culture, especially where there is a strong connection between religious conservatism and nationalism. But religion did not seem to be a particularly powerful force in the Buchan family's life, at least theologically. Rob's parents, Eli and Annie, were married in a Methodist church in 1885, but in the 1891 census, Eli declared himself a Methodist and Annie a Lutheran, whereas the children were listed as English Church. In 1901, the entire family was recorded as Methodist, but in 1911 all declared themselves to be English Church. As Gordon L. Heath argues in Chapter 8 of this volume, religious identities and views were "fluid, adaptive, and contradictory, and they evolved over time and circumstances" (page 181). For the Buchans, church membership was more social than doctrinal.[19] There are no surviving attendance records for Waterdown's Grace Anglican Church, so we don't know if the Buchans were faithful churchgoers, but they were not involved in church governance or committees before 1914. Rob was an active member of the Anglican Young People's Association (AYPA), an organization whose national publications suggest an attempt to inculcate a nationalist, muscular Christianity. For example, a later songbook, probably from the early 1940s, included such selections as "Our Empire's Here to Stay," "There'll Always Be an England," "We'll Never Let the Old Flag Fall," and "When Britain First with One Accord."[20] But the detailed minutes of Grace Church's AYPA meetings tell a different story; regardless of what the nationalist agenda of the organization might have been, local activities focused not on God, King, and Empire, but on party, picnic, and Christmas concert.[21]

There were other institutions in the village and township, but most seem to have followed the AYPA's example, showing far more interest in local matters than in national or international ones. On the basis of surviving accounts, it is difficult to imagine the Sylvia Club or the Waterdown Debating Society inculcating much of anything, and the Waterdown branch of the Women's Institute remained true to its motto (For Home and Country) by devoting more attention to the former than to the latter. During a typical Women's Institute meeting in 1914, a Mrs. Blagden delivered an "ideal Paper on Our flag, and what it stands for," followed by Miss Robson's paper "Simple meals, well cooked and nicely served" and Mrs. Davidson's demonstration of icing a cake.[22] The Women's Institute minute book confirms that home-centred programs outnumbered patriotic ones by a factor of three or four to one. Regardless of the orientation of national headquarters, the local evidence suggests that such institutions were thinly veiled social clubs. Any business to be transacted seems to have been dispensed with quickly, so that the bulk of the time could be given over to food and entertainment. The speed with which villagers set up patriotic organizations when the war began might be read as proof that a nascent war culture was all ready to be coaxed into life. However, it more probably demonstrates that rural society was relentlessly clubbish and looked for any excuse to meet. The existence of the Society for the Recovery of Stolen Horses in Waterdown was not proof that horse theft was endemic in the township. In fact, it was rare and the society's minutes were almost always the same: "There were no horses stolen in East Flamborough." The members of the society simply enjoyed getting together, and the war brought no change to this tendency. If villagers had not met as the Women's Patriotic League, they would have met as something else.

The press is also essential to the formation of war culture, and Eugen Weber posits it as a key mechanism for transforming peasants into Frenchmen during the late nineteenth century.[23] Whether it played the same role in Rob Buchan's world is debatable. The Hamilton and Dundas daily newspapers were certainly available in East Flamborough, and though they were not national publications, the *Spectator*, the *Evening Journal*, and the *Star* were typical of the kind of papers that Weber describes as connecting locals to a larger polity. However, it is impossible to say how widely they sold in Waterdown. The village itself had no newspaper until May 1918, when the weekly *Waterdown Review* was established. It was unapologetically local, like most rural weeklies of the time. The odd bit of international news crept into the pre-printed page blocks supplied by a central news service, but the paper noticed scarcely anything that occurred more than five miles beyond the township's boundaries – and most of those references pertained to some local traveller who was visiting a distant relative while on holiday.

In short, although much of the writing on war culture presupposes its national character, manifestations of national identity are conspicuous by their absence in East Flamborough before 1914. National and imperial organizations certainly did their best to propagate nationalist and imperialist ideas, but they faced rural societies that had more pressing concerns – everything from harvests and livestock to keeping the roads passable. Until the time that Rob enlisted, he led an intensely local life. In this, he was probably typical of much of rural Canada.[24] It should come as no surprise that the forces that allowed Rob to get through battle after battle were intensely local as well.

He didn't join up as soon as the war began. The call for volunteers in August 1914 was directed at men with military experience, and Rob had taken no part in local militia duties. Years earlier, Waterdown mustered a company of the 13th Royal Regiment, but it had long since decamped for nearby Dundas. The 77th

Figure 2.2 Rob Buchan's 36th Battalion on the march in Niagara, 1915. | University of Western Ontario, History Department, Ley and Lois Smith War, Memory and Popular Culture Research Collection.

Wentworth Regiment was not far away, in Hamilton, and a few local men took part in summer manoeuvres, but all evidence suggests that in rural areas such as East Flamborough, militia service was as much a lark as anything. Press accounts of sham battles portray them as something between a Boy Scout camp and a school sports day – taken seriously only by certain unit officers. In the summer of 1914, Stan Sawell of Waterdown tried to convince two friends that they should sign on for the upcoming militia manoeuvres as a vacation; he was outvoted, so the trio went camping for their holidays instead.[25] Any reluctance to join up right away might also be explained by the fact that at the beginning of the war there was nowhere to enlist in Waterdown, or in the entire township of East Flamborough. Those who were eager to enlist had to go to Hamilton, where the cavernous armouries on James Street North had been a magnet for volunteers since August 1914.

In November 1914, Hamilton became home to yet another infantry battalion, the 36th. Now and then, men from East Flamborough rode into the city to join the new unit, but on 19 April 1915 nine decided to enlist together. Seven were friends from Aldershot, the southernmost community in East Flamborough. John Filman, Frank Harrod, and Gordon Horne were all from old East Flamborough families, whereas George Flint and George Taylor were recent immigrants from Britain. So was Tom Humphreys, who followed his older brother,

William, into the CEF. Merv Hopkinson was from Grey County, Ontario, and he worked with George Taylor, stringing line for the Bell Telephone Company. Two Waterdown men went along with them and were attested the following day: Clifford Nicholson and Rob Buchan. Conventional wisdom tells us that, in the heat of battle, men fought for the comrades on either side of them. Evidence from Rob's war suggests that this explanation can be extended and that a soldier's ability to carry on might be sustained by ties to community, carefully nurtured by contact with the most vital reminders of home and the men with whom he enlisted.

The nine friends were split up between various units, but they were careful to keep track of each other as they moved around. A letter from John Filman to his parents in Aldershot is typical of the correspondence that any one of them might have written:

I suppose you have heard that Joe Harrod has gone to the front. He is with the first Battalion and two Waterdown boys Bob Buchan [*sic*] and George Taylor are with the fifteenth Batt at the front. Tom Humphreys is a cook here now ... Gordon Horne is back again. He beat me getting better as he is out on parade now and I am in our hut writing a letter.[26]

On 17 February 1916, Filman wrote to his father from France that he had visited Frank Harrod elsewhere at the front and found that "he looks fine and is getting fat."[27] In these and other letters, we see the ties that linked home and front. The friends saw each other occasionally in Britain and France, for, as a letter from George Taylor explained, "you look forward to meeting your old pals again with the greatest of pleasure."[28] They also used the mail to maintain contact, with their families in East Flamborough acting as conduits for information. The Filman, Harrod, Horne, and Humphreys families all knew each other well; while the young men served together, their parents and siblings worked together in patriotic organizations and Victory Bond drives. Other correspondence in the Filman family papers reveals that they shared mail. A letter to one family was passed around to others, informally at first and later in the pages of the *Waterdown Review,* after it debuted in May 1918.

The *Review* printed three or four letters from soldiers in each edition and was obviously interested in highlighting the local experience at war. Even allowing for the fact that the editor was probably looking for a particular kind of letter, one can only be struck by the degree to which the soldiers were determined to keep in touch with each other while in uniform and, through those contacts, to remain closely connected to their homes. In October 1918, Private Sam Cook, who had been wounded while serving with the 19th Battalion, wrote a letter to his mother (the proprietor of the North American Hotel in Waterdown) that captures how much home ties dominated the thoughts of soldiers: "Met Bob Buchan and had a long talk with him, also young Ireland from Vinegar Hill. He left in a draft for France. I must look up Jim Simmons and Geo. Taylor, as I hear they are at Witley before I arrived here."[29] A few weeks earlier, Taylor, convalescing in Brighton, had written home to East Flamborough in very similar terms:

> It seems a long time since I have written you that I believe I have seen Stanley [Buchan] since. In fact, I saw him more than once, the first time Bob [Buchan] and I took a walk to the camp he was in when he first arrived in England ... Shortly after Stan came up to within a stone's throw of us, and we ran across Austin Tudor besides. They used to come over to my hut for a chat quite often before I went back to France. Once in a while we would go into a restaurant, have a feed and talk over old times. Tudor went out to France about the same time as I went back. He came to see me a few days before I was wounded, being in the 14th Battalion and the same brigade, he did not have very far to go.[30]

At first glance, such letters may seem to offer little to the historian, with their laundry lists of names, some identifiable, some not:

> My Dear Mother:
>
> Say, is Henry Stonhouse over here. I was over to see Earl last night, but I forgot to ask him. I heard he was killed, but I didn't see Lloyd Binkley, but I saw Russell Carey, and he told me the boys were getting along fine. I also saw Vern Willis. I had a letter from Henry Jackson the other day and he says he expects to come to France any day now ...
>
> From your loving son,
>
> Spr. J.A. Morden[31]

But the welter of names in fact gives us profound insights into what mattered to soldiers when they were out of battle and had the opportunity to write home.

Other soldier letters, whether printed in the *Waterdown Review* or held in local archival collections, are very similar in nature – they name East Flamborough soldiers encountered overseas, ask about those who hadn't been seen recently, and after May 1918, request copies of the *Review*. "Hey Liz," wrote one soldier identified only as Will, when are you going to send me some more of these Waterdown Reviews? I haven't had any for over a month now. Please put them in envelopes when you do send any and then I shall be sure, or almost sure, to get them; when you send them in a wrapper I never get them, and I like to have them very much, you see they have so much news in them that you cannot possibly give me in a letter.[32]

And occasionally, there is a reference to someone who had been craving such contact, as in a letter from Private Fred James in France to his mother:

I saw someone here the other day I did not think about, it was Joe Eager, well, of course, Capt. Eager. He is the M.D. of the 78th Batt., and he heard I was here so he looked me up. It was a very pleasant surprise for me. He said I was the first one he had seen from home, and that is two years now.[33]

When James wrote this letter, he was with the 75th Battalion at Camblain-Châtelain, west of Béthune, and Eager's 78th Battalion was just to the north at Rambert. Granted, the distance between the two is not great – a little over five kilometres – and the Canadian Corps was in reserve at the time. Still, for a captain of the medical corps to track down and visit a lowly private from another battalion suggests a deep desire to connect with something tangible from home that could provide stability and security and a much-needed anchor of normalcy.

As many of these letters indicate, Rob Buchan acted as a kind of linchpin for East Flamborough soldiers once he joined the staff of the reserve battalions at West Sandling. Everyone seemed to know where to find him, and he was in a position to act as something of a den-father to local boys who came over. In May 1918, Stan Buchan, Rob's younger brother by six years, was conscripted and within a month was on his way overseas. Rob would have heard from home that Stan was on his way, and a letter to his sister expresses the concern of an older brother, as well as the desire to look out for others from the community:

I have heard nothing of him [Stan] as yet, but we are on the lookout for a big draft any day now and I expect that he will be on it. I will try and find out just as soon as I hear of their landing, and I will write and let you know. I daresay that it would upset you all, being that he was sent away so sudden. I know I kind of felt it myself, but not so much as you people would, and besides I will get over it sooner than you will, for I will be so pleased to see him, but I am very sorry that it was not me landing on the other side of the water, instead of him landing on this side.

Well, I will try and put him on the right road when he gets here and I will try and look after him as much as I can. I don't like to tell you, but I think that it will be best in the long run, that is that they only get from ten to fourteen weeks in England and then they are shot across to France. Of course if things keep quiet over there why he may have longer to stop here, but you can never tell what's going to happen. They will be in segregation for a month after they land here, so it will be some time before he is able to see much of the country. I will try and fix both him and Gordon Bowman up for a leave as soon as it is possible, and find out where they want to go to.[34]

A few days later, Rob wrote again:

I will be on the lookout for Stan when he comes over. We are expecting a big draft in from Canada any day now, so I expect he will be on it and I will try and make it a point to see him as soon as I can and I will try and do all that I can for him, for I know that he will be worse than I was when I first came over here.[35]

It is impossible to know what Rob meant by "worse." Perhaps he meant that Stan's life had changed so much in such a short time – conscripted into the 1st Depot Battalion, 2nd Central Ontario Regiment, on 9 May, he left Canada for England just twenty-five days later, on 3 June. Rob, by contrast, had spent a little over two months in Canada between enlistment and departure. More important is that Rob saw himself as the protector of his brother and of other local men who came through his camp.

But the connection to home wasn't foolproof, as Rob observed in the same letter:

I am sorry that I did not recognize Eddie Crane if I had him in my squad, but you know three and a half years is a long time, and he was only a boy when I left, and besides a uniform makes a big difference in a person. I daresay that a lot of the boys I know in the army now I would not know in three years time with civil clothes on.[36]

Whereas Gordon Bowman never got beyond England, and Stan Buchan reached the 54th Battalion at the front just ten days before the Armistice, Eddie Crane wasn't so lucky. Conscripted on 23 January 1918, he left Canada on 21 February, arriving in England on 4 March. On 29 August, he joined the 54th Battalion in the field, and on 30 September he was killed in action.

The friends who had joined the 36th Battalion with Rob were no more for-tunate. Clifford Nicholson was transferred to the field butchery and returned to Waterdown after the war. Tom Humphreys came back early, invalided out of the 18th Battalion in April 1916 with pleurisy. Gordon Horne, who served with the 1st Battalion, was wounded in June 1916 and never returned to the front. All of the others perished. George Flint was killed in March 1916, with the 18th Battalion, and Frank Harrod died in action three months later as a member of the 1st Battalion. John Filman died just a week after the 15th Battalion's as-sault at Thiepval Ridge of wounds sustained at Courcelette. Merv Hopkinson of the 1st Battalion also died at Courcelette. George Taylor, who was awarded the Distinguished Conduct Medal for gallantry while serving with the 15th Battalion at the Canal du Nord on 27 September 1918, returned to Waterdown after the war; Rob Buchan was a witness at his wedding in 1919. But George's wounds never healed, eventually killing him in January 1921.

All of this evidence affirms that soldiers like Rob Buchan valued and actively cultivated a deep connection with home. Whether this link provided motiv-ation, sustenance, or comfort – or all three – is difficult to say. What is clear, though, is that the civilian world of East Flamborough was not antithetical to the military world of Corporal Robert Oliver Buchan, 15th Battalion. There was no sense of us versus them, or of stay-at-homes whose naiveté about the realities of war made them repugnant to *frontsoldaten*. There were no civilians like the ones whom Siegfried Sassoon satirized so viciously in his poetry – the theatre-goers in "Blighters" cram the music hall to "grin and cackle" at songs about tanks, the squire of "Memorial Tablet" nags and bullies his son to enlist, and the hawkish bishop in "They" is unmoved by the dead, the blinded, and the blasted. Such characterizations have become powerful and popular meta-phors for an unbridgeable gulf separating civilian from soldier. There may indeed have been such a gulf in Rob Buchan's world. The people of East Flamborough could not, in any real sense, understand what Rob and his fellow soldiers went through at Thiepval Ridge; he may not have tried to explain it to them. But that fact never acted as a wedge between home and front. If anything, it made the people at home even more essential to a soldier's morale at the front. It was that local connection, not a nationalist war culture that had indoctrinated and accustomed him to war and militarism, that sustained Rob through trials such as Thiepval Ridge.

Rob's discharge became final on 24 January 1919, after nearly four years in uniform. He returned to the family farm and had no further contact with things military. How had the experience changed him? His discharge certificate de-clared that he was "medically unfit," his wound having left him with a slight stiffness of the wrist, but even that was contentious. In a June 1918 letter to his sister, Rob responded to a friend's comment that she had conveyed to him:

> Tell Jack Dallon that the man that thinks he knows me, don't know me at all, or else he don't know what he is talking about, for I am not a bit more disfigured now than I was when I left Canada and my fingers are not on the bum, so you can tell him that he does not know what he is talking about.[37]

It's impossible to say exactly what he was responding to, but we can guess. Jack Dallon probably predicted that war would be Rob's downfall and that, having been wounded in battle, he would no longer be fit for a hard day's work. Such a suggestion was an affront to any working man but probably doubly insulting to someone who had put his life on hold to do a different kind of work. Rob's rebuttal implies that, in his mind, the war's impact on him had been limited; he would soon be home, and life would go on as it always had. Nothing in Rob's life before 1914 suggests that he was an inherently violent man, but he seems to have assimilated well into a world of violence. He saw his friends killed, and he almost certainly killed men on the other side, and yet toward the end of it all, he insisted that he was essentially unchanged by the experience. Of course, it would be naive to assume that four years in uniform had no impact whatsoever. However, Rob used the vestiges of home – contact with family, friends, news – as a shield against any damage the war could do to him. He left Waterdown to fight, but Waterdown never really left him.

Notes

1 Library and Archives Canada (LAC), Department of Militia and Defence Records, RG 9, series III-D-3, vol. 4924, file 391, reel T-10718, War Diary, 15th Canadian Infantry Battalion, 26 September 1916.
2 Iacobelli notes that two of her three selected soldiers had less than exemplary disciplinary records prior to deserting (pages 256–57).
3 All of the details on Buchan's service are from his personnel file. LAC, RG 150, accession 1992/93, box 1227, file 22, service file of #406684 R.O. Buchan.
4 See, for example, William Philpott, *Three Armies on the Somme: The First Battle of the Twentieth Century* (New York: Alfred A. Knopf, 2010), especially Chapter 2; and Martin Gilbert, *The Battle of the Somme: The Heroism and Horror of War* (Toronto: McClelland and Stewart, 2006), especially 13–21.
5 LAC, Department of Militia and Defence Records, RG 9, series III-D-3, vol. 4876, file 220, reel T-10673, War Diary, 3rd Canadian Infantry Brigade, September 1916, Appendix 50. No Brigade war diaries were written for the month.
6 LAC, War Diary, 15th Canadian Infantry Battalion, 26 September 1916.
7 Kim Beattie, *48th Highlanders of Canada, 1891–1928* (Toronto: 48th Highlanders, 1932).
8 Ibid., viii.
9 Beattie's description of the attack can be found in ibid., 173–81.

10 G.W.L. Nicholson, *Canadian Expeditionary Force, 1914–1919: Official History of the Canadian Army in the First World War* (Ottawa: Department of National Defence, 1962), 177.

11 Harold Bell to mother, printed in the *Cobourg World*, 27 October 1916, Canadian Letters and Images Project, http://canadianletters.ca/content/document-2934.

12 Beattie, *48th Highlanders*, 183.

13 LAC, Department of Militia and Defence Records, RG 9, series III-D-3, vol. 4924, file 391, reel T-10718, War Diary, 15th Canadian Infantry Battalion, 10 June 1917.

14 Henry A. Giroux, "War Culture, Militarism and Racist Violence under Trump," 14 December 2016, Truthout, http://www.truth-out.org/news/item/38711-war-culture-militarism-and-racist-violence-under-donald-trump.

15 See also Jon Simons and John Louis Lucaites, *In/Visible War: The Culture of War in Twenty-First-Century America* (New Brunswick, NJ: Rutgers University Press, 2017); and Kelly Denton-Borhaug, "US War Culture and the *Star Wars* Juggernaut," *Theology and Science* 14, 4 (2016): 393–97.

16 For the full account of East Flamborough's experience during the First World War, see Jonathan F. Vance, *A Township at War* (Waterloo: Wilfrid Laurier University Press, 2018).

17 Ontario, Department of Education, *Report of the Minister of Education, Ontario, 1896* (Toronto: Warwick Bros. and Rutter, 1897).

18 See, for example, Mark Moss, *Manliness and Militarism: Educating Young Boys in Ontario for War* (Don Mills: Oxford University Press, 2001). For earlier ruminations on the subject, see Geoffrey Milburn and John Herbert, eds., *National Consciousness and the Curriculum: The Canadian Case* (Toronto: Ontario Institute for Studies in Education, 1974); and Alf Chaiton and Neil McDonald, eds., *Canadian Schools and Canadian Identity* (Toronto: Gage, 1977).

19 For other interpretations of this point, see David Marshall, *Secularizing the Faith: Canadian Protestant Clergy and the Crisis of Belief, 1850–1940* (Toronto: University of Toronto Press, 1992), 11–12; and John Webster Grant, *The Church in the Canadian Era* (Burlington, ON: Welch, 1988), especially Chapter 5.

20 *The A.Y.P.A. Song Book* (Toronto: Dominion Council of the A.Y.P.A., n.d.).

21 Grace Anglican Church Archives, Waterdown, Ontario, Minute Book of the Anglican Young People's Association of Grace Church, Waterdown, Dominion Branch no. 63, commencing February fifth, nineteen hundred and fourteen.

22 Flamborough Archives, Waterdown, Ontario, Meeting minutes book, Waterdown Branch of the Women's Institute, 7 October 1914.

23 Eugen Weber, *Peasants into Frenchmen: The Modernization of Rural France, 1870–1914* (Stanford: Stanford University Press, 1976), Chapter 18.

24 For an analysis of another rural context that yields similar conclusions, see Jonathan F. Vance, "'Some Great Crisis of Storm and Stress': L.M. Montgomery, Canadian Literature, and the Great War," in *L.M. Montgomery and War*, ed. Andrea McKenzie and Jane Ledwell (Montreal and Kingston: McGill-Queen's University Press, 2017), 41–55.

25 Steven Sawell, ed., *Into the Cauldron: Experiences of a CEF Infantry Officer during the Great War* (Burlington, ON: Privately printed, 2009), 2.

26 Joseph Brant Museum, Burlington, Ontario, Filman Family Records, John Filman to father, 13 October 1915.

27 Ibid., 17 February 1916.

28 George Taylor to Mrs. Cook, undated, in *Waterdown Review*, 19 September 1918.

29 Sam Cook to mother, 30 October 1918, in *Waterdown Review*, 28 November 1918. Alfred Ireland was conscripted in May 1918 but never reached the front. Vinegar Hill is a local name for a relatively steep section of Dundas Street (Highway 5), just east of Grindstone Creek in Waterdown. James Simmons, Waterdown's blacksmith and bell-ringer, enlisted

in the 129th Battalion in January 1916 and served with the Canadian Army Service Corps in England.

30 George Taylor to "Friend," 17 October 1918, in *Waterdown Review*, 7 November 1918. Waterdown native Austin Tudor became a prisoner of war in October 1918 while serving with the 14th Battalion. He returned to the village in 1919.

31 J.A. Morden to mother, France, 6 September 1918, in *Waterdown Review*, 24 October 1918. All of the men mentioned in this letter, including Morden himself, had enlisted in 1916 with the 129th Battalion, and all survived the war. Henry Stonhouse and Henry Jackson cannot be positively identified.

32 Will to Liz, France, 14 July 1918, in *Waterdown Review*, 15 August 1918.

33 F.J. James to mother, 7 June 1918, in *Waterdown Review*, 11 July 1918.

34 Rob Buchan to sister, 13 June 1918, in *Waterdown Review*, 11 July 1918. Gordon Bowman of Waterdown was also a conscript. His brother Percy had joined the 129th Battalion in 1916 but later deserted and died in the village in 1918.

35 Rob Buchan to sister, 19 June 1918, in *Waterdown Review*, 25 July 1918.

36 Ibid.

37 Ibid.

3

The Voiceless Dead: Francis Jenkins, Regina Trench, and Living and Dying on the Western Front

Kyle Falcon

THE BATTLE OF ANCRE HEIGHTS began on 1 October 1916, bringing the Somme offensive into its final stage. During the preceding Battle of Thiepval Ridge (26–28 September), British and dominion forces had failed to advance to the ridge and gain the advantage of observation over the Germans. As part of the renewed offensive in October, the Canadians were tasked with taking unmet objectives, particularly Regina Trench, a heavily fortified German trench system that spanned two thousand metres.[1] Previous attempts had already been

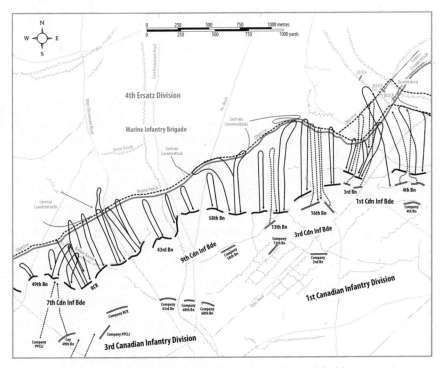

Figure 3.1 Regina Trench, 8 October 1916. | Map by Mike Bechthold.

costly, and the attack on 8 October resulted in one of Canada's deadliest days in the entire First World War.

Before dawn, the 1st and 3rd Canadian Divisions were sent over the top in three brigades, each with two battalions. West of Miraumont Road was the 9th Canadian Infantry Brigade's 43rd Battalion, along with the 58th Battalion to its east. After advancing behind a creeping barrage, the men reached the German trenches only to discover hundreds of yards of thick unbroken barbed wire.[2] In some places, the 58th Battalion managed to make it through the entanglements but was driven back by German counterattacks. The darkness complicated matters. A few men from the 43rd Battalion stumbled upon gaps by chance, but most who followed them into the enemy trenches never returned. When it became clear that the attack had stalled, the Germans in the rear opened fire.[3] Retreating soldiers were forced to lie in shell holes in No Man's Land until the cover of darkness offered safe passage back to their trenches.[4] The 43rd Battalion suffered 353 casualties, including 8 confirmed dead, 224 wounded, and 121 missing; only 73 men remained.[5] A report from the 9th Canadian Infantry Brigade concluded that "the sole reason for the failure appears to be the uncut wire ... [The officers] did all they could have done under the circumstances."[6] Total Canadian casualties for the day were 1,364 dead, wounded, and missing.[7]

The particulars of the assaults on Regina Trench in the fall of 1916 are difficult to distinguish from the greater Somme offensive. Repeatedly, soldiers were mowed down by machine-gun fire because the Allied bombardment had failed to inflict the necessary damage to German defences. Historians still debate the merits of the offensive and Haig's decision to continue the push. Were the failures of the British Expeditionary Force mandatory lessons for solving trench warfare and the casualties unavoidable, given the tactical and technological limitations? Or was the Somme a needless waste perpetrated by incompetent generals who led a generation of young men toward barbed wire and machine-gun fire in hopes of possessing a few miles of wasteland?[8]

The narrative of lions led by donkeys has endured in the popular image of the Somme, and indeed the entire war.[9] Modernist writers such as Robert Graves, Siegfried Sassoon, and Wilfred Owen captured the soldiers' sense of victimization by the war's perpetrators at home and on the front.[10] Early scholarship on their experiences relied heavily on these writings. Paul Fussell's argument that the war exposed the emptiness of high diction and romanticism was founded on a limited sample of texts written by soldiers.[11] The same was true of Eric Leed's *No Man's Land*, which contended that the experience of war irrevocably disintegrated men's identities, thus alienating them from their homelands and their civilized selves.[12] Whereas the questioning of these positions may have represented an advance for historical scholarship, they do not affect the final outcome for those who died in the Great War.

Among these men was Sergeant Francis "Frank" Jenkins. A Scottish-born carpenter from Manitoba, Jenkins enlisted in Winnipeg on 29 June 1915 and was posted overseas with the 43rd Cameron Highlanders of Canada.[13] Jenkins certainly appears to fit the label of a lion. At the time of his death in October 1916 he had been in France for eight months and had been promoted twice. Like hundreds of thousands of soldiers who died in the conflict, he was posthumously granted a British War Medal and Victory Medal for his sacrifice.[14] But there is much we do not know about Jenkins and his experiences. Not unlike the particular battles included under the rubric of the Battle of the Somme, many of the Somme dead are elusive, at risk of being forgotten or subsumed under grander narratives such as victimization. This was evident in the centennial commemorations in Britain and Canada. On 1 July 2016, 1,400 volunteers donned First World War uniforms across the United Kingdom. They refrained from speaking, and instead gave cards to inquisitive spectators that carried a name of someone who was killed on the first day of the Somme.[15] The names of the voiceless Somme dead continue to haunt Britain. In Canada, they have largely been forgotten. Official centennial commemorations failed to recognize Canadian participation on the Somme, focusing instead on Vimy Ridge. If you walk the old battlefields of France and Belgium, you will find striking monuments to Canada's "baptism of fire" at Second Ypres and the "birth of a nation" at Vimy Ridge. But at the site of the Battle of Flers-Courcelette, you must carefully examine the monument's engraving to distinguish it from the nearly identical stones at Mont Sorrel, Bourlon Wood, and the Second Battle of Arras.

What can be said about men like Jenkins, who died on the Somme and left behind a scant record? New scholarship has emerged to reclaim the soldier's agency.[16] As later generations donated surviving wartime letters and diaries across the former British Empire, historians have challenged the narratives of victimization, passivity, and alienation. Although some soldiers were certainly disillusioned by their experiences, many others fondly remembered the camaraderie of the trenches. Nor was there an unbridgeable gap between a soldier's military and civilian identity.[17] As the citizen armies of the British Commonwealth arrived on the Western Front, they brought with them cultural practices of civilian life, including sport and music, and they maintained their domestic identities as sons and husbands through letters home. As Jonathan F. Vance argues in Chapter 2 of this volume, these reference points reminded men of why they were fighting and sustained their morale; in many instances, a soldier "used the vestiges of home ... as a shield against any damage the war could do to him" (page 60). Soldiers were not merely victims of their experiences but also resourceful, resilient, and consenting.

This chapter will tackle these issues directly, arguing that the margin between living and dying at the front was exceedingly thin. In fact, the line between living and dead was blurred on many occasions, with soldiers making use of the dead in their defensive preparations and corpses being "killed" yet again during bombardments. Given the omnipresence of death, front soldiers developed a unique culture, one in which large, impersonal forces were acknowledged, but meaning and agency were bolstered through coping mechanisms such as faith, superstition, trench journals, and entertainments.

Francis Jenkins was born on 19 March 1897 in Ayrshire, Scotland. The third child of Robert and Margaret Jenkins, Francis was fourteen when he and his five siblings moved to Winnipeg in 1911.[18] Winnipeg was a natural settlement for Scottish immigrants, with the largest Scottish demographic of any Canadian city.[19] It is impossible to know precisely why Francis enlisted. There were various social pressures and pragmatic reasons that may have contributed to his decision. Of the 30,617 Canadians who formed the First Contingent, 18,495 (60 percent) were British-born, and they joined in solidarity with their homeland.[20] In the first year of the war, the kilted Cameron Highlanders marched through the streets of Winnipeg to the cheering of enthusiastic spectators.[21] The Jenkins family probably had relatives in the British Isles, which reinforced ties to the empire. As Geoffrey Hayes observes in Chapter 6 of this volume, gendered expectations to do one's duty could also exert considerable pressure on young men. Francis Jenkins's elder brother, Robert, had enlisted sixty-eight days before he did, and their youngest brother, William, followed in the fall of 1915.[22] Their brother-in-law Thomas McIlveen had joined up the previous January. Francis was certainly quick to act, having enlisted only three months after his eighteenth birthday.[23]

Unemployment may also have motivated Francis to enlist. The economy was especially weak in the western provinces, which were home to 40 percent of recruits during the second phase of enlistment.[24] In 1911, Francis began work at the Brown and Rutherford Lumber Company, earning a monthly wage of fifty dollars.[25] The following year, a major fire destroyed the facility on North Buchanan Street. Perhaps these uncertain conditions further pushed him toward enlisting. At the time of his death, Jenkins was receiving $37.20 a month for his military service.[26] This was a salary decrease, but the lure of steady income to support his family may have proven decisive. His pay was given to the family "in full," and according to his former neighbour, he was "highly pleased with being able to assist the family."[27] Whatever his reasoning, Francis Jenkins was

Figure 3.2 Brown and Rutherford Lumber fire, Winnipeg, c. 1912. | University of Alberta, Peel's Prairie Provinces, Postcard 1285, http://peel.library.ualberta.ca/postcards/PC001285.html.

one of many young men of Scottish ancestry who helped fill the ranks of Manitoba's Highlander battalions. These men arrived at the front in time for Canada's engagements at Mont Sorrel and the Somme offensive in 1916.

Upon reaching the front lines of the Somme region, Canadian soldiers passed a statue of the Virgin Mary, which dangled by a thread atop the basilica at Albert. As myth had it, the war would end once the statue finally fell, but so far it had stubbornly stayed in place.[28] Once in the front lines, soldiers encountered a desolate landscape in which the dead lay unburied in No Man's Land. Herbert Richard Butt of the 102nd Canadian Infantry Battalion was among the many soldiers who noticed the heads, feet, torsos, and other strewn body parts rising from the mud in the Somme's Death Valley.[29] These sights served as a reminder of one's possible fate and heightened the sense of powerlessness as victory remained out of reach.

Upon his arrival, Butt was informed that only half of the men who went into the Somme battlefield came out unscathed. "They say it's almost impossible to go in twice without being hit," he wrote in his diary, "but I feel confident of coming through alright myself."[30] The historian Alexander Watson argues that the soldiers of the Great War maintained an unrealistic optimism regarding their fate. He quotes the psychologist C. Stanford Read, who observed it was not unusual for a British soldier to believe "that there is a good chance that he himself will be spared."[31] This was despite the fact that 45 percent of British soldiers became casualties.[32] Unlike Jenkins, Butt lived through the Somme as he predicted, and he participated in the successful capture of Regina Trench. Why did he survive Regina Trench, whereas Jenkins perished? Was it just dumb luck?

The most typical cause of injury and death at the front was artillery fire, accounting for nearly two-thirds of British Army casualties.[33] During major offensives, the risk of death increased substantially. British forces fired approximately 19 million shells on the Somme – 150,000 a day – and the German home front was producing 7 million shells each month.[34] Jenkins arrived in Ypres in mid-February 1916. Between 1 March and 23 August, the 43rd Battalion experienced 483 casualties, for an average of three a day. When the unit entered the Somme on 15 September, the danger escalated dramatically. By 7 October, the 43rd had suffered 269 casualties, for an average of twelve per day.[35]

Much has been written about the "live and let live" philosophy that existed on the front. Of course, this ethic was not in effect in all sectors. For example, Ypres was too strategically important for such a dynamic to develop.[36] The worst moments for the Canadians between the Second Battle of Ypres and the Battle of the Somme came during the Battle of Mont Sorrel in June 1916. There, the 43rd Battalion successfully defended against several German attacks but at a cost of over two hundred casualties (nearly half the total casualties between March and August 1916).[37] Outside of these assaults, soldiers on the salient had to deal with daily artillery and machine-gun fire as well as the threat of snipers. The war diaries of the 43rd Battalion provide a portrait of life in Ypres for Jenkins and his comrades. In the front lines, there were steady casualties from stray bullets, artillery, and machine-gun fire. On 3 March 1916, Private T. Dawson was "hit in the leg by sniper while crossing behind supports."[38] On 31 March, Lance Corporal W. Davidson was "wounded on ration party," whereas three others were killed and four wounded "by shell on machine gun."[39] Nightly working parties were also dangerous. Arthur Jordens of the Saskatchewan Regiment wrote home, "I hate the night work. It takes lots of nerves, you get no fighting chance if you get hit; theirs more casualty than in the front line, for the German gets wise to where you are working and he opens his machine ... and if your not quick enough to flop your a goner."[40] Between 3 and 5 May, five Highlanders were wounded while on working party.[41] These were the everyday dangers that faced Jenkins in Ypres.

It was often a matter of luck whether a soldier's name was on a particular shell or bullet. Near misses were a hallmark of life at the front. Bullets could ricochet, and indirect shellfire struck indiscriminately, perhaps killing one soldier but sparing another. On 8 October, during their assault on Regina Trench, a shell killed a captain of the 43rd Battalion and wounded Lieutenant Colonel Robert McDonnell Thomson. Thomson was being driven to the field hospital when his luck ran out. The ambulance suffered a direct hit, killing him and all others in the transport.[42] In retrospect, some soldiers reflected on the seemingly inconsequential decisions or accidents of fate that spared them death or serious injury. In June 1917, Walter Douglas Darling of the Canadian Machine Gun Corps was walking along a railway line when a shell burst on his right. He paused to remark, "That was a big one," to his runner. Just as he did so, a shell fragment "whizzed within three inches of my feet and crashed into the rail." As he wrote to his fiancée back home, "If I had not stopped for a second, I would have had my foot there."[43]

It is hardly surprising that, in this environment, one key element of soldier culture as it developed was superstition. Soldiers carried lucky charms, talismans, and amulets, and they prayed during moments of peril.[44] As one YMCA worker observed, "Most of the men are fatalists ... in so far as they believe that if it is their fate to get shot, they will be shot. They do their duty and put their faith in luck."[45] Fatalism has been interpreted as a coping mechanism – one way of avoiding depressing reflection about one's mortality. John Mellor Poucher of the 9th Battalion Canadian Railway Troops echoed this view in his diary, commenting that "one thinks and thinks and seems dazed. Seems like a nightmare – a Hell – one don't think about it too much or they would be crazy."[46] After the Battle of Mont Sorrel, Poucher took comfort in his faith in Providence, writing that "in my heart of hearts I do believe in providence and I am sure he will do what is best for me."[47] In a world governed by randomness, soldiers adopted the attitude that their fate was out of their hands, rather than thinking about the possibility of their own deaths.

If fatalism were taken as literally as chaplains feared, it would have fundamentally altered the behaviour of soldiers. It did not prompt men to take absurd risks when convinced of their own invulnerability.[48] Owen Davies observes that the profusion of good luck charms at the front reveals that soldiers sought to alter their futures "through action or engineer the intervention of providence through belief. Indeed, luck more than fate pervades the written experiences of combat."[49] Private Wilfred Leslie Wright in the 75th Canadian Battalion believed that his fate was predetermined by God. "If it is his will to let us come out safe," Wright wrote, "nothing can possibly hurt us." This attitude appears fatalistic, but Wright believed that his survival was dictated by faith and prayer: "And surely I think, and have faith, that with so many faithful friends praying for us ... and our own prayers, we will come out safe and well."[50] Soldiers also carried Bibles in their tunics – some of which occasionally stopped a bullet – and engaged in a "wind up" religion by attending services, receiving Communion, or engaging in prayers before battles, even if they were not deeply religious.[51] Faith and superstition were ways by which soldiers attempted to exert agency in the face of vast impersonal forces.[52]

There is some evidence that religion was important to the Jenkins family.[53] Thomas McIlveen was a Methodist until he married Francis's sister, Mary, at which point he converted to Presbyterianism.[54] In contrast to his brothers, who identified as Presbyterians on their attestation papers, Francis identified as a Wesleyan (Methodist). This suggests that he took his faith seriously, since he was willing to convert to a denomination to which most of his family did not belong. Francis would probably have been familiar with the 43rd Battalion's chaplain, Charles W. Gordon. Approximately one-third of the battalion belonged to his Presbyterian congregation in Winnipeg.[55] Three days before the 43rd attacked Regina Trench, Gordon conducted a Communion service that was "adapted from all Protestant churches." According to him, "the great majority of the battalion came forward," including those who had not been faithful, but who, upon arriving at the Somme, looked for spiritual assurance.[56] Certainly, Francis Jenkins had spiritual resources at his disposal in the struggle to cope with life at the front.

Soldiers did not have to rely entirely on luck or the supernatural. They could take practical steps to reduce their chances of death in the trenches. Alfred "Alf" Arnold of the Royal Army Medical Corps remarked, "A lot of course depends on one's luck but a lot also depends on one's ingenuity."[57] In the event of a high shrapnel shell burst, standard procedure was to tilt the head forward so the rimmed helmet could absorb any harmful shrapnel.[58] This method was not foolproof, and sometimes the shrapnel pierced the helmet, as in the unlucky case of one of Jenkins's comrades in Ypres.[59] Veteran soldiers also claimed that they could predict the trajectory of shells on the basis of their look or sound.[60] Newcomers had to learn through experience. Once they joined the lines, their training or the other soldiers provided them with the basic dos and don'ts of trench warfare. Still, new arrivals sometimes made mistakes or acted recklessly. Two months after Jenkins's battalion arrived in France, one soldier was chastised for carelessly exposing his head above the trenches several times.[61] After spending more than six months in Ypres, Jenkins had had time to adapt to his environment. Although he and his comrades were always prisoners to the whims of fate, they could learn to maximize their chances of survival.

Fortuitous timing of illness or injury could also spare soldiers from participation in major offensives. Sick leave or an injury known as a "blighty" became opportunities for escape from danger. A blighty was just serious enough to get out of the front lines but not so serious as to cause permanent disability. Arthur Jordens envied his brother Wilfred and hometown friend Pete for getting the measles and a gunshot wound to the shoulder, respectively. Only Pete's case was severe enough to see him indefinitely removed from the front lines; Wilfred "didn't have it bad enough."[62] Some soldiers deliberately sought out a blighty. After arriving in Ypres, Garnet William Durham of the Canadian Corps Cyclist Battalion was told by one soldier about a certain spot where "you had only need to put your hand around the corner of the ruin to get a bullet" from a German sniper.[63] As if to prove through demonstration, the man did just that and sure enough was hit by a bullet.

More often than not, soldiers had no need to go looking for injury. Alexander Watson argues that the frequency with which men hoped to get a blighty may explain why they were so confident of their survival. Rather than reflecting a self-delusion, it was an acknowledgment of the regularity of injury over death.[64] For example, Will R. Bird of the 42nd Canadian Battalion recalled one such incident. As he and a group stood behind a ruined wall, believing themselves to be safe, they were stunned when one of them was suddenly shot. They discovered a small gap in the wall. It was at this moment that Bird realized how easy it was to become a casualty.[65]

Jenkins does not appear to have feigned illness to get out of the trenches. He had a nearly perfect bill of health, broken only by a bout of diarrhea toward the end of the Battle of Mont Sorrel. At this point, his battalion was already being relieved, and his sick leave lasted only four days.[66] His endurance made him a good soldier, if not unlucky. Much like a shell or bullet, illness or injury could target indiscriminately but spare someone's life. In April 1917, one of Butt's comrades was struck in the hand by a piece of shrapnel. The damage was negligible, resulting in a bruise and small cut, but he had to be taken out of the line for inoculation only days before the Canadians advanced on Vimy Ridge. "He's damned lucky to get out of this attack," Butt wrote on 7 April.[67] Two days later, he himself was killed by a German sniper during the assault. Such stories were not unfamiliar to families with two or more sons in the Great War. Francis's brother Robert, of the 8th Canadian Infantry Battalion, was in France for less than a month when he was shot in the left knee at Ypres in September 1916. The injury ended his front-line service just as his comrades, including Francis, entered the Somme battlefields never to return.

In many respects then, Francis Jenkins was a victim of his circumstances. His promotion to sergeant and his experience in the trenches suggest that his death was probably not the result of ineptitude. Certainly, soldiers could be killed because of reckless behaviour or inadequate training, but the men who assaulted Regina Trench could do little against fully intact barbed wire and exposure to German firepower. As Poucher observed, "After all, in such a battle, what chance has a fellow against shrapnel, liquid fire, gas and high explosives?"[68] Francis survived Mont Sorrel and the intermittent shellfire of the Ypres salient for several months but was unfortunate to be assigned to the attack on Regina Trench on 8 October. This was the "bigger picture" of his war – the circumstances that dictated his trajectory and the environments he faced. What characterized his own "little battle"? What emotional supports would have been available to him? And what might these reveal about how soldiers exerted agency in the trenches more generally?

Morale at the front was sustained in various ways. Humour, patriotism, faith, and camaraderie all played their part, as did material comforts such as the rum ration and letters and care packages from home. Sporting events and concert parties also offered escape. Soldiers could find some reminder of home at the front that helped them endure. As Jonathan F. Vance explains in his discussion of Rob Buchan, a "local connection, not a nationalist war culture," kept him going (page 59). The same was probably true of Francis Jenkins.

The Western Front necessitated psychological defences, as soldiers shared their living quarters with lice, rats, and corpses. During major offensives such as the Somme, burying the dead was too dangerous, so they became a regular feature of the trench environment. On one occasion, while digging in their trenches, Butt and his comrades unearthed the bodies of German soldiers, their boots later "staring" them in the face while they ate their dinner. Men put corpses to practical use by stepping on them to avoid sinking into the mud. "We don't take any more notice of a dead person now than we do of a rat," Butt wrote.[69] Dark humour served as a cathartic release, since it acknowledged the possibility of death, but in a way that protected the individual from descending into paralyzed fear or hopelessness.[70]

One means of dealing with the front was through reading and writing. Some soldiers, like Poucher and Butt, kept a diary. Others, like Captain Walter Douglas Darling, wrote home on nearly a daily basis and were overjoyed to receive correspondence and parcels from loved ones in Canada and Britain. Single young men like Francis Jenkins relied on the support of their mothers.[71] As Leslie Wright explained to his mother, "you don't know, or can't realize, how much the influence of home helps a fellow to stick to it and do his duty, whatever the result. When a fellow is feeling almost down and out ... the thought that the folks at home are thinking and praying for you ... helps more than you imagine."[72] Gunner E.R. Gill of the 1st Battery Canadian Field Artillery kept a record of all the letters he received and sent home. In five months, he received 136 letters and postcards and sent 120, an average of about 1 letter sent and received every day. He could expect 8 letters each week. Of 250 pieces of correspondence, 62 were from, or sent to, his mother and father.[73]

For married or engaged men, such as Francis Jenkins's brother-in-law Thomas McIlveen, wives and fiancées were critically important. As Darling wrote to his fiancée on 5 December 1916, "don't ever think that I shall tire of your letters, dearest. If you only knew how precious they are to me!" Darling's spirits were lifted each time he received mail, as he told her, "I don't expect much news, just the loving encouragement yourself and your letters always give me."[74] By 1917, Darling's nerves were growing more strained, but during these trials he would think of his fiancée back home:

> I ache for you – some-times it seems that the days will never pass, and each one brings me so much nearer to you! I long for the end of the war so that you and I can begin the reconstruction of our lives together! I love you so much and I long to hug and kiss you and carry you around, as I used to![75]

Because Darling was an officer, he was permitted to enclose his letters in green envelopes, thus bypassing the censor. His correspondence is much more candid than one might expect. Those who were not officers might choose to write in a diary to express their longings for loved ones.

Letters from home reminded soldiers of why they were fighting. "Yesterday I had a nice letter from Rosie, how I wish I could be with her again," Poucher wrote in his diary in the spring of 1917.[76] But he had committed himself to holding out until the war was finally finished to ensure the defeat of Germany. Believing that a victorious Germany would wreak violence on his own family, he declared, "We must win. We must keep in mind her past doing and what might have happened to our wives and sisters. One can't forget. They must pay."[77] In Chapter 7 of this volume, Sarah Glassford demonstrates that the threat of continued German atrocities, especially those perpetrated against women, was used to strengthen support for the war, both at home and on the front lines. Letters could lift a soldier's spirits and remind him of who and what he was fighting for in France; in Poucher's case, his task was to protect family and friends from German savagery. His comments may sound jingoistic, but he was under no illusions about the glory of combat. "Who said there is glory in war?" he asked rhetorically. "It is hell. If ever hell is half as bad. Preserve me from it."[78] Although the war was taking a toll on Poucher, he remained convinced of the need to see it through.

Some soldiers were unable to fully express the realities of life at the front. Poucher lamented in his diary that it was impossible to "write down all my impressions of the day," and he mentioned periods of intense loneliness.[79] Diaries allowed for honest reflection but remained isolated from social networks. Letters also had limitations. Poucher admitted to self-censoring his correspondence home. "I will be glad when I can spare [Rosie] from the worry and trouble which she has now," he wrote. "I always have a bright letter, am afraid mine must be flat and empty at times."[80] The historian Jessica Meyer notes that soldiers used their letters to sustain their own domestic identities. Consoling messages were expressions of the "dutiful son and provident husband."[81] Nevertheless, whether as a result of the limits of language, or masculine expectations to ease anxiety on the home front, diaries and letters made for imperfect outlets of emotion and offered only partial comfort.

It was other men at the front who could best understand and reciprocate a comrade's feelings amidst the hardships. Trench newspapers represented a culture that relied on insider jokes, language, symbols, and shared experiences. They were written for and by the soldiers to offer relief from life at the front.[82] The first issue of the 7th Battalion's *Listening Post* proclaimed, "I'm here to try and break trench monotony."[83] Concerns about monotony were accompanied by promises of humour, and most soldiers' newspapers stressed the need for lighter material that could make trench life bearable. The goal of the *Dead Horse Corner Gazette* was to provide a "merry laugh and entertainment which heralds the breaking down of dull monotony and routine living."[84] The *Growler* stated that "of necessity, our humour must be rather blunt to appeal to men spending their days and nights in wet and muddy trenches, dodging shells ... If we can manage to take their minds off the unpleasant surroundings for an hour every two weeks, we will feel that we have achieved our aim."[85] In their attempts to appeal to the front-line soldier and provide an element of escapism, these periodicals found that humour was the best means for achieving these ends.

Despite the *Growler*'s aim of diverting attention from the unpleasantness of the front, the newspapers commonly addressed these very hardships. Satirical language provided a means of understanding and making light of front-line experiences. The trench papers resembled a typical newspaper or magazine, and features that one would expect to find in journals back home were used to comment on the peculiar nature of life on the front. For example, the *Listening Post* ran an ad for "Rooms to let ... Dug. Inn. Guaranteed to be 50 feet below the surface. Near modern and Historic ruins. Owner left hurriedly on account of health. Long lease. Pumps or anything else which would not necessitate the reappearance of the owner would be installed free, as he is hoping to be absent for several years. Apply Sanitary Dept."[86] The destruction of Ypres and its famous Cloth Hall, routinely cited by soldiers in their letters home, prompted the *Listening Post*'s mention of "Historic ruins." The absent landlord is a not-so-veiled criticism of certain senior officers, who were unwilling to share the dangers of the front.

Trench newspapers have been recognized as a forum in which men could freely criticize leadership.[87] The historian Graham Seal interprets the phenomenon as part of how men negotiated their consent to fight.[88] Even some of the most mundane and silly pieces bear evidence of soldiers' agency in response to horrid conditions and army discipline. For example, until 1916, *King's Regulations*, which governed the physical appearance of soldiers, stipulated that "the chin and lip will be shaved, but not the upper lip. Whiskers, if worn, will be of moderate length."[89] Moustaches were thus practically mandated. In the fall of 1915, the No. 1 Canadian Field Ambulance held two "Mustache Competitions" in four categories: Charlie Chaplin, Ferocious, Non-descript, and Beginners. Sergeant Noble Armstrong won the "Charlie Chaplin Class" in November 1915.[90]

The trench newspapers could also be used to level criticism against the home front. The rum ration was a particularly sore point, given its importance to morale, and soldiers took issue with teetotallers as Canada grappled with temperance during the war (prohibition came to Manitoba in 1916).[91] When it was suggested that the rum ration be replaced with a bi-weekly bowl of pea soup, one writer pointed out that it could not be safely cooked in a front-line trench and was thus often "thrown over the parapet." He went on to suggest that "Perhaps our friends in Canada will learn with surprise," he wrote, "that it is frequently impossible to light fires in the front trenches," referring to the fact that a fire would attract the attention of snipers and be subject to artillery bombardments.[92]

The above illustrates that occasional gaps in understanding did exist between Canadian soldiers and civilians, but those at the front still sought to re-create elements of home in an effort to prevent such gaps from widening. Sporting events were especially popular, and Canadian soldiers indulged in baseball, soccer (frequently identified as football), and other athletics, sometimes not far removed from the fighting.[93] The 4th Battalion's track and field competitions in October 1915 included among its participants men who had just come out of the firing line.[94] Soldier Ross Binkley was killed hours after he pitched for the 3rd Battalion, Canadian Machine Gun Corps in a game against the No. 3 Canadian Field Ambulance.[95] When the 49th Battalion held a day of sporting events, "the rapid pulse of the machine gun" and "the staccato of the rifle fire of warring nations" were audible in the distance. Still, the men made the most of the occasion and enjoyed "the sports of the Brigade as if peace instead of war was in the air."[96]

Initially spontaneous events, sports matches were conducted with whatever materials could be found, but they soon gained the support of senior officers. The Canadian Scottish 16th Battalion held soccer matches in 1915, using only a whistle and a ball, but several months later it joined an organized league thanks to proper supplies and official encouragement.[97] By June 1917, the 1st Canadian Division had nine baseball fields, three football fields, tennis courts, a basketball court, and two boxing platforms. Motor cars were also arranged to transport men to championship matches.[98] Jenkins died before sport became more organized and sophisticated, but his battalion managed to engage in athletic events twice in June 1916.[99]

Troops unsurprisingly preferred sport to drill and work parties. For example, the *Iodine Chronicle*, a trench newspaper produced by the No. 1 Canadian Field Ambulance, proclaimed that "football and baseball ... do more to keep Tommy fit and contented than all the route marches ever invented."[100] It was increasingly recognized that sport was beneficial for morale, physical fitness, and building camaraderie, especially between officers and their men. The No. 1 Canadian Field Ambulance formed an official football club in early 1916, with a warrant officer, captain, and private serving as president, vice-president, and secretary, respectively. The *Iodine Chronicle* saw this de-emphasis of rank as an example "of the democracy of sport" and of the recognition from authorities that sport could be good for the men's spirit and physical fitness.[101] The 49th Battalion's day of regimental sports saw cooperation and competition between officers and the ranks, which one soldier singled out as a symptom of "the good feeling that exists amongst the Canadians," one that he saw as responsible for their success on the battlefield.[102] The historian J.G. Fuller argues that competitive sports created an environment of "class collaboration," allowing privates and working-class men to compete and collaborate with their officers in a way that was not possible on the battlefield.[103]

The popularity of sporting events was rivalled by concert parties – variety shows modelled after the music halls of Britain and Canada. These were made possible by civilian-soldiers who had been part of the cultural scene back home. Basil James Green of the 8th Battalion confessed in his memoir that his knowledge of magic saved his life. Before he enlisted in 1914, Green was an amateur magician in Winnipeg. In November 1915, he was removed from the front lines and given the assignment of assembling a concert party with four other men. With the help of engineers, they spent a week converting an empty hall into a theatre, constructing a stage, cinema screen, and a drop curtain made of burlap. Camouflage paint was used to create the setting of the Canadian Rockies, and floodlights controlled by dimmers were built from "biscuit boxes." "Whatever we may have lacked in polish we gained in ingenuity," he recalled, and the audience "roared their applause."[104]

Green's magic show blended the horrors of the war's mutilated bodies with uncanny entertainment. In his final act, he detached the head of his partner and placed it on a pedestal. To prove that he was not using a dummy, he engaged the head in conversation while the body moved its arms. His penchant for complex magic tricks earned him a reputation among the chaplaincy, and he was eventually removed from front-line service just before the Battle of the Somme. For the remainder of the war, he operated canteens, assisted in the construction of officer clubs, and performed the occasional magic trick.[105]

Green's reversal of fortune filled him with relief but also a sense of guilt. "I could not help but feel, at times, qualms of consciousness [sic]," he explained, "when I compared my good fortune with that of my comrades in the fighting battalions."[106] Feelings of guilt could be assuaged by the acknowledgment that one had done one's bit. The concert shows were organized and performed by men who had seen active service and understood life in the trenches.[107] Trench newspapers and soldiers' correspondence reveal that troops appreciated these shows. Alf Arnold was thrilled when the Canadians brought a YMCA hut with them into his lines. As he stated, their shows were a great relief from the ordinary life of a soldier at the front, reminding him of pleasant things back home: "I hope [the hut] is permanent. I heard piano music today for the first time in 10 weeks ... I hope that this tent has brought Sunday with it. What I look forward to as much as anything is the spending of a real English country Sunday once again."[108]

Participation in these endeavours could be justified on the basis of their importance to morale. The editor of the 49th Battalion's trench newspaper, the *Forty-Niner,* noted that, while the men were advancing, he was staying behind to produce the paper. Reassured by praise from the men, he remarked that "it is a pleasure to know that even though one does not kill Germans, he has been the means of bringing a little pleasure in this none too gay life."[109] As soldiers themselves, they recognized the value of their efforts to curb monotony and combat the gloom of trench life.

The audience could also feel moments of guilt. A report of a concert held for the 49th Battalion noted that "less than three miles away [in] the trenches ... the rattle of the rifles and machine guns" raged on. There were "comrades being wounded, and ... killed, while we sit here listening to the music and enjoying ourselves." But these thoughts were countered by the novelty of the moment. Most of all, the concerts offered a brief escape from the front. As one soldier stated, "when we hear the music and listen to the songs and jest, and join in the rollicking choruses, we forget any little discomforts and our thoughts dwell on pleasanter things. Our minds go back to the bright, sunny days in Alberta, when we used to go gaily marching out behind the band to the tunes we are hearing now."[110] Sporting events and concert parties provided a reminder of home, that place they longed to return to and which they believed they were fighting to protect.[111]

On 16 October 1916, J.S. Davis of the 9th Canadian Field Ambulance reflected in his diary on the devastating toll that the Canadians had suffered on the Western Front. "The Somme fighting has been exceedingly expensive for the Canadians," he wrote. "Many battalions have less than one quarter of their effectiveness ... The decisive break has still to come ... Nothing spectacular is likely to occur on this front for many months."[112] As the Virgin Mary continued to dangle atop the basilica at Albert, Francis Jenkins and thousands of others Canadians were killed and maimed while attempting to capture a few thousand metres of trench. When Davis penned his comment, Jenkins had been missing for over a week and would not be officially confirmed dead for more than a year. For months, his body was one of the unidentified and unburied dead scattered across the Somme landscape that greeted Richard Butt and other new arrivals.[113] But it was not lost forever, and today his remains rest at Regina Trench Cemetery, memorialized by his mother with the epitaph "Asleep till the day break and shadows flee away."[114]

The voiceless dead of the Somme present challenges regarding the nature of individual agency. Most of the soldiers who lived and died on the Western Front were like Jenkins, leaving no record of their experiences. As Peter Farrugia observes in Chapter 4, the empty combat boots neatly arranged in ranks around the Vimy monument for the centenary in April 2017 "tell us little about – and may even occlude in some cases – the past that we claim to commemorate" (page 86). In the wake of the Vietnam War, the "war to end all wars" was characterized as a tragic farce. Today, however, Jenkins's life and death are contested terrain, as revisionist scholars argue against the supposed futility of the Somme.[115]

Jenkins is a fitting exemplar of the voiceless dead of the Great War. Killed in a battle that most Canadians have never heard of, one subsumed under an operation that is most commonly judged by its first bloody day, he left little behind. It does seem that he was a man who took his faith seriously, and judging from his two quick promotions, he was an effective soldier. But our ignorance does not mean that he had no life, exercised no agency. Like his comrades in the 43rd Battalion, Jenkins deployed what weapons he could to transport as much of home as possible to the front. Through faith, superstition, communications – with home and with other soldiers – and entertainments, he reaffirmed that he was living and fought to preserve his humanity.

Notes

1   Robin Prior and Trevor Wilson, *The Somme* (New Haven: Yale University Press, 2005), 248.

2 Library and Archives Canada (LAC), RG 9, series III-D-3, vol. 4898, folder 295, "Appendix C 1: Report on Attack on Regina Trench by the 9th C.I.B. October 8th, 1916," War Diaries, 9th Canadian Infantry Brigade, 29.

3 LAC, "Appendix A: Narrative of Attack by 9th Canadian Infantry Brigade on Regina Trench on October 8th," War Diaries, 9th Canadian Infantry Brigade, 7; LAC, Appendix D: Major W. Grassie, 43rd Canadian Battalion to 9th Canadian Infantry Brigade, 11 October 1916, Appendix D 1: Report on the attack carried out by 58th Canadian Infantry Battalion in pursuance of Operation Order No. 45, 10 October 1916 and "Appendix D 2: Narrative of Report of Accordance with Your G.890," War Diaries, 9th Canadian Infantry Brigade, 30–35.

4 LAC, RG 9, series III-C-3, vol. 4199, folder 6, file 7, Major Commanding 58th Can. Inf. Battalion to G.O.C., 9th Can. Inf. Brigade, 10 October 1916, in "Operations: Ancre Heights (Regina Trench)," 11.

5 LAC, RG 9, series III-D-3, vol. 4938, file 434, "War Diary of the 43rd Canadian Battalion, Volume 9, from 1 October 1916 to 31 October 1916," 4–5; LAC, "Narrative of Attack by 9th Canadian Infantry Brigade on Regina Trench on October 8th," 8.

6 LAC, "Narrative of Attack by 9th Canadian Infantry Brigade on Regina Trench on October 8th," 10.

7 G.W.L. Nicholson, *Canadian Expeditionary Force, 1914–1919: Official History of the Canadian Army in the First World War* (Ottawa: Department of National Defence, 1962), 186.

8 For examples, see Holger Afferbach and Gary Sheffield, "Waging Total War: Learning Curve or Bleeding Curve?" in *The Legacy of the Great War: Ninety Years On,* ed. Jay Winter (Columbia, MO: University of Missouri Press, 2009), 61–90.

9 See Dan Todman, *The Great War: Myth and Memory* (London: Continuum, 2005), 73–120.

10 For a discussion of the extent to which troops were either victims or active agents, see Trevor Wilson, *The Myriad Faces of War: Britain and the Great War, 1914–1918* (London: Polity Press, 1986), 675–84.

11 See Paul Fussell, *The Great War and Modern Memory,* new ed. (Oxford: Oxford University Press, 2013).

12 See Eric Leed, *No Man's Land: Combat and Identity in World War I* (New York: Cambridge University Press, 1979).

13 LAC, Canadian Expeditionary Force (CEF), RG 150, accession 1992-93/166, box 4813-6, Attestation paper, Francis Jenkins, 153344.

14 LAC, CEF, RG 150, accession 1992-93/166, box 4813-6, "Casualty Form – Active Service." Francis Jenkins embarked for France on 20 February 1916 as a lance corporal. He was promoted to corporal on 17 April 1916 and to sergeant on 18 June 1916.

15 See "About," 14–18 NOW, http://becausewearehere.co.uk/we-are-here-about/.

16 Most notably, Tim Cook's recent work, *The Secret History of Soldiers: How Canadians Survived the Great War* (Toronto: Allen Lane, 2018). This study, which covers many topics that I discuss here, appeared while this collection was in preparation. Other useful sources include G.D. Sheffield, *Leadership in the Trenches: Officer-Man Relations, Morale, and Discipline in the British Army in the Era of the First World War* (London: Macmillan, 2000); and Craig Leslie Mantle, ed., *The Unwilling and the Reluctant: Theoretical Perspectives on Disobedience in the Military* (Kingston: Canadian Defence Academy Press, 2006).

17 See, for example, Jessica Meyer, *Men of War: Masculinity and the First World War in Britain* (Basingstoke, UK: Palgrave Macmillan, 2009), 2–5.

18   "Canadian Passenger Lists, 1865–1935," Saint Johns, New Brunswick, December 1910, 8, Ancestry.com, https://search.ancestry.ca/search/db.aspx?dbid=1263.

19   Jim Blanchard, *Winnipeg 1912* (Winnipeg: University of Manitoba Press, 2005), 50.

20   Tim Cook, *At the Sharp End: Canadians Fighting the Great War, 1914–1916* (Toronto: Viking, 2007), 28–29.

21   Jim Blanchard, *Winnipeg's Great War: A City Comes of Age* (Winnipeg: University of Manitoba Press, 2005), 20, 94.

22   LAC, CEF, RG 150, accession 1992-93/166, box 4816-41, Attestation paper, Robert Jenkins, 622306; LAC, CEF, RG 150, accession 1992-93/166, box 4818-8, Attestation paper, William Jenkins, 461365.

23   LAC, Attestation paper, Francis Jenkins.

24   Robert Brown and Donald Loveridge, "Unrequited Faith: Recruiting the CEF 1914–1918," *Canadian Military History* 24, 1 (2015): 67–68.

25   Laurier Centre for Military, Strategic and Disarmament Studies Archives (LCMSDS), Veterans Affairs Canada (VAC) Pension Files, reel 29, Francis Jenkins, 92854.

26   See the payment history in his personnel file, LAC, CEF, Francis Jenkins.

27   LCMSDS, VAC Pension Files, Francis Jenkins.

28   Fussell, *The Great War and Modern Memory*, 142–45.

29   Imperial War Museum (IWM), Private Papers of H.R. Butt, Documents.6771, Diary of Private Herbert Richard Butt, 28 October 1916, 14. In this chapter, I make frequent use of archival material produced by British-born soldiers like Jenkins. Too often, histories of the war have been written from a narrowly national perspective, robbing commentators of vital corroborative evidence to support their conclusions about soldiers' experiences.

30   Ibid., 12.

31   Alex Watson, "Self-Deception and Survival: Mental Coping Strategies on the Western Front, 1914–18," *Journal of Contemporary History* 41, 2 (2006): 256.

32   Ibid., 247.

33   T.J. Mitchell and G.M. Smith, eds., *History of the Great War Based on Official Documents. Medical Services. Casualties and Medical Statistics of the Great War* (London: His Majesty's Stationery Office, 1931), 40.

34   Prior and Wilson, *The Somme*, 302.

35   These numbers were compiled from the daily reports in the 43rd Battalion's war diary. See LAC, "War Diary of the 43rd Canadian Battalion," vols. 2 to 9.

36   Tony Ashworth, *Trench Warfare: The Live and Let Live System* (London: Macmillan, 1980), 21.

37   LAC, "War Diary of the 43rd Canadian Battalion, Volume 5, from 1 June 1916 to 30 June 1916," 5–7, War Diaries, 9th Canadian Infantry Brigade, "Appendix 1: Narrative of Event June 2nd to June 16th, INCLUSIVE"; LAC, "War Diary of the 43rd Canadian Battalion, Volume 6, from 1 October 1916 to 31 October 1916," 4–5.

38   LAC, "War Diary of the 43rd Canadian Battalion, Volume 2, from 1 March 1916 to 31 March 1916," 1.

39   Ibid., 2.

40   IWM, Private Papers of A. Jordens, Documents 18920, Arthur Jordens to mother, 18 August 1916.

41   LAC, "War Diary of the 43rd Canadian Battalion, Volume 4, from 1 May 1916 to 31 May 1916," 1.

42   LAC, "War Diary of 43rd Canadian Battalion, Volume 9, from 1st October to 31 October 1916," 4–5.

43   IWM, Private Papers of W.D. Darling, Documents 3472, Walter Douglas Darling to fiancée, 5 December 1916.

44 For a discussion of charms, see Fussell, *The Great War and Modern Memory*, 124–34; Joanna Bourke, *Dismembering the Male: Men's Bodies, Britain, and the Great War* (Chicago: University of Chicago Press, 1996), 231–33; Michael Snape, *God and the British Soldier: Religion and the British Army in the First and Second World Wars* (New York: Routledge, 2005), 35–38; Vanessa Chambers, "Fighting Chance: War, Popular Belief and British Society, 1900–1951" (PhD diss., University of London, 2007), 35–61; Alexander Watson, *Enduring the Great War: Combat, Morale and Collapse in the German and British Armies, 1914–1918* (Cambridge: Cambridge University Press, 2008), 92–100; Owen Davies, *A Supernatural War: Magic, Divination, and Faith during the First World War* (Oxford: Oxford University Press, 2018), 135–76; and Cook, *The Secret History*, 73–80.

45 David Cairns, ed., *The Army and Religion: An Enquiry and Its Bearing upon the Religious Life of the Nation* (London: Macmillan, 1919), 160.

46 IWM, Private Papers of J.M. Poucher, Documents 6995, John Mellor Poucher Diary no. 3, 18 July–October 1917, entry for 31 July 1917.

47 IWM, John Mellor Poucher Diary no. 1, 7 March 1916–7 January 1917, entry for 30 June 1916.

48 Edward Madigan, *Faith under Fire: Anglican Army Chaplains and the Great War* (London: Palgrave Macmillan, 2011), 188; Cook, *The Secret History*, 74. Certainly, examples can be found of soldiers behaving in these ways because of their fatalism, but not on a scale that would be comparable to the frequency with which soldiers used fatalistic language.

49 Davies, *A Supernatural War*, 136.

50 IWM, Private Papers of W.L. Wright, Documents 20162, W. Leslie Wright to home, 26 December 1916.

51 Watson, *Enduring the Great War*, 97–98; Jason Schweitzer, *The Cross and the Trenches: Religious Faith and Doubt amongst the British and American Great War Soldiers* (London: Praeger, 2003), 187–92; Snape, *God and the British Soldier*, 45–57; Madigan, *Faith under Fire*, 183–96.

52 For a deeper investigation of religion and faith in the war, see Chapter 8 in this volume.

53 According to Jim Blanchard, the Winnipeg Presbyterian and Anglican Churches each had thirty thousand followers. This made them by far the largest two local denominations. See Blanchard, *Winnipeg 1912*, 49–50.

54 Thomas McIlveen first enlisted in January 1915 and identified himself as a "Methodist." He received a discharge through purchase in August 1915, only to re-enlist a week later. This time (and now married to Mary), he identified as a Presbyterian. See LAC, CEF, RG 150, accession 1992-93/166, box 6879, Attestation paper, Thomas McIlveen, 460796. Mary Jenkins married Thomas on 8 May 1915. See E. Kildonan, Manitoba Canada, "Web: Manitoba, Marriage Index, 1881–1937," Ancestry.com, https://search.ancestry.ca/search/db.aspx?dbid=70600.

55 Blanchard, *Winnipeg's Great War*, 167.

56 Charles W. Gordon, ed., *Postscript to Adventure: The Autobiography of Ralph Connor* (New York: Farrar and Rinehart, 1938), 262.

57 IWM, Private Papers of A.J. Arnold, Documents 9691, A.J. Arnold to family, 9 September 1916, 1.

58 Richard Holmes, *Tommy: The British Soldier on the Western Front, 1914–1918* (London: HarperCollins, 2004), 400–1.

59 The incident happened on the 6 April 1916 and was recorded in the battalion diary. See LAC, "War Diary of the 43rd Canadian Battalion, Volume 3, from 1 April 1916 to 30 April 1916," 1.

60 Watson, *Enduring the Great War*, 85–92; Denis Winter, *Death's Men: Soldiers of the Great War* (London: Penguin Books, 1979), 116.

61   LAC, "War Diary of 43rd Canadian Battalion, Volume 4, from 1 May to 31 May 1916," 6.

62   IWM, Arthur Jordens to mother, 29 August 1916, 3.

63   IWM, Private Papers of G.W. Durham, Documents 348, Garnet William Durham, "My Experiences in the War, 1914–1918: Being Extracts from Letters Written by Me during the War and Returned to Me after the Armistice," 87.

64   Watson, *Enduring the Great War*, 103–4.

65   Will R. Bird, *And We Go On: A Memoir of the Great War* (Montreal and Kingston: McGill-Queen's University Press, 2014), 23.

66   LAC, "Casualty Form – Active Service," Francis Jenkins.

67   IWM, Butt, Diary, 7 April 1917, 45.

68   IWM, Poucher, Diary, 12 May 1916.

69   IWM, Butt, Diary, 12 November 1916, 17–18.

70   Watson, *Enduring the Great War*, 92; Tim Cook, "'I Will Meet the World with a Smile and a Joke': Canadian Soldiers' Humour in the Great War," *Canadian Military History* 22, 2 (2013): 48–62.

71   For the relationships between mothers and sons, see Michael Roper, *The Secret Battle: Emotional Survival in the Great War* (Manchester: Manchester University Press, 2009).

72   IWM, Wright to mother, 8 June 1917.

73   IWM, Private Papers of E.R. Gill, Documents 12202, E.R. Gill, "Notes for 1916," in Diary and Notebook 1915.

74   IWM, Darling to fiancée, 5 December 1916.

75   Ibid., 6 June 1917.

76   IWM, Poucher, Diary, 20 May 1917.

77   Ibid., 31 July 1917.

78   Ibid., 15 June 1916.

79   Ibid., 5 May 1916.

80   Ibid., 1 August 1917.

81   Meyer, *Men of War*, 15–17, 29–31.

82   Graham Seal, *The Soldiers' Press: Trench Journals in the First World War* (London: Palgrave Macmillan, 2013), 78–80.

83   "Introduction," *Listening Post*, 10 August 1915, 1.

84   "Our Aims and Hopes," *Dead Horse Corner Gazette*, October 1915, 1.

85   "Introduction," *Growler*, 1 January 1916, 1; Cook, *The Secret History*, 9.

86   "Rooms to Let," *Listening Post*, 10 August 1915, 2.

87   Cook, *The Secret History*, 221–20.

88   Seal, *The Soldiers' Press*, x.

89   Quoted in Holmes, *Tommy*, 365.

90   "Mustache Competition," *Iodine Chronicle*, 15 November 1915, 1.

91   See Tim Cook, "'More a Medicine than a Beverage': 'Demon Rum' and the Canadian Trench Soldier of the First World War," *Canadian Military History* 9, 1 (2000): 6–22; and Fay Wilson, "Booze, Temperance, and Soldiers on the Home Front: The Unraveling of the Image of the Idealised Soldier in Canada," *Canadian Military History* 25, 1 (2016), http://scholars.wlu.ca/cmh/vol25/iss1/16.

92   "Save Us from Our Friends," *Dead Horse Corner Gazette*, December 1915, 14.

93   For more on the development of sport in the Canadian Armed Forces, particularly baseball, see Andrew Horrall, "'Keep-A-Fightin! Play the Game!' Baseball and the Canadian Forces during the First World War," *Canadian Military History* 10, 2 (2001): 27–40.

94   "Sport Gossip," *Dead Horse Corner Gazette*, December 1915, 24.

95   "Sport: Baseball," *Now and Then*, 15 December 1915, 3.

96 "Brigade Sports," *Forty-Niner,* January 1915, 17.

97 R.T.S.S., "Sporting Dope," *Brazier,* 15 February 1916, 8.

98 J.G. Fuller, *Troop Morale and Popular Culture in the British and Dominion Armies, 1914–1918* (Oxford: Clarendon Press, 1990), 88.

99 LAC, "War Diary of the 43rd Canadian Battalion, Volume 4, from 1 May 1916 to 31 May 1916," 2; LAC, "War Diary of the 43rd Canadian Battalion, Volume 5, from 1 June 1916 to 30 June 1916," 3.

100 "Football Once More," *Iodine Chronicle,* 20 January 1916, 3.

101 "Football," *Iodine Chronicle,* 20 January 1916, 3.

102 "Brigade Sports," *Forty-Niner,* January 1915, 17.

103 Fuller, *Troop Morale and Popular Culture,* 93.

104 IWM, Private Papers of Lieutenant B.J. Green, Documents.15073, Basil James Green, The Autobiography of an Almost Nonagenarian, n.d., 32.

105 Ibid., 33–39.

106 Ibid., 42.

107 H. Maylor, "Reports," *Listening Post,* 25 November 1915, 36; Tim Cook, "'The Singing War: Canadian Soldiers' Songs of the Great War," *American Review of Canadian Studies* 39, 3 (2009): 224–41. See also Jason Wilson, *Soldiers of Song: The Dumbbells and Other Canadian Concert Parties of the First World War* (Waterloo: Wilfrid Laurier University Press, 2012).

108 IWM, Arnold to family, 9 September 1916, 1–2.

109 "Editorial," *Forty-Niner,* January 1915, 16; Cook, *The Secret History,* 218.

110 "Our 'Sing-Songs,'" *Forty-Niner,* December 1915, 26–27.

111 Fuller, *Troop Morale and Popular Culture,* 1–2.

112 IWM, Private Papers of J.S. Davis, Documents 1638, J.S. Davis, Diary, 16 October 1916.

113 LAC, CEF, "Casualty Form – Active Service," Francis Jenkins. Jenkins was "presumed" killed for "official paperwork purposes" in May 1917 and confirmed dead in December 1917.

114 "Jenkins, Frank," Commonwealth War Graves Commission, http://www.cwgc.org/find -war-dead/casualty/234983/JENKINS,%20FRANK.

115 See, for example, Gary Sheffield, *Forgotten Victory – The First World War: Myths and Realities,* Kindle ed. (Endeavour Press, 2014), Chapter 7.

4

"Going over the Ground Again": Major Samuel Bothwell, 1st CMR, and Vimy Ridge

Peter Farrugia

History and Memory

The Historial de la Grande Guerre in Péronne, France, is a Great War museum that has become a respected voice in the interpretation of the war since its inception in 1992. It offers a unique perspective, deliberately pursuing a multinational approach and underlining the difficulty of comprehending, let alone representing the war.[1] The development of the Historial project was originally entrusted to Gérard Rougeron, a filmmaker with deep roots in the Somme region, where the Historial is located. Passionate and creative, Rougeron was not daunted by the challenge; instead, he developed many ideas that were designed to convey the enormity of the Great War. In one of the more intriguing, he enclosed a life-sized statue of a French soldier in a plastic booth that was

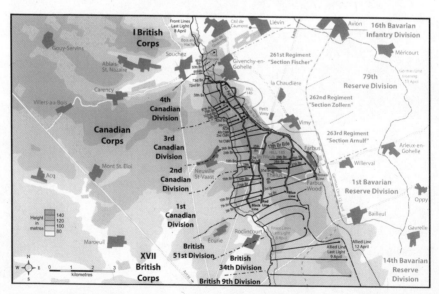

Figure 4.1 Vimy Ridge, 9 April 1917. | Map by Mike Bechthold.

fitted with a piped-in water system to simulate the endless rains of the Somme. With head bowed, the unfortunate *poilu* perpetually hunches over in an effort to protect himself from the rain.

In this one gesture, Rougeron hit on an apt representation of the sacrifice of the individual soldier (whether belonging to the Entente or Central Powers) on the Western Front.[2] He also produced an appropriate symbol of the Sisyphean task of the historian of the Great War, with each generation rolling its rock uphill in the quest to understand the past in the light of the present. Of all the Great War battles, Vimy is, for Canadians, the one most freighted with myth and memory. It is the one that has most frequently been reinterpreted and repackaged, with contemporary concerns figuring prominently in the meaning that has been ascribed to it.

The process of making sense of the past – whether it is a matter of how to represent the predicament of the infantryman on the Western Front or how to mark the victory of the Canadian Expeditionary Force (CEF) at Vimy Ridge – involves the negotiation of the delicate interplay between past and present. The "presence of the past" is a resonant phrase chosen by Roy Rosenzweig and David Thelen as the title for their 1998 volume exploring Americans' vital connections with their past.[3] The authors found that interviewees were heavily invested in exploring their pasts; they used words such as "love" and "passion" to describe their attachment to history.[4] However, they defined their pasts in ways that differed markedly from the analyses of professional historians. Tellingly, when it came to trustworthiness, history professors ranked fourth among those surveyed, lagging behind museums, personal accounts from relatives, and conversations with eyewitnesses on a ten-point reliability scale.[5] Canadians, of course, are not immune to these same forces linking history and memory, past and present. As Margaret Conrad, Jocelyn Létourneau, and David Northrup found when they conducted a similar survey, Canadians were equally engaged with their pasts and determined not to let scholars dictate terms. Indeed, the authors concluded, "historymaking in families, communities, and nations has long been a contested terrain, and this is unlikely to change, even if approaches and preoccupations on the part of professional historians and the larger public begin to converge."[6]

The presence of the past was unmistakable in April 2017, as Canadians marked the centenary of the iconic battle in their history. Across the country, events both large and small were organized to commemorate this moment in the Great War. The ceremony at the Vimy monument itself drew some twenty-five thousand pilgrims,[7] and there were dozens of smaller ceremonies at home. Even in Quebec, where attitudes to Vimy have been complicated, there was interest in the anniversary. Montreal held a ceremony in "the newly inaugurated 'Place de

Vimy' – a section of a west-end park that was renamed in honour of the 1917 battle."[8] Still, it was the nationally televised ceremony, held at the battlefield under the shadow of Walter Allward's imposing monument, that drew the most sustained and rapturous attention. Thousands of combat boots had been placed around the monument, and actors in costume also attended. The *Toronto Star* noted the "empty black combat boots for each of the men who died fighting for the ridge" and added that "actors took on the personas of those who lived through that terrible time, bringing not only soldiers back to life, but also their mothers and fathers, wives and even nurses." The report underlined the impact on the assembled crowds, remarking that the "emotion of the event was too much for some to bear."[9]

And yet, however much such rituals may move participants and spectators, they can assume a two-dimensional quality, as historical nuances are steamrolled by memory, and the dead are remobilized for contemporary purposes. One of the more arresting elements of the commemorations organized by the federal government perfectly captured this struggle between history and memory. The boots lined up in silent ranks along the monument and grounds on 9 April represented the soldiers in whose name Canadians were gathering. Much like the cenotaph (the empty tomb) or the disembodied names on monuments, they may bring us up short or inspire a tear. However, they tell us little about – and may even occlude in some cases – the past that we claim to commemorate.[10] Are we in danger of allowing those who fought at Vimy to become ciphers, "empty boots" into which we can pour whatever judgments, values, and agendas resonate with us today?

For some observers, the "theatre of memory" that was enacted in France on the 100th anniversary of the Vimy assault brought to mind an observation that media theorist Neil Postman had made in a different context.[11] In his exploration of contemporary American culture, *Amusing Ourselves to Death*, Postman declared,

> telegraphy made relevance irrelevant. The abundant flow of information had very little or nothing to do with those to whom it was addressed; that is, with any social or intellectual context in which their lives were embedded. Coleridge's famous line about water everywhere without a drop to drink may serve as a metaphor of a decontextualized information environment: In a sea of information, there was very little of it to use.[12]

The same could perhaps be said of Canada's centenary celebrations of Vimy. In a sea of remembrance, there appeared to be little remembering. Instead, feet firmly planted in current realities, the ceremonies advanced contemporary

Figure 4.2 Combat boots at the Vimy monument, April 2017. | Photo by Jason Long.

agendas, even while they purported to honour the dead. Like Alfred Dreyfus, the wrongly accused French army captain whose 1894 conviction for espionage set off a major controversy, the dead of Vimy would have been uncomfortable with the notion that they were heroes or symbolic of some abstract idea.[13] In this chapter, the story of one soldier who fought at Vimy Ridge, as well as an overview of how the Vimy myth has been used for various purposes since 1917, reveals the intensity of the ongoing struggle between history and memory and underlines the fact that Great War battles continue to be fought today, none more costly than the one at Vimy.

Samuel Bothwell, 1st Canadian Mounted Rifles

Day one of the assault on Vimy Ridge – 9 April 1917 – was the bloodiest of the entire war for the CEF. The number killed more than doubled that of the second-costliest day on our list. This simple but profound fact is often overlooked by Canadians.[14] Acting Major Samuel Bothwell of the 1st Canadian Mounted Rifles (CMR) was among those who died that day. As for other individuals who are the focus of this collection, the historical record contains little to help us understand what he experienced, let alone how he interpreted this battle that has assumed such a critical place in Canadian identity.

An additional complication renders Bothwell even more distant to contemporary Canadians: he does not fit the stereotypical image of a Canadian soldier in the Great War. This image would feature a young man, somewhere around twenty-one years of age, with neither life experience nor martial expertise. Given our emphasis on the *victory* rather than the *cost* at Vimy, Canadians would also probably imagine one of the survivors of the battle, representative of perseverance and strength. Samuel Bothwell is a virtual anti-type of this image. He was born on 1 June 1879, making him thirty-seven when he fought on the ridge.[15] This was not some callow youth but a family man, closer to middle age than to his teen years. He was the father of four children. Equally important, Bothwell was not born in Canada. Like many who served in the CEF, he hailed from the British Isles. In fact, recent scholarship has revealed that 38.3 percent of all those who enlisted were born in the United Kingdom.[16] Bothwell was born in Unionist territory, in Dromara, County Down, Ireland; after emigrating, he settled in Mosside, Alberta, where he took up farming.[17] There was one other peculiar feature that set him apart from his peers: at six foot seven inches, he towered over virtually everyone.[18]

Bothwell was also far more experienced in warfare than the average CEF recruit. He attested, originally to the 66th Battalion, in Edmonton on 2 July 1915 and subsequently joined the 1st CMR on 2 August 1916.[19] But his experience in the armed forces extended much further back. The *Edmonton Bulletin* reported in May 1917 that he possessed a "splendid military record," having served with distinction with the 2nd Life Guards and subsequently the Yeomanry staff in South Africa. He had been decorated for gallantry during the Boer War, receiving the Distinguished Conduct Medal, and had stayed on afterward, serving in Natal during the Zulu Rebellion in 1903.[20] Clearly, this was a man with considerable knowledge of the intricacies of the military world, unlike many of his comrades or many of the individuals studied in this collection.

Samuel Bothwell saw action at Vimy as part of the 1st Battalion of the Canadian Mounted Rifles. The CMR was originally organized in December 1914. It was mobilized in Brandon, Manitoba, and recruited from the Prairies.[21] The 1st CMR disembarked in England on 21 June 1915 and arrived on the Western Front on 22 September 1915. Its designation was changed from regiment to battalion and it ceased to be a unit of cavalry with the formation of the 8th Canadian Infantry Brigade on 1 January 1916.[22] The 1st CMR's battle honours include many of the most significant CEF engagements in the Great War: Mont Sorrel, the Somme, Flers-Courcelette, Vimy, Hill 70, Passchendaele, Amiens, the Hindenburg Line, the Canal du Nord, and Cambrai. Mont Sorrel (or Hill 62) is of particular interest.[23] The 1st and 4th CMR were occupying the 3rd Canadian Division's front lines on 2 June 1916, when the Germans detonated mines and

Figure 4.3 Canadian Mounted Rifles recruitment
poster. | Photo by author, from his own collection.

launched a surprise assault. Canadian positions were overrun, and 557 of the
1st CMR's 692 men were killed, wounded, or captured.[24] This catastrophic engagement is largely forgotten today, but at one time, Mont Sorrel was seen as
among the most significant actions for the Canadians. Indeed, MP Hugh Guthrie
asserted in 1922 that the central Canadian war monument, the one for which
Walter Allward's imposing design had been selected, was supposed "to have
been erected on Hill 62 near the Ypres salient," scene of the disaster for the 1st
CMR in June 1916.[25]

In many respects, the Canadian Mounted Rifles can be read as an apt symbol
of the larger war between 1914 and 1918. The unit produced one of the most
arresting recruiting posters of the period, promising quick transportation to
the adventure of the front with "Canada's crack cavalry corps." At a time when
the propagandist was just beginning to hone his black arts, this poster, with its
calm horsemen surveying the battlefield, was brilliant. Of course, the reality
turned out to be much different for those who enlisted. The Great War was
nothing if not a challenge to military doctrine, and troops who had imagined

themselves winning the day by flashing in decisively on their horses were soon forced to dismount, the CMR among them.[26]

Despite the disappointment of their repurposing, members of the CMR could take solace in having seen action in many of the CEF's best-remembered battles, none more talismanic than Vimy. The 1st CMR played a significant role in the assault on the ridge. Part of the 8th Infantry Brigade, in the 3rd Canadian Division, it was assigned the task of taking the Zwischen Stellung Trench and, after that, La Folie Farm.[27] Little is known of Samuel Bothwell's particular fate.[28] The war diaries of the 1st CMR do offer some assistance, providing glimpses of what transpired during the attack. Prior to the assault, Bothwell had been elevated to second-in-command of Company D. On 9 April, his unit was in the front lines and ready to attack. At 5:30 a.m., the barrage commenced. D Company took the lead, with C in support and B and A behind it. "Keeping close to the barrage," the troops advanced on their primary objective, the Zwischen Stellung, which they reached by 6:05 a.m.[29] The difficulties encountered in the assault have sometimes been glossed over in historical accounts. The war diary notes that "the trenches were unrecognizable, mud beyond belief. The whole of our Battalion frontage was alive with men of the 2nd Division ... who had swung right across our front ... These men were hopelessly lost and without ideas of their flanks."[30] Casualties were extremely high. A Company, now only about 40 strong, had been amalgamated with B Company and placed under the command of Major F.G. Taylor. Still, despite these circumstances, all 1st CMR objectives had been taken by 3:15 and were being held with about 250 men, including 100 from the 5th CMR, which had initially been in reserve. It was only at 9:25 p.m. that the unit was able to get a clear idea of the casualties, Captain (Acting Major) S. Bothwell among them.[31]

There would be no triumphal return to Canada, then, for Samuel Bothwell. He died on the first day of a battle that was not decided until its fourth day; after intense fighting, the infamous "Pimple" was cleared of German defenders only on 12 August.[32] And, of course, we cannot know what Bothwell experienced in the assault that killed him. It is impossible for us to imagine what he was thinking or feeling in those desperate final seconds. Perhaps he was calculating that the immense battle was hanging in the balance, that an individual act of courage was required to spur his men on. Or perhaps he lay wounded in a shell hole, his thoughts turning to the creature comforts of home, as well as his wife and family.

Even on the domestic front, what little we know of Bothwell's life defies neat storylines. Many Canadians, not fully appreciating the reality of the situation in which women found themselves, might be seduced by the stereotypical image of the dutiful wife or sweetheart, forsaking male companionship to remain loyal to the memory of her man. Certainly, the literature of the Great War is replete with examples of grief and devotion of this kind. Vera Brittain captured the desolation she felt at the loss of her fiancé and brother when she admitted, "There seemed to be nothing left in the world, for I felt that Roland had taken with him all my future and Edward all my past."[33] There certainly were women who, wounded beyond all endurance, could never bring themselves to love with the same intensity again. But they were the exception rather than the rule. However much the Great War advanced gender equality, there was no question that inequities persisted. In Chapter 7 of this volume, Sarah Glassford tackles the issues – from policies regarding chaperoning to expectations concerning proper dress and comportment – that faced Canadian nurses in the field. Meanwhile, on the home front, it remained virtually impossible for a woman to live independently of a man. Even where matters of the heart were not the primary consideration, hard economic necessities often dictated a woman's choices.[34] With four children to provide for, Alice Bothwell was in a very difficult situation. She remarried almost exactly three years to the day after the death of her husband, on 13 April 1920. After that, correspondence from the CEF was addressed to Mrs. Alice Morris, 55 Edbrooke Road, London.[35]

The fate of Samuel Bothwell and his family complicates the Vimy myth still further. If the battle marked the birth of a nation, as some have suggested, not all who were midwives to that birth remained to enjoy it. The record is not entirely clear, but it appears that only one of Bothwell's children, a son, stayed in Canada while the others accompanied their mother to London. Just as we cannot imagine the environment on the battlefield, with its cries of the dying, the roar of the barrage, the sense of elation among survivors at making it through, we cannot imagine the mixture of grief, pride, and anxiety occasioned by the sudden loss of a husband and the equally sudden realization that the family's future was in very real jeopardy.

Vimy Ridge in Memory

As arduous as the battle of April 1917 was, the struggle over Vimy's significance has been no less protracted and no less intriguing to the student of history. The assault on Vimy Ridge has evolved from being seen as one victory among many CEF triumphs to being treated as *the* crucial moment in the war, when Canadian nationhood was forged. Although this progression cannot be teased out in detail here,[36] it will be helpful to alight on a few key moments in the development of the Vimy myth and to suggest why it poses a serious challenge to the practitioners of history.

Certainly, the victory of April 1917 did not go unnoticed. One reason was that the ridge had proven exceedingly difficult to win; numerous assaults had failed to yield ultimate victory.[37] In addition, the fact that the attack on Vimy marked the first occasion on which the four Canadian divisions in the CEF fought together was instantly grasped as important, though perhaps not as critical as the myth would have us believe.[38] Finally, the timing of the triumph added to its lustre; coming as it did over the Easter holiday, it seemed providential, confirming that the Allies were engaged in a just war.[39] This sort of connection was part and parcel of an age when faith – as Gordon L. Heath demonstrates in Chapter 8 of this volume – was much more influential than many present-day commentators acknowledge.[40]

Despite all of this, it is equally true that Vimy was *not* instantly and universally recognized as Canada's greatest military achievement, much less its moment of birth. For one thing, the war was not yet won, and there was little leisure for celebration. A job remained to be done. Moreover, the action at Vimy was a diversionary attack. The decisive blow was supposed to be delivered by the French in the Reims-Soissons sector.[41] Even with some time for reflection, not all were convinced that this operation represented Canada's most significant contribution to the war effort. During a 1922 parliamentary debate on war memorials, Sydney Mewburn, who was militia and defence minister from 1917 to 1920, informed the House of Commons that "many of the army officers held that Vimy was by no means the most important battle that was fought by the Canadian corps."[42] Even Arthur Currie himself was dubious about the claims for Vimy's pre-eminence. He was convinced that the Battle of Hill 70, four months later, was "a more 'Canadian' affair and ... a tougher fight."[43]

From the very beginning then, the volatility of memory surrounding the Battle of Vimy Ridge was evident. The image of the assault as the most important engagement for the CEF in the Great War was contested immediately. However, that did not prevent the myth from gaining ground. The building of the Vimy legend began slowly but picked up pace as the decades passed. Absent the voices of those who were present at the battle, Vimy became a national touchstone. In happy times, it could be used to deepen our appreciation of what Canada represented; in darker moments, it could be employed to strengthen national resolve. The fact that there was no unanimity about the true import of the battle was of little consequence. As David Lowenthal suggests, "If the past is a foreign country, nostalgia has made it the foreign country with the healthiest tourist trade of all. But like other tourists, those to the past imperil the object of their quest."[44] Like the visitor who searches for "unspoiled" scenery or "authentic" local cuisine, those who return to Vimy seeking lessons for today risk rewriting the very events they consider instructive.

So where should the tourist begin in the quest for answers? One logical place would be the competition to choose monument designs for the eight sites that were designated as future memorial locations.[45] Walter Allward's entry – which committee member A.Y. Jackson said "went beyond and above anything the framers of the competition conceived of" – presented real problems.[46] Practically, it gave the committee headaches because its grandeur could not be duplicated in all eight sites, as originally intended. At the same time, the idea of achieving any sort of aesthetic harmony between it and the second-place design, Frederick Clemesha's *Brooding Soldier,* was next to impossible; the two sculptures bore no resemblance to one another.[47] Allward's design was no less problematic thematically than it was from a practical standpoint. In explaining its genesis, Allward claimed,

> When things were at their blackest in France, I went to sleep one night after dwelling on all the muck and misery over there, my spirit was like a thing tormented ... I dreamed I was in a great battlefield. I saw our men going in by the thousands and being mowed down by the sickles of death ... Suddenly through the avenue I saw thousands marching to the aid of our armies. They were the dead. They rose in masses, filed silently by and entered the fight to aid the living. So vivid was this impression, that when I awoke it stayed with me for months. Without the dead we were helpless. So, I have tried to show this in this monument to Canada's fallen, what we owed them and we will forever owe them.[48]

Allward's work was not to be a triumphalist monument. Its central message was that the First World War had been, above all else, *costly.*[49] Once again, we cannot ignore the fact that 2,398 men were killed on the first day of the attack on Vimy Ridge, making it the bloodiest day for the CEF in the Great War. It was little wonder, then, that the figure he chose to gaze out over the Douai plain was christened Canada Bereft.

The early emphasis on the cost of the war was further indicated by the fact that the authorities who were charged with commemorating Canada's part in the conflict originally contemplated placing Allward's monument at Hill 62 in Belgium, scene of the Mont Sorrel debacle. Tim Cook suggests that this was a "bizarre choice" given that at least "its first two phases" were "a resounding defeat."[50] It is true that commemoration of failed operations is much less common than commemoration of victories. However, it is not unprecedented. The Australian preoccupation with the Gallipoli campaign of the First World War is a case in point, as is the Canadian fixation on the failed Dieppe Raid in the Second World War.[51]

It is equally important to keep in mind that, in the interlude between the 1921 selection of Allward's design and the 1936 unveiling of his monument, the mood of Europe had been transformed. In 1921, the idea that the carnage of the First

World War might lead to a new international order was reasonable; the sense of citizenship manifested in the typical war memorial of the early post-war years was "expressed in terms of a sacrifice which must never be allowed to happen again."[52] By 1936, this was, at best, a forlorn hope. In the wake of Hitler's rise to power, the remilitarization of the Rhineland, and the mounting threat of a second European conflict, it was very hard to cast the monument's inauguration in a celebratory light.[53]

This refusal to revel in victory, this solemnity in the face of the tragedy of war, has often been counted the Vimy monument's greatest strength. And it may have been its saving grace. Hitler admired the monument precisely because it was less a nationalistic symbol than a meditation on the immense cost of war. Four years after its unveiling, on the heels of Germany's stunningly swift defeat of France, the Führer responded indignantly when Canadian press reports alleged that his troops had vandalized the site. He deliberately paid it a visit to counter claims that it had been damaged.[54] The outrage occasioned by rumours of its desecration hint at the extent to which Vimy was already being enrobed in new layers of meaning.

The process of myth making accelerated in the 1960s. The 1967 centennial has often been described as the signal moment in the reinterpretation of the war and of the battle at Vimy specifically. However, even before 1967, there was a resurgence of interest in the Great War, a trend that was by no means confined to Canada. In Britain, it coalesced around two poles. On the one hand, Alan Clark's *The Donkeys* was published in 1961. This book portrayed British generals – above all Douglas Haig – as callous dunderheads leading their men to senseless death.[55] In contrast, 1963–64 saw the production of a landmark documentary, *The Great War*. A co-production of the BBC and the Imperial War Museum (IWM),[56] this film was much more sympathetic to Haig and his staff. It was not without its controversies, however. At one point, the director of the IWM, Noble Frankland, threatened to cease cooperating with the producers of the documentary due to its use of reconstructions.[57] This one contretemps might seem of limited relevance to a discussion of Canadian perceptions of Vimy. Nonetheless, it underscores the extent to which academic historians were seeing their role in the shaping of historical consciousness diminishing, even before the advent of the post-modernist critique of history and the new technologies that promised to democratize the process of history making. In the 1960s, when the notion of "King and Country" was largely dismissed, when deference to authority was eroding generally, and when the Korean and Vietnam Wars had undermined the image of war as an honourable calling, it was perhaps to be expected that the Vimy monument's message of devotion to peace would resonate.

A push back in the direction of the Great War as noble enterprise did eventually arrive. By 1967, powerful forces in Canada were once again recasting the ways in which the Battle of Vimy Ridge was deployed. Numerous factors contributed to this trend. On the one hand, Canada was seeking a new, distinctive path, a *via media* between Britain and the United States. Evocative symbols such as the new Canadian flag (unveiled in 1965), the role of peacekeeping (after Lester B. Pearson won the Nobel Prize in 1957), and the Order of Canada (instituted in 1967) facilitated this.[58] At the same time, in an era when the people of Quebec were clamouring to be "maîtres chez nous," Prime Minister Pearson sought to reinforce national unity. He reached back to the Great War to make his case. It was in this context that Léo Cadieux, the minister of defence, read the prime minister's words at the fiftieth anniversary ceremony of Vimy. Pearson claimed that "in the broad and colourful pageant of Canadian history past and yet to be enacted, the Battle of Vimy Ridge will stand as a benchmark of courage, gallantry and sacrifice – *the crucible which brought forth and tempered the Canadian identity.*"[59] This statement provided a blueprint for how Vimy could be mobilized for official purposes, one that has been borrowed with increasing regularity in recent years.

Although the temptation to draw from the Pearsonian well in the name of national unity never vanished entirely, it is equally true that the Vimy myth did not enjoy unbroken currency. Even a popular historian such as Pierre Berton – generally considered a member of the "Vimy created Canadians" camp – could still ask,

Was it worth it? Was it worth the cold and the lice, the rats and the mud? Was it worth the long hours standing stiffly in the trenches, praying that no sniper's bullet would find its mark? Was it worth it to crawl out into No Man's Land with a bag of bombs, seeking to mangle the men in the opposite trench before they mangled you? Was it worth that tense, chilly wait on the Easter Monday morning so long ago, when the world finally exploded and the enemy was driven from the heights at a cost in lives and limbs the High Command and the press described as "minimal"?

There was a time, less cynical, more ingenuous, when most Canadians were led to believe that the answer was *yes*. Nations must justify mass killings, if only to support the feelings of the bereaved and the sanity of the survivors. In Canada, long after the original excuses were found wanting – the Great War, after all, was clearly *not* a war to end all wars – a second justification lingered on. Because of Vimy, we told ourselves, Canada came of age; because of Vimy, our country found its manhood.

But was *that* worth it? Was it worth the loss of thousands of limbs and eyes and the deaths of five thousand young Canadians at Vimy to provide a growing nation with a proud and enduring myth? ...

The answer, of course, is *no*.[60]

The emphasis here seems to be more on courage than on victory, cost over reward. This may not necessarily accord with the image of Berton as promoter of Canadian nationalism, but it probably comes close to the mood of soldiers such as Bothwell; the cost *was* significant.

Would Samuel Bothwell have concurred with Berton? We will never know. He was, after all, older than most volunteers, with a growing young family and a medal from a previous conflict to allay the suspicions of patriots. He had every reason *not* to enlist. And yet, he signed up. However, it is likely that he would have appreciated Berton's bristling at the ease with which practised tongues spoke of glory, valour, and nation while eliding the fear, the hot lead, and the terrible suffering endured by those who took the ridge.

In the years after the 1986 publication of Berton's *Vimy*, the tide seemed to shift decisively to the conception of Vimy as the birthplace of the nation. No doubt, what has been called the "memory boom" had something to do with this;[61] however, the change was also political in nature. The ninetieth anniversary of the battle, in 2007, coincided with the refurbishing of the monument. Noting that "every nation has a creation story to tell," Prime Minister Stephen Harper asserted that the "names of all the great battles are well known to Canadians and Newfoundlanders, but we know the name of Vimy best of all, because it was here for the first time that our entire army fought together on the battlefield and the result was a spectacular victory, a stunning breakthrough that helped turn the war in the allies favour."[62]

Five years later, Canadian hockey icon Don Cherry devoted his Coach's Corner segment on *Hockey Night in Canada* to Vimy Ridge. He began by noting that "on the 9th coming up, it is Vimy Day ... It is very important in Canada – and I know the lefties don't like that – but it made us a nation as they say." After emphasizing that the French and British had spent three years trying to win the position, he added that "the Canadians took it in three days – they actually took it in one day." Holding up a hockey jersey emblazoned with an image of the Vimy monument, a gift from General Michel Maisonneuve of Royal Military College Saint-Jean, he declared, "This was the first Team Canada."[63] Many elements of the Vimy legend were discernible in Cherry's diatribe. These included the note of Canadian exceptionalism, the false left-right binary in the debate over the true meaning of the engagement, and the presentation of war as a noble game.

The broad contours of Cherry's sermon accorded with Prime Minister Harper's position at the time. This was illustrated on 4 August 2014, when he marked the centenary of the war's outbreak and cited "our commitment to values" as Canada's motivator for participation in the conflict:

So, as Canadians went to Europe 100 years ago when an old imperialism tore apart the Continent's peace, again in 1939 we entered the fray, this time to defeat fascism. It's why with our allies we joined arms across Europe ... to stem the tide of Communism. It's why we stepped in after September 11, 2001, when the defenders of liberty attacked the terrorists seeking to destroy us.

He concluded, "every time we take a stand to defend the values for which they fought and for which so many died, we remember their stories in the only way that really matters."[64] Clearly, Harper was drawing a direct line from the pitted landscape of Vimy and the beaches of Normandy to the desert of Afghanistan. He was also proclaiming that there was just one valid way of honouring the sacrifices of the past and that was by subscribing to the Vimy legend.

Lest we imagine that this sort of appropriation of the past for contemporary political aims is limited to one party in Canada, we should return to the 2017 centenary celebrations and the statement of Prime Minister Justin Trudeau. "One hundred years ago," it began,

on a gentle slope in France, the four divisions of the Canadian Corps fought for the first time as one. They were ordinary – yet extraordinary – men, *from all corners of the country: Francophone, Anglophone, new Canadians, Indigenous Peoples ...*

Many of the soldiers wearing the Canadian uniform that day were *immigrants to this country.* People of many languages and backgrounds, representing every region in Canada, fought for the values we hold so dear: freedom, democracy, and peace. In the words of one veteran: "*We went up Vimy Ridge as Albertans and Nova Scotians. We came down as Canadians.*"[65]

Where Harper underlined geopolitical considerations, Trudeau stressed unity in diversity, no matter that the "immigrants" of whom he spoke were drawn overwhelmingly from the British Isles rather than from around the globe, as is the case today.[66] And no matter that many of the Indigenous soldiers whom he lauded were denied access to the benefits that their non-Indigenous brothers were given upon their return. No matter that Newfoundland's experience in the war was very different from Canada's.[67] What always gets lost in such monochromatic interpretations of Vimy is the complexity of the moment. Conscription riots in Quebec, war fatigue in rural Canada and among elements of labour, conscientious objection, all are airbrushed out of the picture.[68]

Even as he spoke, Trudeau was probably aware that the vision he trumpeted was not fully operative in public consciousness. An Ipsos-Reid poll conducted in March 2017 had underlined this fact. Ten percent of Canadians polled had stated that the battle was the key event in Canadian history – ranking it behind only Confederation (38 percent) and the drafting of the Charter (33 percent) – but a more detailed breakdown of responses revealed key nuances. Only 4 percent of Atlantic Canadians and 2 percent of Quebeckers saw Vimy in this light. In Quebec, 47 percent of respondents preferred to view the creation of the Charter as the critical moment in Canadian nationhood.[69] Clearly, the idea that the battle at Vimy marked the birth of Canada is not universally held among Canadians.[70]

Going over the Ground Again

Not long before Trudeau marked the 100th anniversary of Canada's most famous battle, the respected military historian Terry Copp delivered a public lecture in an annual series organized by the Great War Centenary Association of Brantford, Brant County, and Six Nations (GWCA).[71] His talk examined the 199th Irish Canadian Rangers, giving a detailed account of the unit's Great War history. But he concluded on a sombre note, suggesting that all his meticulous research, his "grubby empiricism" as he characterized it, counted for very little in the face of powerful forces of memory.[72] In making this assertion, Copp was in accord with Neil Postman, who saw a world drowning in information yet desperately thirsty for truth. Likewise, in an age when memory has been deemed a sacred obligation, one might reasonably ask how much actual remembering is taking place.[73]

How do historians respond to a legend that shows no sign of slowing down any time soon? When a rant during the intermission of a hockey broadcast exerts more influence than a scholarly study of the battle, what is to be done? When politicians reinterpret the battle to suit their own ends, what is the best course of action? In short, how can members of the historical profession "get in the game" and influence public perceptions of an event that all admit was significant for Canada? Recognition that the legend of Vimy Ridge is contested is more than just a matter of minutiae. It strikes at the heart of the historical enterprise. Although we may long ago have given up Rankean visions of seizing hold of Truth, it is not wholly irrelevant either. As the authors of the 1995 volume *Telling the Truth about History* put it, "We are arguing here that truths about the past are possible, even if they are not absolute, and hence are worth struggling for."[74]

The problem is, even when contemporary academics choose to focus on Vimy, their interpretations may differ markedly. Two studies on Vimy Ridge, both written by highly respected Canadian historians, were published to target the 2017 centenary. In October 2016, Ian McKay and Jamie Swift released *The Vimy Trap: Or, How We Learned to Stop Worrying and Love the Great War;* in March 2017, Tim Cook published *Vimy: The Battle and the Legend.*[75] Their analyses could hardly have been more divergent. As its title suggests, *The Vimy Trap* frames Canadian attitudes to Vimy within the wider context of global acceptance of war.[76] The authors' main target is Vimyism, an especially virulent attachment to the legend of the battle, which they define as "a form of martial nationalism that exalts the nation-building process and moral excellence of soldiers."[77] Jamie Swift went so far as to declare that it is fatuous to speak of a Canadian identity or a Canadian psyche, noting that "these constructs imagine the country as an organic, unified being, just as the 'Birth of a Nation' promoters see Canada as a veritable person, born (or perhaps 'coming of age' or 'maturing') on the blood-soaked fields of France and Flanders."[78] Tim Cook traces a less linear path for the legend of Vimy Ridge. He contends that its power has waxed and waned over the one hundred years following the battle, suggesting that, in 1967, "as Canada turned firmly to peace and as it cast away its old symbols Vimy came for many to represent the 'birth of a nation.'"[79] More significantly, though he points out some dubious attempts to memorialize the assault – from naming children after the town to branding tinned salmon with its name – Cook does insist that Vimy is one of those powerful "ideas, myths and icons that persistently carry the weight of nationhood."[80]

Reaction to both books was mixed. A reviewer in the *Winnipeg Free Press* praised Cook, observing, "If his position as military historian at the Canadian War Museum suggests bias or narrowness of viewpoint, his broad strokes and ability to move from documentation to anecdote, from battle description to opposing viewpoints, will satisfy most critical readers."[81] For his part, Jamie Swift, writing in the *Canadian Historical Review,* was less impressed. He concluded that Cook was a

> martial nationalist ... [who] imagines the "nation" to be possessed of a single, unwavering truth about Vimy. Yet this leaves unexamined any understanding of who reinvented in Vimy in the last half of the twentieth century – a cadre of martial nationalists in the federal state, a militant and well-funded war museum, and a host of intellectuals determined to steer Canadians away from the shoals of peace.[82]

Meanwhile, McKay and Swift's volume had also won both admirers and detractors. Joseph Burton lauded the authors for addressing "the institutionalization of memorialization and the rising arms industry that threatens to prolong Vimyism indefinitely."[83] Geoffrey Hayes countered that *The Vimy Trap* was "intended to be a provocative scholarly work, but the clever title, the combative tone, the dearth of original primary research – all suggest that this is a polemic."[84] Interestingly, whereas the book's approach was a black mark for Hayes, suggestive of a dismissal or even a misreading of existing literature, another reviewer was less concerned. He stated that the work was "'presentist' in a good way ... Historians should welcome this approach as a way of demonstrating the usefulness of history, and for its potential to capture the attention of the media, the interested public, and academics in other social sciences and humanities disciplines."[85] One wonders if a similarly "provocative" analysis from a different perspective would have been as warmly received.

Perhaps, in this age of 140-character pronouncements on everything from pop culture icons to geopolitical issues, this sort of polarization should be expected. But are we missing an important point? Could it be possible to acknowledge both the creeping militarization that inures people to the horrific violence of war *and* the sort of complexity that allows us to hate war as a tragic waste of life and yet retain respect for the individuals who waged it – like the men and women whose stories form the backbone of this collection?

The search continues for understanding of the Great War. Despite recent warning against relying too heavily on war poets when making sense of the conflict,[86] perhaps it would be useful to turn to one of their number, Edmund Blunden, by way of conclusion. In the preface to his collection *Undertones of War,* Blunden writes movingly of the Great War's power over him. He claims that "I must go over the ground again. A voice, perhaps not my own, answers within me. You'll be going over the ground again, it says, until that hour when agony's clawed face softens into the smilingness of a young spring day."[87] Blunden knew that he, like the men and women whose stories are told in this volume, had been shaped, irrevocably, by his wartime experience; he would continually mine it, discovering new fragments, integrating them into his larger understanding of 1914–18, calibrating his interpretations. Going over the ground. It is what the farmer does when preparing the soil, planting, watering, weeding, and harvesting. It is what teachers and students do in classrooms and on battlefield tours. It is also what academic historians must do. Terry Copp has done it with his fascinating web-based study, Montreal at War, 1914–1918.[88] And it is what the Great War Centenary Association has done, in its exploration of the more than five thousand volunteers from Brantford, Brant County, and Six Nations who served in the war.[89]

Without question, large set-piece encounters between prominent historians with clashing viewpoints may be useful in helping us better understand the meaning of Vimy. However, victory on the ridge was the result of the obscure arts of echo ranging and muzzle flashing as much as the often-cited innovation of the creeping barrage, of tactics learned from the French at Verdun as much as Canadian guts.[90] So it is when combatting the legend of Vimy. Articles in the popular press, interviews on local radio stations, and websites that tell individual stories but also reveal the work of the professional historian all contribute to a more complete and nuanced vision of our nation's most recognized military engagement. They give us the chance to fill the empty boots of 9 April 2017 with blood and bone. Without them, we cede the field to politicians who are eager to remobilize the boys of '17 in support of their latest foreign policy position, or to corporations seeking to boost profits by tapping into popular understandings of an event.

This ability of corporations to latch onto historical events in order to boost sales was epitomized by a 2014 advertisement for the Sainsbury grocery chain. Released in November and co-sponsored by the Royal British Legion, the ad depicts a famous incident from the unofficial Christmas truce of 1914, when German and British troops emerged from their trenches to fraternize and even play a friendly game of soccer in No Man's Land. The ad focuses on an English soldier named Jim and a German soldier named Otto. When the men return to their trenches, Otto discovers a gift from Jim in his greatcoat pocket – a bar of Sainsbury's chocolate.[91] The ad won plaudits in some circles for its production values and for its creators' willingness to consult with the legion, as well as with Great War costume expert Taff Gillingham and Andrew Hamilton, grandson of Captain Robert Hamilton of the 1st Battalion, Royal Warwickshire Regiment, who was an eyewitness to the event. However, a number of its elements were not necessarily accurate. These included the identity of the first soldier to emerge from the trenches, the attitude of officers to the suspension of hostilities, and the importance accorded the soccer match among the events that took place as troops mingled.[92]

Still, the accuracy of the Sainsbury ad was only one problem that drew attention. The larger question for many critics was the true purpose of the commercial. On this sanitized Western Front, foes could lay down their arms and see each other, however briefly, as fellow human beings. But the ad's tagline "Christmas is for sharing" was as much about commerce as any sense of shared humanity. The true aim of the production was the stimulation of sales, particularly of the chocolate bar that featured in the spot.[93]

This is why going over the ground again truly matters. History is not meant to win votes, to move product, or even to reinforce a flattering Canadian self-image. Whatever purpose Samuel Bothwell died for on 9 April 1917, it was none of these.

Notes

1 Jay Winter, *Remembering War: The Great War between Memory and History in the Twentieth Century* (New Haven: Yale University Press, 2006), 226–33. For a fuller exploration of the challenges of depicting war, see Jay Winter, "Museums and the Representation of War," *Museum and Society* 10, 3 (November 2012): 150–63. Also valuable is Jennifer Wellington, *Exhibiting War: The Great War, Museums, and Memory in Britain, Canada, and Australia* (Cambridge: Cambridge University Press, 2017).

2 Winter, *Remembering War*, 224. I have intentionally chosen the word "sacrifice" to describe the suffering of the poilu. In public consciousness, the theme of futility is commonly associated with the Great War. For a dissenting view, challenging the centrality of futility in the Great War experience, see Dan Todman, *The Great War: Myth and Memory* (London: Continuum, 20075, especially Chapter 4, 121–52.

3 Roy Rosenzweig and David Thelen, *The Presence of the Past: Popular Uses of History in American Life* (New York: Columbia University Press, 1998).

4 Ibid., 177.

5 Ibid., 21. The mean score for each of the top four sources was 8.4 (museums), 8.0 (relatives), 7.8 (eyewitnesses), and 7.3 (professors).

6 Margaret Conrad, Jocelyn Létourneau, and David Northrup, "Canadians and Their Pasts: An Exploration in Historical Consciousness," *Public Historian* 31, 1 (Winter 2009): 33–34.

7 See "Canadians Attend Memorials for Vimy Ridge Centennial Country-Wide," *CTV News*, 9 April 2017, https://www.ctvnews.ca/canada/canadians-attend-memorials-for-vimy-ridge-centennial-country-wide-1.3361326. Even more impressive was the television audience for the ceremony. The CBC's flagship news program, *The National*, earned an average minute audience (AMA) of 511,500 on 9 April. The preceding day had seen it garner an AMA of 461,600, and on the following day its AMA was 432,400. I am indebted to Nancy-Jane Collard, integrated account lead at CBC/Radio-Canada, for sharing these statistics with me.

8 Just a year earlier, the City had endured withering criticism when its executive committee voted to rename Vimy Park in Outremont for the recently deceased former sovereigntist premier, Jacques Parizeau. Jeremy Diamond, executive director of the Vimy Foundation, was predictably disappointed, stating, "To replace Vimy with another story doesn't do the respect that Vimy deserves." See Morgan Lowrie, "Montreal Decision to Rename Vimy Park in Honour of Parizeau Sparks Criticism," *Canadian Press* (Toronto), 16 June 2016.

9 Lee Berthiaume, "Thousands of Canadians Gather in France to Mark 100th Anniversary of Vimy Ridge," *Toronto Star*, 9 April 2017. Reactions to the ceremony, however, were not universally glowing. Logistical problems – inadequate washroom facilities, long waits to leave while dignitaries were ushered away, limited water supply for those standing in the hot sun – ruined the experience for many of those who travelled to France. See Tom Spears, "'Shame Shame on You!' Hundreds Complain to Veterans Affairs about Disorganized Vimy Ridge Ceremony," *National Post*, 11 December 2017.

10 The boots were meticulously arranged in ranks throughout the park by Canadian and French youth. That this particular touch created a lasting impression is suggested by the fact that the Canadian government initiated a program allowing educators to "borrow a boot" to stimulate reflection and discussion. "Borrow a Boot!" Veterans Affairs Canada, 14 February 2019, http://www.veterans.gc.ca/eng/remembrance/information-for/educators/learning-modules/vimy-ridge/borrow-a-boot.

11 The phrase "theatre of memory" was coined by Raphael Samuel, whose study of that name remains a classic. See Raphael Samuel, *Theatres of Memory: Past and Present in Contemporary Culture* (New York: Verso, 1994). Samuel contends that "memory, so far from

being merely a passive receptacle or storage system, an image bank of the past is, rather an active, shaping force ... It is dynamic – what it contrives symptomatically to forget is as important as what it remembers – and ... it is dialectically related to historical thought, rather than being some kind of negative other to it." Ibid., xxiii.

12 Neil Postman, *Amusing Ourselves to Death* (New York: Penguin Books, 1986), 67.

13 According to Jean-Denis Bredin, Dreyfus did not want "his martyrdom to make him a public personality or fuel any sort of notoriety." Jean-Denis Bredin, *The Affair: The Case of Alfred Dreyfus*, trans. Jeffrey Mehlman (New York: George Braziller, 1986), 490.

14 The *National Post* noted Canadian ignorance of the cost of this battle, adding that fewer than 200 soldiers died on the Plains of Abraham and only 267 were lost in the entire Boer War. Tristin Hopper, "The Germans Considered It a Victory, Too: Rare Images Showing Everything You Didn't Know about Vimy Ridge," *National Post*, 6 April 2017.

15 "Appendix 2: Lest We Forget: The Men of Vimy Ridge" (research compiled by students at Smiths Falls District Collegiate Institute under the direction of Blake Seward), in *Vimy Ridge: A Canadian Reassessment*, ed. Geoffrey Hayes, Andrew Iarocci, and Mike Bechthold (Waterloo: Wilfrid Laurier University Press 2007), 332. The Canadian Virtual War Memorial and Commonwealth War Graves Commission mistakenly list his age at death as forty-one. Canadian Virtual War Memorial, "Major Samuel James Bothwell," Commonwealth War Graves Commission, Veterans Affairs Canada, 26 February 2020, http://www. veterans.gc.ca/eng/remembrance/memorials/canadian-virtual-war-memorial/detail/ 297014?Samuel%20James%20Bothwell.

16 Chris Sharpe, "Enlistment in the Canadian Expeditionary Force, 1914–1918: A Re-evaluation," *Canadian Military History* 24, 1 (2015): 17–60 For further discussion of the composition of the CEF, see Richard Holt, *Filling the Ranks: Manpower in the Canadian Expeditionary Force, 1914–1918* (Montreal and Kingston: McGill-Queen's University Press, 2017).

17 "Major Samuel James Bothwell," Canadian Great War Project, http://www.canadiangreat warproject.com/searches/soldierDetail.asp?ID=14964.

18 Library and Archives Canada (LAC), Canadian Expeditionary Force (CEF), RG 150, accession 1992-93/166, box 903–14, Personnel file for Samuel Bothwell, "Medical History Sheet" and "Casualty Form Active Service." Desmond Morton claims that the average height of men in the CEF was five foot five. See Desmond Morton, "A Canadian Soldier in the Great War: The Experiences of Frank Maheux," *Canadian Military History* 1, 1 (1992): 79.

19 LAC, "Medical History Sheet."

20 *Edmonton Bulletin*, 17 May 1917, quoted in "Major Samuel James Bothwell," Canadian Great War Project.

21 "1st Canadian Mounted Rifles – History," http://canadianmountedrifles.yolasite.com/1cmr -history.php.

22 Ibid.

23 "Battle Honours of the Canadian Army: The North Saskatchewan Regiment," Regimental Rogue, http://regimentalrogue.com/battlehonours/bathnrinf/37-nsaskr.htm.

24 Tim Cook, *At the Sharp End: Canadians Fighting the Great War, 1914–1916* (Toronto: Viking, 2007), 351.

25 Canada, *House of Commons Debates* (22 May 1920), 2100. For a fuller discussion of the deliberations of the committee entrusted with the siting of Canadian memorials, see John Pierce, "Constructing Memory: The Vimy Memorial," *Canadian Military History* 1, 1 (1992): 5.

26 For a fascinating examination of the merits and flaws of the CMR as well as the reasons for its reconfiguration from cavalry to infantry see William Stewart, "The Barrier and the

Damage Done Converting the Canadian Mounted Rifles to Infantry, December 1915," *Canadian Military History* 24, 1 (2015): 285–319.

27 "Appendix 1: Order of Battle – Vimy Ridge," in Hayes, Iarocci, and Bechthold, *Vimy Ridge,* 324; "Battalion Operation Order No. 44," War Diary, 2nd Battalion Canadian Mounted Rifles, 7 April 1917, Canadian Great War Project, http://canadiangreatwarproject.com/WarDiaries/diaryDetail.asp?ID=15089.

28 All that is recorded of Bothwell is that "this officer was leading 'C' Company, in the attack on VIMY RIDGE, when he was hit by enemy machine gun bullets and instantly killed." See LAC, RG 150, accession 1992-93/314, 156, Circumstances of Death Registers, Surnames Border – Boys.

29 LAC, Online MIKAN no. 2004667 War Diaries of the First World War; War Diaries, 1st Battalion, Canadian Mounted Rifles (outside dates: 1915/09/01–1919/02/28), 9 April 2017, 7 (Item 242). See also G.W.L. Nicholson, *Canadian Expeditionary Force, 1914–1919: Official History of the Canadian Army in the First World War* (Ottawa: Department of National Defence, 1962), 252–61.

30 LAC, War Diaries, 1st Battalion, Canadian Mounted Rifles, 9 April 1917, 9 (item 244).

31 LAC, Online MIKAN no. 2004667 War Diaries, 1st Battalion, Canadian Mounted Rifles 14, (item 249).

32 A vivid account of the ferocious battle to dislodge elements of the elite 4th Prussian Guards from its heavily fortified positions on the high ground of the Pimple can be found in Tim Cook, *Vimy: The Battle and the Legend* (Toronto: Allen Lane, 2017), 127–29.

33 Vera Brittain, *Testament of Youth* (London: Fontana, 1979), 190.

34 See Virginia Nicholson, *Singled Out: How Two Million Women Survived without Men after the First World War* (London: Penguin, 2008), for an exploration of the economic hurdles and social stigma faced by single women.

35 LAC, RG 150, accession 1992-93/166, box 903–14, CEF Personnel file, Separation Allowance Form.

36 This is, after all, the goal that Tim Cook set himself in *Vimy: The Battle and the Legend.* It is equally the project of Ian McKay and Jamie Swift in their unapologetically polemical study of the Battle of Vimy Ridge, *The Vimy Trap: Or, How We Learned to Stop Worrying and Love the Great War* (Toronto: Between the Lines, 2016).

37 See Michael Boire, "The Battlefield before the Canadians, 1914–1916," in Hayes, Iarocci, and Bechthold, *Vimy Ridge,* 51–61. Boire summarizes the situation neatly when he writes, "By the time the Canadian Corps marched from the Somme to relieve IV British Corps at Vimy in October 1916, this ground had been fought over many times, claiming over 300,000 French, British and German casualties." Ibid., 59.

38 Brigadier Alexander Ross famously declared that Vimy represented "Canada from the Atlantic to the Pacific on parade. It was the birth of a nation." Tim Cook underlines that Ross made this comment in the foreword to fellow vet D.E. McIntyre's *Canada at Vimy,* published in *1967* not *1917.* Cook, *Vimy: The Battle and the Legend,* 316.

39 See Jonathan F. Vance, *Death So Noble: Memory, Meaning, and the First World War* (Vancouver: UBC Press, 1997).

40 Heath begins by remarking that "surprisingly, most accounts of the war either ignore faith and religion outright or merely mention them in passing. Whereas this exclusion may reflect the present-day marginalization of religion from Canadian public life and national vision, it certainly does not do justice to the remarkable influence of the wartime churches or to the religious identity of the young dominion" (page 175).

41 See Nicholson, *Canadian Expeditionary Force,* 236–37 and Gary Sheffield, "Vimy Ridge and the Battle of Arras: A British Perspective," in Hayes, Iarocci, and Bechthold, *Vimy Ridge,* 15–29.

42   Canada, *House of Commons Debates* (22 May 1922), 2099.

43   Douglas E. Delaney, "Rethinking the Battle of Hill 70," *Journal of Military and Strategic Studies* 18, 2 (2017): 258. See also LAC, MG30-E100, Arthur William Currie Papers, Arthur Currie, Personal diary, 15–18 August 1917; and Mark Osborne Humphries, ed., *The Selected Papers of Sir Arthur Currie: Diaries, Letters, and Report to the Ministry, 1917–1933* (Waterloo: LCMSDS Press of Wilfrid Laurier University, 2008), 48–49. For a fuller study of the Battle of Hill 70, see Douglas E. Delaney and Serge Marc Durflinger, eds., *Capturing Hill 70: Canada's Forgotten Battle of the First World War* (Vancouver: UBC Press, 2016).

44   David Lowenthal, *The Past Is a Foreign Country* (Cambridge: Cambridge University Press, 1985), 4.

45   These were St. Julien, Passchendaele, Observatory Ridge, Vimy Ridge, Drury Crossroads, Bourlon Wood, Courcelette, and Hospital Wood. Canada, *House of Commons Debates* (22 May 1920), 2098. There is a striking similarity between this list and the one for the costliest days of the CEF.

46   A.Y. Jackson, "Letter to the Editor," *Canadian Forum* 11, 18 (March 1922): 559.

47   Cook, *Vimy: The Battle and the Legend*, 184–85.

48   Laura Brandon, "The Sculptures on the Vimy Memorial," Canadian War Museum, https://www.warmuseum.ca/the-battle-of-vimy-ridge/the-sculptures-on-the-vimy-memorial/#tabs.

49   What the Vimy legend tends to overlook is precisely this cost.

50   Cook, *Vimy: The Battle and the Legend*, 185.

51   For Gallipoli, see K.S. Inglis, *Sacred Places: War Memorials in the Australian Landscape* (Melbourne: Melbourne University Press, 2001), especially 441–43; and Bruce S. Scates, "Manufacturing Memory at Gallipoli," in *War Memory and Popular Culture: Essays on Modes of Remembrance and Commemoration*, ed. Michael Keren and Holger H. Herwig (Jefferson, NC: McFarland, 2009), 57–76. For Dieppe, contrast Norm Christie, *The Suicide Raid: The Canadians at Dieppe, August 19th, 1942* (Ottawa: CEF Books, 2001), with David R. O'Keefe, *One Day in August: The Untold Story behind Canada's Tragedy at Dieppe* (Toronto: Alfred A. Knopf Canada, 2013).

52   Jay Winter, *Sites of Memory, Sites of Mourning* (Cambridge: Cambridge University Press, 1995), 95. For the role of veterans in interwar pacifist organizations, see Martin Ceadel, *Pacifism in Britain, 1914–1945: The Defining of a Faith* (Oxford: Clarendon Press, 1980).

53   Eric Brown and Tim Cook, "The 1936 Vimy Pilgrimage," *Canadian Military History* 20, 2 (2011): 42–43.

54   Serge Durflinger, "Safeguarding Sanctity: Canada and the Vimy Memorial during the Second World War," in Hayes, Iarocci, and Bechthold, *Vimy Ridge*, 291–305.

55   Alan Clark, *The Donkeys* (London: Hutchinson, 1961). For an excellent analysis of Clark's impact on thinking about the Great War, see Todman, *The Great War*, 199–203. The West End production *Oh! What a Lovely War* built on many of the themes that were articulated in *The Donkeys*. Todman, *The Great War*, 104–11.

56   The CBC was also a collaborator. See Imperial War Museum Archives (IWM), ROADS/DD1/04/007/1-2, BBC Great War Series, Christopher Roads to Alasdair Milne, 13 August 1963.

57   IWM, EN3/2/11/11 BBC, Noble Frankland to Sir Hugh Greene KCMG, Dir. General of BBC, 24 September 1964. The practice of using archival footage from one engagement to represent another remains fairly common. Experts at the IWM were horrified by the extent to which *The Great War* was relying on reconstructions, however. Most notoriously, the opening credits featured an exhausted Tommy in a trench surrounded by corpses. This was actually a collage of two separate images; the soldier in the composite had initially been surrounded by smiling comrades. (See *The Great War*, Season 1, Episode 1, "On the

Idle Hill of Summer," https://www.youtube.com/watch?v=KjHCkVVTTHg.) For an exploration of reconstructed images more generally, see Roger Smither, "'A Wonderful Idea of the Fighting': The Question of Fakes in the *Battle of the Somme,*" *Imperial War Museum Review* 3 (1989): 4–16.

58 These and various other key factors are discussed in Cook, *Vimy: The Battle and the Legend,* 303–10.

59 *Montreal Gazette,* 10 April 1967, quoted in ibid., 322 (emphasis added).

60 Pierre Berton, *Vimy* (Toronto: Anchor Canada, 1986), 307–8 (emphasis in original). The suggestion that the battle created Canadians can be found on page 337.

61 Winter, *Remembering War,* 26–51.

62 "Text of Prime Minister Stephen Harper's Speech," *CTV News,* 9 April 2007, http://www.ctvnews.ca/text-of-prime-minister-stephen-harper-s-speech-1.236701. For analysis of Stephen Harper's consistent efforts to reshape Canadian perceptions of the past, see Reg Whitaker, "Harper's History: Does the Right Hand Know What the Other Right Hand Is Doing?" *Labour* 73 (Spring 2014): 218–21.

63 "Coach's Corner," *Hockey Night in Canada,* 7 April 2012, https://www.youtube.com/watch?reload=9&v=2lY8UvP-UhA.

64 "PM Delivers Remarks on the 100th Anniversary of the Start of the First World War," 4 August 2014, Dailymotion, https://www.dailymotion.com/video/x2yzc99.

65 "Statement by the Prime Minister of Canada on the 100th Anniversary of the Battle of Vimy Ridge," 9 April 2017 (emphasis added), http://pm.gc.ca/eng/news/2017/04/09/statement-prime-minister-canada-100th-anniversary-battle-vimy-ridge. There has been limited scholarly attention paid to the shift in how the Canadian past is being mobilized under Trudeau. One useful contribution to this discussion was a piece in the *Globe and Mail,* which observed that the incoming Minister of Heritage, Mélanie Joly, referred to her portfolio as the "ministry of symbols." The article further noted her assertion that "It's very interesting to be in charge of symbols of progressiveness. That was the soul of our platform." Robert Everett-Green, "Mélanie Joly to Reset 'Symbols of Progressiveness' as Heritage Minister," *Globe and Mail,* 6 November 2015.

66 See Sharpe, "Enlistment in the Canadian Expeditionary Force," 55.

67 Paul Gough, "Sites in the Imagination: The Beaumont Hamel Newfoundland Memorial on the Somme," *Cultural Geographies* 11, 3 (July 2004): 235–58; David Macfarlane, *The Danger Tree* (Toronto: HarperCollins, 1991).

68 For the fear of ethnic conflict over conscription, see Brock Millman, *Polarity, Patriotism, and Dissent in Great War Canada, 1914–1919* (Toronto: University of Toronto Press, 2016). For changing rural attitudes to the war, see Mourad Djebabla, "'Fight or Farm': Canadian Farmers and the Dilemma of the War Effort in World War I (1914–1918)," *Canadian Military Journal* 13, 2 (2013): 57–67. For labour's growing opposition, see Craig Heron, "National Contours: Solidarity and Fragmentation," in *The Workers' Revolt in Canada, 1917–1925,* ed. Craig Heron (Toronto: University of Toronto Press, 1998), 268–304. For conscientious objection, see Amy J. Shaw, *Crisis of Conscience: Conscientious Objection in Canada during the First World War* (Vancouver: UBC Press, 2009).

69 Ipsos Public Affairs, *The 100th Anniversary of the Battle of Vimy Ridge* (Toronto: Ipsos, March 2017), 11. The situation deteriorated even further in the year following the splashy ceremonies. A press release lamented that just under a year after the centenary celebrations, "recognition of the famous monument has fallen by 3 points to just 16 percent ... The monument at Vimy Ridge is featured on both the $20 bill and the $2 coin, and yet 70 percent of those polled were unwilling to even hazard a guess, saying that they 'didn't know' the distinctive shape of the Vimy Memorial, one of Canada's great examples of public art." Some even mistook the memorial for the Washington Monument or the Twin

Towers in New York. See "Press Release Ipsos Public Affairs April 9, 2018." Ipsos Public Affairs, "One-Year Removed from Vimy Centenary, Recognition of Vimy Monument Falls to just 16%," Press release, 9 April 2018.

70 A particularly scathing denunciation of the myth is offered by Martin Masse, "Vimy Ridge: Can a War Massacre Give Birth to a Nation?" *Le Québécois libre* 102 (13 April 2002), http:// www.quebecoislibre.org/020413-2.htm.

71 Concentrating on Brantford, Brant County, and Six Nations of the Grand River Territory, the GWCA was founded in 2013 to "preserve and make available to the public, a permanent and evolving record of our community's involvement during the First World War." "About the GWCA," Great War Centenary Association, http://doingourbit.ca/node/4854.

72 Terry Copp, "The Irish Canadian Rangers: From Easter Rebellion to the Western Front" (lecture presented at the Great War Centenary Association, Brantford, ON, 27 March 2017).

73 The uproar that began in April 1994 over the Smithsonian's exhibition featuring the *Enola Gay*, which dropped the atomic bomb on Hiroshima, is a perfect example of the volatility of memory and the passions it can arouse. For a good overview of the controversy, see Michael J. Hogan, "The Enola Gay Controversy: History, Memory and the Politics of Presentation," in *Hiroshima in History and Memory*, ed. Michael J. Hogan (Cambridge: Cambridge University Press, 1996), 200–32. A useful website, with many primary documents of interest, is the Enola Gay Controversy, History on Trial, http://digital.lib.lehigh. edu/trial/enola/.

74 Joyce Appleby, Lynn Hunt, and Margaret Jacob, *Telling the Truth about History* (New York: Norton, 1995), 7.

75 Ian McKay is the L.R. Wilson Chair in Canadian History at McMaster University. At Queen's University (1988 to 2016) and then McMaster, he has supervised or co-supervised ninety-four graduate theses and cognate essays. His 2008 study, *Reasoning Otherwise: Leftists and the People's Enlightenment in Canada, 1890–1920*, was awarded the John A. Macdonald Prize by the Canadian Historical Association. "Meet the Wilson Institute," McMaster University, Faculty of Humanities, https://wilson.humanities.mcmaster. ca/2016/10/27/meet-the-wilson-institute-dr-ian-mckay/. Tim Cook is a historian at the Canadian War Museum (CWM) and an adjunct research professor at Carleton University in Ottawa. He was curator of the First World War permanent gallery at the CWM. Author of several award-winning books, many of which were award winning, he has received the Pierre Berton Award for service to public history and is a member of the Order of Canada. "Tim Cook," Carleton University, Department of History, https:// carleton.ca/history/people/tim-cook/.

76 The subtitle is a play on the title of Stanley Kubrick's brilliant 1964 anti-war satire, *Dr. Strangelove or: How I Learned to Stop Worrying and Love the Bomb*.

77 McKay and Swift, *The Vimy Trap*, 10.

78 Jamie Swift, "Review of Tim Cook, *Vimy: The Battle and the Legend*," *Canadian Historical Review* 98, 3 (September 2017): 603.

79 Cook, *Vimy: The Battle and the Legend*, 325.

80 Ibid., 228, 7.

81 Ron Robinson, "Cook's Vimy History a Big, Balanced Beauty," *Winnipeg Free Press*, 1 April 2017, https://www.winnipegfreepress.com/arts-and-life/entertainment/books/cooks -vimy-history-a-big-balanced-beauty-417852953.html.

82 Swift, "Review of Tim Cook," 605.

83 Joseph Burton, "Review of *The Vimy Trap: Or, How We Learned to Stop Worrying and Love the Great War*," *Canadian Historical Review* 98, 2 (June 2017): 405.

84 Geoffrey Hayes, "Review of Ian McKay and Jamie Swift *The Vimy Trap: Or, How We Learned to Stop Worrying and Love the Great War*," *Canadian Military History* 27, 1 (2018): 17.

85   Nathan Smith, "Review of Ian McKay and Jamie Swift *The Vimy Trap: Or, How We Learned to Stop Worrying and Love the Great War*," *Ontario History* 60, 1 (Spring 2018): 110–11.

86   See, for example, Todman, *The Great War*, 153–86.

87   Edmund Blunden, "Preface to the 1924 Edition," in Edmund Blunden, *Undertones of War* (London: Penguin, 2000), xii.

88   An attractive and informative website produced by Copp and his collaborators, Montreal at War, 1914–1918 (https://montrealatwar.com) integrates his research on the Irish Canadian Rangers. The added advantage of such a website is that it allows Copp to pull back the veil on the work of the academic historian, offering insight into relevant secondary and primary sources. See, for example, "Links," https://montrealatwar.com/links/; and "Primary Documents," https://montrealatwar.com/primary-documents/.

89   "We Remember: WWI Records Search," Great War Centenary Association, http://www. doingourbit.ca/records-search. The GWCA has also organized public commemorative ceremonies and worked collaboratively with Six Nations scholars to develop school curriculums, especially material sensitive to issues surrounding First Nations involvement in the war.

90   Tim Cook, "The Gunners at Vimy: 'We Are Hammering Fritz to Pieces,'" in Hayes, Iarocci, and Bechthold, *Vimy Ridge*, 105–24; Nicholson, *Canadian Expeditionary Force*, 250.

91   "1914 | Sainsbury's Ad | Christmas 2014," 12 November 2014, YouTube, https://www.you tube.com/watch?v=NWF2JBb1bvM.

92   Kathryn N. McDaniel, "Commemorating the Christmas Truce: A Critical Thinking Approach for Popular History," *History Teacher* 49, 1 (November 2015): 95. See also "The Supermarket and the Christmas Truce – Lesson Plan and Resources," MrAllsopHistory. com, https://www.mrallsophistory.com/revision/the-supermarket-and-the-truce -sainsburys-christmas.html. Both of these explorations of the commercial demonstrate that it is possible to engage with it to get to a more complex reading of the Christmas truce and the Great War more generally.

93   McDaniel, "Commemorating the Christmas Truce," 94–96. See also Ally Fogg, "Sainsbury's Christmas Ad Is a Dangerous and Disrespectful Masterpiece," *The Guardian*, 13 November 2014.

5
Soldier or Ward? Hill 70 and the Lived Experience of Private Wilfred Lickers

Evan J. Habkirk

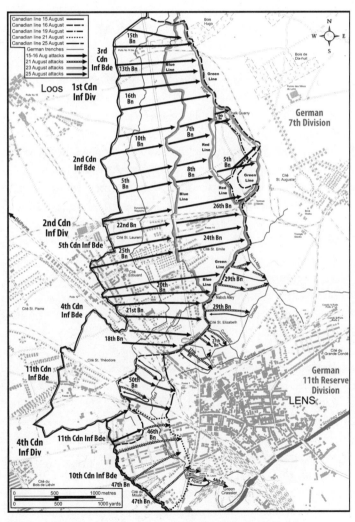

Figure 5.1 Hill 70, 15 August 1917. | Map by Mike Bechthold.

A NUMBER OF HISTORIANS have argued that, between the 1870s and the end of the First World War, First Nations people were under constant surveillance by the Canadian state, mostly by the Department of Indian Affairs (DIA), with military scholars noting an increased meddling in the lives of Indigenous veterans through the issuing of veterans' benefits.[1] By following one Indigenous soldier, Private Wilfred Lickers, from his first battle at Hill 70 until his death in 1960, I demonstrate that surveillance and interference in the lives of Indigenous soldiers began well before they were discharged from service. In some cases, federal intrusion began before they entered the military, continued while they were dealing with the pressures of battle and news from home, and endured into their post-war lives.

Lickers was born on 1 October 1891 on the Six Nations Territory at Grand River, just east of Brantford, Ontario. The third child of George and Minnie Lickers, Wilfred had two older sisters, Cassie and Liddie (Lydia), and was the elder brother of Leonard, Elmer, and Minnie (Ellen).[2] Although his First World War attestation lists him as a labourer, as he worked on various farms, including his father's, he was also a member of the militia, having joined the 37th Haldimand Rifles in 1909.[3]

For Six Nations men, enlistment in the militia system was not uncommon. To combat the constant regulation and supervision by the DIA, some First Nations men sought outlets beyond their reserve communities, where they would be treated as equals or could achieve the self-sufficient manhood that was idealized in Canada at the time.[4] Many Six Nations men chose to enter the service, which they saw as a natural extension of their traditional military support of the British Crown.[5] Wishing to avoid the segregation that characterized many segments of the Canadian military, they flocked to the ranks of the 37th Haldimand Rifles, among them Wilfred's father, George, who was a long-serving bandsman.[6] During the 1890s, more than half of its members, and all of its musical band, were Six Nations men.[7]

With the passing of the Indian Act in 1876, First Nations people became wards of the Crown and a heavily policed population. First, by relocating them to reserves, the DIA tried to isolate them from the non–First Nations community.[8] It hired Indian agents and superintendents, inspectors, commissioners, clerks, matrons, stockmen, farm instructors, ration issuers, interpreters, tradespeople, medical personnel, teachers, and police, thus ensuring that every aspect of life on the reserve would come under scrutiny and that the traditional economic, political, social, and cultural freedoms of First Nations people would be limited and replaced with those of the dominant Euro-Canadian society.[9] Where Indigenous and settler communities lived in close proximity, as was the case with the Six Nations and Brantford, the DIA could count on other forms of supervision. By interviewing or employing local justices of the peace, game wardens, fishery and timber inspectors, public health officers, valuators, missionaries, farmers, merchants, contractors, surveyors, politicians, and academics, the DIA could garner further information about the living conditions on any reserve.[10] The department even employed First Nations community members, who, sometimes unknowingly, became part of its surveillance network.[11] Others inside and outside of the First Nations community could also write to the DIA about issues that they saw as unfair or bothersome.

Through this web of surveillance, the DIA created tabular statements about the lives of its wards, gathering detailed information regarding their income, education, material possessions, morality, farm improvements, and used and unused land. Although the accuracy of the statements could be suspect, these aspects of First Nations life were measured, judged, and compared against those of other First Nations and even their non-Indigenous neighbours to assess their progress toward "civilization."[12] On the basis of these statements, Ottawa could legislate any social controls against First Nations people that were deemed necessary by the dominant culture. These controls and surveillance techniques would be expanded when a First Nations person entered the Canadian armed forces under the constant gaze of military authorities.

For the Six Nations of the Grand River, government systems of control were imposed slowly before 1876. By the 1840s, the Six Nations had been consolidated onto a portion of its territory in the Haldimand Tract, namely Tuscarora Township, in Brant County. Agents and commissions were also appointed to investigate the affairs of the Six Nations; among other topics, they examined financial affairs, enfranchisement, and public health. In 1858, at the request of merchants in Brantford, the government set up a commission to investigate financial accounts between Six Nations individuals and Brantford merchants. It concluded that delinquent accounts should be paid in full, using monies from the Six Nations trust fund.[13] Founded on the monies from Six Nations land sales and leases, the trust fund was to be used for the public good of all Six Nations people by their Confederacy Council of Chiefs, but the government appropriated funds from it without the authority of the Council.[14]

In 1874, another commission investigated why the Six Nations opposed the Gradual Enfranchisement Act of 1869. William Patterson, Liberal MP for the Brant riding, interviewed missionaries, clergy, physicians, and Brantford merchants, as well as Chiefs and other members of the Six Nations. To form his conclusions, Patterson only interviewed eighteen people, ten being non-Six Nations, and eight being Six Nations members whose occupations heavily linked them economically to the Euro-Canadian community.[15] The commission also dealt with concerns that lay beyond its investigative scope, with some interviewees reporting on the attendance of Six Nations children in day schools and the debate over whether an elected band council should replace the Confederacy Council of Chiefs as the official government of Six Nations.[16]

One of the lengthier DIA investigations of the Six Nations was that of Inspector J.A. Macrae in 1899. Macrae was sent to probe sanitary conditions and the state of health on the Six Nations territory. His report found that the rumours of ill health and poor sanitary conditions had been exaggerated by the appointed physician to the Six Nations, Dr. Levi Secord, who hoped to have a hospital built in the territory.[17] Again, most of the evidence cited in Macrae's report came from doctors, missionaries, and other non-Indigenous people, including ethnologist David Boyle.[18] Like other observers, Macrae reported on matters that were beyond his mandate, such as the Brantford Farmers' Market, liquor traffic, Six Nations religious practices, including the growth of the traditional Longhouse beliefs relative to Christianity, and the relationship between the City of Brantford and the Six Nations.[19]

Alongside these investigations were the reports of the DIA superintendents at Six Nations. From 1862 to 1891, the reserve was supervised by Jasper Gilkison. He was succeeded by E.D. Cameron, who was then replaced by Gordon J. Smith in 1906.[20] Not only did these men oversee the affairs of the Six Nations, but they also attended and reported on Confederacy Council of Chiefs meetings, whose decisions they were empowered to overrule. The DIA also hired Six Nations employees to aid in its administration of the territory, starting with interpreters.[21] The father of poet E. Pauline Johnson, G.H.M. Johnson, for example, was hired as an interpreter, path master, and timber inspector.[22] Others were later employed by the DIA to work in its office in downtown Brantford and were asked to report on the Grand River Territory.

Given their experience at the hands of the repressive Canadian government throughout the nineteenth century, one would expect that Six Nations men would not be eager to enlist during the First World War. In fact, the opposite proved true.[23] With the outbreak of the war, over three hundred Grand River men joined the Canadian Expeditionary Force, many with the 114th Battalion.[24] Born out of the 37th Haldimand Rifles, the 114th began recruiting in late 1915. With many men from Six Nations already in the 37th, the 114th became known locally as the All Six Nations Battalion. For other First Nations men, it acted as a Pals Battalion, with many recruits coming from Indigenous communities in Ontario and Quebec. The battalion's official nickname was Brock's Rangers, in honour of the Six Nations men who had fought at Queenston Heights with General Isaac Brock during the War of 1812. The name celebrated the continued military support shown by First Nations people toward the British Crown, and the loyalist roots of the people from Haldimand County.

Figure 5.2 Wilfred Lickers and his first wife, Eva. |
Courtesy of the Lickers family and University of
Calgary, Libraries and Cultural Resources, Indigenous-
Canadian Military History Collection.

Wilfred Lickers was among the recruits who joined the 114th. The year 1916 was a turbulent one for the twenty-five-year-old Lickers. Not only would he enlist in the 114th but he would also become a father and a widower. His wife, Eva, who was from the neighbouring reserve at New Credit, died in April 1916. By July, the 114th had been sent to Camp Borden.[25] Given a home furlough in October before heading overseas in November, Lickers would see some of his relatives for the last time; his father, George, would die in late November.[26] Before leaving for Europe, Lickers paid for Eva's headstone and, possibly following the matrilineal traditions of the Six Nations, arranged for his daughter, Eva Jane, to be cared for by his mother-in-law at New Credit.[27] In early November 1916, the 114th Battalion arrived safely in England.

Once overseas, the 114th was broken up for reinforcements, with the battalion band staying behind to tour Scotland. After this tour ended, the band too would be used as reinforcements.[28] For First Nations soldiers who had enlisted with their friends, this fragmenting of battalions was traumatic. Leaving their friends and being placed in units where they were greatly outnumbered by Euro-Canadians caused many to suffer homesickness and depression, as they coped with life in the trenches and the norms of non-Indigenous culture.[29] With many other Six Nations men, Lickers transferred into the 107th "Timber Wolf" Battalion, the other "All First Nations Battalion." Whether he chose the 107th because he sought the comfort of serving with other First Nations people or because he wanted to stay with his friends, Lickers would find his way to the front line just in time for the unit's August assault on Hill 70.[30]

The Battle of Hill 70 was part of a diversionary attack on the French town of Lens, which was part of a larger diversionary attack ordered by Field Marshal Douglas Haig, the commander of the British Expeditionary Force. To prevent the Germans from reinforcing the Flanders and Passchendaele sectors, Haig ordered an attack on Lens.[31] Lieutenant General Arthur Currie, along with members of the British First Army, felt that a direct attack on Lens would be too costly and proposed an assault on Hill 70, which lay just north of the city.[32] Currie hoped that once the Canadians had captured the hill, the Germans would naturally mount a counterattack, which would render them too exhausted to hold Lens.[33]

Before the assault could commence, Currie called for intense counter-battery operations to eliminate German strong points. For four days, with the use of infantry, forward artillery observation officers, Royal Flying Corps patrols – specifically No. 16 Squadron RFC – and newly deployed wireless radios, Lieutenant Colonel Andrew McNaughton's artillery cleared barbed wire obstacles, machine-gun nests, and the majority of German guns.[34]

The attack called for Currie's famous bite and hold tactics, in which limited objectives would be captured and held against counterattacks to inflict maximum damage to the enemy.[35] After practising their assault on taped-out courses,[36] the 1st, 2nd, and 3rd Divisions took their positions on the front line. On 15 August 1917, at 4:30 a.m., the 1st and 2nd Divisions attacked the hill while the 3rd Division launched a diversionary assault on Lens.[37] The 107th Battalion followed in the wake of the 3rd and later 2nd Brigades of the 1st Division. The brigades stormed the hill under the protection of a creeping barrage and smoke screens produced by gas shells and flaming drums of oil,[38] ultimately capturing their objectives and fortifying what was left of the German trenches. The 107th, under the same fire, aided in building defences, constructing communication trenches, running supplies, and covering for the attacking troops.[39]

The 107th had begun as an infantry battalion. Like the 114th Battalion, it started recruiting in late 1915 and attracted many First Nations enlistees from the Canadian Prairies. Unlike the 114th, which was broken up for reinforcements once overseas, the 107th changed its designation and became a pioneer battalion. This type of battalion consisted of both infantrymen and engineers; they were trained to fight but were primarily tasked with the construction and breaching of obstacles.[40] At Hill 70, they crossed three to five hundred yards of battlefield, carrying the gear, weapons, and ammunition of a standard infantryman (sixty to eighty pounds), with each company issued an additional 27 spools of barbed wire, 200 sandbags, 100 shovels, picks and axes, 12 large wire cutters, 6,000 rounds of Lewis gun ammunition, and 100 grenades.[41] During the first day of the battle, the 107th suffered 151 casualties.[42] Despite these losses, the unit continued digging trenches into the limestone hill at a rate of six hundred yards a day while also carrying construction materials up the line.[43]

Once the hill was captured, the Germans, as expected, counterattacked. Again, through the coordinated effort of forward artillery observation officers, the RFC, infantry and spotters, and artillerymen, many of these counterattacks were broken up before they could reach the Canadian defenders.[44] By dividing his gunners into six shifts, McNaughton was able to guarantee continuous fire on the German front line, making counterattacks and repair of the lines almost impossible.[45] Machine-gun fire plans strengthened the captured positions. Machine guns were situated every thirty-five yards, and many were used for cover and indirect fire as much as for actual defence during the counterattacks.[46] From 15 August until 18 August, the Germans launched twenty-one counterattacks, the heaviest of which included a bombardment of fifteen to twenty thousand gas shells.[47]

After working to build defences under these conditions, members of the 107th were pulled from the front lines and held in reserve. Many volunteered as stretcher-bearers where light trams and field ambulances could not evacuate the wounded.[48] When the 10th Battalion ran into heavy resistance, stretcher-bearers from the 107th came to its aid.[49] In fact, the 107th evacuated many men from the 10th Battalion at the cost of another eighty-eight casualties, some of whom were victims of a concentrated mustard gas attack.[50] The unit was finally pulled out of the front lines on 17–18 August 1917.[51] It is hard to say with any certainty where Lickers would have been during this battle.[52] Before it began, some men from the 107th were set aside as a reserve force, and only three companies of the battalion went into the front line. Additionally, the list of those who were engaged was either not recorded in the 107th battalion war diary or has been lost.[53]

In all, from 15 to 21 August, the Canadians experienced approximately 5,400 casualties at Hill 70, with 3,527 coming on the first day and 1,800 occurring during the counterattacks. For the Germans, the initial assault and their costly counterattacks led to an estimated 12,000 to 15,000 casualties.[54] Of the 5,400

Canadian casualties, 249 were from the 107th Battalion, 21 of whom were former Brock's Rangers.[55] Although the follow-up attacks on Lens from 21 to 25 August did not force the Germans to surrender the town, and though the victory at Vimy Ridge overshadowed the Battle of Hill 70 during the post-war years, Currie and Haig were quick to praise the operation. Currie stated, "It was altogether the hardest battle in which the Corps has participated."[56] He continued, "Congratulatory messages were received from the Commander-in-Chief, General [Herbert Charles] Plumer, General [Julian] Byng ... General Gordon Lennox and many others. It was a great and wonderful victory. [General Headquarters] regard it as one of the finest performances of the war."[57] Douglas Haig called the operation "one of the finest minor operations" of the war.[58] For its part, the 107th was commended by Currie, and the commanding officer of the 10th Battalion sent it a letter of appreciation for its help in evacuating his wounded men.[59] Even Canon Frederick Scott, though not mentioning the 107th by name, was quick to praise all pioneer battalions and their role in the success of the attack: "Our Pioneer Battalion[s] did splendid work in digging trenches under heavy fire, in order to connect our advanced positions."[60]

The 107th continued its work in the front lines until May 1918. Due to casualties and the reorganization of Canadian engineering and construction battalions, it was broken up and redistributed among the engineering components of the 1st, 2nd, and 3rd Canadian Infantry Battalions.[61] This again would fracture the First Nations community that the 107th had fostered for its soldiers. Lickers was reassigned to the 3rd Canadian Engineering Battalion in June 1918.[62] Although he remained on active duty until the end of the war and was not listed as being wounded overseas, he would later note that he had been gassed while working in the trenches.[63] Whether this occurred at Hill 70 is undetermined.[64]

While as he was losing his new battalion family, Lickers was also dealing with lingering personal problems that began in 1916 and were exacerbated by the DIA. He experienced the war like any other veteran, but he had very little control over the way in which his life was managed back home. Although he could choose whether to fight and die for Canada, his post-war life was highly influenced by the surveillance and bureaucratization of the DIA, which had the final say in the lives of all First Nations people. Before heading overseas, Wilfred had left his daughter, Eva Jane, with his wife's family and had assigned some of his pay to a trust fund for her care.[65] While he was fighting and building trenches, the DIA, without consultation, changed the terms of his assigned pay. Now, some of his salary would be assigned to his ex-mother-in-law, who continually made demands for greater support.[66] Once he learned of this, following the passing of his father, George, in November 1916, Lickers petitioned the Department of Militia to change his assigned pay, allocating nothing to his ex-mother-in-law and assigning it to his widowed mother, who was now caring for the family farm and Lickers's invalid brother.[67] Although the Department of Militia supported his decision, it was overruled by the DIA and the Canadian Patriotic Fund Brantford Branch. Instead, they took more of his pay, assigning portions to Lickers's mother, and created a new allowance to support his ex-mother-in-law.[68] Lickers fought these decisions from May 1917 to December 1918 but could do nothing to change them. He was required to fund his mother, his ex-mother-in-law, and his daughter's trust fund through his pay.

Lickers returned to Canada at war's end in 1919. Upon arriving home, he sought to re-establish his life. He remarried and applied for entry into the Soldier Settlement Program. The program granted him a loan of $1,800 ($800 for implements and $1,000 for erecting buildings), making him one of the few First Nations veterans to be accepted by the program. He was given a lot on the Grand River territory beside his father's farm.[69] Although the program purchased twenty to thirty thousand settlement farms for former soldiers,[70] only 130 loans had been given to First Nations veterans by 1920. Of this number, one-third were granted to veterans from the Six Nations.[71]

For Lickers, the loan may have seemed a stroke of good fortune, but he and the other First Nations veterans who were awarded money were now subjected to another level of government surveillance as a result. Because they were wards of the Crown, the administration of all their programs was handed over to the DIA. This fact, combined with their legal status as dictated by the Indian Act, meant that they were not permitted to own their farms. Since most of the land granted to them lay within Indian reserves – a cost-saving measure implemented by Deputy-Superintendent of Indian Affairs Duncan Campbell Scott – they received only a certificate of possession, as no individual could own land on a reserve.[72] In rare cases, limited mostly to Ontario, First Nations veterans did receive off-reserve land and, if they managed to pay off their loans, were able to gain full ownership of their farms.[73]

The Soldier Settlement Program also raised issues about the sovereignty of the Confederacy Council of Chiefs. Before the implementation of this program, the Council had held the right to decide who occupied the land in Six Nations Territory. The Soldier Settlement Program was managed by the DIA, which meant that the department had the authority to assign Six Nations land to individuals without the consent of the Council. The Council was also concerned about defaulted loans: If a veteran failed to repay his loan, what would happen to the land? Would it return to the Six Nations, or would it become private property and be taken out of the Six Nations holdings?[74] In October

1919, the DIA explained to the Council that defaulted properties would not be given to non–Six Nations individuals; the wider issue of who had the authority to allot land within Six Nations Territory was never resolved.[75]

The main problem with the DIA handling the Soldier Settlement Program was that it lacked the administrative mechanisms to manage this and other veterans' programs. Many post-war programs for First Nations veterans were handled in a haphazard manner. Some, such as the Veterans Insurance Plan, received virtually no attention; the DIA head office in Ottawa sent just one circular on the subject to all Indian agencies.[76] Others, such as the Last Post Fund and Veterans Allowances and Pensions, suffered from bureaucratic in-fighting at the DIA. In addition, some detractors insisted that these two programs were redundant as the DIA already gave all First Nations people, including veterans, a pension – though it was half of what non–First Nations veterans received. For Euro-Canadian vets, the Last Post Fund covered all funeral expenses, including a headstone, but the DIA version extended only to a rough-cut casket without a headstone.[77]

The Soldier Settlement Program suffered similar inconsistences between what was offered to First Nations and non–First Nations veterans. The on-reserve contact for most First Nations communities was their local Indian agent. The Six Nations had a local superintendent, and two agricultural representatives assigned to administer the program. Robert H. Abraham was appointed overall program supervisor for the First Nations communities of Walpole Island, Sarnia, Muncey, Cape Croker, Rama, Georgina Island, Moraviantown, New Credit, and Six Nations of the Grand River. A Six Nations man, Hilton Hill, was charged with the supervision of agriculture at Grand River.[78] These men would advise on the issuing of loans and what the DIA needed to distribute to the soldier-settlers. In 1924, Elliott Moses, a Six Nations man who had trained at the Ontario Agricultural College, was added to the staff at the Brantford Indian Office to help administer the program.[79] In 1923, some eighty Six Nations men had been accepted into the program, with at least seventy-five of them remaining in good standing; no farms had required foreclosure or other intervention by the DIA.[80]

Early reports show that the Soldier Settlement Program was a success in the Grand River territory. Duncan Campbell Scott himself stated that the program was benefitting many First Nations communities across Canada.[81] The 1923 report claimed that First Nations settlers had paid 78 percent of what they owed on their loans for 1922.[82] The 1924 report claimed that, despite the bad farming season of 1923, First Nations settlers were meeting their loan obligations.[83] However, some observers detected problems. During his 1923 investigation into the affairs of the Six Nations, Commissioner Andrew Thompson, the former commander of the 114th Battalion, was apprised of some concerns. Robert

Abraham reported to him that some veterans were having trouble paying back their loans due to crop failures, and he noted that many supplies bought for the program had been purchased at a time when prices were inflated.[84] In light of the deflation that began in the 1920s, and would continue into the 1930s, many of the Six Nations veterans were calling on the Canadian government to re-evaluate their loans.[85]

By March 1927, the situation had worsened. E.J. Sexsmith, Abraham's replacement, complained to Duncan Campbell Scott that the settlers had received no seed and argued that they would have no fall harvest if it did not arrive soon.[86] The DIA managed to get seed to the settlers by the end of April.[87] From 1928 to 1934, there were no reports on how well First Nations soldier-settlers were doing, but the DIA often asked the Soldier Settlement Board for more money.[88] Many lists were issued by the DIA of Six Nations men who were not meeting their loan obligations.[89] Scott had noted this trend in 1924, when he pointed out to Superintendent C.E. Morgan, successor to Gordon J. Smith, that some soldier-settlers had not made a single payment on their loan in four years.[90]

The sudden downturn in the Soldier Settlement Program was due mainly to the program itself and to declining agricultural markets; it was not the fault of individual settlers. The situation would be exacerbated by the Great Depression of the 1930s. With the fall of markets in 1921, the soldiers, who had bought their farms and initial supplies at prices inflated due to the war, carried high debt loads and were also making less from their land. Under these conditions, they could never pay off their loans. In 1923, 30,604 soldiers remained on their farms.[91] By 1930, the number had dropped to 10,907.[92] With the failure of the markets and with so many settlers still on the land, Ottawa had no choice but to come up with new ways of keeping them in place.[93] In 1930, it wrote off $11.3 million in settler debts.[94] A year later, it abolished the Soldier Settlement Board.[95] By 1939, only 8,000 soldier-settlers remained on the land across Canada.[96]

From 1924 to 1930, understanding that the failures of Six Nations soldier-settlers simply reflected the larger national failure of the Soldier Settlement Program, E.J. Sexsmith and Superintendent C.E. Morgan clashed with Duncan Campbell Scott on the cases of individual settlers. Claiming that Scott was not aware of the circumstances of the soldier settlers in the Six Nations Territory,[97] Sexsmith and Morgan used every means at their disposal to stop the DIA from foreclosing on farms.

For First Nations soldier-settlers, the failure of the agricultural markets translated into a prolonged decline in income. Between 1929 and 1933, their total annual income plunged from $2,388,435 to $1,269,510. This 53 percent drop was not shared by their non-Indigenous counterparts, whose total annual income fell by 17 percent.[98] Furthermore, their rebound potential was not as strong as that of non-Indigenous soldier-settlers. By 1940, the total annual income for First Nations farmers had risen to $1,709,818, whereas non-Indigenous farmers surpassed their 1929 income levels.[99] This was, in large part, due to the failures of the federal government and the DIA. Although the DIA did establish loans for the Soldier Settlement Program, the federal government did not allow First Nations farmers to take out loans for new equipment after the initial loan was given.[100] Although the Soldier Settlement Board and the Department of Soldiers' Civil Re-establishment allowed for loans for this purpose,[101] these loans were not available to First Nations veterans due to the Indian Act, which prohibited Indigenous people from accessing credit, unless it came from and was supervised by the DIA.[102] Thus, First Nations veterans were forced to use outdated farming equipment and practices that demoralized them and led to the economic stagnation of their properties.

The soldier settlement file for Wilfred Lickers reads like a triumph-to-tragedy story. In 1920, he had cleared forty acres of his fifty-acre settlement and had petitioned for a further loan to expand.[103] By 1921, he had acquired more land, cleared fifty acres, moved a home onto the property, erected a small barn, and purchased two horses and two cows, as well as a cream separator. He was also contemplating buying out his sister's share of his father's farm.[104] Everything seemed to be going well until 1923, when his barn caught on fire. Since it was partially built on his sister's property, insurance would not cover its repair.[105] Due to crop failures, Lickers was unable to make his usual $200 loan repayment for the 1923–24 year and was reduced to a payment of only $40. This trend of making partial or no payments continued into the 1930s.[106]

Using the reports of many DIA employees, Duncan Campbell Scott blamed Lickers, not the economic slump, for the failing farm. In 1929, Scott instructed E.J. Sexsmith to "point out to him [Lickers] that he must do better, and, if in your judgment, there is no prospect of improvement, you should recommend the cancellation of his loan and give to some other member the opportunity which Lickers does not appreciate."[107] Scott even wrote to Lickers directly, stating,

> You are not making a success of farming because you do not keep up with your work and do not do your seeding on time. The Department must insist on you using more energy on your work and also in making payments on your loan, otherwise, such action will have to be taken as will protect the interests of the Department.[108]

In 1929, Scott advocated cancelling Lickers's loan, even though Sexsmith advised against it. In a letter to Sexsmith, Scott stated, "Evidently this settler is not trying to make a success of farming and ignores all the attempts of the DIA to induce him to live up to his agreement, and it would seem that the time has arrived to cancel his loan."[109] Although the loss of the farm seemed imminent, a family tragedy would save Lickers from foreclosure.

First Nations people commonly fell prey to bureaucratic infighting within the DIA. Such was the case for Wilfred Lickers, whose private life became the focus of a squabble between four Indian agents – Gordon Smith and later C.E. Morgan at Six Nations and William C. Van Loon and later Maurice Winger at nearby New Credit in Mississauga territory. These men controlled the lives of the people under their supervision through a variety of means, including the band membership lists for the two territories. However, maintaining the lists was not always easy. Families from the two communities frequently intermarried, causing bureaucratic nightmares for Indian agents who strove to keep a strict accounting of the individuals on their band's list.

Before going overseas, Lickers, a Six Nations man, had a daughter, Eva Jane, with his wife from New Credit. After his wife died in 1916, Lickers willingly gave Eva Jane to her grandmother in New Credit to care for while he was away. In 1924, Lickers put in a custody claim for Eva Jane after learning that the grandmother had died in 1921 and that his daughter had been living with an uncle at New Credit since then.[110] This caused an argument to erupt between the Indian agents at New Credit and Six Nations. Although Eva Jane's father was from Six Nations, her residence at New Credit put her on the New Credit band list, and William Van Loon sought to keep it that way. The issue even divided the child's New Credit family: her uncle George felt that she should go to Lickers, whereas her uncle, John, recommended she be placed at the Mohawk Institute residential school.[111] This may have spurred Lickers's 1924 bid for custody. Unfortunately, due to his status as ward of the Crown, this matter was out of his hands. Under the direction of Van Loon and her uncle John, eight-year-old Eva Jane was placed in the Mohawk Institute Residential School against the wishes of her father. The DIA file notes that Lickers continued to provide for her through the trust fund he had established during his overseas military service, now valued at $1,276.[112] Although the administrators of the Mohawk Institute used this trust fund to purchase items for Eva Jane, its records listed her as an orphan whose mother had died and whose father had been killed in action during the war.[113] Through her uncle George, however, we do know that Eva Jane understood that her father was alive, loved her, and wanted her home.

In January 1929, tragedy struck. On the twenty-fourth, Eva Jane was confined to bed with what was thought to be a cold. By the next day, she had lapsed into a diabetic coma, and she died soon afterward.[114] Only thirteen, she was laid to rest beside her mother in a cemetery at Grand River. Lickers paid the funeral expenses through his trust fund.[115]

Immediately after Eva Jane's death, concerns arose about her trust fund: To whom would it be allotted? Once again, as a ward of the Crown, Lickers had no say regarding the money he had set aside for his daughter. Following the lead of his predecessor Van Loon, Maurice Winger wanted the money to go to Eva Jane's family at New Credit, as her uncle John and his mother had cared for her.[116] Lickers himself wrote to Duncan Campbell Scott, pleading his case that the money was rightfully his, as it came from his military service.[117] After two years of departmental haggling,[118] the DIA assistant secretary, J.D. McLean, applied the bulk of the trust fund directly to repaying Lickers's soldier settlement loan and gave a hundred dollars to Eva Jane's uncle John. The DIA correspondence gives no hint as to how Lickers felt about the death of his daughter.[119] Nonetheless, with the application of $842 toward his loan, he became one of "the lucky and the strong" soldier-settlers, paying off his entire loan in 1934.[120]

As was the case for other returned First Nations veterans, no one asked why Lickers, who had risked his life in the war, was seemingly unable to make his own decisions regarding his post-war life. Due to their legal status as wards, Lickers and other First Nations veterans had to rely on the DIA and the paternalistic federal government, who monitored and documented their every move, to make their decisions for them. Ottawa reviewed its practices after the Second World War,[121] but the DIA and other government agencies continued to monitor Lickers until his death in 1960. He had witnessed some of the worst fighting of the Great War, had become a successful farmer, and had proven a model citizen of the Grand River Territory, who would rejoin the Haldimand Rifles and help raise two generations of his family on his farm.[122] Nevertheless, his status as a ward of the Crown ensured that, not only would he be constantly scrutinized by the state, but also that he was effectively treated as a child under Canadian law. Whatever their reasons for enlisting during the Great War, it is hard to imagine that First Nations soldiers envisioned this sort of treatment at the hands of a government that actively recruited them in 1915 and that continues to do so today.

Notes

1 Sarah Carter, *Lost Harvests: Prairie Indian Reserve Farmers and Government Policy* (Montreal and Kingston: McGill-Queen's University Press, 1990); Keith D. Smith, *Liberalism, Surveillance, and Resistance: Indigenous Communities in Western Canada, 1887–1927* (Edmonton: University of Athabasca Press, 2009); E. Brian Titley, *A Narrow Vision: Duncan Campbell Scott and the Administration of Indian Affairs in Canada* (Vancouver: UBC Press, 1986); E. Brian Titley, *The Indian Commissioners: Agents of the State and Indian Policy in Canada's Prairie West* (Edmonton: University of Alberta Press, 2009); Robin Brownlie, *A Fatherly Eye: Indian Agents, Government Power, and Aboriginal Resistance in Ontario, 1918–1939* (Toronto: University of Toronto Press, 2003); Evan J. Habkirk, "'The Six Nations'

Veteran," in Evan J. Habkirk, "Militarism, Sovereignty, and Nationalism: Six Nations and the First World War" (master's thesis, Trent University, 2010), 121–56; Eric Story, "'The Awakening Has Come': Canadian First Nations in the Great War Era, 1914–1932," *Canadian Military History* 24, 2 (2015): 11–35.

2 Tammy Martin, email message to author on behalf of the Six Nations Genealogy Society, 5 August 2014.

3 Library and Archives Canada (LAC), reel T-16671, Nominal Rolls of the Haldimand Rifles, 1867–1914, G Company, 15 June–26 June 1909 (Camp Niagara).

4 For more on ideals of manliness, see Chapter 6 in this volume, which focuses on Talbot Papineau. The shared pressure that Papineau and Lickers felt is all the more striking when one considers their dissimilar social standing. Papineau enjoyed every possible social advantage, whereas Lickers was surveilled and denied the rights that other Canadians enjoyed, especially soldiers and veterans of the Canadian Expeditionary Force.

5 L. James Dempsey, *Warriors of the King: Prairie Indians in World War I* (Regina: Canadian Plains Research Centre, 1999), vii, 10, 46; Janice Summerby, *Native Soldiers – Foreign Battlefields* (Ottawa: Veterans Affairs Canada, 2005), 8; L. James Dempsey, "The Indians and World War One," *Alberta History* 31, 3 (1983): 34.

6 See R. Scott Sheffield, "Indifference, Difference and Assimilation: Aboriginal People in Canadian Military Practice," in *Aboriginal Peoples and the Canadian Military: Historical Perspectives,* ed. P. Whitney Lackenbauer and Craig Leslie Mantle (Kingston: Canadian Defence Academy Press, 2007), 57–71; LAC, reel T-16670, Nominal Rolls of the Haldimand Rifles, 1867–1914, 1 Company, 15 September–26 September 1896 (Camp Niagara) and 1 Company, 4 June–18 June 1898 (Camp Niagara).

7 LAC, reel T-16671, Nominal Rolls of the Haldimand Rifles, 1867–1914.

8 Smith, *Liberalism, Surveillance, and Resistance,* 8–9. According to Smith, this isolation was a double-edged sword for the DIA, as it also acted as a safe haven for Indigenous people where they could congregate and keep their traditional culture alive.

9 Smith, *Liberalism, Surveillance, and Resistance,* 14, 16.

10 Ibid., 16.

11 Ibid.

12 Ibid., 16, 17.

13 LAC, RG 10, vol. 242, J. Thorburn to R. Pennefather 30 September 1858.

14 Ibid. The Six Nations Confederacy Council of Chiefs is the traditional governing body and was the federally recognized government on the Six Nations territory at Grand River. Post-war conflicts caused turmoil between the council and the DIA, resulting in a 1924 RCMP raid on the Grand River Territory and the outlawing of the council. In its place, the DIA installed an elected band council, as dictated by the Indian Act. The Confederacy Council of Chiefs still operates in the Grand River territory but is not recognized by the federal government.

15 LAC, RG 10, vol. 1935, file 3589, "Report of the Select Committee of the Affairs of the Six Nations Indians in Brant and Haldimand," 8 May 1874. Six Nations interviewees included farmers, chiefs, doctors, and clergy.

16 Ibid.

17 Reverend J. Bearfoot, cited in J.A. Macrae, "Report re Sanitary and Some Other Matters: Six Nations Reserve, 26 October 1899," in *Annual Report of the Department of Indian Affairs for the Year Ended 31st December 1899* (Ottawa: Department of Indian Affairs, 1900), 619.

18 Ibid. David Boyle was the secretary of the Ontario Historical Society, the provincial archaeologist, and curator of the Ontario Provincial Museum. His field research among the

Six Nations was published in many reports and papers, including the *Archaeological Report Being the Appendix to the Report of the Minister of Education Ontario* (Toronto: Warwick Brothers and Rutter, various years).

19 Macrae, "Report re Sanitary," 616.

20 E.M. Chadwick, *People of the Longhouse* (Toronto: Church of England, 1897), 53; Michael St. Amant, "Major Gordon James Smith: Second President of the Brant Historical Society," *Brant Historical Society News Letter* 3 (2016): 4.

21 It is difficult to determine when the British Indian Department began to hire official interpreters. In many cases, the individual treaties negotiated with the British and Canadian governments identified various individuals as interpreters. After Joseph Brant, both John Norton and John Brant took on this role. John Smoke Johnson and later his son, G.H.M. Johnson, were appointed government interpreters. The New England Company also had interpreters for its missionaries. G.H.M. Johnson was listed as its interpreter in 1838.

22 Horatio Hale, "Chief George H.M. Johnson, Onwanonsyshon," *Magazine of American History* (February 1885): 137.

23 For more on this, see Habkirk, "The Six Nations' Veteran."

24 This number comes from Paula Whitlow and Tammy Martin's tabulation for the Woodland Cultural Centre in Brantford, Ontario, in 2014.

25 LAC, RG 10, vol. 6778, file 452-195, W.C. Van Loon to the Assistant Deputy and Secretary of the Department of Indian Affairs, 8 March 1918.

26 "Ohsweken," *Brantford Expositor,* 24 November 1916.

27 LAC, RG 10, vol. 6778, file 452-195, W.C. Van Loon to the Assistant Deputy and Secretary of the Department of Indian Affairs, 8 March 1918 and 5 September 1918.

28 "Edinburgh Sees Real Red Indians" and "Indian Tribesmen Visit Glasgow," *Brantford Expositor,* 27 and 28 December 1916.

29 Story, "'The Awakening Has Come,'" 20, 21; Habkirk, "The Six Nations' Veteran," 126–31.

30 According to his service file, Lickers was transferred to the 107th in May 1917, a few months before the Battle of Hill 70, but his participation in the attack cannot be proven beyond a shadow of a doubt. Although the 107th war diaries do not name the individuals who took part in the assault, the list of 107th members who were killed and wounded during it includes many former members of the 114th Battalion. Wilfred's arrival in May 1917, his receipt of a good conduct badge in late June 1917 while with the 107th in the field, and the close proximity of his regimental number to others in the 107th make it likely that he did join the attack on Hill 70. See 107th Canadian Pioneer Battalion War Diaries, Library and Archives Canada, http://collectionscanada.gc.ca/pam_archives/index.php?fuseaction= genitem.displayEcopies&lang=eng&rec_nbr=2004952&rec_nbr_list=2004952, 4216812,4168164,4168166,4168165,1889591,4250742,4226820,4228958,2040843&title= War+diaries+-+107th+Pionneer+Battalion+%3D+Journal+de+guerre+-+107e+ Bataillon+de+pionniers.&ecopy=e001465455.

31 Douglas E. Delaney, "Introduction," in *Capturing Hill 70: Canada's Forgotten Battle of the First World War,* ed. Douglas E. Delaney and Serge Marc Durflinger (Vancouver: UBC Press, 2016), 10.

32 Ibid., 12; Nikolas Gardner, "Higher Command: First Army and the Canadian Corps," in Delaney and Durflinger, *Capturing Hill 70,* 30; John Ferris, "Seeing over the Hill: The Canadian Corps, Intelligence, and the Battle of Hill 70 July–August 1917," *Intelligence and National Security* 23, 3 (2007): 356.

33 Delaney, "Introduction," 13.

34 Ibid., 15. See also Tim Cook, "The Fire Plan: Gas, Guns, Machine Guns, and Mortars," in Delaney and Durflinger, *Capturing Hill 70,* 102–3, 108; Geoffrey Jackson, "Hill 70 and Lens, the Forgotten Battles: The Canadian Corps in the Summer of 1917" (master's thesis,

University of Calgary, 2006), 13, 20, 21, 47; Serge Durflinger, "Assault on Hill 70," *Legion Magazine*, 31 July 2017, https://legionmagazine.com/en/2017/07/assault-on-hill-70/; and Dan Jenkins, "Fight for Hill 70, 15 August 1917," *Esprit de Corps* 7, 9 (2000): 21. Due to inclement weather that delayed the attack, the RFC spotting was imperfect, leaving some artillery and enemy strong points active. Gardner, "Higher Command," 39; Cook, "The Fire Plan," 117. For more on the use of RFC battlefield photography and of technology for battlefield reporting, see Chapter 1 in this volume.

35 Gardner, "Higher Command," 36; Cook, "The Fire Plan," 106, 120; Jackson, "Hill 70 and Lens," 16.

36 Ferris, "Seeing over the Hill," 352, 360.

37 Cook, "The Fire Plan," 108–9.

38 Ibid., 119; Durflinger, "Assault on Hill 70"; Jackson, "Hill 70 and Lens," 25n78; Jenkins, "Fight for Hill 70," 22; Bob Gordon and Thomas Gordon, "The Battle of Hill 70, August 15–22, 1917: In the Seesaw Battles of Attrition on the Western Front, the Cost in Lives Was Steep – Often Just a few Hundred Meters of Captured Ground," *Esprit de Corps* 18, 6 (2011): 34.

39 Cook, "The Fire Plan," 119–20; Gardner, "Higher Command," 36; Jackson, "Hill 70 and Lens," 16.

40 Steven A. Bell, "The 107th 'Timber Wolf' Battalion at Hill 70," *Canadian Military History* 5, 1 (1996): 73.

41 Ibid., 75.

42 Ibid.

43 Ibid.

44 Delaney, "Introduction," 13; Gordon and Gordon, "The Battle of Hill 70," 34.

45 Jackson, "Hill 70 and Lens," 14.

46 Ibid.; Gordon and Gordon, "The Battle of Hill 70," 34.

47 Jenkins, "Fight for Hill 70," 22; Gordon and Gordon, "The Battle of Hill 70," 34.

48 Bell, "The 107th 'Timber Wolf' Battalion," 76; Andrew Iarocci, "Sinews of War: Transportation and Supply," in Delaney and Durflinger, *Capturing Hill 70*, 157; Robert Engen, "Force Preservation: Medical Services," in Delaney and Durflinger, *Capturing Hill 70*, 171, 172.

49 Bell, "The 107th 'Timber Wolf' Battalion," 76, 77. For an in-depth look at the 10th Battalion's experience at Hill 70 and the chalk quarry, see Daniel G. Dancocks, *Gallant Canadians: The Story of the Tenth Canadian Infantry Battalion, 1914–1919* (Calgary: Calgary Highlanders Regimental Funds Foundation, 1990), 128–35.

50 Bell, "The 107th 'Timber Wolf' Battalion," 76.

51 Ibid.

52 For personal accounts of the engagement, see Frederick George Scott, *The Great War as I Saw It* (Toronto: F.D. Goodchild, 1922), 198; and Kenneth Walter Foster, "Foster, Kenneth Walter Memoir," Canadian Letters and Images Project, https://www.canadianletters.ca/content/document-4021. See also Deward Barnes, *It Made You Think of Home: The Haunting Journal of Deward Barnes, Canadian Expeditionary Force: 1916–1919*, ed. Bruce Crane (Toronto: Dundurn Group, 2004), 106–18; and Arthur LaPointe, *Soldier of Quebec (1916–1919)*, trans. R.C. Fetherstonhaugh (Montreal: Editions Edouard Garand, 1931), 52–65.

53 See LAC, 107th Canadian Pioneer Battalion War Diaries.

54 Durflinger, "Assault on Hill 70"; Jackson, "Hill 70 and Lens," 72.

55 LAC, 107th Canadian Pioneer Battalion War Diaries. Of the twenty-one casualties, two were killed, nine were wounded, nine were gassed, and one was missing in action.

56 Mark Osborne Humphries, ed., *The Selected Papers of Sir Arthur Currie: Diaries, Letters, and Report to the Ministry, 1917–1933* (Waterloo: LCMSDS Press of Wilfrid Laurier

University, 2008), 48. For more on how Vimy came to overshadow other First World War battles, see Chapter 4 in this volume.

57   Humphries, *The Selected Papers of Sir Arthur Currie*, 48–49.
58   Douglas Haig, quoted in Durflinger, "Assault on Hill 70."
59   Bell, "The 107th 'Timber Wolf' Battalion," 77.
60   Scott, *The Great War as I Saw It*, 199.
61   Bell, "The 107th 'Timber Wolf' Battalion," 78; LAC, 107th Canadian Pioneer Battalion War Diaries.
62   LAC, Wilfred Lickers Casualty Form, http://central.bac-lac.gc.ca/.item/?op=pdf&app=CEF&id=B5636-S070.
63   LAC, RG 10, vol. 7516, file 25,023-96, Wilfred Lickers Application: Indian Soldier Settlement, no date.
64   Of the 249 casualties suffered by the 107th at Hill 70, ninety-three reported being gassed. Others, such as Six Nations and 107th veteran O.M. Martin, did not report being gassed at Hill 70 until after the war.
65   LAC, Van Loon to Assistant Deputy and Secretary of the Department of Indian Affairs, 8 March 1918.
66   LAC, RG 10, vol. 6778, file 452-195, Director of Separation Allowances and Assistant Paymaster for the Department of Militia and Defence to the Secretary of the Department of Indian Affairs, 23 May 1918; Captain F. Shaw, Paymaster, 3rd Canadian Engineering Battalion, to Paymaster General, 7 June 1918; W.C. Van Loon to the Secretary of the Department of Indian Affairs, 17 June 1920.
67   LAC, Shaw to Paymaster General, 7 June 1918.
68   LAC, RG 10, vol. 6778, file 452-195, F.W. Thompson, Canadian Patriotic Fund Brantford Branch, to Account and Paymaster, Department of Militia and Defence, 19 July 1918.
69   LAC, RG 10, vol. 7516, file 25,023-96, Gordon J. Smith to the Secretary of the Department of Indian Affairs, 26 May 1920.
70   E.J. Ashton, "Soldier Land Settlement in Canada," *Quarterly Journal of Economics* 39, 3 (May 1925): 496; Joseph Schull, *Veneration for Valour* (Ottawa: Veterans Affairs Canada, 1973), 23; Jonathan F. Vance, "Aftermath," *The Beaver* 80, 5 (October–November 2000): 25.
71   John Leonard Taylor, *Canadian Indian Policy during the Inter-War Years, 1918–1939* (Ottawa: Indian and Northern Affairs Canada, 1984), 38. By 1927, the number of soldier settlement loans given to First Nations veterans had expanded to 224 nationwide, with most being granted to veterans in Ontario. Fred Gaffen, *Forgotten Soldiers* (Penticton, BC: Theytus Books, 1985), 184.
72   Dempsey, "The Indians and World War One," 8; LAC, RG 10, vol. 7484, file 25001, Duncan Campbell Scott to Arthur Meighen, 15 August 1918.
73   Gaffen, *Forgotten Soldiers*, 36.
74   LAC, RG 10, vol. 7504, file 25,023-1, Excerpt from the Six Nations Council Minutes, 9 June 1919; LAC, RG 10, vol. 1743, file 63-32, Gordon J. Smith's Summary of Six Nations Council Minutes for 1, 2, 8, 15, and 22 October 1919.
75   LAC, Excerpt from the Six Nation Council Minutes, 8 October 1919; LAC, Gordon J. Smith's Summary of Six Nations Council Minutes for 1, 2, 8, 15, and 22 October 1919.
76   LAC, RG 10, vol. 6771, file 452-34, Circular from Duncan Campbell Scott to Indian Agencies, 20 November 1920.
77   LAC, RG 10, vol. 6771, file 452-37, Arthur H.D. Hair to A.F. MacKenzie, 19 January 1928 and A.F. MacKenzie to Arthur H.D. Hair, 21 January 1928.
78   LAC, RG 10, vol. 7484, file 25001, R.H. Abraham to Duncan Campbell Scott, no date.
79   LAC, RG 10, vol. 7484, file 25,001-1A, pt. 1, Duncan Campbell Scott to C.E. Morgan, 9 July 1924.

80 LAC, RG 10, vol. 3231, file 582,103, Andrew T. Thompson, Report on the Six Nations, 1923.
81. LAC, RG 10, vol. 7484, file 25,001, Duncan Campbell Scott to unknown, 26 November 1920.
82 LAC, RG 10, vol. 7484, file 25001-1A, pt. 1, Duncan Campbell Scott to John Bennett, 27 March 1923.
83 LAC, RG 10, vol. 7484, file 25001-1A, pt. 1, Duncan Campbell Scott to John Bennett, 3 April 1924. One contradiction in the Soldier Settlement Program is that the reserve land First Nations veterans were given was already owned by their band. Therefore, they were making payments on land that they already owned by virtue of their band membership.
84 LAC, Thompson, Report on the Six Nations, 1923.
85 Ibid. Thompson's report also refers to a salvage sale of the assets owned by a defaulting soldier-settler, where chattels issued by the program were sold at extremely low prices.
86 LAC, RG 10, vol. 7484, file 25001-1, pt. 3, E.J. Sexsmith to Duncan Campbell Scott, 28 March 1927.
87 LAC, RG 10, vol. 7484, file 25001-1, pt. 3, E.J. Sexsmith to Duncan Campbell Scott, 30 April 1927
88 RG 10, vol. 7484, file 25001-1, pt. 3, Duncan Campbell Scott to J.G. Rattray, 15 November 1927, 11 November 1928, 29 August 1929, and 19 December 1930 and A.S. Williams to T. Magladery, 19 May 1932 and 19 April 1934.
89 RG 10, vol. 7484, file 25001-1, Department of Indian Affairs, no date; LAC, RG 10, vol. 7484, file 25001-1, pt. 3, List of Six Nations Settlers Whom Notices Were Sent, no date and S.S. Loan Balances Six Nations, no date, Gordon Smith to Charles Stewart, 6 June 1922; LAC, RG 10, vol. 7504, file 25,032-1A, pt. 1, Hand Written List, 1924–1925 and C.E. Morgan to Secretary of the Department of Indian Affairs 10 March 1924; LAC, RG 10, vol. 7504, file 25,032-1B, Indebtedness on Instalments due on Soldier Settlement Loans Six Nations Reserve, 22 June 1926; RG 10, vol 2285, file 57169-1B, pt.3, Gordon J. Smith to Charles Stewart, 6 June 1922.
90 LAC, RG 10, vol. 7504, file 25,032-A, pt. 1, Duncan Campbell Scott to C.E. Morgan, 29 February 1924.
91 Desmond Morton and Glenn Wright, *Winning the Second Battle: Canadian Veterans and the Return to Civilian Life, 1915–1930* (Toronto: University of Toronto Press, 1987), 153.
92 Ibid., 204.
93 Schull, *Veneration for Valour*, 23–24.
94 Morton and Wright, *Winning the Second Battle*, 209.
95 Vance, "Aftermath," 25.
96 Morton and Wright, *Winning the Second Battle*, 223.
97 LAC, RG 10, vol. 7504, file 25,032-1A, pt. 1, C.E. Morgan to Duncan Campbell Scott and A.F. MacKenzie, 20 October 1924 and 4 February 1930.
98 Taylor, *Canadian Indian Policy*, 92.
99 Ibid.
100 Dempsey, *Warriors of the King*, 76.
101 Ashton, "Soldier Land Settlement in Canada," 494; Morton and Wright, *Winning the Second Battle*, 137.
102 Elliott Moses, "Seventy-Five Years of Progress of Six Nations of the Grand River," *Waterloo Historical Society* 56 (1968): 21. According to Moses, Six Nations farms that bordered on those owned by non-Indigenous people had the best record of success because their owners could borrow equipment from their neighbours. The farm machinery that did exist at Six Nations was used, rundown, and bought from non-Indigenous farmers. Ibid., 22.
103 LAC, RG 10, vol. 7516, file 25,023-96, Gordon J. Smith to the Secretary of the Department of Indian Affairs, 26 May 1920.

104 LAC, RG 10, vol. 7516, file 25,023-96, Gordon Smith to the Secretary of the Department
     of Indian Affairs, 12 January 1921 and 23 January 1921; Report of the Assistant Agriculture
     Supervisor to the Secretary of the Department of Indian Affairs, 16 May 1921.
105 LAC, RG 10, vol. 7516, file 25,023-96, Duncan Campbell Scott to R.H. Abraham, 23 May
     1923.
106 LAC, RG 10, vol. 7516, file 25,023-96, C.E. Morgan to Secretary of Department of Indian
     Affairs, 1 December 1924, and Duncan Campbell Scott to Wilfrid Lickers 1 October 1925,
     October 1927, 1 October 1928, 1 October 1929, and 7 October 1930.
107 LAC, RG 10, vol. 7516, file 25,023-96, Duncan Campbell Scott to E.J. Sexsmith, 25 February
     1929.
108 LAC, RG 10, vol. 7516, file 25,023-96, Duncan Campbell Scott to Wilfred Lickers, 14 January
     1927.
109 LAC, RG 10, vol. 7516, file 25,023-96, Duncan Campbell Scott to E.J. Sexsmith, 22 October
     1929. Although some may argue that these reports and inspections of Lickers's farm did
     not amount to government surveillance, their level of detail leaves little to the imagination.
     Every year, inspectors recorded how many acres had been planted and what crops were
     under cultivation, the number of buildings on the property, and the number of livestock,
     among other details. Their reports were sometimes supplemented with hand-drawn maps
     of the layout of house and farm. Although this style of reporting may also have been ap-
     plied to non-Indigenous soldier-settlers, when these reports are added to those of local
     superintendents, Indian agents, DIA staff, and outside investigators, the Soldier Settlement
     Program clearly became part of a comprehensive system of surveillance for First Nations
     people.
110 LAC, RG 10, vol. 6778, file 452-195, C.E. Morgan to the Secretary of the Department of
     Indian Affairs, 20 September 1924.
111 After learning that his brother planned to put Eva Jane into the Mohawk Institute, George
     coaxed her away from his brother's farm while she was milking and dropped her off with
     Lickers. A truant officer at Six Nations retrieved the child and later, on Van Loon's recom-
     mendation, she was placed her in the care of the Mohawk Institute. LAC, RG 10, vol. 6778,
     file 452-195, W.C. Van Loon to the Secretary of the Department of Indian Affairs, 23
     September and 15 October 1924. John and the truant officer were paid fees of four and
     two dollars respectively for delivering Eva Jane to the school. LAC, RG 10, vol. 6778, file
     452-195, Voucher 94, 15 October 1924 and Voucher 95, 13 September 1924.
112 LAC, RG 10, vol. 6778, file 452-195, C.E. Morgan to the Secretary of the Department of
     Indian Affairs, 20 September 1924.
113 LAC, RG 10, vol. 6778, file 452-195, A.M. Rogers to the Department of Indian Affairs, 16
     March 1927.
114 LAC, RG 10, vol. 6200, file 466-1, pt. 2, Quarterly Report of A.M. Rogers, 31 March 1929.
115 LAC, RG 10, vol. 6778, file 452-195, J.D. McLean to Maurice Winger, 9 February 1929.
116 LAC, RG 10, vol. 6778, file 452-195, Maurice Winger to the Secretary of the Department
     of Indian Affairs, 6 February 1929, 16 February 1929, 22 March 1929.
117 LAC, RG 10, vol. 6778, file 452-195, Wilfred Lickers to Duncan Campbell Scott, 27 March
     1931.
118 This haggling included a scheme advocated by Winger, in which the DIA would use the
     entirety of the trust fund to repay an education loan that Eva Jane's mother had been
     granted but had not repaid at the time of her death. This scheme was put to rest by J.D.
     McLean, DIA assistant deputy and secretary, who notified the department that since the
     money was the assigned pay of Lickers, it all had to go to him. McLean would backtrack
     on this ruling after Winger protested, claiming that Eva Jane's family deserved some of
     the money as her rightful heirs. Although the New Credit family had no legal claim, a

hundred dollars was issued to Eva Jane's uncle John. LAC, RG 10, vol. 6778, file 452-195, J.D. McLean to Maurice Winger, 6 March 1929; Maurice Winger to J.D. McLean, 22 March 1929; J.D. McLean to Maurice Winger, 27 May 1929.

119 In Chapter 10 of this volume, Cynthia Comacchio discusses the impact of "contemporary expectations as to how grief should properly be managed and expressed" during the Great War (page 226). Thus, the social norms of the day dictated that, at least publicly, men did not show emotion, especially grief. Nevertheless, the death of Eva Jane as a result of the inhuman policies of the DIA would undoubtedly have had a marked effect on Lickers.

120 Morton and Wright, *Winning the Second Battle*, 223; LAC, RG 10, vol. 7516, file 25,023-96, Deputy Superintendent General of the Department of Indian Affairs to Elliott Moses, 16 April 1936.

121 See Special Joint Committee of the Senate and the House of Commons Appointed to Examine and Consider the Indian Act, *Minutes of Proceedings and Evidence,* (Ottawa: King's Printer, 1946); and Special Joint Committee of the Senate and the House of Commons Appointed to Examine and Continue and Complete the Examination and Consideration of the Indian Act, *Minutes of Proceedings and Evidence,* (Ottawa: King's Printer, 1947).

122 LAC, RG 24, vol. 31022, file 869-L-122, Lickers, W.G. – Corporal, Haldimand Rifles, 30 October 1928.

6

Talbot Papineau:
The Life and Death of an Imperial Man

Geoffrey Hayes

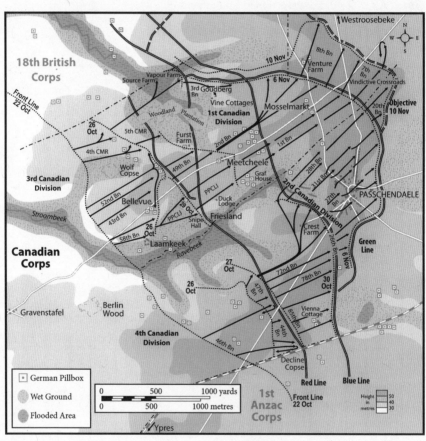

Figure 6.1 Passchendaele, 30 October 1917. | Map by Mike Bechthold.

MAJOR TALBOT MERCER PAPINEAU was killed on 30 October 1917, during the Canadian Corps attack on Passchendaele village in Flanders. He was thirty-four years old and one of the 849 soldiers in the Canadian Expeditionary Force (CEF) to die that day. By the grim measure of fatalities, Papineau died on Canada's sixth-worst day of the war. Another gauge of the day's fighting may come from the fact that 69 percent (580) of the Canadian dead were never found or identified, including Papineau. Their names are inscribed on the walls of the Menin Gate in Ypres, Belgium, a monument to British and imperial troops who, as the inscription notes, "stood here from 1914 to 1918 and to those of their dead who have no known grave." The stark columns list nearly fifty-five thousand names of British, British West Indian, British Indian, Australian, South African, and Canadian troops. Major Talbot Papineau, MC, is listed on panel ten just below the name of his unit, the Princess Patricia's Canadian Light Infantry.

Talbot Papineau is easily among the best known of the nearly seventy thousand soldiers who died fighting with the CEF. In her masterful 1992 study, *Tapestry of War*, Sandra Gwyn tapped into Papineau's rich wartime correspondence to portray an ambitious though tragic figure whose promising political future was snuffed out in the mud of Passchendaele. Gwyn helped to introduce many students of Canadian history to the very public exchange between Papineau and his cousin, the Quebec nationalist Henri Bourassa, in the summer of 1916. She concluded that their conversation about Canada's wartime role "defined with eloquence and urgency the terms of a debate about the character of Canada that continues today."[1] In the constitutional climate of the 1970s and 1980s, it was easy to draw parallels between Bourassa and Papineau during the Great War and René Lévesque and Pierre Trudeau a half-century later. Brian McKenna went one step further when he cast as Papineau Justin Trudeau in his 2007 docudrama *The Great War*.[2] Whether as a symbol of the French-English divide in Canada or of the tragedy of war, Papineau has seemed in recent decades a very useful historical figure.

Geoff Keelan's close reading of the Papineau-Bourassa correspondence through the lens of wartime "cultural mobilization" offers another, more nuanced understanding of Papineau's legacy. Keelan makes the important point that Papineau's urgent plea for all patriotic Canadians to support the war marked a form of coercion that Henri Bourassa and many others simply rejected. Indeed, Keelan acknowledges that, however Papineau's message may have earned him supporters in 1916, his "voice faded quickly after the war ended."[3]

Whether as an eloquent voice of a future bicultural, bilingual nation or as a tragic hero, Talbot Papineau can be understood in many ways. This chapter draws upon a selected reading of his "cultural products," both public and private. It argues that Papineau negotiated a complicated path driven by Canadian wartime politics and persistent notions of Victorian masculinity that lingered well into the twentieth century. Papineau was a tragic figure, increasingly out of touch with the shifting political currents back home. However tempting it may be to see him as a forerunner to Justin Trudeau, it might be more accurate to measure him against Raymond Asquith, a talented, ambitious member of a prominent British political family who returned to, and died in, the trenches during the fall of 1916. In Papineau's ideas, dilemmas, and choices, we find someone who was trying to measure his ambitions against the persistent Victorian ideal of the imperial man.

Papineau was exceptional in many ways. His wealth, social standing, and education stand in glaring contrast to that of, for example, a First Nations soldier such as Wilfred Lickers, the subject of the preceding chapter in this volume. Papineau also held what Keelan calls a "complicated" cultural identity.[4] He moved easily between the elites of three countries, Canada, the United States, and the United Kingdom. He listed his place of birth as Montebello, Quebec, on the seigneury of his great-grandfather, Louis-Joseph Papineau. The nationalist politician who had led an armed rebellion seemed to have little in common with a great-grandson who shared his surname. Sandra Gwyn describes Talbot as enjoying a very comfortable upbringing under the gaze of an adoring and ambitious mother, Caroline Rogers, an American who had raised her son as a Presbyterian at the centre of Philadelphia society. Unlike his great-grandfather and his much older cousin, Henri Bourassa, Talbot had strong imperial connections. He had attended Oxford on one of the first Rhodes scholarships awarded to a Canadian, studying law before returning to a private law practice in Montreal in 1908.[5] Nevertheless, those who tried to place Talbot Papineau during the years ahead would continue to draw parallels, however forced, between Louis-Joseph and Talbot.

1914

When war came in August 1914, Papineau was in Vancouver, speaking at the national convention of the Association of Canadian Clubs. He represented the Montreal chapter, which had first gathered in 1905 to draw upon the city's business and political elite to discuss issues of economic, social, and international importance. Its founding member was Papineau's law partner, Andrew McMaster.[6] One admirer later recalled that Papineau's address "made a profound impression on the convention," especially when he protested that Canada had had no say in the imperial decision to go to war.[7]

Nevertheless, Papineau wanted desperately to join the fight. That month, he gained an appointment as a lieutenant in the Princess Patricia's Canadian Light Infantry, a unit raised and financed by one of Montreal's wealthiest men, Andrew

Figure 6.2 Captain Talbot Papineau (left) and Brigadier
General Henry Burstall (right), July 1916. | LAC, Ministry
of the Overseas Forces of Canada fonds, a000434.

Hamilton Gault. Gault's imperial sympathies were reflected in the unit's name.
Princess Patricia was the daughter of the Duke of Connaught, who was then
Canada's governor general and the third son of Queen Victoria.

Gault no doubt saw in Papineau something of himself and the exclusive
English Montreal society to which they both belonged. Gault was a Boer War
veteran and a kind of imperial adventurer, who preferred that his appointees
have some military experience. He made an exception in Papineau's case. Both
had gone to McGill and Oxford. Papineau's lean figure remained well sculpted
from his time rowing and playing hockey. Fluently bilingual, ambitious, handsome, well educated, and well connected, he was obviously officer material.

But first, he would have to prove himself. An old friend later recalled, "It did
not take much experience of the war to make us realize that besides a knowledge
of barrack square drill many other qualifications were essential in a good officer.

These he [Papineau] possessed in an unusual degree."[8] When he enlisted, Papineau lacked a moustache, then a sign of masculine authority, but that was corrected by regimental edict. That he was single may have quietly raised other questions. An ambitious, handsome professional man driven by an imperial adventure and the chance for personal and political advancement, Lieutenant Papineau sailed for England with the Patricias in the fall of 1914.[9]

The country he left that autumn must have seemed remarkably united. The debate that had divided Prime Minister Wilfrid Laurier and his protégé Henri Bourassa over Canada's role in the South African war in 1899 was a distant memory. Laurier's proposal for a Canadian navy in 1910 further enraged Bourassa, who founded *Le Devoir* as a nationalist journal that year. The election of 1911 that brought Conservative Robert Borden to power was equally divisive. Yet in the fall of 1914, Bourassa (who had barely escaped from Europe through the summer of 1914) cautiously endorsed the war effort. The Opposition Liberal Party, led by the aging Laurier, had also promised early on to support Borden's wartime government. But this fragile consensus was short-lived. Old political divisions would re-emerge as Borden's government fell from favour. The festering debate over Regulation 17, which restricted French language school instruction in Ontario, would further alter the Canadian political landscape in ways that Papineau would never appreciate.[10]

Bourassa had long since changed his mind about the war when he replied to Papineau's open letter in the summer of 1916. The elder cousin dismissed the war as an imperialist folly, countering that "the excitement of warfare and the distance from home have obliterated in his [Papineau's] mind the fundamental realities of his native country." As we shall see, there was some truth in that.

Papineau's military career almost ended before it began. In December 1914, the tent he shared with another officer caught fire.[11] Both Papineau and Charles Stewart were badly burned, and they missed the Patricias' departure for Belgium to join the British 27th Division. Papineau joined the unit in January 1915 in the salient that surrounded the besieged town of Ypres in Flanders. The next month, he led a group of bomb throwers, who helped destroy a German trench near St. Eloi. One former comrade, W. Stewart Thomson, later recalled the time "when we introduced the trench raid to the 23rd Bavarians and blazed a trail along which the Canadians have since distinguished themselves time and again. [Hamilton] Gault earned his D.S.O. [Distinguished Service Order] that morning, while Papineau, Crabbe and Colquhoun got the Military Cross – my own share was a Hun bullet!"[12] Standing against repeated German attacks on Bellewaerde Ridge in May 1915 cost the battalion nearly half its strength.[13] But it held. Papineau emerged as one of the few "Originals" to survive the fighting, and one of the first Canadians to be awarded the Military Cross for the attack at St. Eloi;

he was then Mentioned in Dispatches for his actions in June. His reputation as a brave, popular, even heroic officer was coming into focus.

The Fox Correspondence

If John Tosh is correct that manliness was "one of the key concepts in the moral universe of the Victorians," then Talbot Papineau had emerged from the fighting that spring close to attaining that enduring manly ideal.[14] Maintaining that ideal posed a real challenge. The emotional effects of the fighting were apparent in June 1915, when Papineau began an intimate correspondence with Beatrice Fox, a woman whom he would never meet. This remarkable exchange of letters helped him negotiate what Michael Roper terms his secret battle for emotional survival. Roper's study examines how wartime letters, often written between soldiers and their mothers, reveal the breadth and depth of this struggle.[15] Papineau's letters to his mother, Caroline, reflected a close, often professional relationship in which Papineau looked to her as both an advisor and gossip, as well as a nurse, valet, and purveyor of goods.

Papineau imagined Beatrice Fox as an idealized wife who could empathize with his mood swings and frustrations. It was to Beatrice that he admitted to the boyish violence of male camaraderie, as he detailed wrestling with his bunkmates:

Last night I was rolling off my puttees when the Baron, who is a pugnacious devil, suddenly swung round and batted me on the foot with his cane. I naturally went for his throat. We each secured a stranglehold and for several moments dust and clothes and legs and arms rose and fell in confusion. Eventually we arranged terms of peace. Later, for some reason which I cannot recall I fired five rounds of ammunition with accuracy against Barclay's candle, which was extinguished; Barclay then retaliated on my bottle with equal success ... We behaved disgracefully, I admit.

It was difficult for Papineau to reconcile such rough-and-tumble childishness with the idealized vision of masculinity. As he wrote again to Beatrice, "I shrink from the naked disclosure of human passions – I dislike intensely loss of control, drunkenness, insanity, hatred, anger, they fill me with a cold horror and dread. But to see a man afraid would be worse than all."[16] Like so many of his generation and class, Papineau was deeply concerned with how his behaviour revealed his moral character.[17]

But he also struggled with the physical temptations proffered by London's dark streets and nightclubs, which teemed with unescorted women. Remarkably, he admitted to Beatrice near the end of his leave in October 1915 that he had sought the hollow shams of easy and immediate gratifications. Because life might suddenly end, I have not waited for the slow and doubtful realizations. I wanted affection – beauty – laughter – companionship – I wanted them immediately and so I bought them – the cheap, ready-made articles, and so I have cheapened myself until I was sick with disappointment and glad that tomorrow I go back to the front and so perhaps end it all.

As it turned out, Papineau was sick with more than disappointment. His medical records detail repeated hospital visits in November 1915 and January 1916 to treat a case of gonorrhea.[18]

Though he saw the battlefield as a place of manly redemption, Papineau decided to pursue a series of staff appointments that kept him out of the fighting from the start of January 1916 to May 1917. His secondment to the Canadian Corps Headquarters as the aide de camp to the corps commander Edwin Alderson was a plum appointment, probably arranged through his friendship with Sir Max Aitken, then the most powerful Canadian in London.[19] When Alderson was sacked in the spring of 1916, Papineau remained on the headquarters staff to work for Julian Byng. If he deftly negotiated the political intrigues of the Canadian senior command, his staff work also distanced him from political realities in Canada.

Papineau's staff positions gave him the opportunity to write his famous open letter to his cousin Henri Bourassa. Entitled "What of the Soul of Canada?" the letter is an intriguing document, as Papineau exhorts, then threatens his cousin to support the war. Geoff Keelan suggests that through this letter, "Papineau had an active role in the cultural mobilization of Canadians during the Great War." He maintains that Papineau "tied English-Canadian imperialism to French-Canadian nationalism, uniting them in a shared struggle against a German menace and the promise of a new and better Canadian nation. Followers of both, he believed, were ready to endure hardship so that an imagined Canada could survive."[20]

It is hard to judge the letter's impact on Canadian public opinion at such a crucial moment in the war. Andrew McMaster urged Papineau to tone down the letter, for it left unclear his Liberal Party allegiances. The Conservative *Globe* praised Papineau's stand, but the Liberal *Toronto Star* printed the full exchange, along with a remarkably balanced appraisal of Bourassa.[21] The correspondence gained no mention in Robert Borden's diaries of the time. That should not surprise. Borden was a Conservative, Papineau a Liberal. Between complaining about his endless correspondence (usually requests for patronage appointments) and detailing the results of his fishing trips and his gardening, Borden tried to keep abreast of current arguments about Canada's position in the empire.

In May, he concluded that Arthur Keith's *Imperial Unity and the Dominion* "shows much insight but deductions not always accurate."[22] In June, he dined with J.S. Ewart and discussed Lionel Curtis's ideas for imperial federation.[23] The last line in his diary entry for 10 June 1916 is striking: "I think a Republic better with some close and binding alliance with rest of Empire and with U.S."[24] Possibly his strained relationship with the governor general, the Duke of Connaught, was spilling over here.

Indeed, Borden was concerned about many things in 1916. The "very unwholesome" divorce proceedings of Hamilton Gault found their way to his cabinet in March. The growing criticisms about the Ross rifle and the never-ending rants by his irrepressible Militia and Defence minister, Sam Hughes, exasperated Borden, who knew that a drop in voluntary enlistments posed a real challenge to his government. When Hughes suggested instituting a registry of males who were eligible for military service, Borden "told him confidentially that registration means in end conscription and that might mean Civil war in Quebec."[25]

Papineau's pleas to help win the war by uniting English Canadian imperialism and French Canadian nationalism were increasingly out of step with the ever-changing Canadian political mood. But when a *Times* article of August 1916 reviewed his letter favourably, he must have been pleased. The piece represented Papineau as the "Soul of Canada" and praised his arguments, including his veiled threat that the returning veteran would "inflict" upon dishonest politicians, the unscrupulous businessman, and those who did not support the war effort "the punishment they deserve – not by physical violence, for we shall have had enough of that – nor by unconstitutional or illegal means, for we are fighting to protect, not to destroy, justice and freedom – but by the invincible power of our moral influence."[26] Such rhetoric may have gone over well in imperial circles. In Canada, not so much.

Fall 1916

The year 1916 was a difficult one for the Canadians on the Western Front, and for the Patricias especially. Already, the unit had seen one commanding officer, F.D. Farquhar, killed near Ypres in March 1915. Having joined the 3rd Canadian Division, the Patricias suffered terribly at Mont Sorrel in June 1916. There, another commanding officer, H.D. Buller, was killed, and Hamilton Gault lost a leg in the same action. Then the Canadians moved south to take their place in the battles being waged along the Somme River through the late summer into November. They suffered twenty-four thousand casualties, including some eight thousand dead.

While the Canadians fought desperately for Regina Trench through October 1916, Papineau toured the battlefields and worked in Max Aitken's London office, writing dispatches for British and Canadian audiences. In private, he was touchy about how he was perceived. He wrote to his mother in October, "I am angry enough as it is to have been [through all (?)] the Somme fighting & to have people think me comfortably in London on Sir Max's Staff."[27] Of course, Papineau *was* living a comfortable life and was scheming about his political career. His partner and political advisor Andrew McMaster wrote from Montreal that fall, suggesting that Papineau should return to Canada to help with recruiting and to position himself for the election that everyone knew was coming. McMaster assured him that Liberal fortunes were on the rise and that he and Laurier had offered Papineau a chance to run in the riding that included Montebello, the Papineau seigneury.[28] To that end, McMaster warned Papineau to distance himself from Aitken, whose Tory politics were tied to the increasingly unpopular figure of Sam Hughes. Indeed, Papineau was in a delicate position, seeking favour in a highly politicized staff organization while harbouring political ambitions as a Liberal. In October, he was offered another staff appointment at the corps headquarters. Perhaps this was a way out of the brambles, away from Aitken and partisan politics, and a return to real soldiering.

Still, Papineau wanted to make a political statement. In December 1916, he spoke at the Canadian Corps School in Pernes, France. The title of his talk was "The War and Its Influences upon Canada." He began on an optimistic note, anticipating that hostilities would be over by spring, or summer's end at the latest. His views on the future of Canada were equally optimistic. He anticipated that a "strong, self-reliant spirit of Canadian Nationality" would run "side by side" with a "powerful current of 'Imperial Patriotism' – or a realization of the advantages to be had from a form of union and solidarity with the other nations of the old British Empire, with whom, during the war, we have fought side by side in such complete harmony and to such victorious issue." His faith in imperial union had clear racial overtones: "If, as so many believe, lasting peace may only come to the world by reason of the strong alliance between certain nations of an equal civilization who will act together in the control and discipline of lower civilizations, then surely in the present union of the nations of the Empire we have the nucleus for that broader, international union."[29] That the "nations of an equal civilization" had started such a costly war obviously eluded him.

Papineau was not alone in believing that a reformed empire would propel Canada to a new level of authority in world affairs. He anticipated that America, "deeply influenced by Canadian public opinion," would enter into a continental defence alliance with its northern neighbour to police both North and South America and beyond. Free trade would widen trade networks with Europe and especially France. In the future, "I think all Canadians after the war will endorse any policy of commercial or diplomatic character which will place us side by side with France in the search for human welfare, and the assuring of the world's peace."[30]

Notions of masculinity also played an important part in Papineau's vision, as he stressed the transformative power of the returning soldier. A strong peacetime military force, boosted by compulsory military training, would provide "an insurance against aggression, [be] a means of improving the physique of a nation, and [act] as an admirable disciplinary measure." The moral force of the returning veterans would transform politics themselves. "Freed from the shackles of purely party politics," the vets would wield "an invincible power and, I believe, always a power of good."[31]

But dangers lurked, especially if the veterans sought too much on their return. Papineau thought it would be disastrous if they were "pampered and petted, to be given free land and easy living, to be pensioned and supported, and to have jobs found for them." He wondered if those who "have lived and fought like men" overseas would "become mollycoddles when we return to Canada."[32] Papineau feared that the state and civilian life could steal everything that the war had created by weakening, even emasculating, returning veterans.

He also warned his audience of another male type, the "false hero." This was

the old soldier who, having never been in France, or never in the firing line, returns with great stories of his prowess and adventures and so secures advantages over more deserving, but more modest men. Already there are many cases of this which I know of personally. Men who have been tragic failures here but whose record was not known elsewhere and who have returned to Canada or England and have been showered with the gifts of an honourable and sentimental enthusiasm. Nothing is more disgusting to the real soldier.[33]

Papineau suggested that a "bureau of information" be set up to help police the war records of individuals, which must have seemed a stretch. It is unclear whether he saw himself as a real soldier or a false hero.

Compulsory military training; Canadian membership in continental and imperial police forces; a stingy approach to veterans' benefits to avoid mollycoddling; and a surveillance service to uncover overly boastful officers. In Canada, where volunteer enlistment rates continued to drop, such ideas were hardly going to gain traction. Was such bold talk a way to assuage his own guilt for leaving the Patricias for the relative comfort of a staff position? Perhaps, but it was also a political non-starter.

A new staff appointment to the Canadian Corps Headquarters early in 1917 gave Talbot more opportunities to advance his career. Juicy gossip and important names spilled from his letters to his mother. In March 1917, he gloated when

Douglas Haig's headquarters asked about his language skills: "I am wondering what it may mean. Rather nice to have an appointment at G.H.Q. [General Headquarters] wouldn't it!"[34] The news that the Americans were entering the war in April was "splendid": due to their contribution, it might end by the summer, and he would also have a chance to lecture to American army officers on the challenge of raising an army.[35] In May, he described his highly successful tour of the battlefields of Verdun: "We saw the whole famous battle ground & slept the night in the citadel. Next day many visits & luncheon with the Army Commander."[36]

Papineau was having a very good war indeed, so his decision in May 1917 to give up his staff position and return to the Patricias must have shocked those closest to him. A letter to his mother, dated 22 May 1917, uncovers a lingering motive: "Why, oh why am I so ambitious, my dear mother? Could we not be happy with less honour or glory and more security and comfort." Caroline was equally ambitious for her son, but his contemplated return to the Patricias probably horrified her. He received conflicting advice. Julian Byng, who was soon to leave the Canadian Corps after its costly success at Vimy Ridge, urged him to return to regimental duty; Arthur Currie, who succeeded Byng as corps commander, thought it better that Papineau take another staff job. With such connections, Papineau could easily have finished the war in England. But, he noted emphatically, "the opinions I value most are in favour of regimental duty."[37]

Certainly, he had ambitions to return to the Patricias as the unit's second-in-command.[38] But he explained and understood his decision to return as a highly gendered act. His vision of the manly veteran, hardened by a brotherhood of physical effort and shared danger, may seem naive in retrospect. But he meant it. As he wrote to his mother,

> I shrink from the fresh discomforts, the physical fatigues and the narrowness of the existence but I realize that if I have the necessary courage & character to see it through I shall have proved myself much more of a man than I can ever do as a scribe. Better to share in the making of history than in the writing of it.[39]

A powerful sense of noblesse oblige was also evident here. Above all, his job as an officer was to look out for his men's comforts, their worries, and their entertainments, so that he could lead them into battle, and if necessary, die with them.[40] Papineau understood these obligations, as he confided to his mother: "Yet we have to win this war and those who win it are the men in the field. They [the soldiers] must be encouraged. Their dangers and hardships must be shared and lightened."[41]

A certain degree of fatalism may have been at work here too. As Kyle Falcon rightly points out in Chapter 3 of this volume, fatalism often acted as "a coping mechanism – one way of avoiding depressing reflection about one's mortality" (page 69). Given that returning to the Patricias would expose him to increased danger, it is hardly surprising that Papineau might assume a fatalistic air. Another imperial man, Raymond Asquith, was not quite five years older than Papineau, but the two had followed similar paths, first in their legal studies at Oxford and then in their political ambitions. Despite Raymond's age (thirty-seven) and pedigree, being the brilliant eldest son of the British prime minister Herbert Asquith, he gave up a promising political career to lead the men of the Grenadier Guards into the second Somme offensive. He died on the first day, 15 September 1916.[42]

The *Times* reported Asquith's death just weeks after proclaiming Papineau the "Soul of Canada." One of the many tributes to Asquith came from a Labour MP who pronounced him "a man of fine character." The member, Mr. Thomas, noted that Asquith had written "in lead pencil" from the trenches to explain why he was not in a staff position – because "he sought no privilege not accorded to an ordinary soldier." The MP observed that his own constituency of railway men would mourn "the death of a husband and father as the nation did the loss of a hero."[43] Was Raymond Asquith's heroic, selfless choice a guide then to Papineau's decision to rejoin the Patricias?

The return to regimental duty must have been difficult. Few familiar faces were left. Nonetheless, his letters to his mother continued to be chatty and deflecting, seeking to allay her fears. In July 1917, he wrote to his "Dearest mother" about mucking through the trenches in "rotten miserable weather." However, "I am certainly not as much in the trenches now as I used to be on the Staff," he stated, perhaps truthfully. Caroline remained concerned for his social standing, pushed him about why he had left the staff, and asked after his promotion prospects. He replied that he had been promoted to the rank of major, noting vainly that it would allow him to "put up my crown" (the symbol of a major) on a new tunic.[44] The status of a battlefield promotion, not one gained through staff work, was important.

Still, his correspondence could be remarkably forthright about the risks he faced. In a 5 July letter to his mother, he detailed how his friend Percy Molson, a prominent athlete and member of the famous Montreal family, had died when "a big trench mortar bomb ... exploded" between him and another officer. Hamilton Gault, the wealthy founder of the Patricias, remained a reassuring presence, even with the loss of his left leg. On 10 July, Talbot observed that Gault had broken his "best leg" in a polo match. As the letter closed with a mention of having a friend over to tea, he wrote ominously, "Bad news from the north. Hope it is not so bad as Germans claim." The Third Battle of Ypres had just begun.[45]

As Jessica Meyer and others note, a soldier's correspondence helped maintain bonds to a domesticated life at home, or in Talbot's case, to his mother's impressive address in central London.[46] Like all soldiers, he kept a careful record of his meals in his letters. Referring to food was one way of assuring Caroline that he was living in some style and comfort. He reported of one luncheon in July 1917 that included sardines on toast, fried meat, potatoes, spinach, custard, and tea: "What more could I want[?]" Apple slices shared by a fellow officer prompted an almost childlike excitement: "we fell upon them with glee."[47] Later in the month, he thanked his mother for the cake she had sent him but reminded her that "parcels should be unusual treats or delicacies rather than real food." Talbot's letters nearly always included a request for high-quality items, as if to reassure Caroline that he was still a man of some refinement. Cigarettes were crucial; he asked his mother to set up a standing order at his London tobacconist. Henry Maxwell's, a high-end London bootmaker, supplied his shoes and laces; the collars he ordered had to be refitted. And, as an officer, he naturally needed a good fountain pen "in special bottle with filler for a cork & a case. I also want some Gillette razor blades."[48] Always, there were reminders of his position and of the masculine expectations he had of himself.

Twice in July 1917, he closed his letters by referring to an impending election in Canada: "Perhaps I shall be asked to run." Talbot Papineau was not asked to run in the Canadian general election Robert Borden called that fall. After failing to convince Wilfrid Laurier to join a coalition government, the beleaguered prime minister created a Union government with Liberals who supported conscription for overseas service. However attractive Papineau may have thought himself as a political candidate, he faced substantial liabilities. Would he have defected to the Unionists or supported Laurier? And where would he have won a nomination? Despite his name, he was still a pro-war (and probably pro-conscriptionist) Protestant in an overwhelmingly Catholic province. He was also a soldier on active service who, despite his influence within the CEF, had little immediate connection to political organizers back in Canada. His political bona fides were also suspect, for, as his partner Andrew McMaster had warned him, associating with Tory Max Aitken would not help him to acquire a Liberal Party nomination.

Two examples suggest that Papineau had little chance of winning any riding in Quebec. In the predominately anglo riding of Brome in the Eastern Townships, Andrew McMaster was elected as an anti-conscriptionist Laurier Liberal. He defeated the Unionist candidate, Brigadier General Dennis Draper.

Despite his impressive military credentials (he had led an infantry battalion onto Vimy Ridge the previous April), Draper could not even win an anglo riding in Quebec. The electoral success of another Louis Joseph Papineau is instruct- ive as well. First elected in the riding of Beauharnois as a Liberal in 1908, he jumped to the Conservatives and held the seat in 1911. Five years later, he retained it as a Laurier Liberal and then held it for a fourth time (as a Mackenzie King Liberal) in 1921.[49] To survive Quebec politics through the First World War era, a Papineau had to navigate treacherous waters.

Idealized in Battle and in Death

If Talbot was not able to position himself as soldier-politician, he seemed hon- estly to relish the roles of idealized, paternal officer and devoted son. This was not at all unusual, for a soldier's martial and domestic identities "were in no way mutually exclusive."[50] His reassuring letters thanked his mother for her endless supplies, the socks and pencils, the cake, sardines, chocolate, and tinned fruit. Despite the cold and wet, he insisted that he was always comfortable, staying warm with the help of a small dog that he took into the trenches with him. Always, there was the need to stay clean: "I am wild to get my clothes off." He admitted that lice were a problem, but he managed to shave every day. The possibility of a bath brought special mention.[51] A man of his stature could not let the mud of the battlefield cling for too long.

Papineau had one more leave back to the United Kingdom in October. There, he enjoyed the company of his mother at her London home. Then it was back to the lines, this time in western Belgium. It seems remarkable that, despite the heavy losses on the battlefield and the political situation in Canada, corps commander Arthur Currie would commit his Canadians to the capture of Passchendaele village. But he did. As the Canadians approached the sodden trenches near the ruins of Ypres, Talbot wrote a final note to his mother. It was dated 27 October 1917:

> By the time you receive it I shall be all right or you will have news to the contrary
> – so you need have no anxiety. I am in a tearing hurry to finish my remaining
> preparations & to get to sleep. I am enjoying the whole thing enormously so far
> & I have as yet not the least nervousness. I have issued most minute & careful
> orders & I hope foreseen every eventuality. My men & officers are splendid. I have
> every confidence in them. We are all in fine spirits. Never did I less regret my
> decision than at this moment. Always know that if I do get killed I was completely
> happy and content to the last minute and that my only regret is due to the sorrow
> it will cause you and the boys [Talbot's three brothers]. It is all worth while and
> as time goes by you will realize this feeling too. Remember dearest that if I can

my spirit will be with you to comfort you and that my only unhappiness will be yours. I say this just in case in order that you may know what my last thoughts were. I have a sensible feeling however that my chances are good & that I can still write you gallant tales![52]

In this letter, he seems to have attained a masculine ideal as both a devoted son and an able, supportive officer, a caring father to his troops.

The Canadian Corps joined the Third Battle of Ypres in October 1917. It had been launched by the British with some success the previous summer, in hopes that they could even reach the Belgian coast and disrupt German submarines. But wet weather and near-constant artillery fire through the fall had churned the battlefield into a quagmire. After a series of costly attacks by the British, Australians, and New Zealanders in October, the Canadians were pressed into battle. Their objective was the ruins of Passchendaele, which marked the heights east of Ypres, only about two kilometres distant. The Canadians launched the first of three advances on 26 October. It continued for two more days, costing nearly 2,500 casualties, including 585 killed. The second push, on 30 October, was even more deadly, with over 800 killed (including Papineau) and more than 1,400 wounded. During the third push, of 6 November, the Canadians reached the rubble of Passchendaele. When they were relieved in mid-November, they had suffered 15,654 battle casualties.[53]

It did not take long for comrades, friends, and politicians to interpret Talbot Papineau's legacy. One comrade recorded what were allegedly his final words: "You know, Hughie, this is suicide."[54] Such sentiments fit nicely into a persistent post-war view that the battles for Passchendaele represented the very futility of war. The lines from Siegfried Sassoon's "Memorial Tablet," first published in 1919, still embody these ideas a century later: "I died in hell, they called it Passchendaele."[55] By this measure, Papineau emerges as a brave, fatalistic, even cynical soldier.

It would take time for such associations to gain purchase in Canada. Those who mourned Papineau back home saw his life and death within the context of French-English relations. Toronto's *Globe* concluded that his death "removes a young French-Canadian leader who, because of his aptitude for public affairs as well as his ancestry, commanded the respect and support of many of the younger generation throughout the Province of Quebec." Imagining Papineau as a patient father figure to Quebecers, the editors wrote,

May his death in freedom's cause stir like a bugle call the people of his beloved Province, whose failure to rise to a great opportunity saddened and perplexed him, but never destroyed his faith in and affection for the French-Canadian race.

English-speaking Canadians will not soon forget that from the same historical stem sprang Henri Bourassa, the anti-British demagogue, and Talbot Papineau, soldier and patriot, who died that liberty might not perish from the earth.[56]

In the heat of a divisive election campaign, the Conservative English press saw in Papineau's death some form of redemption for French Canada.

Other comrades and acquaintances published letters of condolence that elevated Papineau to a heroic masculine ideal. Back in 1914, W. Stewart Thomson had gone overseas with the original Patricias. In a letter to the *Globe*, he employed a familiar trope that stressed how Papineau's ability, courage, and patriotism had earned him the love of his regimental community.[57] Thomson remembered

> our late comrade [as] one of the best loved men in the regiment; his name had a distinctive Canadian flavor, and that, perhaps carried no great weight with the original Pats, but his lovable personality soon made itself felt, and it was with genuine regret that we had to leave him behind on the 20 December 1914, when we sailed for France.

In Thomson's view, the very things that had brought Papineau self-doubt, especially his decision to leave the regiment in 1915, had helped him attain a masculine ideal. Papineau's range of attributes made him "a rare spirit – a scholar, a gentleman, a soldier, and worthy company for real men (in the Patricias) like Farquhar, Buller and Gault." To raise Papineau to the exalted company of such "real men" was possible only because he had died in battle. In death, he had passed the ultimate test of manhood. Thomson finished by stealing a line from the Roman poet Catullus, a Victorian favourite:

> May the earth lie light on his breast. Those of us who knew him best will miss him most. To know him was to realize that he had a brilliant future ahead of him, and Canada has suffered grievous loss. To read of men like this laying down valuable lives as sacrifices on the altar of their country's freedom, and then turn over to column upon column of drivel about the referendum – well, it simply passes human understanding.[58]

Thomson saw Papineau's heroic masculine ideal in stark opposition to the sordid election campaign (for most Canadians, a referendum on conscription) then under way.

James Cobourg Hodgins was a Unitarian minister, Tory pamphleteer, and self-published poet.[59] He was moved enough by Papineau's death to pen "Carmina."

Inspired by the popular fascination with the classical and medieval worlds, Hodgins imagined Papineau as a courageous knight who, without hesitation, entered the fray to defend a weakened empire. Papineau's real strength came from how he was among the first to answer the call to arms: "Among the very first – Immortal band! / clear, with invincible gaze, you gasped the truth, / Saw, in a flash, the threat against all peace, all honor and all joy, and drew your sword."[60] Papineau represented a gallant imperial hero who was among the first to defend Britain from peril.

In January 1920, friends and admirers gathered at Montreal's Canadian Club to remember Talbot Papineau. In a nice gesture, a club member read the talk that Papineau gave at Pernes in December 1916. Its views on compulsory military service, imperial reform, and continental defence must have seemed rather dusty four years on, and two years into the peace. But the club membership wanted to remember Papineau the man. Club president Major George McDonald (who may have been a brother officer) fondly recalled a childhood scrap that marked Papineau's rise as a man: "It was an affair of honour. He acted with courage and with chivalry and earned the admiration and respect of all his schoolfellows." So it was when he joined the Patricias. When some questioned his lack of military experience, his manly, paternal qualities shone through. According to McDonald, "His personal courage, his untiring energy and his resourcefulness soon proved his sterling worth. He served with his battalion in the trenches during the first hard winter and he was in the forefront of all the engagements in which it was concerned during that period."[61]

The idealized masculine forms of remembrance were by then familiar. Papineau had

> won the love and respect of his men and of his brother officers. He always looked after the comfort of his men before thinking of his own and he never ordered his men to do anything or go anywhere that he did not personally lead them. He was a pioneer in the aggressive form of trench warfare for which the Canadians afterwards became famous.

His secondment to the Canadian Corps, McDonald insisted, was "on account of his experience and intimate knowledge of trench tactics ... In this capacity he proved of particular value to the new troops then arriving in France. It was at this time that he wrote the letter to Henri Bourassa, which was so widely circulated, and which received the distinction of a long editorial in the *Times*."[62]

Like remembering the war itself, memorializing Talbot Papineau meant invoking a form of selective amnesia. His long stint as a staff officer could not be explained fully by his tactical prowess. It was also best to avoid the reaction that his remarks may have provoked in Canada. After all, he had died just before the hotly debated election won by Borden's Unionist coalition. Everyone who was present at the Montreal Canadian Club meeting could recall the bloody riots over conscription that racked Quebec City in April 1918 and the military occupation that followed.[63]

As so many had before, the chairman closed the meeting by comparing Talbot Papineau to his famous great-grandfather, who had "earned the title of Patriot. I don't know anyone who is more worthy of that title than his great-grandson Talbot Papineau. He has given his life – he has given more to his country."[64] For whatever purpose his memory served, it was Talbot Papineau the man whom people sought to remember.

Talbot Mercer Papineau's life and death can be understood in many different ways. To some, he was an aspiring politician, a patriot, even the "Soul of Canada" whose enormous potential was tragically cut short by war. To his fellow officers, he embodied a decorated hero, courageous, beloved by everyone in uniform. In his chivalry, his devotion to honour and duty, some elevated him to a kind of imaginary knighthood. He was a "real man."

Papineau's public and private writings reveal how he navigated the kind of man he aspired to be. His path was a difficult one, dictated by the fluid realities of Canadian politics and the pervasive rules for masculinity. In embracing an imperial world view that found little support at home, he thwarted his political ambitions. Although he was a decorated war hero, the social and sexual forays detailed in his personal correspondence reveal a man uncertain of who he was.

Manly ideals were important to Papineau, and they may also have guided him in making his most pressing choice. He could easily have sat out the war as a staff officer and writer, but would that have made him vulnerable to accusations that he was a "false hero" or, even worse, a "mollycoddle"? In the end, he decided on neither politics nor a comfortable position behind the lines. Like Raymond Asquith, Talbot Papineau returned to the front to die with his unit. As his final letter to his mother reveals, that decision reconciled his role as a careful, caring officer with that of a devoted son.

Notes

1 Sandra Gwyn, *Tapestry of War: A Private View of Canadians in the Great War* (Toronto: HarperCollins, 1992), 325, 401.
2 Lee-Anne Goodman, "Justin Trudeau Makes Acting Debut in CBC Docudrama," *Toronto Star*, 4 April 2007, https://www.thestar.com/entertainment/2007/04/04/justin_trudeau_makes_acting_debut_in_cbc_docudrama.html.
3 Geoff Keelan, "Canada's Cultural Mobilization during the First World War and a Case for Canadian War Culture," *Canadian Historical Review* 97, 3 (2016): 398–99, doi:10.3138/chr.97.3.

4   Ibid., 379. I am indebted to Geoff Keelan for his insights and for the generous use of his transcripts of the Papineau correspondence in Library and Archives Canada. I cite these transcripts below.

5   Sandra Gwyn, "Papineau, Talbot Mercer," *Dictionary of Canadian Biography,* http://www. biographi.ca/en/bio/papineau_talbot_mercer_14E.html.

6   Canadian Club of Montreal, "History," http://www.cerclecanadien-montreal.ca/en/about/ history/, accessed 15 August 2018.

7   George McDonald, "Preface," in Talbot Papineau, *The War and Its Influences upon Canada: Address Delivered by the Late Major Talbot Papineau, M.C., to the Canadian Corps School at Pernes in February, 1917: Read to the Members of the Canadian Club of Montreal, on Monday, January 26th, 1920, by Mr. E. Languedoc, K.C.,* 1920, 1, http://archive.org/details/ McGillLibrary-128705-4858.

8   Ibid.

9   See Sandra Gwyn's brilliant description of Talbot's early life in *Tapestry of War,* 90–106.

10 Keelan, "Canada's Cultural Mobilization," 385.

11 Ralph Hodder-Williams, *Princess Patricia's Canadian Light Infantry, 1914–1919* (Toronto: Hodder and Stoughton, 1923), 2:16.

12 W. Stewart Thomson, "The Late Major Papineau," *The Globe,* 7 November 1917, 6. D.S.O. refers to the Distinguished Service Order.

13 David Jay Bercuson, *The Patricias: The Proud History of a Fighting Regiment* (Toronto: Stoddart, 2001), 5.

14 John Tosh, "What Should Historians Do with Masculinity? Reflections on Nineteenth-Century Britain," *History Workshop* 38 (1 January 1994): 180.

15 See Michael Roper, *The Secret Battle: Emotional Survival in the Great War* (Manchester: Manchester University Press, 2009).

16 Quoted in Gwyn, *Tapestry of War,* 213–14, 215.

17 Tosh, "What Should Historians Do?" 182.

18 See Gwyn, *Tapestry of War,* 224. See also LAC, RG 150, accession 1992-93/166, box 7559-19, Talbot Papineau Personnel File, http://central.bac-lac.gc.ca/.item/?op=pdf&app=CEF&id =B7559-S019.

19 See "Chapter 18: The Soul of Canada," in Gwyn, *Tapestry of War.*

20 Keelan, "Canada's Cultural Mobilization," 392–93.

21 On McMaster's urgings, see Gwyn, *Tapestry of War,* 320; see also Papineau's letter and Bourassa's reply in Arthur Hawkes, *Canadian Nationalism and the War* (Montreal: Toronto Star, 1916), 27, https://hdl.handle.net/2027/umn.31951002022145d.

22 Robert Laird Borden, *The Diaries of Sir Robert Borden, 1912–1918* (Ottawa: Library and Archives Canada, unpublished), transcribed by Dr. Kathryn Rose, entry for 25 May 1916, https://research.library.mun.ca/2428/5/1916.pdf.

23 On this point, see Daniel Gorman, "Lionel Curtis, Imperial Citizenship, and the Quest for Unity," *Historian* 66, 1 (2004): 67–96. My thanks to Professor Gorman for pointing out his work.

24 Borden, *The Diaries,* entry for 10 June 1916.

25 Ibid., 10 March 1916, 12 June 1916, 15 June 1916.

26 "The Soul of Canada," *Times* (London), 22 August 1916, Times Digital Archive.

27 LAC, MG 30-E52, Letters from Talbot Papineau to Caroline Rogers Papineau, 26 October 1916 (transcript by Geoff Keelan).

28 The riding of Labelle (later Argenteuil) was the same riding that cousin Henri Bourassa had represented as a Liberal and would later represent as an independent, both before the war and in the 1920s. See Keelan, "Canada's Cultural Mobilization," 380.

29 Papineau, *The War and Its Influences*, 3, 4, 5.

30 Ibid., 7.

31 Ibid., 10.

32 Ibid.

33 Ibid., 11.

34 LAC, Talbot to Caroline, 6 March 1917 (transcript by Geoff Keelan).

35 LAC, Talbot to Caroline, 4 April 1917 (transcript by Geoff Keelan).

36 LAC, Talbot to Caroline, 11 May 1917 (transcript by Geoff Keelan).

37 LAC, Talbot to Caroline, 22 May 1917 (transcript by Geoff Keelan).

38 In a 10 May 1917 letter to the commanding officer of the Patricias, Agar Adamson, Papineau claimed that it was his turn to be second in command of the regiment: "I am now due as second in command." Quoted in Tod Strickland, "Creating Combat Leaders in the Canadian Corps: The Experiences of Lieutenant-Colonel Agar Adamson," in *Great War Commands: Historical Perspectives on Canadian Army Leadership, 1914–1918*, ed. Andrew Godefroy (Kingston: Canadian Defence Academy Press, 2010), 233n56.

39 LAC, Talbot to Caroline, 22 May 1917.

40 On the pervasive notion of noblesse oblige in the British army officer corps, see G.D. Sheffield, *Leadership in the Trenches: Officer-Man Relations, Morale, and Discipline in the British Army in the Era of the First World War* (London: Macmillan, 2000).

41 LAC, Talbot to Caroline, 22 May 1917.

42 See John Buchan's eulogy to his friend Raymond Asquith in *Memory Hold-the-Door* (London: Hodder and Stoughton, 1940), 56–69, http://archive.org/details/in.ernet.dli.2015.97446.

43 "Labour Member's Tribute to Mr. Raymond Asquith," *Times* (London), 25 September 1916, 9, Times Digital Archive.

44 LAC, Talbot to Caroline, 1 and 5 July 1917 (transcript by Geoff Keelan).

45 LAC, Talbot to Caroline, 5 and 10 July 1917 (transcript by Geoff Keelan).

46 Jessica Meyer, *Men of War: Masculinity and the First World War in Britain* (Basingstoke, UK: Palgrave Macmillan, 2009), 33–34, 65–66.

47 LAC, Talbot to Caroline, 8 and 3 July 1917 (transcript by Geoff Keelan).

48 LAC, Talbot to Caroline, 27 July 1917 (transcript by Geoff Keelan).

49 Parliament of Canada, "Papineau, Louis-Joseph, K.C., B.C.L.," https://lop.parl.ca/sites/ParlInfo/default/en_CA/People/Profile?personId=1673, accessed 29 August 2017. Louis Joseph Papineau was probably a distant cousin of Talbot Papineau.

50 Meyer, *Men of War*, 44.

51 LAC, Talbot to Caroline, 1, 2 October 1917 (transcript by Geoff Keelan).

52 LAC, Talbot to Caroline, 27 October 1917 (transcript by Geoff Keelan).

53 G.W.L. Nicholson, *Canadian Expeditionary Force, 1914–1919: Official History of the Canadian Army in the First World War* (Ottawa: Department of National Defence, 1962), 320, 323, 327.

54 Gwyn, "Papineau, Talbot Mercer."

55 Siegfried Sassoon, "Memorial Tablet," First World War Poetry Digital Archive, http://ww1lit.nsms.ox.ac.uk/ww1lit/collections/item/9660. Wyndham Lewis had a similarly dark image of the Battle of Passchendaele, stating that its "very name, with its suggestion of *splashiness* and of *passion* at once, was subtly appropriate. This nonsense could not have come to its full flower at any other place but at *Passchendaele*. It was preordained."

56 "Papineau – Soldier and Patriot," *The Globe*, 5 November 1917, 6.

57 See Meyer, *Men of War*, Chapter 3.

58 Thomson, "The Late Major Papineau," 6. Interestingly, the works of Catullus were translated for Victorian readers by a British soldier, Charles Abraham Elton, 1778–1853.

59 For an example of his work, see James C. Hodgins, *Fugitives* (Toronto: Daniel Rose Printer, 1891), Microform, http://archive.org/details/cihm_01240.

60 James Cobourg Hodgins, "Carmina," http://www.warmuseum.ca/firstworldwar/wp-content/mcme-uploads/2014/08/2-b-1-i-carmina-kl.pdf.

61 McDonald, "Preface," 2.

62 Ibid.

63 Martin F. Auger, "On the Brink of Civil War: The Canadian Government and the Suppression of the 1918 Quebec Easter Riots," *Canadian Historical Review* 89, 4 (1 December 2008): 503–40.

64 "Closing Remarks by the Chairman," in Papineau, *The War and Its Influences*, 12.

7

Fallen Sisters: Gender, Military Service, and Death in Canada's First World War

Sarah Glassford

IN MAY 1918, GERMAN PLANES bombed a British military hospital complex at Étaples, France. Canadian nursing sister Dorothy Ellis Collis vividly described the experience: "It was dreadful. We could see the fires through the window, hear the men shouting and calling. Hear bombs dropping, the guns would all stop until the machines came within range ... We were sure the next one would hit us."[1] This devastating air raid was precisely the sort of thing that, in popular understandings of the Great War, Canadian women were not supposed to get

Figure 7.1 The Canadian nursing sisters' close proximity to danger is evident in this image of No. 1 Canadian General Hospital at Étaples after it was bombed in May 1918. | Canadian War Museum Archives, Photo Archives O.3823.

anywhere near. It was the sort of thing, in fact, that Canadian soldiers were fighting to *protect* women from. During the Étaples raid of 19–20 May 1918, three nursing members of the Canadian Army Medical Corps (CAMC) were killed: Katherine Macdonald, Gladys Wake, and Margaret Lowe. They and the other CAMC nurses who died as a direct result of their service were gender anomalies, military women killed in what was supposed to be solely a man's war. Canadian women filled strictly non-combatant roles in the Great War, so, unlike other chapters in this book, this one does not revolve around a particular battle. However, as demonstrated by the Étaples bombing, being non-combatants did not mean that Canadian women escaped the wide-ranging impacts of the war.

Canadians of the Great War era held deeply entrenched ideas about the proper roles and natural abilities of men and women, understanding them in terms of contrasting but complementary sets of qualities: men were strong, women were weak; men were aggressive, women were nurturing; men were worldly, women were domestic.[2] First World War developments sometimes overturned these beliefs, but far more often they were reflected and even reinforced in varied realms, including recruitment tactics, trench culture, voluntary and paid work on the home front, and rituals of mourning.[3] Overseas military nursing and specifically the deaths of Nursing Sisters Macdonald, Wake, and Lowe, offer one avenue by which to consider this much broader canvas of gendered wartime experience. To do so, this chapter explores three key questions. First, to what extent were Macdonald, Wake, and Lowe representative of other Canadian military nurses? Second, what gave them licence to diverge so blatantly (through their military service and proximity to the front lines) from wartime expectations for other Canadian women? Third, how did constructions of femininity work together with those of masculinity to shape notions of what military service, citizenship, and/or death meant? The answers demonstrate that the years 1914–18 were coloured by gendered ways of understanding and responding to the Great War and the changes it wrought in the lives of Canadians.

Sister Soldiers: Who Were the CAMC Nursing Sisters?

During the First World War, 2,845 women enlisted as nursing sisters in the CAMC – Katherine Macdonald, Gladys Wake, and Margaret Lowe among them. As Cynthia Toman points out, the nurses constituted a tiny part of the total Canadian Expeditionary Force (0.5 percent), but they had a disproportionate impact: each of the 761,635 patients admitted to a CAMC medical unit came into contact with them.[4] Macdonald, Wake, and Lowe were all hospital-trained graduate nurses, unmarried with no children, and in good physical condition – basic characteristics that made a woman eligible for service in the

CAMC (though eighty-five *were* married). None of the three had pre-war military nursing experience, but by the time they were posted to Étaples, each had accumulated between one and two years of active service overseas and had nursed with three or four CAMC units.[5] Only twenty-five years old, Katherine Macdonald of Brantford, Ontario, was the baby of the trio. Scottish-born Winnipegger Margaret Lowe was thirty in 1918, and thirty-four-year-old Gladys Wake had been born in Esquimalt, British Columbia, but was living with her parents in Malvern, England, when she enlisted in January 1916. Wake was initially posted to the British front at Salonika (in Greek Macedonia), making her not only the oldest and longest-serving of the three women examined here, but also the most experienced in the conditions of war: the deprivations encountered by combat troops and medical staff in Salonika were particularly gruelling.[6]

Macdonald, Wake, and Lowe are reasonably representative of CAMC nurses. Like more than two-thirds of the group, they were Protestants. All three were unmarried, as were 97 percent of their colleagues. They were also white, like almost all nursing sisters, thanks to the racially biased acceptance criteria of most nurse training schools. Two were Canadian-born, as were the overwhelming majority of CAMC nurses, unlike the disproportionately British-born soldiers in the Canadian Expeditionary Force during the early war years. Agewise, Macdonald, Wake, and Lowe also reflected CAMC nursing norms: the average age on enlistment was 29.9 years, and the most frequently reported age was 27.0, with the average age increasing as the war went on. The CAMC nurses possessed a variety of civilian professional experience and came from a diverse array of family relationships, educational backgrounds, and economic circumstances. But in the essentials of age, marital status, religion, and geographic origins, Macdonald, Wake, and Lowe resembled many of their peers.[7]

These similarities notwithstanding, the only reason that this chapter discusses them in tandem is because all three were killed when German planes bombed No. 1 Canadian General Hospital on the fateful night of 19–20 May 1918. Margaret Lowe and Katherine Macdonald had been there for a little over two months, arriving one week apart in early March 1918, but Gladys Wake was merely five days into her first week with the unit when Étaples came under fire. Macdonald's personnel file states merely that she was "killed in action (enemy air raid)," but other sources reveal that "a piece of shrapnel severed her femoral artery and she died of blood loss." Wake was severely wounded in the leg, resulting in a fractured femur and the diagnosis "dangerously ill." She died two days after the air raid. Lowe suffered a gunshot wound that punctured her chest and a compound fracture to her skull. Nine days after the raid, she too died. All three are buried in the Étaples Military Cemetery, along with 11,514 other military personnel.[8]

Figure 7.2 Katherine Maud Macdonald. | Brant
Museum and Archives, 979.106.1.

Dianne Dodd's research shows that at least sixty CAMC nursing sisters died
of war-related causes, twenty-one as a result of enemy action during May and
June 1918 (including Macdonald, Wake, and Lowe). Six were killed by German bombs, and fifteen drowned at sea – fourteen of them on a single lifeboat
that went down when the hospital ship *Llandovery Castle* was torpedoed.[9] Living
and travelling in war zones, nursing sisters were vulnerable and were regularly
exposed to a variety of infections and diseases. They accepted these occupa-
tional hazards and "were particularly anxious to serve in forward medical units,
arguing that this was 'real' war nursing."[10] Despite the dangers, the deaths of
Macdonald, Wake, and Lowe were atypical of CAMC nursing sisters overall:
their non-combatant status put them at significantly lower risk of death than
was true for ordinary CEF soldiers. Roughly 2 percent of all nursing sisters died
as a result of their military service, as compared to 10 percent of CEF soldiers
who died during the war from illness or injury.[11]

Officers and Ladies: How Did Canadian Nurses End Up in the Army?

Under international humanitarian law, neither hospitals nor medical and nursing personnel were acceptable military targets during the First World War.[12]

The Germans bombed Étaples in May 1918 because the British operations there included both a medical facility *and* an extensive military training complex. In a similar blurring of distinctions, the Canadian nurses at Étaples were fully enlisted, commissioned officers of the CAMC, with the rank of "lieutenant/ nursing sister" – in other words, they were nurses and soldiers (albeit non-combatant ones). Unlike the military nurses of the other Allied nations, who served in all-female auxiliary organizations such as the American Red Cross nursing service or the Queen Alexandra's Imperial Military Nursing Service, CAMC nursing sisters were members of the otherwise all-male Canadian military.[13]

With the outbreak of war, military nursing "offered nurses opportunities for steady work, economic gain, social visibility, and demonstration of personal patriotism," as well as adventure – much like the enticements that drew men to the CEF.[14] Women applied in droves, and the CAMC quickly filled its initial quota. As the war went on, male enlistment plummeted, but the rank, pay, and opportunities for adventure and service offered by military nursing proved so attractive to women that there was a lengthy waiting list until the Armistice.[15] Meanwhile, some two thousand women who lacked graduate nurse qualifications served as Voluntary Aid Detachment (VAD) nurses with the Canadian St. John Ambulance Association, and hundreds of Canadian nurses worked in the nursing services of other countries. The latter included Edith Anderson Monture, who trained in New York before serving overseas with the American Army Nursing Corps. Monture's Indigenous heritage meant she was not welcome in either Canadian nurse training programs or the CAMC. The institutional racism displayed by these exclusions was more severe than that encountered by young First Nations men who tried to join the CEF: as discussed by Evan J. Habkirk in Chapter 5 of this volume, Indigenous men met with ambivalence from the military establishment, but were eventually allowed to enlist.[16]

Although some feminists and pacifists retained their anti-war stance after August 1914, the majority of Canadian women responded to the British Empire's call to arms as eagerly as their male counterparts and were "actively engaged in wartime society and deeply affected by the vagaries of war." Women were urged to lead and participate in voluntary work for war charities, to conserve food, to raise funds for everything from warm socks to machine guns, to encourage men to enlist, and to take on clerical jobs and certain types of factory labour that were traditionally done by men. The federal government even allowed nursing sisters and the close female relatives of CEF soldiers to vote in the 1917 election, expecting that they would support its conscription agenda.[17] Observers lavishly praised women's efforts as proof that they were capable, contributing citizens. Women themselves took advantage of these new opportunities and revelled in the various benefits they brought, including increased income, expanded authority, greater public influence, and the personal satisfaction of feeling they were making a difference.[18] Yet, the period remained deeply marked by traditional ideas about the appropriate roles of men and women. For instance, employment in a factory was seen as more acceptable for working-class and unmarried women than for their middle-class or married counterparts. And though women temporarily made up a significant proportion of the labour force in munitions factories, inequality of the sexes remained the norm in terms of pay scales and who held supervisory roles.[19]

The persistence of pre-war gender norms is most obvious in relation to the battlefields: *fighting* was exclusively a man's job. The printed attestation forms signed by nurses Macdonald, Wake, and Lowe contained only the pronouns "he," "him," and "his," and although English speakers at that time often applied male pronouns to mixed-gender groups, at least one contemporary indicated that they were *not* gender-inclusive when it came to joining the army. Major David Donald (CAMC), who conducted Gladys Wake's medical examination in January 1916, took the time to cross out "him" and replace it with "her" before he signed on the dotted line to approve Nurse Wake for overseas service.[20] Nor was the "men-only" expectation limited to overseas service. Early in the war, a few local efforts were made to establish women's home guard units in Canada, but they were treated as bizarre curiosities and quickly folded.[21]

War work that was considered appropriate for men revolved around notions of "protection" – of women, children, home, or innocent Belgians. Men could join the army or home guard, labour in munitions factories, run industries, farm to supply the army, and govern. By contrast, women's war work sprang from traditions of "service" – to the country, the empire, or the fighting men overseas. Women could do needlework, roll bandages, furnish comforts and medical supplies, visit convalescing soldiers, and prepare food parcels. They could also *temporarily* do non-traditional paid labour, and they could nurse.[22] The distinction was so clear to contemporaries that transgressions were considered ridiculous. In March 1915, the *Illustrated War News*, which was read by Canadians, Newfoundlanders, and Britons, reprinted a cartoon from a German comic newspaper that suggested the British Army was about to be reinforced by a uniformed regiment of four thousand women. The cartoon depicted the regiment as a collection of undisciplined oddballs in all shapes and sizes (reproducing familiar suffragette stereotypes). This suggested that women would make laughably terrible soldiers, but it also functioned as propaganda, implying that the British Army was both pathetic as a fighting force and desperate for recruits. The *Illustrated War News* drew its humour from German stupidity – actually believing that Britain would send women to the front lines! – and from the very idea of female combat soldiers, which at that point was as amusing to Britons as to their foes.[23] As American general William Westmoreland would assert in 1979, "No man with gumption wants a woman to fight his nation's battles."[24] Given this antipathy toward women in the military, how did nurses end up as officers in the Canadian army during the First World War?

From the CAMC's perspective, taking this course was the sensible option. Trained female nurses had proven their worth to modern armies as far back as the Crimean War of 1853–56, when Florence Nightingale famously ministered to British sick and wounded, and a handful of Canadian military nurses had served proudly and effectively with the British Expeditionary Force during the South African War (1899–1902). Thanks to the political influence of Georgina Fane Pope, a nurse who had participated in the South African campaign, two nurses were included when the CAMC was reorganized in 1904. In 1910, Colonel Guy Carleton Jones, head of the CAMC, was impressed by a speech given by CAMC nurse Margaret Macdonald on the importance of recognizing the military nurse as a specialist. When war was declared in August 1914, Jones summoned Macdonald to Ottawa and asked her to mobilize Canadian nurses for the conflict, drawing from those with prior training in military nursing as well as the larger civilian nursing workforce. She was ultimately appointed as matron-in-chief of the CAMC nursing sisters, with the rank of major – the first woman to hold this rank anywhere in the British Empire.[25]

Staffing CAMC hospitals with military nurses was one thing; the decision to integrate them within the military structure itself was quite another. This move encompassed two innovations: first the CAMC created an all-female rank of "nursing sister" and then it granted those nursing sisters officer status (they enlisted as lieutenants and could later be promoted). These choices were thoroughly pragmatic. As Toman writes, "the CAMC enlisted its nurses as soldiers in order to have control, not only over their behaviour and activities as women in the all-male domain of war, but also over their movements and postings."[26] In 1914, a first-class military medical service included female nurses, but if the CAMC had to deal with women it was determined to do so on its own terms.

Since nursing sisters constituted a semi-separate rank within the CAMC, they held authority "over other nursing sisters, assistants in the various hospital units and, most importantly, their patients." However, they took orders from senior officers as any soldier would, and their authority did not extend beyond the medical wards. This effectively confined their disruptive potential to a tiny portion of the Canadian military landscape. Some male officers initially opposed the granting of officer status to nursing sisters, but in the minds of CAMC leaders the benefits of bringing them under control far outweighed any drawbacks.[27] There would be a persistent tension, however, between their gender and their status as officers. In 1918–19, the head of the CAMC in France fought to gain recognition for CAMC nursing sisters who displayed notable valour during the German air raids of 1918. The Military Cross was the appropriate gallantry medal for junior officers, but British military officials refused to grant it to nurses, awarding them the Military Medal instead, which was reserved for "other ranks." In protocol terms, this was equivalent to a gender-based slap in the face. "If nurses were to get top gallantry awards," as Katherine Dewar notes, the implication seems to have been "that it would somehow diminish the award for soldiers."[28]

As this example suggests, one characteristic feature of virtually all women's experiences during the Great War was the way in which traditional attitudes frequently undercut roles and opportunities that challenged gender norms. For instance, women's voluntary work for charities such as the Red Cross involved considerable organizational, financial, and executive ability, as well as significant labour and skill, but contemporaries spoke of it as "caring" and "mothering" work that drew upon women's supposedly natural domestic and maternal qualities. Similarly, in praising female munitions workers, newspaper articles were careful to emphasize "that their work did not make them less feminine" and that it was in fact not unlike some of their traditional domestic duties.[29]

In the same way, a variety of language, imagery, privileges, and restrictions emphasized the femininity of CAMC nurses and distinguished them from the military men they nursed as well as those with whom they worked. Their official title of "nursing sister," for instance, was affectionately shortened to "sister" by the men in their care – a term also used for female siblings and nuns. These connotations set the nurses apart from the French or Belgian farm women, *estaminet* (tavern) keepers, and prostitutes whom soldiers might regularly encounter overseas. Their working uniform further marked them as distinct: their long blue dresses and white bibbed aprons earned them the pretty nickname "bluebirds." Their woollen dress uniforms and greatcoats had a more military air, brass buttons and all, but the impractical starched white collars, cuffs, and veil of their regular nursing garb made for an attractively feminine and decidedly unmilitary uniform.[30] Nursing sisters themselves wished to look and feel feminine despite the trying conditions in which they lived and worked, and they spent their free time in stereotypically feminine pursuits, including "shopping, sewing, decorating wards and living quarters, partying, going on picnics, gardening, bicycling, and serving tea and dinners to one another." Such activities, Toman writes, "reassured both the military and families [back home] that nursing sisters would still be suitable as daughters, sisters, and wives after the war."[31] As reassuring as the activities may have been, the sisters engaged in them because they saw them as meaningful. As Kyle Falcon asserts in Chapter 3 of this volume, "given the omnipresence of death, front soldiers developed a unique culture, one in which large, impersonal forces were acknowledged, but meaning and agency were bolstered through coping mechanisms such as faith, superstition, trench journals, and entertainments" (page 66). The CAMC nurses were similarly resilient and resourceful, making the most of their intermittent leisure time to help themselves cope with the physical, emotional, and mental strains of their work.

Susan Mann points out that, like many civilian nursing uniforms of this period, those of the CAMC evoked the housedress of a wife, the apron of a servant, the collar and cuffs of a schoolgirl, and the veil of a nun.[32] Like the term "sister," this array of visual connotations largely emphasized women in non-romantic, non-sexual roles. Since the late nineteenth century, nursing's status as a suitable peacetime career for young women had been carefully built on the foundation of an asexual image: intimate contact between respectable women and the bodies of strangers – especially male bodies – was considered socially acceptable only if the nurses' own sexuality were concealed and policed. Thus, their uniforms "represented non-sexual femininity that legitimized their place in the work-force, on the streets, and at the bedside."[33] Even so, their sexuality remained a concern. Postcards depicting nurses seductively posed with military patients show that the fantasy (or fear, for wives and sweethearts back home) of the sexy nurse was in circulation during the Great War.[34] To combat notions of sexual transgression between nurses and patients, the late-nineteenth- and early-twentieth-century nursing profession largely accepted only those women whom it considered respectable (white, often middle-class, and of good character). It emphasized the rigorous education and practised skill that went into the work and maintained strict codes of behaviour in hospitals and training schools, insisting on obedience and deference to authority.[35]

During peacetime, the nurse's place in the medical system was understood in terms of gendered metaphors of family: as Kathryn McPherson explains, "graduate nurses assumed a subordinate wifely position relative to the male doctor and a maternal position relative to the dependent patient." A physician's authority over the health care team paralleled that of a (male) head of household, and "the personal service tasks demanded in patient care were deemed natural for women to execute," as would a wife or mother.[36] The importance of these gendered hierarchies in medical settings is demonstrated by the fact that the wartime CAMC refused to employ male nurses or female doctors, both of which did exist in small numbers. There were three women doctors who joined the CAMC, but they did so as nursing sisters and were limited to nursing duties.[37]

These highly gendered understandings of nursing were reinforced during the war years, when women's home front efforts were popularly understood as "mothering" work: military nurses became an overseas extension of civilian women's maternal care. Nursing sisters referred to their soldier patients as "lads" and "boys," and extolled their brave stoicism as a reason to make sacrifices for them – all of which reinforced the metaphor of a (non-sexual) familial relationship of care between nurses and servicemen. Contemporaries saw motherliness as a critical element of good military nursing care and a valuable antidote to the dehumanizing carnage of the Western Front. Joshua Goldstein argues that because women have traditionally been excluded from combat roles, "part of the power of [female] army nurses comes from the message that, if one is in the presence of women, one is no longer in combat but connected with home." In other words, the simple fact that the sisters were women offered the healing, comforting message "that the battlefield is finite and the other world still exists."[38] Images of angelic nurses cradling wounded soldiers on the battlefield cropped up regularly in fundraising posters and popular songs. The public rarely distinguished between CAMC nurses, Red Cross personnel, members of the Queen Alexandra's Imperial Military Nursing Service, and VADs, lumping them all under one idealized umbrella as angels of mercy. The popular 1918 song "The Rose of No Man's Land" is a good example, with its refrain "Mid the war's great curse / Stands the Red Cross Nurse / She's the rose of No Man's Land."[39]

The desexualizing aspects of CAMC nurses' language, dress, and behaviour were important because the presence of women in the war zones, and in the CAMC, had the potential to disrupt the military machine or to undermine the sisters' professional status and personal reputations. One perk of their military rank was being allowed to socialize with male officers – a coveted privilege that non-CAMC nurses lacked.[40] Many of the off-duty social events, excursions, and sports that the sisters organized involved mixed-gender groups. Close friendships and romances flourished between medical and nursing staff – and perhaps also between some pairs of nurses.[41] Starved for female company, male patients also freely admired, flirted with, and occasionally tried their luck with nurses. As Canadian VAD Jane Walters observed, "Patients had a habit of falling in love with [nurses]." She added, "to be thrown in with men like that, all kinds from all over the world, it took some doing to keep level, not have your head turned. But you had your heart hurt very often."[42]

These romantic entanglements unfolded under the watchful eye of the unit's matron, a senior nurse who supervised both the work and the leisure time of nurses, in a manner similar to that of nurse training schools. The closer the unit was to the fighting front, the less liberty sisters had in how and where to spend their off-duty time. To tour in certain areas, they required permission and sometimes army escorts, and at some points in the Mediterranean theatre they were scarcely allowed to leave their unit at all, "lest something or someone snatch us up and run off with us," as Nursing Sister Alice Ross wrote.[43] The army also strove to protect CAMC nurses in their own dwelling places. Male guards were sometimes assigned to keep them safe in camp, their living quarters were segregated from those of male medical personnel, and during one relocation, they were not permitted to billet in Boulogne, a city that was deemed a bad moral influence. They were expected to uphold an image of womanly propriety, so exposing them to the rampant carousing and prostitution of Boulogne would never do.[44]

For a variety of reasons, then, the Canadian military considered it sensible – if not entirely unproblematic – to enlist women. The concession was a small one: they would carry no weapons, engage in no combat, be barred from the active fighting zones, require impeccable character references, be chaperoned and guarded when necessary, and work only within the limited sphere of CAMC hospital facilities. The payoff was surely worth the irregularity of allowing women into this sacred male preserve.

Military Service and Death: What Did It All Mean?

Although enlisting women in the Canadian Army marked a departure from gender norms, their role in the CAMC was highly traditional. Early-twentieth-century Canadians viewed nursing as a quintessential form of "women's work," believing women's biological role as mothers inherently suited them to nurture and care for others. In an era before universal hospital insurance or medicare, most Canadians convalesced at home (and many were born and/or died there, too), cared for by their mothers, sisters, daughters, maiden aunts, or trained private duty nurses. Female nursing had also become standard in Canadian hospitals by this period.[45] Professional nursing was skilled and vital work: germ theory was well known, but antibiotics did not exist, so the task of maintaining sterile and hygienic conditions fell to nurses. Yet contemporaries tended to focus on the fact that many aspects of nursing resembled women's domestic work. Nurses did a great deal of cleaning – of wounds, patients, floors, linens, and implements – and monitoring patients' conditions and relieving their pain appeared to mimic a mother's care for her children.

These perceptions of nursing and womanhood contributed to some of the most powerful Allied propaganda of the Great War. The German invasion of Belgium in August 1914 brought a wave of Belgian refugees to Britain, who spread tales of German atrocities that were subsequently confirmed in May 1915 by Britain's Committee on Alleged German Outrages. Throughout the British Empire, newspapers published excerpts from the report, stirring up anti-German sentiment with a gruesome litany of murder, mass rape, arson, and mutilations, including "cutting off of children's hands and women's breasts." The alleged atrocities (later shown to be based on false testimony) immediately became fodder for Allied propaganda revolving around one central theme – women in peril. As Peter Buitenhuis writes, "in poster and report and appeal, Belgium [was] the raped and mutilated maiden, left to die."[46] This metaphor of Belgium as a woman violated by the enemy was powerful on its own, but the Allied propaganda machine in 1915 received further fuel when a German submarine sank the British passenger ship *Lusitania,* and German authorities executed British nurse Edith Cavell. Cavell was head nurse in a Belgian hospital at the time of the invasion and was arrested for helping Allied prisoners escape into the Netherlands. She was convicted of espionage and executed by firing squad in October 1915. Although the charge was to some extent justifiable, the British government and the Allied press celebrated Cavell as a martyr, "a glowing example of Christian British womanhood who selflessly risked her life to care for enemy wounded, and, despite her innocence, bravely confronted death." The theme of women in peril remained a constant throughout the war, and resentment was stoked with the sinking of the Canadian hospital ship, *Llandovery Castle,* in 1918. In that same year, Universal Studios released a film about Kaiser Wilhelm *(The Beast of Berlin),* whose North American promotion campaign featured giant cut-outs of the kaiser pointing a sword at a terrified woman.[47] Anti-German propaganda of this type fuelled incidents such as that described by Gordon L. Heath in Chapter 8 of this volume, in which residents and soldiers in Berlin, Ontario, threw a bust of the kaiser into a local lake (page 196n62).

Depictions of innocent women and children suffering at the hands of German invaders were central to mobilizing volunteer-based armies in the British Empire. They painted the enemy as uncivilized and depraved, offered the liberation of Belgian women and children as a reason to fight, and implied that the women and children of the British Empire would be equally vulnerable if the Germans were not defeated.[48] The notion of protecting one's own women and children has historically been an important component of masculinity across many cultures, despite rarely being necessary; consequently, this was a potent appeal.[49] From the mid-nineteenth to the mid-twentieth century, a particular "cult of manliness" held sway in the Anglo-American world: the ideal man was strong, physically able, loyal, morally upright, and dutiful to his country/empire, and religion. He was decisive, shunned weakness of any kind, held his emotions in check, and strove as nearly as possible to be "a manly warrior."[50] As Geoffrey Hayes details in Chapter 6 of this volume, in his exploration of Talbot Papineau's war experience, the power of this ideal was very strong.

The advent of war in 1914 provided a tailor-made outlet for this vision of manhood, in the form of military service. Young men could now put their courage and stoicism to the test on real battlefields. In an increasingly urbanized, industrialized Canada, where many social critics feared that men were becoming soft, "the war simplified the transition from youth to manhood: being a soldier meant being a man."[51] Nor was the appeal limited to the young, as fighting for one's country at any age was proof of manhood. So ingrained was this idea that men who could not or would not enlist suffered shame and public castigation. As Amy Shaw demonstrates, conscientious objectors were accused not only of being cowardly, weak, arrogant, and anti-democratic, but also of being both childish and effeminate for "refusing to accept one of the public responsibilities of manhood."[52] Meanwhile, more than 100,000 Canadian men encountered a problem of their own: they were eager to enlist in the CEF, but disability or poor health made them inadmissible. If their reason for being deemed medically unfit were not readily visible, they faced the same public condemnation experienced by conscientious objectors but without the internal support of conscience to sustain them. According to Nic Clarke, "the nagging guilt and often all-consuming self-doubt about their masculinity and social and biological worth ... could be crippling." Some rejected volunteers went into self-imposed social exile for the duration of the war, and a few are known to have committed suicide.[53] The distinction between those who served and those who stayed home still carried weight during the Great Depression, when veterans made claims to state assistance based on their military service, as opposed to "Weak and old men forced to stay / With other men* of softer clay (*Eligibles)."[54] Those who served in the military are explicitly contrasted with those who were ineligible to serve on the basis of age or debility and those who were eligible to serve but chose not to do so. The implication is that soldiers were "real" men – and therefore entitled to state assistance.

Of course, Canadian men had many reasons for enlisting. These included "social pressure, unemployment, escape from a tiresome family or a dead-end job, self-respect," plus loftier reasons such as idealism, a sense of duty, or ties to Britain. Desmond Morton notes that by 1916, most unenlisted Canadian men were engaged in war-related service of some type, whether through farming, industry, or voluntary work.[55] And, like the home front work of Canadian women, these contributions were hailed as valuable aspects of the war effort. Yet, military service remained the litmus test for masculinity. Newspapers, books, films, popular songs, advertisements, sermons, and school lessons – and especially anything published by the Canadian War Records Office – fed Canadians a steady diet of romanticized portrayals of the men of the CEF. The prevailing image was "that the Dominion's valiant and manly northern warriors were laying the seeds for ever-lasting national glory." Even factual narratives by combatants tended to focus on courage, cheerful endurance, and daring exploits, while keeping mum about the fear, tedium, deprivation, and trauma of life on the front lines.[56] Jeff Keshen suggests that, although Canadian soldiers' expectations of adventure and glory were swiftly dashed, a combination of military censorship and "the desire of recruits to bear the brunt like real men" limited their truth telling to battalion publications that the Canadian public never read.[57]

Back home, the mythology of Canada's unflagging warriors inspired a range of campaigns to boost home front efforts through comparison to the men of the CEF. Adolescent boys were recruited for farm labour as "Soldiers of the Soil," and women were enticed into VAD nursing with praise for their voluntary efforts as a form of feminine "soldiering." War charities such as the Canadian Red Cross and the Canadian Patriotic Fund devised slogans that likened civilian donations and charitable labour on the home front to the sacrifices being made by servicemen. The fund's slogan "Fight or pay," for example, urged civilian men and women to donate money as their equivalent to military service.[58] The mythology of the CEF burned so brightly that others could bask in its reflected glow.

Posters produced by the Military Hospitals Commission to promote its retraining scheme for wounded Canadian soldiers featured the slogan "Once a Soldier Always a Man" – suggesting that the mere act of enlisting guaranteed a man's masculinity regardless of what befell him during the war. But this was not the case. The instinct for self-preservation that prompted some soldiers to desert was punished by execution or imprisonment and incurred lasting public shame for the family that had produced such an undutiful coward.[59] Equally devastatingly, soldiers who suffered from shell shock came to be seen as weak and effeminate. The compassionate "rest cure" approach of early in the war gave way to painful alternatives such as electric shock, in an attempt to force patients back to health and thence to the fighting lines. After the war, shell-shocked veterans were not eligible for pensions, as they were thought to have shirked their manly duty by purposefully avoiding danger.[60] The masculinity of the CEF therefore had clear boundaries. In many ways, it was defined by what it was not – the supposedly feminine qualities of emotionality or weakness – and it made no space for universally experienced human emotions such as fear.

These powerful gendered ideals had a significant impact on the way in which Canadians understood military service and death in wartime. Dewar's study of Prince Edward Island military nurses notes that "each nurse's safe return to P.E.I. from the war was only recorded in a few lines on page eight of the *Island Patriot*, in a column titled 'Of Local Interest,'" whereas the return of soldiers from the Island "was usually front-page news with a big write-up detailing their heroic participation in the major battles of the war." Soldiers' decorations were made much of, whereas "nurses' decorations were seldom mentioned."[61] The clear difference in the public response to the service of women and men extended well beyond Prince Edward Island and into the post-war era. Dodd's study of major national commemorations of nursing casualties finds that during the war years, nursing sisters "were applauded for their bravery," but like the praise for executed nurse Edith Cavell, it was usually for propaganda purposes. In the 1920s and 1930s Dodd sees "ambivalence and reluctance to acknowledge nurses' military role." Even the national memorial to CAMC nursing sisters that was unveiled in Ottawa in 1926 features nurses in "the traditional role of mourner and/or nurturer" without directly addressing the fact that some of them lost their lives in the course of their military service. Only in recent years have memorials begun to reflect the sisters' own perceptions of themselves as soldiers. Notably, after years of advocacy by local historian and archivist Sherri K. Robinson, a mountain near Pemberton, British Columbia, was named for Gladys Wake in 1998.[62]

This approach to post-war commemoration stems in part from how the nurses themselves chose to remember and forget their wartime experiences. In crafting their monographs, both Dewar and Toman drew upon extensive writings by nursing sisters, proving that, "in spite of official prohibitions against personal diaries and photographs, a surprising number of nurses felt compelled to record and photograph the war from their own perspectives."[63] Yet, "very few nursing sisters ever published their own accounts,"[64] and both Dewar and Toman relied heavily on letters and diaries from private family collections. In the case of Prince Edward Island, Dewar found that a century later, "some relatives are still hesitant to share those diaries and the secrets they contain – secrets still seen as too personal for public airing."[65]

Matron-in-Chief Margaret Macdonald hoped that the story of her nurses' hard work under gruelling conditions and their critical contribution to overseas medical care would be an integral aspect of Canada's war memory. After all, thanks in large part to their labour, an unprecedented 93 percent of soldiers who reached treatment survived their wounds, and disease killed fewer servicemen than did the enemy.[66] Instead, their story faded into a footnote. During the early 1920s, Margaret Macdonald attempted to write a history of CAMC nursing during the Great War but did not succeed, likely because her request for contributions from rank-and-file nurses produced few responses.[67] Nor did her public appearances establish a realistic image of CAMC nursing sisters in the evolving memory of the war. Press coverage often drew more attention to her clothing than to her successful military career, reminding readers that "in spite of ... her proximity to war, she was essentially feminine." Macdonald used her speaking engagements to talk about wartime nursing's parallels to women's domestic work and its origins in a feminine ethic of service – a highly selective account engineered to reassure her (usually female) listeners that the CAMC nurses and women on the home front had mothered the troops in similar ways.[68] Only in the early twenty-first century would Great War nursing sisters begin to emerge from the mists of the past as flesh-and-blood professionals who forged a central role for women in the Canadian military medical service, thanks to scholars such as Susan Mann, Cynthia Toman, Katherine Dewar, and Mélanie Morin-Pelletier.[69]

Scholars have attributed military nurses' silence on their work in the Great War (evident beyond Canada as well) to various factors, including professional discretion, concerns about censorship, a desire to subordinate their stories to those of their soldier patients, and the difficulty of contradicting the image of nurses as angels of mercy. Their reticence may also have been a coping mechanism; silence may have seemed "an appropriate balm" after the traumatic war years.[70] Many male veterans opted for silence as well, either refusing to speak of their experiences or restricting their accounts to amusing anecdotes and the comradeship they enjoyed in the army.[71]

Even if many men wished to forget, Canadian society had a great deal to say about their service, indulging in a decades-long collective grieving period for the sixty thousand of them who did not come home. As Jonathan Vance demonstrates, Canadians understood men's military service and death in combat in very particular ways. The male soldier fighting in Europe was portrayed as a just warrior defending Canada, the British Empire, Western civilization, and Christianity – and helping to bring his country to maturity in the process. Accordingly, his death in battle was seen as a sacrificial and purifying gift to his country, akin to that of Christ, which guaranteed his immortality. In his youthful vigour, he represented both the culmination of Canada's history and the promise of its future. The language and imagery of cenotaphs, stained glass windows, war art, honour rolls, poems and novels, and other public and private memorials that accumulated during the interwar years reinforced the notion that the men of the CEF did not "lose" their lives, but "gave" them. This wording offered consolation to bereaved loved ones by affirming a larger meaning for the entire war and upholding the image of the Canadian soldier as courageous and dutiful. "To lose one's life was a tragedy," writes Vance, but "to give one's life by making the supreme sacrifice was the ultimate in selflessness." In this context, the society-wide duty to honour and remember the fallen soldier, and to build a country worthy of his sacrifice, was unambiguous.[72]

Most Canadian Great War memorials either do not include women or present them in purely allegorical roles such as Sacrifice, Victory, or Grief. This lack

Figure 7.3 Funeral procession for Gladys Wake. | LAC, Ministry of the Overseas
Military Forces of Canada fonds, 002562.

speaks to the absence of nursing sisters from the Canadian understanding
of the Great War's meaning. Male soldiers were nation-builders, holy warriors,
defenders of civilization; nursing sisters were not. There was no equivalent
mythology for their service, let alone their deaths. The angel of mercy image
was powerful but narrow in scope. It limited nurses to a single purpose – comforting wounded men – and emphasized not a medical role but an emotional
one. More broadly, both pre-war ideologies and wartime propaganda reinforced
the notion that women were victims, not victors, and healers rather than heroes.
However, commemorating the role of nurses as healers could muddy the waters. When the Nursing Sisters' Memorial was unveiled in the Hall of Honour
at the Parliament Buildings in Ottawa in 1926 it placed the Great War service of
nurses within the broader context of women's healing work. By doing so it ended
up downplaying the deceased military nurses whose commemoration was its
original purpose.[73] Victims *could* be successfully memorialized, but Edith
Cavell's larger-than-life mythology as a martyr to German frightfulness vastly
eclipsed the memory of CAMC nursing sisters who died in the course of duty.
    At the vast Commonwealth War Graves Commission cemetery in Étaples,
the tension inherent in the status of CAMC nursing sisters as both women and

officers is made tangible in the inscriptions chosen for the gravestones of Katherine Macdonald, Gladys Wake, and Margaret Lowe. Macdonald's stone, taking the time-honoured approach of identifying an unmarried woman with her parents, is inscribed, "Killed in Action Beloved Daughter of Angus and Mary Maud Macdonald Brantford, Canada." Wake's marker invokes the religious meanings that many Canadians ascribed to the war: "The Noble Army of Martyrs Praise Thee." Lowe's headstone takes a patriotic stance and most explicitly evokes the soldiering ethos attached to the men of the CEF: "She Did Her Duty for King and Country."[74] No coherent and socially resonant meaning for the deaths of nursing sisters emerged from the war, as the diversity of these inscriptions attests. The pre-war ideas about gender that framed male and female roles were largely to blame: women were not supposed to be in the army, let alone to die as a result.

As Peter Farrugia explains in Chapter 4 of this volume, Canadians' understandings of their collective past are malleable and highly contested. It is important to note, therefore, that Canadian memorials to Great War military nurses *do* exist. Prince Edward Islanders named a Charlottetown military hospital after Nursing Sister Rena MacLean, who drowned when the *Llandovery Castle* was torpedoed. Some nursing sister casualties appear with male Canadian military casualties in gracing honour rolls, plaques, posters, and certain war memorials. CAMC nursing sisters collectively commemorated their war service through a beautiful white marble memorial in the Parliament Buildings in Ottawa, as mentioned above, and through the formation of a veterans' group called the Overseas Nursing Sisters Association.[75] Still, Edith Cavell occupies some of the most prominent Canadian commemorative real estate: as of 2020, a mountain, a lake, a glacier, a meadow, a hiking trail, and at least three public schools bore her name, whereas, as Dianne Dodd puts it, the CAMC nurses remain "largely invisible in the commemorative terrain."[76] Even the two military nurses in the National War Memorial in Ottawa are easy to miss, overwhelmed by the twenty men in the sculpture. In terms of proportionate numbers of those who served, this is not inappropriate, but it is also an apt metaphor for the place of military nurses in Canada's myth and memory of the Great War.[77]

SINCE THE 1960S, SCHOLARS have debated whether the First World War had a positive or a negative impact on the status of women. After sixty years of weighing the evidence, the question remains difficult to answer. Some things changed positively for some women, but for others the changes were temporary, negative, incomplete, undermined, or non-existent. Class, race, ethnicity, politics, religion, region, age, marital status, and a host of other markers of identity played a role in the degree to which the war years altered women's lives and expectations, making it impossible to generalize. The best answer to the question (borne out by the example of the Canadian nursing sisters) may simply be "it's complicated." Sarah Glassford and Amy Shaw argue that the years 1914 to 1918 did not usher in a radical transformation of Canadian women's status overall, but suggest that on a personal level, the war transformed the lives of many women. In this view, the war can be seen "as a time of shifts and repositionings – as a milepost rather than as a finish line in the great transformation that was the twentieth century."[78] What can be said with complete certainty, however, is that male and female experiences of the Great War were deeply shaped by contemporary understandings of gender, on both the home front and the front lines, and that the war itself opened spaces for gender roles to begin making those shifts. But neither phenomenon was simple or straightforward. Nursing Sisters Katherine Macdonald, Gladys Wake, and Margaret Lowe broke gender norms by serving as officers in the CAMC. Yet their military service and their deaths were not ascribed the same meanings as the military service and deaths of male soldiers. Why should this matter a century later?

Acknowledging the gendered ways in which early-twentieth-century military service was perceived encourages a rereading of nursing memoirs, one that looks past the stereotypes of caring mothers and angels of mercy to recognize the labour, skill, and professional competence they demonstrate, as well as how nurses themselves understood their service. Doing so reveals that the sisters viewed themselves very much as soldiers, worked incredibly hard, were taxed to the utmost both mentally and physically, witnessed the carnage of battle on a daily basis, valued their ability to contribute to the war effort in a direct and tangible way, and braved illness, mental strain, and even death, alongside the men they nursed.

Being attuned to the influence of gender roles and expectations in wartime offers new insights into the reasons why men and women behaved in certain ways and how they made sense of what they experienced. It also enables us to better understand the war's long legacy in Canada, not only in terms of politics, economy, or even women's rights and status, but also on an individual level. Male veterans were expected to reintegrate into civilian society with little support, and those who had difficulty in doing so were sometimes characterized as weak and effeminate. Real men were supposed to be tough and self-reliant. In return, veterans used their numbers and the discourses of manly military citizenship to push back and demand state support.[79] Some CAMC nurses faced equivalent struggles in reintegrating into civilian life and coping with what they had seen and done during the war. But unlike many male veterans, they had their professional training already in hand and some had developed nursing specialties through their war service. Marriage was a viable "career" path, and the expanding fields of public health nursing and social work absorbed many nursing sister veterans who might otherwise have struggled to reintegrate.[80]

Finally, it is important to study gender because failing to do so helps erase the female portion of the population from the pages of Canadian history. As the contributions of military nurses faded into the background of Canada's Great War memory, the more mundane home front efforts of women – lauded in 1919 as "generous, continuous, persistent" and valued to the tune of tens of millions of dollars – practically vanished from that memory altogether.[81] No statues were raised to them; no honour rolls were compiled and mounted on schoolhouse walls. Not until the late twentieth and early twenty-first centuries would scholars – newly interested in the gender dynamics of the past – rediscover these forgotten histories and write women into a more holistic narrative of how Canada experienced the crucial years of conflict. Women have reclaimed their places in the scholarly record of the Great War, but they remain precariously placed on the fringes of popular memory even today.

Notes

1   Dorothy Ellis Collis, Diary, 19 May 1918, quoted in Debbie Marshall, "Nursing Sister Gladys Maude Wake," 4 February 2010, Finding the Forty-Seven: Canadian Nurses of the First World War, http://rememberingfirstworldwarnurses.blogspot.ca/2010/02/nursing-sister -gladys-maude-wake.html.

2   See views from 1878–1918 excerpted in Ramsay Cook and Wendy Mitchinson, eds., *The Proper Sphere: Woman's Place in Canadian Society* (Toronto: Oxford University Press, 1976), 5–91.

3   For example, see Tim Cook on vocabulary and soldier masculinity in "Fighting Words: Canadian Soldiers' Slang and Swearing in the Great War," *War in History* 20, 3 (2013): 323–44; and Suzanne Evans on women's central role in mourning practices in "Marks of Grief: Black Attire, Medals, and Service Flags," in *A Sisterhood of Suffering and Service: Women and Girls of Canada and Newfoundland during the First World War,* ed. Sarah Glassford and Amy Shaw (Vancouver: UBC Press, 2012), 219–40. On the relationship between war and gender throughout Canadian history, see Tarah Brookfield and Sarah Glassford, "Home Fronts and Front Lines: A Gendered History of War and Peace," in *A Companion to Women's and Gender History in Canada,* ed. Carmen Nielsen and Nancy Janovicek (Toronto: University of Toronto Press, 2019), 151–69. For the impact of the war on gender roles, see also Chapters 6 and 10 in this volume.

4   Cynthia Toman, *Sister Soldiers of the Great War: The Nurses of the Canadian Army Medical Corps* (Vancouver: UBC Press, 2016), 219.

5   Katherine Macdonald's attestation papers indicate she officially enlisted on 20 March 1917 in London, Ontario, but another document in her file indicates she enlisted earlier and nursed in a CAMC hospital in Military District No. 1 (Canada) beginning in November 1916. She served in the following overseas CAMC units between April 1917 and March 1918: No. 10 Canadian Stationary Hospital (Hastings, England, and later France); and No. 14 Canadian General Hospital (Eastbourne, and later Basingstoke, England). She arrived at No. 1 Canadian General Hospital, in Étaples, on 8 March 1918. Margaret Lowe enlisted on 24 March 1917 in Winnipeg and served in the following CAMC units between June

1917 and March 1918: Ontario Military Hospital; No. 16 Canadian General Hospital (Orpington, England); and No. 10 Canadian Stationary Hospital (England and later France). She arrived at Étaples on 16 March 1918. Gladys Wake enlisted on 10 January 1916 in London, England, and served in the following CAMC units between January 1916 and May 1918: Duchess of Connaught Canadian Red Cross Hospital (Taplow, England); No. 1 Canadian Stationary Hospital (Salonika); No. 4 Canadian General Hospital (Shorncliffe [?], England); and No. 11 Canadian General Hospital (Moore Barracks, England). She reached Étaples on 14 May 1918. All Library and Archives Canada (LAC), RG 150 (CEF), accession 1992-93/166, box 6748-49, file Macdonald, Katherine Maud, NS; box 5768-43, file Lowe, M., NS; box 9989-48, file Wake, Gladys Maude Mary. On nurses' marital status see Toman, *Sister Soldiers*, 50.

6 LAC, Macdonald, Katherine Maud, NS; Lowe, M., NS; Wake, Gladys Maude Mary. Toman, *Sister Soldiers*, 84–93 (Salonika).

7 Toman, *Sister Soldiers*, 47, 49–50.

8 LAC, Macdonald, Katherine Maud, NS; Lowe, M., NS; Wake, Gladys Maude Mary; Toman, *Sister Soldiers*, 66 (Macdonald); Commonwealth War Graves Commission, "Find War Dead and Cemeteries: Étaples Military Cemetery," https://www.cwgc.org/find/find -cemeteries-and-memorials/results?name=Etaples%2BMilitary%2BCemetery&country =France&firstwar=true.

9 Dianne Dodd, "Canadian Military Nurse Deaths in the First World War," *Canadian Bulletin of Medical History* 34, 2 (2017): 339; Katherine Dewar, *Those Splendid Girls: The Heroic Service of Prince Edward Island Nurses in the Great War, 1914–1918* (Charlottetown: Island Studies Press, 2014), 116.

10 Toman, *Sister Soldiers*, 101–2, 73.

11 Of the 619,000 enlisted members of the CEF, 60,000 died during the war. Toman, *Sister Soldiers*, 11; see also Desmond Morton, *When Your Number's Up: The Canadian Soldier in the First World War* (Toronto: Random House, 1993), 181.

12 Caroline Moorehead, *Dunant's Dream: War, Switzerland and the History of the Red Cross* (New York: Carroll and Graf, 1998), 45. The first Geneva Convention on ameliorating the condition of the sick and wounded in war was signed in 1864 and revised in 1906.

13 Toman, *Sister Soldiers*, 3–4.

14 Cynthia Toman, "'Help Us, Serve England': First World War Military Nursing and National Identities," *Canadian Bulletin of Medical History* 3, 1 (2013): 146.

15 Toman, *Sister Soldiers*, 3–4.

16 See also Linda J. Quiney, "Gendering Patriotism: Canadian Volunteer Nurses as the Female 'Soldiers' of the Great War," in Glassford and Shaw, *A Sisterhood of Suffering*, 103, 109; Toman, "'Help Us,'" 147, 154; Alison Norman, "'In Defense of the Empire': The Six Nations of the Grand River and the Great War," in Glassford and Shaw, *A Sisterhood of Suffering*, 35; and Cynthia Toman, "'My Chance Has Come at Last!' The Weston Hospital, the Women's Christian Temperance Union, and Indian Nurses in Canada, 1917–1929," *Native Studies Review* 19, 2 (2010): 95–119.

17 Glassford and Shaw, "Introduction: Transformation in a Time of War?" *A Sisterhood of Suffering*, 2 (quotation), 11–14. The Military Voters Act (1917) gave the federal vote to all members of the CEF, including nursing sisters. The Wartime Elections Act (1917) enfranchised women who had husbands, brothers, or sons in the CEF, but it disenfranchised men and women of certain ethnic and racial groups.

18 See, for example, the treatment of women's Red Cross work in Sarah Glassford, "'The Greatest Mother in the World': Carework and the Discourse of Mothering in the Canadian Red Cross Society during the First World War," *Journal of the Association for Research on Mothering* 10, 1 (2008): 219–33.

19 Kori Street, "Patriotic, Not Permanent: Attitudes about Women's Making Bombs and Being Bankers," in Glassford and Shaw, *A Sisterhood of Suffering*, 148–70.

20 LAC, Wake, Gladys Maude Mary, Certificate of Medical Examination.

21 Glassford and Shaw, "Introduction," *A Sisterhood of Suffering*, 2, 15; Robert Rutherdale, *Hometown Horizons: Local Responses to Canada's Great War* (Vancouver: UBC Press, 2004), 195.

22 Rutherdale, *Hometown Horizons*, 194–95.

23 "A Monstrous Regiment of Women! A German Caricature Suggesting That British Suffragettes Are to Fight at the Front," *Illustrated War News*, 31 March 1915, 47, http://war timecanada.ca/sites/default/files/documents/The%20Illustrated%20war%20News.%20 March%2031%2C%201915.pdf. Based on a report of Lady Castlereagh forming a uniformed Women's Volunteer Reserve.

24 Joshua Goldstein, *War and Gender: How Gender Shapes the War System and Vice Versa* (Cambridge: Cambridge University Press, 2001), 283.

25 Toman, *Sister Soldiers*, 15, 17; Susan Mann, *Margaret Macdonald: Imperial Daughter* (Montreal and Kingston: McGill-Queen's University Press, 2005), 69–72.

26 Toman, *Sister Soldiers*, 16.

27 Ibid.

28 Dewar, *Those Splendid Girls*, 160–63, quotation on 163.

29 Glassford, "Greatest Mother in the World"; Street, "Patriotic, Not Permanent," 164–65.

30 Toman, *Sister Soldiers*, 150–55.

31 Ibid., 158.

32 Susan Mann, ed., *The War Diary of Clare Gass* (Montreal and Kingston: McGill-Queen's University Press, 2000), xxii.

33 Kathryn McPherson, *Bedside Matters: The Transformation of Canadian Nursing, 1900–1990* (Toronto: University of Toronto Press, 2003), 16.

34 Toman, *Sister Soldiers*, 170.

35 Mann, *The War Diary of Clare Gass*, xviii–xix; McPherson, *Bedside Matters*, 15.

36 McPherson, *Bedside Matters*, 15.

37 Morton, *When Your Number's Up*, 183; Toman, *Sister Soldiers*, 43–44.

38 Glassford, "Greatest Mother in the World;" Toman, *Sister Soldiers*, 183; Mann, *The War Diary of Clare Gass*, xxii, xxxiii; Goldstein, *War and Gender*, 308.

39 Sarah Glassford, *Mobilizing Mercy: A History of the Canadian Red Cross* (Montreal and Kingston: McGill-Queen's University Press, 2017), 97–98.

40 Mann, *The War Diary of Clare Gass*, xxv.

41 Toman, *Sister Soldiers*, 160–65, 170–76, 185–86. In *War Torn Exchanges: The Lives and Letters of Nursing Sisters Laura Holland and Mildred Forbes* (Vancouver: UBC Press, 2016), Andrea Mackenzie explores one such relationship in depth.

42 Mrs. Jane Walters, quoted in Daphne Read, ed., *The Great War and Canadian Society: An Oral History* (Toronto: New Hogtown Press, 1978), 147–48.

43 Toman, *Sister Soldiers*, 172, 148–49.

44 Mann, *The War Diary of Clare Gass*, xxii–xxiv.

45 McPherson, *Bedside Matters*, 1, 4.

46 Peter Buitenhuis, *The Great War of Words: British, American, and Canadian Propaganda and Fiction, 1914–1933* (Vancouver: UBC Press, 1987), 12, 27; Jeffrey Keshen, *Propaganda and Censorship during Canada's Great War* (Edmonton: University of Alberta Press, 1996), 14; Goldstein, *War and Gender*, 362–63.

47 Buitenhuis, *The Great War of Words*, 29; Keshen, *Propaganda and Censorship*, 14 (quotation), 20. On the Cavell phenomenon, see Katie Pickles, *Transnational Outrage: The Death and Commemoration of Edith Cavell* (Basingstoke, UK: Palgrave Macmillan, 2007).

48 The significance of these atrocity stories to Canadian understandings of the war is shown by their persistence through the 1920s and 1930s. Jonathan F. Vance, *Death So Noble: Memory, Meaning, and the First World War* (Vancouver: UBC Press, 1997), 20–26.

49 Explored in Goldstein, *War and Gender*, Chapter 6.

50 Amy J. Shaw, *Crisis of Conscience: Conscientious Objection in Canada during the First World War* (Vancouver: UBC Press, 2009), 124–26; Mark Moss, *Manliness and Militarism: Educating Young Boys in Ontario for War* (Don Mills: Oxford University Press, 2001), 14.

51 Keshen, *Propaganda and Censorship*, 128–29; Shaw, *Crisis of Conscience*, 126.

52 Shaw, *Crisis of Conscience*, 121, 126.

53 Nic Clarke, *Unwanted Warriors: The Rejected Volunteers of the Canadian Expeditionary Force* (Vancouver: UBC Press, 2015), 3–5.

54 From a veteran-penned poem in the *Legionary*, April 1932, 7, quoted in Lara Campbell, "'We Who Have Wallowed in the Mud of Flanders': First World War Veterans, Unemployment, and the Development of Social Welfare in Canada, 1929–1939," *Journal of the Canadian Historical Association* 11 (2000): 136.

55 Morton, *When Your Number's Up*, 51–52, 63.

56 Keshen, *Propaganda and Censorship*, x, 13, 16, 31–33.

57 Ibid., xvi, 133.

58 Ibid., 53; Quiney, "Gendering Patriotism," 119; Desmond Morton, *Fight or Pay: Soldiers' Families in the Great War* (Vancouver: UBC Press, 2004), vi; Glassford, *Mobilizing Mercy*, 107, 119.

59 On courts martial and CEF members, see Chapter 11 in this volume.

60 Morton, *When Your Number's Up*, 197–98, 250.

61 Dewar, *Those Splendid Girls*, 145.

62 Dianne Dodd, "Commemorating Canadian Military Nurse Casualties during and after the First World War: Nurses' Perspectives," in *Routledge Handbook on the Global History of Nursing*, ed. Patricia D'Antonio, Julie A. Fairman, and Jean C. Whelan (New York: Routledge, 2013), 55–56, 69.

63 Toman, *Sister Soldiers*, 8.

64 Ibid., 6.

65 Dewar, *Those Splendid Girls*, 131.

66 Morton, *When Your Number's Up*, 181.

67 Mann, *The War Diary of Clare Gass*, xxvi.

68 Mann, *Margaret Macdonald*, 159–61.

69 See Mélanie Morin-Pelletier, *Briser les ailes de l'ange: Les infirmières militaires canadiennes, 1914–1918* (Outrement: Athéna, 2006); and Mélanie Morin-Pelletier, "Héritières de la Grande Guerre: Les infirmières militaires canadiennes durant l'entre-deux-guerres" (PhD diss., University of Ottawa, 2010).

70 Toman, *Sister Soldiers*, 5–6; Dewar, *Those Splendid Girls*, 131; Mann, *The War Diary of Clare Gass*, xxv.

71 Vance, *Death So Noble*, 74–85, 109–10.

72 Ibid., 36–40, 44, 50–51 (quotation), 136, 157, 199.

73 Kathryn McPherson, "Carving Out a Past: The Canadian Nurses' Association War Memorial," *Histoire sociale/Social History* 29, 58 (1996): 417–29.

74 Commonwealth War Graves Commission, "Find War Dead and Cemeteries," https://www.cwgc.org/find-records/find-war-dead/.

75 Toman, *Sister Soldiers*, 212–14; Dewar, *Those Splendid Girls*, 115, 197.

76 Dodd, "Commemorating," 56. There are Edith Cavell schools in Moncton, Vancouver, and St. Catharines. A fourth, in Windsor, Ontario, closed in 1987. Mount Edith Cavell and its associated geographic features and hiking trail are in Alberta's Jasper National Park.

77 Glassford and Shaw, "Conclusion: A 'Sisterhood of Suffering and Service,'" *A Sisterhood of Suffering*, 320–21; Toman, *Sister Soldiers*, 212.

78 Glassford and Shaw, "Introduction," *A Sisterhood of Suffering*, 20.

79 Mark Humphries, "War's Long Shadow: Masculinity, Medicine, and the Gendered Politics of Trauma, 1914–1939," *Canadian Historical Review* 91, 3 (2010): 503–31; Campbell, "'We Who Have Wallowed'"; Desmond Morton and Glenn Wright, *Winning the Second Battle: Canadian Veterans and the Return to Civilian Life, 1915–1930* (Toronto: University of Toronto Press, 1987).

80 Toman, *Sister Soldiers*, 195–97.

81 J. Castell Hopkins, *Canada at War: A Record of Heroism and Achievement* (Toronto: Canadian Annual Review, 1919), 257 (quotation), 246.

8
Religion and the Great War: The Canadian Experience

Gordon L. Heath

IN THE EARLY DAYS OF August 1918, it was obvious to the Allied troops that a big push was imminent. On 4 August, Canadian chaplains conducted a pre-battle day of prayer.[1] There is no list of who attended services, but among those hoping to receive consolation and inspiration could have been Ontario-born lieutenant Solon Albright of the 15th Battalion.[2] The invitation to the services would be his last.

This chapter examines religion and the war, from both the perspective of those in Canada and those at the front, to place Albright's religious identification in context. However, due to the relative paucity of sources from the front and an overabundance of material that originated in Canada, the balance of the analysis will tilt toward the home front. In doing so, it demonstrates that there is no single, straightforward narrative; whereas religion certainly bolstered support for the war effort, it also undermined pervasive national, imperial, and martial narratives and motivated conscientious objectors.

Surprisingly, most accounts of the war either ignore faith and religion outright or merely mention them in passing. Whereas this exclusion may reflect the present-day marginalization of religion from Canadian public life and national vision, it certainly does not do justice to the remarkable influence of the wartime churches or to the religious identity of the young dominion. Increasingly, researchers of religion in Canada are noting the important role that faith has played in public life and, more specifically, in the discourse for and against the Great War.[3] Stated simply, to overlook faith is to ignore one primary way in which soldiers and citizens interpreted their world and gave meaning to its trials and tribulations.[4] Such neglect also masks the work of institutions that invested a remarkable degree of practical support for the war effort, or, conversely, denominations or dissenters that refused to be swept up in the war hype. Regrettably, though great strides have recently been made regarding religion and the war on the home front, there has not been sustained attention to the

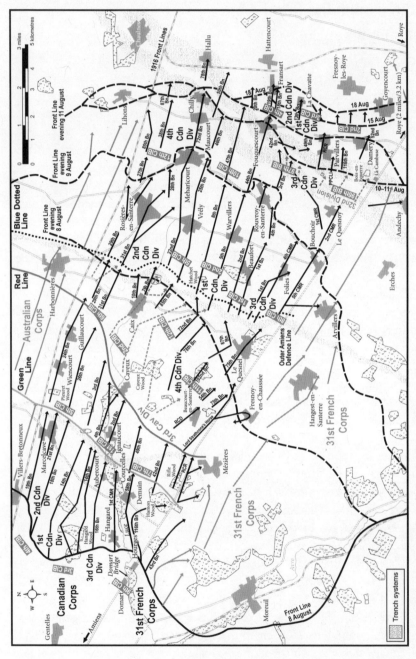

Figure 8.1 Amiens, 8 August 1918. | Map by Mike Bechthold.

faith of Canadian soldiers in the trenches, such as Albright, that has been directed elsewhere to American or British soldiers.[5] All this is not to say that religion was necessarily the sole or even primary motivating factor for enlistment; nor is it a claim that those who identified with this or that denomination on a census form or church membership list were zealous Christians. As Jonathan F. Vance points out in Chapter 2 of this collection, there was a cultural and communal aspect of religion apart from political, theological, or personal convictions. He suggests that "local activities focused not on God, King, and Empire, but on party, picnic, and Christmas concert" (page 52). Nevertheless, the response of organized religion to the war did play a role, not only in personal piety, but also in the public discourse of both clergy and politicians. In addition, religion shaped pervasive notions of masculinity, an idealized "muscular" Christianity that directly influenced motives for enlisting.

Without further evidence, it is difficult to say how seriously Solon Albright took his religious affiliation. On his attestation form of 1916, he professed to be being "Baptist," placing his experiences within the larger religious – and almost exclusively Christian – context of wartime Canada. Canadian churches had an influence on society unlike any other institution at the beginning of the twentieth century, and Protestant and Catholic leaders and organizations were committed to shaping national identity in the decades following Confederation.[6] In 1911, Canada boasted just over 7 million people. Of them, 2,833,000 were Catholics, comprising just under 40 percent of the population. The Methodists, Presbyterians, Anglicans, and Baptists were the largest and most influential Protestant denominations at that time, with 1,079,000 Methodists, 1,115,000 Presbyterians, 1,043,000 Anglicans, and 382,000 Baptists, for a total of just over 50 percent of the population.[7] Lutherans accounted for roughly 3 percent of the population (229,864), with numerous other Christian groups hovering around 1 percent or less.[8] Non-Christian religious groups were relatively small: 74,564 Jews, 14,562 Confucians, 11,840 Pagans, 10,012 Buddhists, 1,758 Sikhs and Hindus, 797 Muslims, 26,027 no religion, and 3,110 agnostics.[9]

Although growing tensions in Europe were noted during the months before the war, and were commented on in denominational papers, synods, presbyteries, and the like, many Canadian religious leaders and congregants entered the summer of 1914 with no idea of the horrors on the horizon. After the insatiable demands of total war touched all aspects of religious life, priests and parishes struggled with meeting the needs of the afflicted, and the losses incurred meant that ministries suffered or were curtailed. Church-based women's groups on the home front did their best to support the war effort while living with uncertainty over the return of sons and husbands.[10] Developing an effective military chaplaincy in the face of government opposition and church squabbling also proved a challenge.[11] The seemingly never-ending carnage could also gnaw at faith in a providential and benevolent God.

It is hard to know how much this affected Albright. Born in 1890 in Berlin, Ontario, to Abraham and Frances Albright, he remained in the city, becoming an accountant and eventually marrying Ruth Margory Steveley in 1916. Together they had a daughter, Ruth Maud Antoinette, in early 1917.[12] In late 1915, Albright enlisted and was cleared for overseas deployment in 1916. He subsequently reverted in rank, which allowed him to be shipped off with his unit just over a year later in 1917.[13] He settled in well with his unit as an officer, gained the respect of his comrades, and proved popular with locals. One memoir remarked that he was among "the most soldierly and best-posted men in the regiment. Is popular with men and officers alike ... The girls all said, 'Too bad he is married.'"[14] Although this provides no "smoking gun" for those who seek to understand why he enlisted, Albright's brief response of "Baptist" gives a glimpse of the role of faith in the experience of Canadians.

As early as October 1914, Ontario and Quebec Baptists pledged to "do everything in our power to support the cause of Great Britain in this present terrible and deplorable war."[15] Wartime stresses and lack of students meant that denominational universities, such as the Baptist McMaster University, experienced a financial crisis due to falling student enrolment.[16] Nonetheless, by 1916, the chancellor of McMaster framed the current conflict as a "stand against oppression and the 'outrageous theology' that one nation is the vice-regent of God charged with the task of 'crucifying' lesser breeds."[17]

It would also seem that other religious bodies enthusiastically and uncritically endorsed the war effort. The four largest British-origin Protestant denominations, as well as French and English Catholics, early and openly expressed their support. Even relatively small and new movements such as the Salvation Army and Mormons followed suit.[18] The most ardent supporters in that spectrum were the Anglicans, and the least enthusiastic were French Quebec Catholics.[19] Despite these differences, the sermons and official statements of all these denominations shared the same content.

Those who endorsed involvement in the war believed that it was being fought for high ideals such as righteousness, freedom, and civilization. Although there were excesses – such as recruitment from pulpits, the discourse of holy war, and even a jingoistic celebration of empire – the churches' attitude was just as often nuanced and critical, shaped by either the classic just war paradigm of just cause (*jus ad bellum*) and just means (*jus in bello*) or pacifism's outright rejection of violence. Church leaders who were imbued with the often radical ideals of the social gospel saw the war not only as a defence of justice in Europe, but also as

Figure 8.2 Captain Solon Albright (centre) with his comrades in Company B of the 118th Battalion, Berlin, Ontario, May 1916. | Courtesy of the Waterloo Historical Society and the Grace Schmidt Room, Kitchener Public Library, P2682.

an opportunity to apply a more radical approach to state control of industry – or morals, in the case of prohibition – for the Christianization of the nation. It was widely anticipated in pulpits and pews that the sacrifice of sons and wealth would lead to a renewed and reinvigorated Christianity and nation, and that the "war to end all wars" would usher in a new world order.[20]

The churches were not monolithic in their response to the conflict, but a number of common themes did dominate their discourse, which citizens and soldiers such as Albright would have encountered on a continual basis. First, the war was being fought for justice or righteousness. In an article titled "The Crusaders," the *Presbyterian Record* declared, "if ever cause of war was holy and right, and worthy of highest, noblest, purest manhood, that cause is the present one."[21] Although it was not always overtly stated as such, the response was cast in traditional "just war" language. One key consideration was that such a war must be fought for defensive purposes, and it was believed in 1914 that the present conflict met that criterion. Germany had initiated hostilities by invading France and Belgium, actions that made it the aggressor and the British cause one of legitimate justice. Furthermore, the "scrap of paper" that the German chancellor Theobald von Bethmann-Hollweg had so cavalierly dismissed was viewed in Britain and in Canada as a compelling legal obligation to come to the defence of beleaguered Belgium.[22] The nature of the invasion also generated a fervent sense of moral obligation to defend Belgium. Accounts of the German Army's conduct during its advance through that country played an important role in galvanizing popular opinion. The sinking of passenger ships such as the *Lusitania* seemed to confirm suspicions of German barbarism, and thus the moral obliga-tion to fight against such injustice was strengthened. The war against the Muslim Ottoman Turks was also cast in this light and as a just cause due to the hor-rendous mistreatment of the Christian Armenians within their borders.[23] The Armenian genocide started in April 1915, and estimates of the disaster usually range between 1 and 1.5 million deaths.[24] Commentary in the four largest Protestant churches stressed that defeating Germany meant an end to genocide by the Turks.[25]

Second, the war was framed in the language of purging and renewal. Since the latter part of the nineteenth century, apprehension had been expressed in the press and pulpits regarding the moral condition of British society. This had been a concern in the early months of the South African War and had become more pressing during the Great War. Had the sins of the past and present finally caught up with Britain and its empire? Religious leaders called for national days of prayer and repentance. Simultaneously, churches advocated daily spirit-ual renewal and revival to battle against national sins, thus transforming the young country of Canada into a truly Christian one. Robert A. Wright argues that the churches hoped that the war would contribute to many of their social reform aims: the elimination of oppression, an increased spirit of sacrifice among citizens, the establishment of a more cooperative and less exploitive way of doing business, and a removal of class barriers.[26] In this way, the social gospel agenda and the war effort were amalgamated.[27] The concern for moral purity also worked its way to the front. Military chaplains had a number of responsibilities, including regular hospital visits. When Albright was hospital-ized for bronchitis and a number of times with trench fever, he would have had access to a chaplain.[28] However, chaplains did more than simply console the troops; they dealt with the moral turpitude of the CEF. With his comrades, Albright would often have been obliged to listen as chaplains exhorted them to honour their Christian confession by avoiding brothels, blasphemy, and other such sins.[29]

Third, the war-related discourse of the churches was permeated with assumptions, terms, and aspirations regarding nation and empire. For instance, Samuel D. Chown, the Methodist general superintendent, published an open letter in the *Christian Guardian* that stressed the rectitude of fighting for both righteousness and empire: "We are persuaded that this war is just, honorable and necessary in defence of the principle of righteousness and the freedom of our Empire in all its parts."[30] Blending spiritual metaphors with empire, one commentator in the *Wesleyan* claimed that Canadian mothers were expected to offer up their sons on the Altar of God, nation, and empire.[31] And as Murray Angus notes, there was a sense that, when fighting for King George, one was also fighting for King Jesus.[32] English-speaking Catholic Church leaders were enthusiastic supporters of the empire too. For instance, Bishop Alexander MacDonald of Victoria proclaimed,

> Canada is a part of the British Empire. Canadians are British subjects; we are all under the manifold obligation to the Motherland; the parliament of our country has decided by unanimous vote to discharge, some measure, our obligation. It is, I conceive, the strict duty of every citizen of Canada to respect that act of our parliament ... The present crisis to my mind, is emphatically one in which the words of our Blessed Lord find an appropriate application: "He that is not for me is against me, and he that not gathereth with Me scattereth."[33]

Another Catholic bishop, Michael Francis Fallon of London, Ontario, believed that the war provided an opportunity for his flock to develop an identity as patriotic citizens, and his endorsement of it must be seen through the lens of what Adrian Ciani calls his "tripartite loyalties": to the British Empire, to Ireland and Irish Catholics, and to Roman Catholicism.[34] Declarations of loyalty to the empire were also part of the French Quebec Catholic hierarchy's rhetoric. Prominent clergy such as Montreal archbishop Paul Bruchési and Quebec cardinal Louis-Nazaire Bégin all spoke in favour of the war effort, and Quebec bishops signed a pastoral letter in support of it to be read in all churches.[35]

A second glance, however, reveals that wartime religion was far from uniform. Albright listed himself as a Baptist, but one cannot assume that all Baptists – or all Protestants – shared the same view of the conflict. In fact, there was significant diversity in and between various denominations. Religious views were remarkably similar and static in many cases, but they were also fluid, adaptive, and contradictory, and they evolved over time and circumstances. Opinions differed widely, even among organizations that formally supported the war effort. As for those denominations or persons who opposed it, harsh criticism from others led to disruptions, divisions, and resentments that lingered long after the guns went silent.

Positions on the war evolved for a variety of reasons. The most immediate *volte-face* was by Ukrainian Catholic bishop Nykyta Budka. As tensions rose in July 1914, he circulated a pastoral letter urging immigrants to return to eastern Europe to fight for the Austro-Hungarian Empire. Soon afterward, when Canada went to war against that very empire, he retracted his message. However, as will be discussed below, his initial statement made things quite difficult for eastern Europeans and Catholics, whose loyalty remained suspect throughout the war.[36]

Reports of German atrocities and Turkish genocide shifted the church discourse from a just war to a holy war. As hostilities churned on, accounts of German and Turkish misconduct were commented on in the media, and the cause became a holy crusade to end the evils of tyrannical rulers and save Western civilization from the spread of barbarism. To cite but one case, the sermons of Presbyterian minister Thomas Eakin changed their emphasis from just war to holy war.[37] Trips to the front also militarized the views of some clergymen; this was true for Methodist Samuel D. Chown, who visited the front in 1917, and for Baptist T.T. Shields, who did so in 1915, 1917, and 1918.[38]

French Quebec Catholic attitudes altered in response to changes in government policy. Roman Catholics were criticized by English Canadians for being unpatriotic and for failing to carry their fair share of the war effort. Tensions were exacerbated when all four of the largest Protestant denominations officially sided with the Borden government's controversial decision to revoke its promise and implement conscription.[39] This move rankled Quebec Catholics, who saw it as a betrayal, and the Quebec clergy withdrew its support from the Borden government to match popular resentment, even though it had earlier issued statements to sanction the war effort. This reversal was a significant departure from the hierarchy's historic support for government.[40]

After the Armistice, there was a radical swing in the churches away from wartime perspectives. Within a few years, the writings of clergy and denominational statements were widely and openly voicing approval for pacifism. Their mood reflected the pervasive disappointment that no brave new world had been born from the war to end all wars.[41]

The four largest Protestant denominations expressed approval for the war effort, but military recruitment from their ranks varied considerably, and support was soft in some cases. Anglicans made up more than 46 percent of the CEF, Presbyterians followed with close to 20 percent, Methodists at just over 10 percent, and Baptists at slightly above 5 percent. Anglicans were proud of their prominent role, but the Methodist leadership was embarrassed by the low numbers of Methodist volunteers and responded by establishing the Army and

Navy Board in 1915. After more than a year of work by the board, Methodist volunteers had reached only 10 percent, as mentioned above.[42]

Artifacts, diaries, and correspondence can reveal why individuals enthusiastically joined the CEF,[43] but personal letters can also provide some insight into reticence. None of Solon Albright's letters survived the war, but other correspondence shows that the decision of whether to enlist could be difficult. Such was the case for the letters between Reverend James H. White, the Methodist Home Missions superintendent, and his sons. One son wrote in November 1915, "It is certainly hard to know just what is the wisest thing to do. Personally, I am not at all anxious to enlist, if I did it would be from a pure sense of duty and not that I was keen to go." He never did join up. Another son wrote in December 1915 that – despite White's advice that it was unnecessary to enlist – he was torn over what to do and did not want to bring shame to the family. He eventually enlisted, partially because he fearing getting squeezed out of jobs when veterans returned en masse after the war. Filled with pathos, the letters give a glimpse of the struggles over whether or not to enlist, even in a prominent religious family.[44]

In sanctioning the war effort, churches often took quite nuanced positions, which should give pause to anyone who feels tempted to make sweeping and simple generalizations on the topic. First, despite their approval for conscription, the Protestant denominational papers did not resort to the vicious anti–French Canadian rhetoric that characterized much of the secular press.[45] In addition, their pro-conscription stance was not unqualified. The Military Service Act of 1917, which initiated conscription, needed to be applied with care and maybe even revised, as in the case of farmers who needed help on their farms.[46] More significantly, some denominational publications saw the Wartime Elections Act of the same year as sheerest folly. It enfranchised the wives, mothers, and sisters of Canadian soldiers who were serving overseas while simultaneously disenfranchising many Canadians who had emigrated from enemy countries. The papers argued that extending the vote to some women while excluding others was indefensible, that revoking the privileges of enfranchised immigrant Canadians was an affront to the principles for which Canada and the empire were fighting, and that the act could set a dangerous precedent for the future.[47] Second, though the papers may have favoured participation in the war, they often printed dissenting positions through articles or letters to the editor.[48] Sometimes the editors criticized the opinions expressed in their own papers, but they provided a platform for their critics nonetheless. Not every reader appreciated editorial perspectives. When the *Christian Guardian* voiced outspoken support for conscription, significant numbers dropped their subscription in protest.[49] Third, the papers were greatly concerned about the growth of militarism in Canada. They had articulated their unease during the South African War, but it became more pressing in the Great War. Concomitant with the jingoistic excesses emanating from pulpit and church press were calls for restraint lest Canada become tainted by the militarism that had corrupted Europe (and especially Germany).[50] A distinction between jingoism and imperialism was often made by clergy and commentators, for true imperialism sought to bless nations, whereas jingoism or militarism sought to exploit. Fourth, the habit of praying to God for victory was not without its critics. As Melissa Davidson notes, Anglicans debated extensively over the appropriateness of this practice.[51] The debate indicates that not every clergyman embraced the "God and Empire" rhetoric that was prevalent among some leaders and in the liturgy. Thus, though we can correctly state that certain denominations approved the war effort, the examples mentioned above demonstrate that there was a range of support, and any statements about them need to be suitably nuanced.

Yet another complicating factor when it came to religion and the war was that of ethnicity, an issue certainly encountered by those of German background, such as Albright. Whereas denominational affiliation played a role in enlistment, country of birth seems to have been equally significant: during the early year of the war, most CEF recruits were British-born.[52] A letter from Captain Bellenden S. Hutcheson reveals the pull of ethnic ties:

> You ask concerning my motives for joining the Canadian army: They were rather mixed. In the first place, I was in great sympathy with the Allied cause, secondly I am chiefly of English descent; my great grandfather served under Lord Nelson and lost an eye in the battle of Trafalgar and my paternal grandfather came to the U.S. from England in the 1840's and was Captain and adjutant on a New York regiment during the Civil War.[53]

However, one must be cautious about making assumptions regarding ethnic loyalties and attitudes. Mark McGowan notes that Catholicism was not confined solely to French Canadians, and that almost 700,000 English-speaking Catholics (mainly Irish) lived in Canada.[54] In that community, support for the war effort permeated commentary in the pulpit, religious press, and lay organizations. In fact, the level of English-speaking Catholic enlistment resembled that of English Canada. However, English-speaking Catholics were often subject to the exasperating misperception that they were disloyal. It was a case of guilt by association. Protestant English Canadians were upset by the lack of support for the war among Quebec French Catholics, and though some distinguished between French and Irish Catholics,[55] many simply assumed that both shared the same antipathy to the empire and the war.

An example of the mounting suspicion regarding those who opposed militarization came on 7 June 1918, when the Jesuit Novitiate of St. Stanislaus near Guelph, Ontario, was raided by military police, ostensibly in search of draft evaders. Although Albright was overseas at the time, it is fair to assume that he would have learned of this episode because it received so much attention in the Canadian press and because Guelph lay only twenty-five kilometres from his family in Kitchener.[56] Besides illustrating the problems between government agencies and the bungling of the application of the Military Service Act, the raid reveals the simmering tensions between Protestants and Catholics. English (Protestant) Canadians had long condemned Catholics for failing to endorse the war effort. However, with the 1917 inception of the Military Service Act, their fears and outrage intensified, and rumours spread over alleged Catholic disloyalty and attempts to avoid conscription.[57] In Guelph, local Orangemen and clergy from the Guelph Ministerial Association focused on the students at the Jesuit seminary, claiming that it was hiding conscription evaders. Seeking to appease a powerful southern Ontario Protestant lobby, Minister of Militia and Defence Sydney Mewburn issued an order that led to Captain A.C. Macauley's raid. At dusk, Macauley and his men surrounded the building, carried out a search, interrogated residents, and arrested three young men (one of whom was Marcus Doherty, son of the federal justice minister, Charles Doherty).

Macauley's aggressive actions were more than Mewburn had intended, and the government was quickly forced to backtrack. After a flurry of communication between church, military, and government authorities, Macauley was ordered to retreat empty-handed. Nothing nefarious was discovered at the school, and none of its students turned out to be slackers posing as candidates for the priesthood; the raid's sole achievement was to exacerbate the animosity between Protestants and Catholics. Hoping to avert a public-relations fiasco, the government prohibited any reporting on the event. Within weeks, however, newspapers across the nation weighed in on the raid, politicians debated in Parliament, church leaders preached sermons, and a royal commission was struck to sort out the mess. Defenders of the raid saw it as an attempt to protect the British ideals of fair play and loyalty to the imperial cause, whereas critics saw it as yet another example of anti-Catholicism. Over a year later, newspapers were still discussing the event.[58]

A number of smaller Protestant groups encountered questions and fears related to their ethnic identity and national loyalty.[59] No research has been carried out specifically on German Baptist attitudes to the war, though Norm Threinen notes that "German Lutherans volunteered for war service but they generally lacked the great enthusiasm of the British, and they responded to the war effort more out of a sense of duty than patriotism." Official statements by the Lutheran clergy and church structures did voice support for the cause. In June 1915, the Central Canada Synod passed a patriotic resolution: "We commend the hearty loyalty of our people to our beloved British Empire in the present war crisis. Our loyalty as Lutherans to the flag of the country whose protection we enjoy is historic."[60] The Lutherans also expressed their loyalty by supporting relief and patriotic funds. Despite such public declarations, however, they could not escape the difficult fact that they were German and were thus categorized as enemy aliens by the government and many citizens. The anti-German nativist pressures that prompted the city of Berlin to change its name to Kitchener in 1916 significantly motivated those who enlisted to demonstrate their loyalty to nation and empire, one of whom might have been Solon Albright, as he was of German descent.[61]

Further incidents underline the importance of contemporary anti-German feelings. On 16 February 1916, following a recruitment rally in Albright's hometown, civilians and a group of soldiers from the 118th battalion broke into the offices of the Concordia Club, a German social organization, and vandalized the building, This vandalism was repeated in May when soldiers broke into the Acadian Club, a social organization for single German men in the neighbouring town of Waterloo, and destroyed considerable property. In a July letter to the under secretary of militia affairs, the club's president noted that "when this occurrence took place, twenty-eight of the members had already enlisted, while four others were rejected as medically unfit."[62] Federally, the Wartime Elections Act, passed on 20 September 1917, stated that all Germans in Canada who had been naturalized after 31 March 1902 were "enemy aliens" and were stripped of their right to vote. This was followed with an Order-in-Council on 2 October 1918 in which the government prohibited publication of any newspaper in German.[63] Included in this ban were German church papers that were published by the Lutheran bodies in the United States but could not legally be imported into Canada. Throughout the war, Lutherans experienced hostility and abuse, and many lost jobs and fled to rural German communities, all this despite the fact that the Lutheran clergy publicly approved of the war effort.

Many Catholic or Orthodox Ukrainians sought to enlist but were rejected because of their status as enemy aliens.[64] Some did manage to join up, often by giving false information regarding their country of origin. However, this did not readily win them acceptance by the dominant Anglo-Saxon communities or the federal government. Eastern Europeans had begun to arrive in Canada in noticeable numbers by the 1890s.[65] It is difficult to determine how their religion initially informed their understanding of Canada's national and imperial identity. Bishop Budka's retraction of his pastoral letter indicates support for the nation and empire at the highest ecclesiastical level. In it, he stated,

This is our great duty, to stand in the defence of Canada, because this is the country that embraced us, gave protection under the banner of freedom of the British Empire ... This is our sacred obligation, to be ready to give our possessions and blood for the good of Canada, because this is our new homeland, to which we pledged our faith.[66]

For some in the Ukrainian community, this should have assuaged fears.

Budka's comment was clearly a positive statement of support, but everyone remained too focused on his earlier pastoral letter to notice his retraction. Government officials, as well as newspaper editors, columnists, and letter writers, frequently expressed alarm at the influx of non-British immigrants, whom they saw as undermining Canada's imperial identity and loyalty.[67] As one critic claimed, "you cannot make Anglo-Saxondom of Doukhobors, Galicians, and Finns"; their arrival thwarted attempts to "build up a race which shall hold and develop Canada for the Empire."[68] The grim reality was that, for some, the ethnic and religious identity of eastern Europeans simply did not fit the nationalistic visions of an Anglo-Saxon Canada that was firmly situated within the empire.[69] Even socially conscious churchmen, such as J.S. Woodsworth, could espouse this view.[70] Sadly, despite ample displays of patriotism for the imperial cause, and supportive statements such as Budka's, roughly eighty thousand Ukrainians had to register as enemy aliens, and over eight thousand (mainly young men, but some women and children) were rounded up into twenty-four concentration camps.[71]

More research is needed into the views and actions of non-Europeans or non-Christians in Canada, in particular how their religion shaped visions of national and imperial identity. What little work has been done on Canada's black community indicates that black Baptists in the Maritimes expressed significant support for the war effort. For instance, a sermon at the African Baptist Association meeting in Bridgewater, Nova Scotia, was summarized by a listener:

With the war as an outstanding theme for the base of his remarks he dwelt on the criticalness of the present age ... He pictured the relationship of Pharaoh with the children in Israel to the Kaiser's attitude toward the allied nations, but history records that God has ever been on the side of right. Blessed is he who stands firmly for the right.[72]

The Allies were seen as standing for the right. Reverend William White, the black Baptist chaplain for the 2nd Construction Battalion (Coloured), echoed similar themes in his preaching in France.[73] More than a decade earlier, First

Nations men had fought for Canada in the South African War, a trajectory that continued into the First World War (3,500 Indigenous people served overseas).[74] As Evan J. Habkirk makes clear in Chapter 5 of this volume, Wilfred Lickers was but one of the First Nations soldiers who served with distinction in the CEF, at a time when government policy persisted in marginalizing and infantilizing Indigenous men.[75] In similar fashion, much as they did during the South African War, Canadian Jews responded with widespread support for the war effort.[76] It is estimated that roughly 2,600 to 4,300 Jews served overseas in the CEF.[77] Nonetheless, ethnic and religious minorities faced obstacles to enlistment and often suffered discrimination once in the CEF.[78] Their relatively small numbers also complicated issues related to chaplaincy at the front: a Metis chaplain could not find a placement and was sent back to Canada; a Jewish chaplain was ruled out because there were not enough Jews in a single unit to justify the posting.[79]

Adding yet another layer to the complexity was the fact that some denominations were theologically committed to a pacifist position.[80] Confronted with the problem of what to do with those who sought to opt out of military service for religious reasons, the government sought to strike a balance between preserving religious liberty and marshalling resources for the waging of total war. In reality, however, it enacted troubling measures of censorship, spying on enemy aliens, creating internment camps, and imprisoning conscientious objectors.[81] The historic peace churches, such as the Quakers and Mennonites, had a centuries-long history of opposition to participating in any military conflict, and their response to the Great War did not depart from it (although a number of men did break ranks and enlist – much to the chagrin of their religious communities). Both denominations had made previous arrangements with the Canadian government concerning their stance on war, which the government respected during the early years of hostilities. However, as the casualty lists grew, those who were not willing to "carry their fair share" of the nation's burden became the focus of resentment. Robynne Healey notes that the Quakers and Mennonites received quite different responses from the populace at large.[82] Though both were criticized, Quakers, with their Anglo-Celtic heritage and tradition of public engagement, encountered less antipathy than the Mennonites, with their German heritage and tradition of isolation. Mennonites were also affected by the War Measures Act of 1914, which, among other things, banned German-language publications, a significant hardship for a community whose mother tongue was German. The passing of the Military Service Act in 1917 meant that conscription was imminent, and the Mennonites' status under the act was uncertain for a time.[83] The Non-Resistant Relief Organization was created late in 1917 to unite the relief efforts of the Mennonites, Tunkers, and Amish, as well as to guard their interests.[84] Despite their participation in alternative service, conscientious objectors were deeply resented by many who had sacrificed for the cause.

Another mistreated religious body was the tiny movement of fewer than six hundred people called the Bible Students (eventually known as Jehovah's Witnesses).[85] Their position was decidedly anti-war, and they refused to enlist. As a result, they were subject to government censorship and were denied formal recognition as a legitimate religion, thus disqualifying them from claiming conscientious objector status. Their literature was banned, homes raided, and members fined or imprisoned. Because they publicly criticized clergy who endorsed the war effort, a number of Protestant and Catholic clergy approved of the government's repressive policy. Things would only get worse for the Bible Students in the Second World War.

It is in this context of religious and ethnic tensions that the experiences of the soldiers on the front lines must be interpreted. In the early months of 1918, the prospects for victory had looked bleak. Whereas the war against Germany and its allies had been relatively successful on the oceans and in German colonies,[86] years of offensives on the Western Front had gained little and cost much. Even the highly touted Canadian victory at Vimy Ridge (1917) seemingly did little, if anything, to hasten the advent of peace, and as Peter Farrugia points out in Chapter 4 of this volume, the military and political establishment initially doubted that Vimy was Canada's most significant contribution to the conflict. The collapse of Russia in 1917 also meant that Germany could transfer significant forces to the western theatre of operations and launch a massive offensive early in 1918. There were even rumblings on the domestic front about cost and conscription. The only real bright light on the horizon was the entrance of the United States into the war in April 1917 and the promised arrival of American troops.

By the summer of 1918, the military situation looked much more auspicious. The Allies had managed to contain the great German spring offensives, albeit with great difficulty, and began to consider offensive operations against a weakening and over-extended German Army. One such operation was an attack near Amiens in Picardy, France. The Battle of Amiens (8–12 August 1918), also known as the Third Battle of Picardy, was the beginning of a series of offensives that are often referred to as the Hundred Days. Their aim was to expel German troops from occupied France and Belgium. As in previous assaults, chaplains conducted pre-battle services, which offered inspiration, comfort, and consolation for those such as Albright who were about to face the horrors of modern war.

The battle itself is noteworthy for a number of reasons. On the first day, the Allied troops made gains of up to eight miles, a dazzling improvement on previous offensives, where advances were measured in yards. Good planning played a major role in the success of the operation. Secrecy was critical, and great efforts were taken to ensure that the Germans did not learn of the operation or of the arrival of the Canadians. In fact, a Canadian unit was sent north to Flanders to suggest to German intelligence that the Canadian Corps was transferring to that front. The last of the Canadian soldiers arrived at Amiens the day before the battle was scheduled to start, bearing in mind that for days their paybook had carried the clear instruction "KEEP YOUR MOUTH SHUT," so as not to give away their position.[87] A second reason for success was a rethinking of tactics. Extensive use of aerial photography ensured the accuracy of artillery.[88] To further guarantee surprise, the traditional days-long bombardment was dropped, and as the troops quickly advanced, catching the Germans unaware, artillery was used to take out German guns rather than to soften up trenches and fortifications. It then shifted to a creeping barrage, behind which the troops advanced. The extensive use of tanks was the final tactical innovation that contributed to the stunning success. With tank support, infantry could advance into the teeth of extensive fire, and using tanks en masse was an important development that helped to break the stalemate of trench warfare and to create a more fluid battlefield.

The plan at Amiens was for the Canadian Corps to advance with the British Fourth Army on the far left, the Australian Corps on the immediate left flank of the Canadians (this was the first time the two colonial corps would fight side-by-side), and the First French Army on the right. In the opening hours of the battle, Albright moved forward with his platoon, through a heavy fog. The men advanced swiftly, but after coming under heavy fire, many lay wounded. Albright began to provide first aid but was quickly injured himself by artillery shells and machine-gun fire. He was hit in the head, both arms, and left leg. His men carried him back from the front to receive medical attention, but his wounds were too severe and he died the next day. For Albright, the much touted Battle of Amiens had lasted barely twenty-four hours.[89]

The willingness of over fifteen thousand German soldiers to surrender prompted German general Erich Ludendorff to describe the opening of the offensive as the "schwarzer Tag des deutschen Heeres" (black day of the German Army).[90] The battle raged for a few more days but with only minimal gains. Amiens is considered a major turning point in the war, and the cascade of Allied offensives that followed it advanced northeast toward the German border. Canadians prided themselves on participating in the Battle of Amiens, but that claim to fame came at a cost. The CEF experienced close to twelve thousand casualties, with almost four thousand of those on the first day.[91] One of those casualties was Solon Albright. Concerning his role in the battle, the battalion's war diary stated, "Lieut. Albright, who afterwards died of his wounds was a particularly capable officer and his works throughout the day had been marked by great coolness and daring."[92]

THROUGHOUT THE GREAT WAR, religion played a multi-faceted role. It also regularly provided comfort for the grieving. In the final months of hostilities, Canadians pored over newspaper accounts of the Battle of Amiens, celebrated yet another demonstration of Canada's prowess, and even read of such exploits in their denominational papers.[93] In the midst of the glowing reports, Ruth Albright received a terse notice of her husband's death, as well as $240 from the Canadian government for his sacrifice.[94] Thus, she joined the swelling ranks of widows who were left responsible for a child,[95] and she probably followed the path of tens of thousands who sought assistance from pastors or priests. In such cases, the role of religion shifted from that of motivation to consolation. That consolation carried over into the post-war years, when religious services and memorials contributed to the construction of memory, meaning, and myth that provided hope in the midst of agony, uncertainty, and despair.[96] As for Albright's local Baptist church, it proudly claimed ownership of him and its other thirty-one congregants who enlisted.[97]

Despite the great hopes and aspirations of soldiers such as Albright, or distraught widows such as Ruth, who longed to find some comfort and meaning in the sacrifice of her husband, the war led to neither a reinvigorated faith nor

Figure 8.3 Plaque commemorating Solon Albright's sacrifice in the Great War, Highland Baptist Church, Kitchener, Ontario. | Photo by Peter Farrugia.

to peace. There was no radical post-war decline in religion, but neither was there a widespread revival. People returned to life as best they could and, in many cases, sought solace in religion and religious communities. The much anticipated "end to war" was also elusive, for the Treaty of Versailles (1919) and the League of Nations (1919) failed to solve intractable problems. The interwar period was marked by a reconsideration of support for war, and at the outbreak of the Second World War, many religious bodies, sobered by their post-war experience, entered the new conflict chastened though generally supportive of the war effort.

Notes

1 Duff Crerar, *Padres in No Man's Land: Canadian Chaplains and the Great War* (Montreal and Kingston: McGill-Queen's University Press, 1995), 131.
2 See Library and Archives Canada (LAC), Canadian Expeditionary Force (CEF), RG 150, accession 1992-93/166, box 70–35, Solon Albright personnel file. Like many soldiers in the Canadian Expeditionary Force, Albright did not remain in a single unit throughout the war. He enlisted with the 118th Battalion on 27 November 1915 and was later transferred to the 241st Battalion, which was subsequently folded into the 5th Reserve Battalion on 7 May 1917. Finally, on 28 August 1917, he was taken on strength with the 15th Battalion, with whom he would fight at Amiens a little under a year later. See LAC, Solon Albright personnel file, Casualty Form Active Service, 43.
3 For instance, see Marguerite Van Die, ed., *Religion and Public Life in Canada: Historical and Comparative Perspectives* (Toronto: University of Toronto Press, 2001); Gary Miedema, *For Canada's Sake: Public Religion, Centennial Celebrations, and the Re-making of Canada in the 1960s* (Montreal and Kingston: McGill-Queen's University Press, 2005); Gordon L. Heath and Paul Wilson, eds., *Baptists and Public Life in Canada* (Eugene: Pickwick, 2012); and Gordon L. Heath, ed., *Canadian Churches and the First World War* (Eugene: Pickwick, 2014).
4 Richard M. Gamble, *The War for Righteousness: Progressive Christianity, the Great War, and the Rise of the Messianic Nation* (Wilmington: ISI, 2003); Philip Jenkins, *The Great and Holy War: How World War I Became a Religious Crusade* (New York: Harper One, 2014). Duff Crerar's *Padres in No Man's Land*, an examination of Canadian chaplains at the front, is one of the most helpful accounts of front-line religion.
5 Jonathan H. Ebel, *Faith in the Fight: Religion and the American Soldier in the Great War* (Princeton: Princeton University Press, 2010); Michael Snape, *God and the British Soldier: Religion and the British Army in the First and Second World Wars* (New York: Routledge, 2005).
6 For instance, see Phyllis D. Airhart, "Ordering a Nation and Reordering Protestantism, 1867–1914," in *The Canadian Protestant Experience, 1760–1990*, ed. George Rawlyk (Burlington: Welch, 1990), 98–138; Terence Fay, *A History of Canadian Catholics: Gallicanism, Romanism, and Canadianism* (Montreal and Kingston: McGill-Queen's University Press, 2002); and Mark G. McGowan, "Rendering unto Caesar: Catholics, the State, and the Idea of a Christian Canada," *Canadian Society Church History Historical Papers* (2011): 65–85.
7 *Bulletin XII. Fifth Census of Canada: Religions of Canada for the Year 1911 as Enumerated Under Date of First June* (Ottawa: Census and Statistics Office, 1913).
8 Ibid. Smaller Christian denominations included 88,507 Greek Church, 18,834 Salvation Army, 15,971 Mormons, 10,493 Doukhobors, and dozens of other even smaller groups.

9 Ibid. These headings are the actual ones used in the census.

10 Lucille Marr, "Paying 'the Price of War': Canadian Women and the Churches on the Home Front," in Heath, *Canadian Churches*, 263–83; Penny Bedal and Ross Bartlett, "The Women Do Not Speak: The Methodist Ladies' Aid Societies and World War I," *Canadian Methodist Historical Society Papers* 10 (1993–94): 63–86.

11 See Crerar, *Padres in No Man's Land;* and Duff Crerar, "Dismissed: Military Chaplains and Canadian Great War History," in Heath, *Canadian Churches*, 241–62.

12 Jeff Outhit, "'Daring' Officer Left His Wife, Daughter Behind," *Waterloo Regional Record*, 30 May 2014, https://www.therecord.com/news/waterloo-region/2014/05/30/daring -officer-left-his-wife-daughter-behind.html.

13 It does appear that Albright was invested in the cause of war, although it remains unclear what motivated his actions in this regard. What is clear is that, on 10 August 1917, he reverted to the rank of lieutenant from captain, in order to see action more quickly. LAC, Solon Albright personnel file, Casualty Form Active Service, 42/48.

14 William T. Gregory, *From Camp to Hammock with the Canadian Scottish Borderers* (Leamington, ON: Post News, 1917), 19.

15 "The Patriotic Resolution," *Canadian Baptist*, 5 November 1914, 8, quoted in Michael A.G. Haykin and Ian Clary, "'O God of Battles': The Canadian Baptist Experience of the Great War," in Heath, *Canadian Churches*, 174.

16 Charles M. Johnston, *McMaster University: The Toronto Years* (Toronto: University of Toronto Press, 1976), Chapter 7.

17 Haykin and Clary, "'O God of Battles,'" 174.

18 The Salvation Army's endorsement was ubiquitous; from chaplains to canteens, its members seemed everywhere in support of the war effort. As for Mormons and the war, see Howard Palmer, "Polygamy and Progress: The Reaction to Mormons in Canada, 1887–1923," in *The Mormon Presence in Canada*, ed. Brigham Y. Card et al. (Edmonton: University of Alberta Press, 1990), 124.

19 The enrolment statistics for the CEF show how men in the pew responded to exhortations to join up. In 1917, Anglican enlistment was the most impressive, with 12–16 percent of all Anglicans in uniform, the highest percentage among Protestants. Simon Jolivet notes the need to distinguish between French Catholics in Quebec and French Catholics elsewhere in Canada. He argues that enrolment in Quebec differed from that in the rest of Canada and the rest of French Canada: French Quebec Canadians comprised only 2 percent of the CEF, and of the thirty-five thousand French Canadians in the CEF only fifteen thousand came from Quebec. Jolivet suggests that French Canadian enrolment outside of Quebec mirrored that of English Canada. Also noteworthy is that the enrolment figures of Quebec were low despite the fact that the province's higher clergy supported the war, and official statements encouraged enlistment. See Simon Jolivet, "French-Speaking Catholics in Quebec and the First World War," in Heath, *Canadian Churches*, 75–101; Mark G. McGowan, "'We Are All Involved in the Same Issue': Canada's English-Speaking Catholics and the Great War," in Heath, *Canadian Churches*, 65; Mark G. McGowan, *The Imperial Irish: Canada's Irish Catholics Fight the Great War, 1914–1918* (Montreal and Kingston: McGill-Queen's University Press, 2017); Melissa Davidson, "The Anglican Church and the Great War," in Heath, *Canadian Churches*, 153; David B. Marshall, "'Khaki Has Become a Sacred Colour': The Methodist Church and the Sanctification of World War One," in Heath, *Canadian Churches*, 114; Robert Craig Brown and Donald Loveridge, "Unrequited Faith: Recruiting and the CEF, 1914–1918," *Canadian Military History* 24, 1 (Winter/Spring, 2015): 61–87. Desmond Morton, *When Your Number's Up: The Canadian Soldier in the First World War* (Toronto: Random House, 1993); René Durocher, "Henri Bourassa, les évêques et la guerre de 1914–1918," *Canadian Historical Association Papers*

6, 1 (1971): 254–69; and Chris Sharpe, "Enlistment in the Canadian Expeditionary Force, 1914–1918: A Re-evaluation," *Canadian Military History* 24, 1 (2015): 17–60.

20 For an examination of millenarianism resulting from the Great War, see Kyle Falcon, "The Ghost Story of the Great War: Spiritualism, Psychical Research and the British War Experience, 1914–1939" (PhD diss., Wilfrid Laurier University, 2018), 41–45.

21 "The Crusaders," *Presbyterian Record,* March 1915. Methodism's response to the Great War has received the most attention from historians. Marshall, "Khaki Has Become," 102–32. See also David Marshall, "Methodism Embattled: A Reconsideration of the Methodist Church and World War I," *Canadian Historical Review* 66 (March 1985): 48–64; Bedal and Bartlett, "Women Do Not Speak"; Robert MacDonald, "The Methodist Church in Alberta during the First World War," *Canadian Methodist Historical Society Papers* 10 (1994): 145–69; and Samuel J. Richards, "Ministry of Propaganda: Canadian Methodists, Empire, and Loyalty in World War I" (master's thesis, Salisbury University, 2007).

22 The Treaty of London (1839), signed by Britain, required signatory nations to defend the territorial integrity of Belgium.

23 Gordon L. Heath, "'Thor and Allah in a Hideous, Unholy Confederacy': The Armenian Genocide in the Canadian Protestant Press," in *The Globalization of Christianity: Implications for Christian Ministry and Theology,* ed. Steve Studebaker and Gordon L. Heath (Eugene: Pickwick, 2014), 105–28.

24 Vahakn N. Dadrian, *The History of the Armenia Genocide: Ethnic Conflict from the Balkans to Anatolia to the Caucasus* (New York: Berghahn Books, 2003). To be added to these figures are approximately 250,000 Assyro-Chaldeans of the Church of the East who died in battle or were massacred. See David Gaunt, *Massacres, Resistance, Protectors: Muslim-Christian Relations in Eastern Anatolia during World War I* (Piscataway: Gorgias, 2006).

25 As of yet, there has been no examination of Canadian Catholics and the genocide.

26 Robert A. Wright, "The Canadian Protestant Tradition, 1914–1945," in Rawlyk, *The Canadian Protestant,* 143–45.

27 Richard Allen, *The Social Passion: Religion and Social Reform in Canada, 1914–28* (Toronto: University of Toronto Press, 1973).

28 Albright's medical records indicate that he suffered from PUO (commonly referred to as trench fever) in February and March 1918.

29 Crerar, *Padres in No Man's Land;* McGowan, *The Imperial Irish,* Chapter 4.

30 *Christian Guardian,* 16 September 1914, quoted in J.M. Bliss, "The Methodist Church and World War I," *Canadian Historical Review* 49, 3 (September 1968): 215.

31 *Wesleyan,* 21 June 1916, quoted in Murray E. Angus, "King Jesus and King George: The Manly Christian Patriot and the Great War, 1914–1918," *Papers of the Canadian Methodist Historical Society,* 12 (1997–98): 128.

32 Angus, "King Jesus," 124–32.

33 *Casket,* 12 November 1914, quoted in McGowan, "'We Are All Involved," 39.

34 Adrian Ciani, "'An Imperialist Irishman': Bishop Michael Fallon, the Diocese of London and the Great War," *Historical Studies* 74 (2008): 73–94.

35 Jolivet, "French-Speaking Catholics."

36 Stella Hryniuk, "Pioneer Bishop, Pioneer Times: Nykyta Budka in Canada," *Canadian Catholic Historical Association Historical Studies* 55 (1988): 21–41. For copies of the original letter and the retraction, see Vladimir J. Kaye, *Ukrainian Canadians in Canada's Wars: Materials for Ukrainian Canadian History,* vol. 1 (Toronto: Ukrainian Canadian Research Foundation, 1983).

37 Stuart Macdonald, "For Empire and God: Canadian Presbyterians and the Great War," in Heath, *Canadian Churches,* 133–51.

38 Marshall, "Khaki Has Become," 115; Doug Adams, "The Call to Arms: The Reverend Thomas Todhunter Shields, World War One, and the Shaping of a Militant Fundamentalist," in *Baptists and War: Essays on Baptists and Military Conflict, 1640s–1990s*, ed. Gordon L. Heath and Michael A.G. Haykin (Eugene: Pickwick, 2014), 115–49.

39 Gordon L. Heath, "The Canadian Protestant Press and the Conscription Crisis, 1917–1918," *Historical Studies* 78 (2012): 27–46.

40 Jolivet, "French-Speaking Catholics."

41 Gordon L. Heath, "'We Are through with War': The Rise and Fall of Pacifism among Canadian Baptists between the Two World Wars," *Baptistic Theologies* 9, 2 (2017): 37–53.

42 Davidson, "The Anglican Church," 153; Marshall, "Khaki Has Become," 114.

43 Michelle Fowler, "Faith, Hope and Love: The Wartime Motivations of Lance Corporal Frederick Spratlin, MM and Bar, 3rd Battalion, CEF," *Canadian Military History* 15, 1 (2006): 45–60.

44 For the correspondence, see United Church Archives, Victoria College, Vancouver, box 467, file 27.

45 Heath, "Canadian Protestant Press."

46 "Farmers and the Military Service Act," *Presbyterian and Westminster*, 13 June 1918, 561; "The Question of Cancelled Exemptions," *Presbyterian and Westminster*, 25 July 1918, 77.

47 "An Unwise Measure," *Presbyterian and Westminster*, 13 September 1917, 259; "The War-Time Elections Act," *Presbyterian Witness*, 22 September 1917, 1.

48 "National Repentance," *Canadian Churchman*, 27 January 1916, 59.

49 "Please Stop My Paper," *Christian Guardian*, 2 January 1918, 6.

50 "The War Sermon," *Canadian Churchman*, 27 January 1916, 51–52.

51 Davidson, "The Anglican Church," 156–59.

52 Brown and Loveridge, "Unrequited Faith," 67.

53 "Wartime Letter from Captain Bellenden S. Hutcheson," 14 February 2019, Veterans Affairs Canada, http://www.veterans.gc.ca/eng/remembrance/those-who-served/diaries-letters-stories/first-world-war/bellenden.

54 McGowan, "We Are All Involved," 34–74; and McGowan, *The Imperial Irish*. For further studies on non-francophone Catholics, see Mark G. McGowan, "Harvesting the 'Red Vineyard': Catholic Religious Culture in the Canadian Expeditionary Force, 1914–1919," *Historical Studies* 64 (1998): 47–70; Mark G. McGowan, "Sharing the Burden of Empire: Toronto's Catholics and the Great War, 1914–1918," in *Catholics at the "Gathering Place": Historical Essays on the Archdiocese of Toronto, 1841–1991*, ed. Mark G. McGowan and Brian P. Clarke (Toronto: Canadian Catholic Historical Association, 1993), 177–207; and Charles G. Brewer, "The Diocese of Antigonish and World War 1" (master's thesis, University of New Brunswick, 1975).

55 "Canada's Plain Duty," *Christian Guardian*, 15 August 1917, 5.

56 Brian F. Hogan, "The Guelph Novitiate Raid: Conscription, Censorship and Bigotry during the Great War," *Canadian Catholic Historical Association, Study Sessions*, 45 (1978): 57–80.

57 An underlying tension concerned the unequal treatment of seminarians. Under the terms of the Military Service Act, Protestant seminarians were not defined as clergy until they graduated, which meant that they were not exempt from conscription until that time. However, Catholic seminarians who were preparing for life in a religious order were exempt, even as students.

58 For further discussion of the raid, see Kevin Anderson, "'This Typical Old Canadian Form of Racial and Religious Hate': Anti-Catholicism and English Canadian Nationalism, 1905–1965" (PhD diss., McMaster University, 2015), 73–80; Mark Reynolds, "The Guelph

Raid: When Police Routed Alleged World War I Draft Dodgers – Including a Cabinet Minister's Son – In a Catholic Seminary in the Heart of Orange Ontario, a National Scandal Erupted," *The Beaver* 82, 1 (February–March 2002): 25–30; and Robert Rutherdale, *Hometown Horizons: Local Responses to Canada's Great War* (Vancouver: UBC Press, 2004), 178–91. For examples of newspaper coverage, see "Royal Commission Will Probe Guelph Novitiate Affair," *Montreal Gazette,* 8 April 1919; "Both Ministers Acted Properly in Guelph Raid Affair," *Montreal Gazette,* 4 November 1919, 8; and "Hear the Counsel Sum Up Argument in Novitiate Case," *Toronto World,* 13 September 1919, 11. For a Catholic response to the raid, see Catholic War League, *The Facts of the Raid on the Jesuit Novitiate* (Toronto: Catholic Truth Society of Canada, 1918).

59 Gordon L. Heath, ed., *Empire from the Margins: Religious Minorities in Canada and the South African War, 1899–1902* (Eugene: Pickwick, 2017).

60 Norm Threinen, "Canadian Lutherans and the First World War," in Heath, *Canadian Churches,* 202, 205. Unless noted otherwise, the information in this paragraph comes from this essay. See also W.H. Heick, "The Lutherans of Waterloo County during World War I," *Waterloo Historical Society* 50 (1962): 23–32.

61 "Albright" is an English form of the German surname "Albrecht."

62 "Letter from the Acadian Club President to the Under Secretary of Militia Affairs," 18 July 1916, Berlin and the First World War, University of Waterloo Special Collections, https://uwaterloo.ca/library/special-collections-archives/berlin-and-the-first-world-war. The collection contains further evidence of anti-German feeling: When a bust of Kaiser Wilhelm was stolen and thrown into the lake at Victoria Park, it was rescued by a team of locals on 23 August 1914. The collection possesses a photograph of the salvage operation. See also P. Whitney Lackenbauer, "Soldiers Behaving Badly: CEF Soldier 'Rioting' in Canada during the First World War," in *The Apathetic and the Defiant: Case Studies of Canadian Mutiny and Disobedience, 1812–1919,* ed. Craig Leslie Mantle (Kingston: Canadian Defence Academy Press, 2007), 204–9.

63 Herbert K. Kalbfleisch, *The History of the Pioneer German-Language Press in Ontario* (Toronto: University of Toronto Press, 1968), 106.

64 Material on Ukrainians is taken from Frances Swyripa and John Herd Thompson, eds., *Loyalties in Conflict: Ukrainians in Canada during the Great War* (Edmonton: Canadian Institute of Ukrainian Studies, 1983); and Thomas M. Prymak, *Maple Leaf and Trident: The Ukrainian Canadians during the Second World War* (Toronto: Multicultural History Society of Ontario, 1988). For brief commentary on the Ukrainian response to the South African War, see Gordon L. Heath, "Empire from the Margins: An Introduction," in Heath, *Empire from the Margins,* 5–9.

65 In 1900, there were roughly twenty-seven thousand Galician immigrants in Canada (most were Ukrainians, some Polish, and others ethnic Germans from eastern Europe). They were primarily located in the Prairie provinces. See Vladimir J. Kaye, *Early Ukrainian Settlements in Canada, 1895–1900* (Toronto: University of Toronto Press, 1964), 361.

66 Ibid., 17.

67 Lubomyr Luciuk, *Searching for Place: Ukrainian Displaced Persons, Canada, and the Migration of Memory* (Toronto: University of Toronto Press, 2000), Chapter 2. See also F. Swyripa, *Ukrainian Canadians: A Survey of Their Portrayal in English-Language Works* (Edmonton: University of Alberta Press, 1978).

68 Luciuk, *Searching for Place,* 13.

69 Barry Ferguson, "British-Canadian Intellectuals, Ukrainian Immigrants, and Canadian National Identity," in *Canada's Ukrainians: Negotiating an Identity,* ed. Lubomyr Luciuk and Stella Hryniuk (Toronto: University of Toronto Press, 1991), 304–25; and Orest T.

Martynowych, *Ukrainians in Canada: The Formative Period, 1891–1924* (Edmonton: Canadian Institute of Ukrainian Studies Press, 1991).

70 J.S. Woodsworth, *Strangers within Our Gates: Or Coming Canadians* (Toronto: F.C. Stephenson, 1909).

71 Mark Minenko, "Without Just Cause: Canada's First National Internment Operations," in Luciuk and Hryniuk, *Canada's Ukrainians,* 288–303.

72 *Minutes of the Sixty-Third Annual Session of the African Baptist Association of Nova Scotia,* 1916, 4–5. This is published, but no publication information is found on the document, See https://archives.acadiau.ca/islandora/object/special%3A597.

73 Gordon L. Heath, "The Wartime Diaries of Canadian Baptist Military Chaplain William A. White, 1917–1918," *Baptist Quarterly* 49, 4 (2017): 12. For further analysis of black Canadians and the war, see Calvin W. Ruck, *Canada's Black Battalion: No. 2 Construction, 1916–1920* (Halifax: Society for the Protection and Preservation of Black Culture in Nova Scotia, 1986); Richard Holt, "Filling the Ranks: Recruiting, Training, and Reinforcements in the Canadian Expeditionary Force, 1914–1918" (PhD diss., University of Western Ontario, 2011); John G. Armstrong, "The Unwelcome Sacrifice: A Black Unit in the Canadian Expeditionary Force, 1917–1919," in *Ethnic Armies: Polyethnic Armed Forces from the Time of the Habsburgs to the Age of the Superpowers,* ed. N.F. Dreisziger (Waterloo: Wilfrid Laurier University Press, 1990), 1–26; and James W. St. G. Walker, "Race and Recruitment in World War I: Enlistment of Visible Minorities in the Canadian Expeditionary Force," *Canadian Historical Review* 70 (March 1989): 1–26.

74 Katherine McGowan, "'In the Interest of the Indians': The Department of Indian Affairs, Charles Cooke and the Recruitment of Native Men in Southern Ontario for the Canadian Expeditionary Force, 1916," *Ontario History* 102, 1 (Spring 2010): 109–24; Walker, "Race and Recruitment"; Fred Gaffen, *Forgotten Soldiers* (Penticton, BC: Theytus Books, 1985); L. James Dempsey, "The Indians and World War One," *Alberta History* 31, 3 (1983): 1–8; Evan J. Habkirk, "Militarism, Sovereignty, and Nationalism: Six Nations and the First World War" (master's thesis, Trent University, 2010).

75 Habkirk discusses the paternalistic behaviour of the Department of Indian Affairs with respect to the financial situation of Lickers, presenting it as an egregious example of governmental denial of First Nations soldiers' rights.

76 For works on Canadian Jews and the war, see Zachariah Kay, "A Note on the Formation of the Jewish Legion," *Jewish Social Studies* 29 (July 1967): 171–77; Joe Spier, "Israel Joseph Friedman: A Fallen and Forgotten Soldier – Remembered," *Western States Jewish History* 42 (Fall 2010): 117–22; and Gerald J.J. Tulchinsky, *Branching Out: The Transformation of the Canadian Jewish Community* (Toronto: Stoddart, 1998).

77 For the difficulties of determining a more exact figure, see Harold Pollins, "Jews in the Canadian Armed Forces in the First World War: A Statistical Research Note," *Jewish Journal of Sociology* 46 (2004): 44–58.

78 Walker, "Race and Recruitment."

79 Crerar, *Padres in No Man's Land,* 68.

80 There was also a peace tradition independent of formal church structures. See Thomas Socknat, *Witness against War: Pacifism in Canada, 1900–1945* (Toronto: University of Toronto Press, 1987).

81 Brock Millman, *Polarity, Patriotism, and Dissent in Great War Canada, 1914–1919* (Toronto: University of Toronto Press, 2016); Amy J. Shaw, *Crisis of Conscience: Conscientious Objection in Canada during the First World War* (Vancouver: UBC Press, 2009).

82 Robynne Rogers Healey, "Quakers and Mennonites and the Great War," in Heath, *Canadian Churches,* 218–40. See also S.F. Coffman, "Mennonites and Military Service," in *A Brief*

History of the Mennonites in Ontario, ed. Lewis J. Burkholder (Toronto: Livingstone Press, 1935), 258–72; S.F. Coffman, "The Non-Resistant Relief Organization," in Burkholder, *A Brief History of the Mennonites,* 273–76; Blodwen Davies, "From Militia Tax to Relief," *Mennonite Life* 5 (October 1950): 27–28; Allen Teichroew, "World War I and the Mennonite Migration to Canada to Avoid the Draft," *Mennonite Quarterly Review* 45 (July 1971): 219–49; and H. Jane Southgate, "An Examination of the Position of the Mennonites in Ontario under the Jurisdiction of the Military Service Act, 1917" (master's thesis, Wilfrid Laurier University, 1976).

83 Southgate, "An Examination of the Position"; Coffman, "Mennonites and Military Service."

84 Coffman, "The Non-Resistant Relief Organization." Canadian Mennonites showed appreciation for their exemption from conscription by raising money, gathering food, and providing relief workers. In the decades after the conflict, these activities became an integral part of the Mennonite response to war and suffering around the world. See Davies, "From Militia Tax to Relief," 27–28.

85 M. James Penton, *Jehovah's Witnesses in Canada: Champions of Freedom of Speech and Worship* (Toronto: Macmillan, 1976), 35–80.

86 The German forces in East Africa would not be defeated until late 1918. On the African campaign, see Edward Paice, *World War I: The African Front* (Cambridge: Pegasus, 2010); and Byron Farwell, *The Great War in Africa, 1914–1918* (New York: Norton, 1986).

87 Tim Cook, *Shock Troops: Canadians Fighting the Great War, 1917–1918* (Toronto: Viking, 2008), 411.

88 For an exploration of the emerging role of the Royal Flying Corps in battle, see Chapter 1 in this volume.

89 Outhit, "'Daring' Officer Left His Wife."

90 Erich Von Ludendorff, *Ludendorff's Own Story, August 1914-November 1918, Volume Two* (New York and London: Harper & Brothers Publishers, 1919), 326.

91 See J.L. Granatstein, *The Greatest Victory: Canada's One Hundred Days, 1918* (Don Mills: Oxford University Press, 2014), especially 40–41, where Granatstein quotes Field Marshal Paul von Hindenburg's assessment that the "failure of August 8th was revealed to all eyes as the consequence of an open weakness" in the German military position.

92 War Diary of the 15th Infantry Battalion, quoted in Outhit, "'Daring' Officer Left His Wife."

93 For instance, see "Foch's Great Stroke," *Canadian Baptist,* 15 August 1918, 8.

94 Outhit, "'Daring' Officer Left His Wife."

95 On the challenges that widows faced, see Chapter 4 in this volume.

96 Jonathan F. Vance, *Death So Noble: Memory, Meaning, and the First World War* (Vancouver: UBC Press, 1997), 266–67.

97 The church's history lists Albright among those who served. Solon Albright is buried in Crouy British Cemetery, Crouy-sur-Somme, plot V, B. 4. See Commonwealth War Graves Commission, "Solon Albright," https://www.cwgc.org/find/find-war-dead/results?first Name=solon&lastName=albright.

9

Replacing Leaders: Lieutenant Roy Duplissie and the Hundred Days Campaign

Lee Windsor

THE FIRST DAY IN COMBAT as a platoon leader for newly commissioned twenty-two-year-old lieutenant Roy Duplissie was 28 September 1918. The end of the Great War lay barely six weeks away. Not much time had elapsed since his completion of the three-month course at the Bexhill Canadian Training School for Infantry Officers in late August before the Royal Canadian Regiment called him forward to France in September to take over a platoon.[1] Lieutenant Duplissie then had seven days to get acquainted with his sergeant, four section commanders, and forty-odd men before they were ordered to the front to mount their first operation together. By late morning of 28 September 1918, on the outskirts of Cambrai, some three hours into his first trial by fire as a platoon leader, Roy was dead, killed by a bullet through the head. His story as a youthful, newly trained officer killed while leading a band of seasoned troops through uncut barbed wire under the withering dragon's breath of machine-gun bullets and bursting shell splinters rings out like a Hollywood cliché,[2] symbolic of the mad folly of another pointless Great War battle. His was another life wasted in the unstoppable industrial carnage of 1914–18.

But then, history is always a matter of perspective. Roy's record of military service and those of the units with whom he served reveal a more complex story behind his life and death. His story is intertwined with the emerging technologies and combined arms practice that contributed to Entente victory in 1918. Artillery, tanks, aircraft, electronic communication systems, and motor vehicles all became essential to the British and dominion fighting system in the second half of the war. So too were modern infantry platoons, organized around light machine guns, grenades, and grenade launchers, led by lieutenants who were empowered under an increasingly decentralized leadership structure.[3] But the last desperate German efforts to hold on and the continued lethality of modern weapons ensured that the Western Front consumed human lives through to the last weeks of war, especially among junior officers in the infantry who exposed themselves on the battlefield to coordinate small-unit actions. Canadian Corps

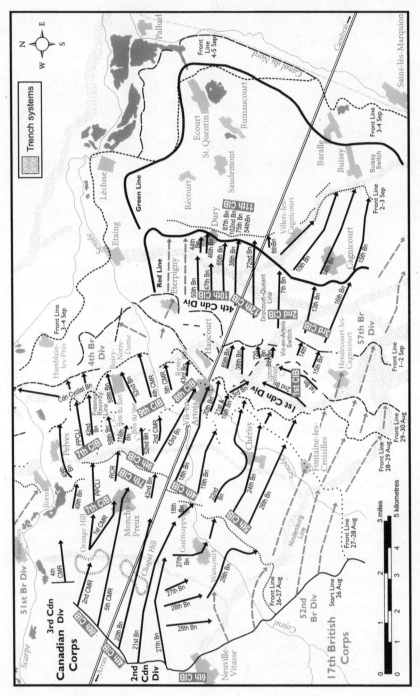

Figure 9.1 D-Q Line to Marcoing Line, 2 September 1918. | Map by Mike Bechthold.

participation in the intense final wave of attacks that finished off the German Army in the Hundred Days campaign demanded a steady supply of replacements in officers and men for the forty-six thousand casualties that were incurred during the offensive.[4] The arrival of the first twenty-four thousand Canadian conscripts in France in late 1918 partly explains how this demand was met in the ranks but not among the officers.[5]

Roy Duplissie's case sheds light on how the Canadian Corps grew and sustained its stock of junior infantry leaders through its costliest actions in the last eighteen months of hostilities. The combat effectiveness of the corps depended on the process of finding and training suitable lieutenants to fill a reinforcement pipeline, which was made all the more important given the high casualty rates among junior officers and NCOs in late 1918. In this respect, the army was not dissimilar to the fledgling Royal Flying Corps, whose recruitment and training measures are discussed by Graham Broad in Chapter 1 of this volume.[6] Roy Duplissie was one of thousands who cycled through the new training system. The criteria for making him an officer had nothing to do with advanced education, social status, or civilian occupation. Like most officers in Great War Canadian infantry battalions, Duplissie was selected because he had proved his value in combat as a non-commissioned soldier.[7] His short time in action as a platoon leader was years in the making. The day he died marked the end of a four-year process of training, front-line service, reconstitution, and professional military development. The investment paid off. Duplissie's leadership and individual action during his last day on earth proved critical to the dramatic chain of events that defeated the Central Powers and ended the First World War.[8]

Duplissie's military personnel record reveals that he first volunteered for the part-time Active Militia in 1914, with the 81st Regiment of Windsor, Nova Scotia. He volunteered for overseas service the next year, at the age of nineteen. Roy then trained full-time for eighteen months in Nova Scotia and the United Kingdom through 1916 and early 1917. The chain of command recognized his leadership ability during his earliest months in service and promoted him accordingly.[9] In April 1917, he formed part of a draft of officers and men who were dispatched to France to fill the holes shot in the ranks of the Royal Canadian Regiment (RCR) after the Battle of Vimy Ridge. The same draft included the newly promoted lieutenant Milton Fowler Gregg, a 1915 combat veteran and early product of the infantry officer reinforcement system.[10]

During the next seven months, Duplissie became a seasoned infantry veteran. In December 1917, after the Battle of Passchendaele, his superiors chose him as an officer candidate and pulled him from the front to rest and then undertake the specialized course, covering the skills and particular knowledge of platoon command. Meanwhile, in his absence, there was no respite for the Canadians. After the intensity of the 1918 spring offensive, launched on 21 March 1918, came the riposte, beginning with the Battle of Amiens on 8 August. As J.L. Granatstein points out, the "sensational success at Amiens" led to a complete overhaul of Allied strategy. In the wake of Amiens, "the idea was to maintain the pressure on the enemy with a series of all out offensives."[11] A key objective now was the critical hub of Cambrai. However, standing in the way of this prize was the Drocourt-Quéant Line. It was here that the vaunted Hindenburg Line intersected the German defences that ran north to the Ypres sector; in short, the D-Q was a hinge, whose taking could threaten defensive positions on either flank.[12]

Even as the Allies were preparing to strike at Cambrai, the brutal logic of the Western Front was beginning to have dire consequences for the Canadian Expeditionary Force. Casualties were outstripping enlistments for the first time since August 1917. To complicate matters, junior officers were suffering disproportionately. Typical was the situation in the 1st Canadian Mounted Rifles,

Figure 9.2

Male enlistments and casualties, Canadian Expeditionary Force, August 1914–August 1919

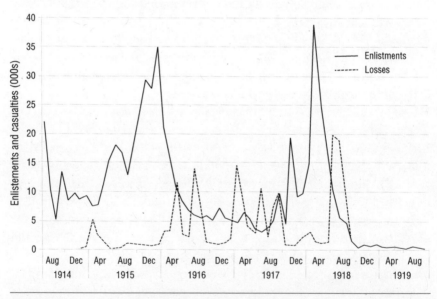

Source: Christopher Sharpe, "Recruitment and Conscription (Canada)," 22 June 2015, International Encyclopedia of the First World War, https://encyclopedia.1914-1918-online.net/article/recruitment_and_conscription_canada (graph based on Nicholson, *Canadian Expeditionary Force*, Appendix C, 546–48).[13]

which had taken heavy losses at the D-Q Line. Lieutenant Ivan Maharg of A Company reported that "all of the officers in one of his battalion's four companies had been killed or wounded."[14]

Duplissie was probably aware of the situation. Weeks after he finished the course and entered the replacement system in the Nova Scotia Regiment Depot, the RCR chose him to take over a platoon in D Company.[15] The officer then commanding that company was none other than Milton Gregg, who just days earlier had earned a bar for his Military Cross. On 28 September, Duplissie and his platoon followed Gregg into the Marcoing Line, between Bourlon Heights and the city of Cambrai. Leading the company vanguard through a deep belt of uncut barbed wire that shielded the Marcoing Line, Gregg and Duplissie established a foothold in the German defences. Roy was then killed while directing light machine-gun fire against a German counterattack.[16] Under that covering fire, Milton Gregg led a grenade charge, which broke the enemy attack and secured the RCR breach. The day stands among the most famous in the history of Canada's oldest regular force infantry regiment.

Officers from the Ranks

During the Great War, the process of selecting and preparing officers to lead Canada's armed forces differed strikingly from that of the Second World War. The education, employment experience, and intellectual capacity of new Second World War volunteers largely determined whether they entered the officer or non-commissioned streams of service, in a system much like the one of today.[17] Education certainly mattered during the Great War, especially in the artillery and engineers, but the most important criterion for selecting and training potential infantry officers was combat experience, at least after 1915.[18] The Canadian policy of choosing officers from veteran members of the ranks dated to the aftermath of Second Ypres, when the 1st Canadian Division struggled to replace its six thousand casualties. The infamous Militia and Defence minister, Sir Sam Hughes, had taken an interest in selecting officers and initially resisted the idea. According to Desmond Morton, Hughes "had personally chosen the officers for the First Contingent, and he did so again for the Second Contingent." Political patronage and social status also influenced the process.[19] After Hughes left his ministerial post in 1916, extracting infantry officers from the pool of combat veterans became normal practice.[20]

By 1917, the process for replacing Canadian infantry officers had evolved into its final form. "Non-commissioned officers and men granted commissions in the field or at the conclusion of service in the field" provided "a regular supply of cadets" from "France for training at the Canadian Cadet School, Bexhill." It was up to battalion and company commanders at the front to observe the performance of their soldiers and to flag the ones that had officer potential. As a 1918 government report noted, "Practically no exceptions were made to the general policy which provided that officer reinforcements for the Canadian Corps should be drawn from the rank and file serving in France."[21] The search and training process had to generate enough graduates to sustain a five-month pool of reinforcement officers, who would be held in readiness in depots from England through to the Canadian Corps Reinforcement Camp in France.[22] Milton Gregg was among the first soldiers who was recommended for commissioning when the system first took shape in 1915. Private Duplissie followed in his footsteps after the system became regularized.

Nothing in the record of Roy Duplissie's early years suggested that he was destined to become an army officer. As was true for Rob Buchan, whom Jonathan F. Vance discusses in Chapter 2 of this volume, the contrast between his early life and the military achievements that would mark his service could hardly be more striking. Roy was born in Saint John, New Brunswick, on 25 August 1896, not far from Milton Gregg's home in Snider Mountain, Kings County. The proximity was no accident, given Canadian policy first to form regional units followed later in the war by regional reinforcement depots to maintain units at the front. Roy was one of two boys born to John and Susan (Blake) Duplissie. The brother apparently died in childhood, for Roy's military records do not list any siblings who were alive at the time of his enlistment. Roy's father died early in his life. His mother married Laban Seymour O'Brien of Little River, Albert County, New Brunswick, in 1910. Roy's relationship to his stepfather raises more questions than answers. His military records make no mention of a father or stepfather other than to indicate that the former was dead and that Roy himself was not the "sole support" for his remarried mother, now Susan O'Brien. Some time after the marriage, the family moved to Newport in Hants County, not far from Windsor, Nova Scotia. Newport was then the scene of a growing gypsum mining and shipping industry that lay along the fertile St. Croix River Valley between itself and Windsor.[23] Perhaps the prospect of steady work around the bustling mine drew Roy, his mother, and her new husband to Hants County. Roy worked as a labourer in that rich mining and agricultural region. The slim, blue-eyed, light-haired young man was raised a Methodist. It is not clear how much schooling he completed before heading to work, but he must have been taught how to think, read, write, and communicate well enough to be considered as officer material.[24]

Without letters, diaries, or some other clear evidence, it is impossible to know exactly why men volunteered for wartime military service. Roy Duplissie first did so in 1914, with the 81st Hants Regiment of the Active Militia, which was based in Windsor. The 81st was a new eight-company infantry unit formed in

1914 to enlarge the capacity and reach of the Truro-based 76th Colchester and Hants Regiment.[25] It was one of several voluntary Active Militia units that were revitalized or formed anew in the years leading up to the war.[26] For whatever combination of reasons, Roy chose to join Canada's part-time volunteer defence force in the year that hostilities were declared.

The controversy over Great War Canadian mobilization inefficiencies is well known. Duplissie's case suggests that the militia system did offer a vehicle to rapidly expand the Canadian Expeditionary Force and to identify the leaders it needed to make it effective. By late 1915, the Canadian government was heavily engaged in growing the Canadian Corps in France beyond the two divisions then at the front. New regionally based battalions led by "prominent citizens" were authorized to recruit across Canada in late 1915 to help produce Prime Minister Borden's promised 250,000-man force. That pledge doubled to 500,000 on New Year's Day 1916.[27] In this context, the Militia Department in Ottawa designated Lieutenant Colonel Hadley Tremain, a lawyer and Member of Parliament for Hants County, to raise the 112th (Nova Scotia) Battalion in the western Nova Scotia counties from Yarmouth to Hants, including the south shore.[28] Tremain was the same man who had raised and then commanded the 81st Hants Regiment, whose members formed the initial wave of 112th Overseas Battalion volunteers who mustered at the Fort Edward Armoury on the heights above Windsor in December 1915. Early in 1916, other west Nova Scotia militia units, from the Yarmouth Field Artillery and the 75th Lunenburg Regiment on the south shore to the 69th Annapolis Regiment in "the Valley," assembled companies for the new battalion at their own armouries. At each location, experienced militia officers and NCOs processed new recruits and introduced them to basic soldiering. This small-town force-generation process formed part of Sam Hughes's short-lived recruiting and billeting policy during the winter of 1915–16, which was intended to rapidly increase the Canadian Corps.[29] A cursory glance at the nominal rolls suggests that a third or more of the 1,126 officers and men taken on in the 112th Battalion began their service in the militia.[30]

By March, the battalion neared full strength, approaching 1,000 all ranks. They carried on assembling and training as dispersed companies around western Nova Scotia until the early summer of 1916. During that time, Tremain and his officers in Windsor were the first to flag the nineteen-year-old Duplissie as part of the Militia Department's new policy of identifying the "most efficient of the recruits" to be "chosen as officers and NCOs."[31] Tremain authorized Duplissie's promotion to lance corporal in April, and to corporal in May 1916 as the unit built on its Active Militia core with hundreds of raw new volunteers in need of basic military training.[32]

On 5 July 1916, members of the 112th Battalion were officially "warned for drafts overseas" and requested to update next-of-kin details on their particulars of family forms before heading to France. Later that month, their turn came to sail from Halifax to Liverpool aboard the White Star Line's SS *Olympic*, an iconic troopship. The 112th disembarked at Liverpool on 31 July 1916 and travelled by train to its new training camp at Oxney, part of the British Army Aldershot training area in Hampshire.[33] That same day, Tremain promoted Corporal Duplissie to acting sergeant. At five foot eight and a half, with a lean thirty-three-inch chest, Roy was not the tallest or broadest of his cohort. A surviving photograph reveals him as a handsome, slim type, standing proud if not imposing among his peers.[34] Physical bearing can be an element of infantry leadership, but certainly something in Duplissie's character and ability convinced his superiors that he was worthy of holding senior non-commissioned rank.

When Duplissie and his fellow western Nova Scotians in the 112th Battalion arrived at Oxney Camp in the summer of 1916, they expected to serve together in another new Canadian infantry division. In hindsight, Prime Minister Borden's pledge to increase the Canadian force to 500,000 soldiers manning five or six field divisions proved unsustainable for a nation of 8 million people, especially given the gravity of loss rates sustained during the Canadian Corps participation in the Somme offensive from September to November 1916.[35] Still, the regional battalions that were raised as part of the 1915–16 expansion scheme assembled the officers, men, and ultimately the organization to build the rudimentary replacement system that took shape in late 1916. That structure made it possible to reinforce the four divisions of the Canadian Corps in service at the front through the hard fighting at the Somme in 1916 and on into 1917, even if this foiled the hopes of officers and men in the newly arrived units. The 112th (Nova Scotia) Battalion played its role, training in the United Kingdom through the fall of 1916, when three drafts totalling some 374 men volunteered to be transferred out and sailed for France to help rebuild the battle-worn 25th (Nova Scotia) Battalion at the front. For whatever reason, Acting Sergeant Duplissie remained with Tremain and the 112th Battalion, either to stay with his west Nova Scotia unit mates or perhaps his long-time commanding officer.

The main body of the 112th Battalion "family" stayed together for over a year, through a second Christmas season in the winter of 1916–17 at Oxney Camp. Any hope that the 112th might serve together ended in January 1917, when the unit was broken up to feed the new provincially based reserve battalion system. Duplissie and most members of the 112th transferred to the 26th Reserve Battalion, not to be confused with the 26th (New Brunswick) Battalion at the front. The 26th formed as part of the depot to supply reinforcement officers and men for Nova Scotia's 25th and 85th Battalions as well as the Royal Canadian

Regiment.[36] The reserve battalions became part of the growing Canadian administration and training installation at Bramshott, a few miles east of the Oxney Camp.

Sergeant Duplissie trained with the 26th Reserve Battalion for ten more weeks, waiting to see which unit would call him forward. Recently commissioned, Lieutenant Milton Gregg was already with the 26th at Bramshott when Duplissie arrived. He was some four years older than Duplissie and had served as a non-commissioned stretcher-bearer with the 13th Battalion (Black Watch) at Second Ypres in April 1915. He was wounded the next month at Festubert. Gregg was subsequently chosen for the earliest batch of efficient non-commissioned members to be developed as infantry officers, based on their combat service.[37]

Their wait ended with the April 1917 Battle of Vimy Ridge. During the fighting from the Grange Tunnel mouth to Bois de la Folie, the RCR lost 12 officers and 274 other ranks killed, wounded, or missing.[38] The losses were not as high as in some units at Vimy, but the gaps in the RCR ranks were wide nonetheless. As the Canadian Corps rested and consolidated its hold on Vimy Ridge, calls went back through the administrative network to dispatch replacements from the reserve battalions in south England. The 25th and 85th Battalions drew heavily on the 26th Reserve Battalion that month, but Lieutenant Gregg and Sergeant Duplissie found themselves assigned to the RCR.[39]

Interestingly, Duplissie refused to join the RCR at the front with a sergeant's rank. On 16 April, he reverted to the rank of private at his own request.[40] Perhaps, after two years of militia and active service, he was willing to play a junior leadership role in a unit that had no combat experience but was not prepared to do so in a unit that was both Permanent Force and battle-proven in the hard fighting at Mont Sorrel, the Somme, and Vimy Ridge. Gregg and Private Duplissie landed in France together on 22 April 1917. Around that time, the RCR pulled out of the line to rest billets in Villers-au-Bois, a little north of Mont St. Eloi and safely behind the Artois Heights and Vimy Ridge. There, in comparatively comfortable huts away from the trenches and bursting shells, the unit began integrating its new replacement draft of five new officers and ninety-four other ranks.[41]

Gregg, Duplissie, and the rest of the newly arrived reinforcements formed up on the grass parade square to, in the words of the regimental war diarist, "learn our ways and customs," while the veteran members rested, trained, and blew off steam in inter-unit sports. Time was taken to integrate replacements carefully. When the veteran RCR members returned to the front on 7 May for a week of defence construction work on Vimy Ridge followed by a week on watch at the front, only the new officers who had battle experience went with them. Duplissie and the other untested reinforcements remained behind to continue training up to the regiment's latest standard of infantry skills and tactics. Only three weeks later, when the unit returned to the Villers-au-Bois rest camp, was Private Duplissie's reinforcement draft assigned to train with its new rifle companies. The men practised with all the latest weapons, now routinely part of the British and dominion platoon tactical system, which was based around Lewis light machine guns, hand grenades (bombs), and rifle grenade launchers.[42]

For the rest of 1917, Duplissie stayed with the RCR. His first test in combat came in June 1917, during the 7th Canadian Brigade's major night raid around the Avion Railway between Vimy Ridge and Lens, the same action in which Lieutenant Gregg acquired both a Military Cross and a painful wound in the buttocks.[43] Duplissie came through the raid unscathed and spent the summer in the Vimy-Lens sector. The RCR was not part of the initial assault at Hill 70 on 15 August 1917; instead, it came forward to relieve exhausted units and to defend the newly won ground against the anticipated German counterattacks. In early October 1917, the Canadian Corps pulled off the line and prepared to take a turn in the ongoing British and dominion offensive in Flanders.[44]

In late October, the RCR took on the support and carrying party tasks during the 7th Canadian Brigade's grim attack along the Bellevue Spur off Passchendaele Ridge. From 26 October to 4 November, RCR companies and platoons carried everything across the mud-caked battlefield, from ammunition and duckboards forward to hundreds of wounded men coming back. RCR platoons also reinforced shattered assault battalions as they consolidated the Canadian hold on the Bellevue Spur and fought off German counterattacks.[45] The great valour and catastrophic losses of the assault battalions have received ample attention; still, the demanding physical work of moving around the great grey lake of death between Gravenstafel Ridge and the new front line in October and November was no less vital to the capture of Passchendaele Ridge. In fact, it resulted in 14 officers and 374 men killed, wounded, and missing, more than the number lost during the RCR's Vimy assault.[46]

At some point during the actions at Avion, Hill 70, and on the Bellevue Spur, Private Duplissie's superiors observed his potential as a combat leader. After Passchendaele, he was promoted to lance corporal and made second-in-command of a section when the RCR moved back to France to the Rely rest and training camp west of Lens in December 1917. In January 1918, Lance Corporal Duplissie also earned a two-week leave to enjoy the comforts and sights of Paris, safely away from the front line and from army life. Leave passes were commonplace during the winter of 1917–18 as part of plans to rest and reconstitute the Canadian Corps before German reinforcements arrived from the Eastern Front and the 1918 campaigning season opened in earnest.[47]

The RCR chain of command had more in store for Duplissie than section leadership. On his return from the City of Lights, he was sent back to the Nova Scotia Regiment Depot in England, "with a view to attending the Cadet School" and becoming an officer.[48] Before he could start his course, however, he fell ill with a painful venereal disease. It seems that Duplissie experienced more of Paris than tourist sites and cafés. The illness landed him in bed for most of February and March 1918 in Bramshott and added him to the oft-referenced high rates of venereal disease among the Canadian Corps. For some Great War soldiers, acquiring an avoidable sexually transmitted illness resulted in severe consequences,[49] and it certainly delayed Duplissie's assignment to the Canadian Training School. Yet his indiscretion came in the midst of the manpower crisis and the implementation of conscription in Canada. With his combat experience, he was too valuable an asset for his officer development track to be terminated. As soon as his health permitted in April 1918, Duplissie resumed his training. His next step was the small-arms instructor course at the Canadian School of Musketry at Mytchett camp, where he learned to teach others to master the revolver, rifle, and Lewis light machine gun. The only whiff of punishment for his earlier indiscretion was a promotion to acting sergeant without pay.[50]

Finally, in May 1918 Officer Cadet Duplissie began the three-month program for infantry officers at the Canadian Training School at Bexhill-on-Sea in Sussex. The Canadian infantry officer selection and development system may have placed a premium on combat-proven candidates, but it did not presume that combat experience alone could prepare infantry lieutenants to do their jobs. The training at Bexhill included more than parade ground drill and bayonet fighting. At least some attention was paid to the rapid evolution of the Great War battlefield and the possibility of adapting the British Field Service Regulations and other training manuals to transform the Canadian Corps from a force that could defend entrenched positions to one that could "advance and defeat the enemy masses" by reducing their defences, "winning a prolonged fire fight," and making "greater use of cover, both natural and artificial." The program at Bexhill put a premium on understanding basic principles of war and acquiring military knowledge "built up by study and practice until it has become an instinct." By 1917–18, Duplissie and his fellow prospective infantry lieutenants had learned that "the subordinate leader of today requires greater dash, resource, and initiative than ever before since the range of the modern weapons increased the distance at which reconnoitering troops must work." In that vein, Bexhill cadets studied map reading, selecting platoon formations "to minimize loss, how to direct their platoon's firepower, the management system for replenishing stores and ammunition, [and] the preparation of defences."[51]

Duplissie passed the Bexhill program in August 1918, in the midst of the Battle of Amiens. He was subsequently commissioned as a lieutenant in the Nova Scotia Regiment Depot at Bramshott and almost immediately started his way back through the reinforcement pipeline. The timing was critical. Early September found the Canadian Corps back in the Arras sector, fighting through the Drocourt-Quéant Line in the first phase of its offensive down the Arras-Cambrai highway. In the middle of that heavy fighting in early September, Lieutenant Duplissie relocated to the Canadian Corps Reinforcement Camp in France.[52] The Canadian officer reinforcement system worked in 1917–18 not least because the Bexhill school vigorously churned out new officers at the same time that the Canadian Corps battled and bled at the front.

The intense week of action from Arras to the Drocourt-Quéant Line cost over 11,000 Canadian casualties. The Royal Canadian Regiment's portion totalled 196 killed, wounded, and missing, including 2 captains and 9 lieutenants; the recently minted lieutenant Duplissie and other replacement officers would have to fill these gaps.[53] Once German counterattacks had spent themselves on the newly won Canadian positions along Dury Ridge, General Arthur Currie ordered an operational pause to prepare the corps for its next challenge. Before it lay a new switch belt of German defences that were anchored on the Canal du Nord, protecting the approaches to the communications hub town and German forward base at Cambrai. Attack preparations included moving the corps artillery, communications, and administrative operation forward behind the new front, gathering intelligence, and preparing detailed plans and orders. But Currie also understood that during the three-week pause, he and his staff had to rest the survivors and reconstitute units that had been depleted in the fighting of August and early September.[54]

The Royal Canadian Regiment took its turn out of the line in mid-September, first for a week in reserve positions behind the front and then for a second week of rest, hot meals, and training at Berneville, west of Arras. During the two weeks, officers and men trickled into the RCR from the corps reinforcement camp, but it was during the second week that Lieutenant Colonel C.R.E. "Dick" Willets invested in integrating and training the new men. Duplissie arrived with four other reinforcement officers on 20 September, the day after the RCR reached Berneville. They added to the five who had come a week earlier and three more who returned from courses or leave. This brought the battalion slate of officers back to a workable number of four per company after the losses sustained fighting at the D-Q Line. No majors remained, and all company commanders were lieutenants. Other than C.R.E. Willets, the only remaining officer whose rank was higher than lieutenant was the regimental adjutant, Captain Francis McCrea.

At Berneville, the new officers, all of whom were experienced veterans, worked on refresher platoon "specialist" training, small-arms skills, and the use of captured German machine guns.[55] In that short time, Duplissie got to know or reacquainted himself with his new platoon and his fellow D Company officers. The Canadian system of regional recruiting and officer selection seems in this case to have created social continuity. Duplissie already knew one of his two fellow platoon leaders very well. Lieutenant John Millett was one of three brothers who had served in the 112th (Nova Scotia) Battalion with Roy back in 1916. Millett had also served with Roy in the militia.[56] The two had followed a remarkably similar path. D Company's senior platoon leader, Lieutenant David Porter, was from Saint John and had served with the RCR on the Somme before being wounded at Vimy. He had returned to the regiment as an officer earlier in 1918 and had served with it since the start of the Hundred Days campaign at Amiens. All three platoon leaders knew their company commander, Lieutenant Milton Gregg, who had just taken over D Company after leading the RCR's C Company through the tough fight earlier that month near Monchy-les-Preux.[57] They also knew the company sergeant major, Charles Pope, who had been awarded the Distinguished Conduct Medal and the Military Medal.[58] It is highly likely that they knew other members of the company as well.

All in all, the RCR integration timeline was far tighter than when Duplissie had first joined the unit in April 1917, but the demands of war in September 1918 left little alternative. After Amiens, Field Marshal Douglas Haig was convinced "that the time had come for an all-out effort against the enemy who was feeling that this is the beginning of the end for him."[59] Everyone in the RCR now realized that, after their short break, they would be joining the rest of the 3rd Canadian Division "in a continuation of the Canadian Corps great offensive." On 26 September, for better or for worse, the 23 officers and 588 other ranks in the RCR were ordered to assemble behind the Canal du Nord.[60] Even with reinforcements, the unit was understrength, especially in light of the mission it was about to undertake. In his diary, Milton Gregg recorded that D Company's drive back to the front was "mixed with strange emotions." The troops in the back of his truck sang "songs on the way, such as 'Home Sweet Home' and 'Till the Boys Come Home,'" while Gregg and Duplissie rode in the truck cab with the driver. "I remembered Duplissie sticking his head in and shouting 'For the love of Mike, sing something cheerful.'"[61]

Cambrai, 1918

The twenty-eighth of September 1918 marked the halfway point in the Hundred Days campaign, which ultimately defeated the German armies on the Western Front and ended the Great War. The assault on the Canal du Nord, which included a highly sophisticated supporting artillery fire plan, stands among the greatest feats of arms in Canadian military history.[62] German units defending the D-Q Line, the Canal du Nord, and Bourlon Wood were smashed and fell back in disorder, although reinforcements shifted in from other fronts to stabilize the situation. In that context, it was not clear until late on 27 September whether General Currie should exploit the victory with a deep thrust or deliver one more deliberate attack against the remaining defences that shielded Cambrai.[63]

Of course, Currie's options for action were weighed carefully before the assault on the Canal du Nord began. After crossing it and winning Bourlon Heights, he famously planned to feed the 3rd Canadian and 11th British Divisions through the narrow bridgehead to join the 1st and 4th Canadian Divisions, which would already be in the fight. The RCR and the 3rd Division would then drive east, essentially fixing the Cambrai garrison against a direct threat, while the remainder of the reinforced Canadian Corps fanned out to the northeast, enveloping the city and engaging as many enemy units as possible away from General Julian Byng's Third Army assault south of the city. Currie aimed "to gain as much ground as possible" toward Cambrai, "provided the enemy resistance is not more than can be overcome by open warfare tactics" and "a limited amount of artillery." Canadian Corps orders specified that if the enemy holding east of Bourlon Heights "cannot be overcome without considerable artillery support," forward divisions were to consolidate, reorganize, secure a good jump-off line, and haul up the necessary guns and ammunition for a barrage to support a broadening four-division advance on 28 September.[64] Canadian Corps senior staff knew that the German Marcoing Line lay on the western fringe of Cambrai, but they could not know its details, or how well it was manned, until Canadian troops got a close look.[65]

Mounting a second and wider deliberate attack one day after launching one of the more complicated operations in Canadian history and penetrating five kilometres inside a well-defended enemy zone was asking a lot. Elite German alarm and counterattack divisions such as the 1st Guards and 26th Wurttemberg had recently arrived at Cambrai to block the Canadian thrust. Most of the Canadian Corps Heavy Artillery and ammunition columns were still on the move across the canal to new fire positions that were better able to reach Cambrai. Canadian signallers were still laying new telephone cables and moving up telephone exchanges. In the early hours of 28 September, Canadian divisional field batteries and hastily laid phone lines were mostly in position, but there had been little or no time to register their guns on observable aiming points.[66] The divisional field gunners were backed by a comparatively small number of Canadian and British heavy guns, and all of them knew virtually nothing about the new enemy gun positions, forward strong points, or barbed wire entanglements in front of them. The 3rd Divisional Artillery fired a small harassing fire plan in the last hours of darkness but did not engage in sustained high-explosive, wire-cutting, or obstacle destruction shooting. In comparison, the entire Canadian Corps Heavy Artillery had fired a week-long wire-cutting program along the Canal du Nord defences to blow and hold open lanes for the great attack thirty-six hours earlier.[67] The single available British heavy artillery brigade that had moved up in the 3rd Division's area on the night of 27–28 September prepared itself mainly for long-range counter-battery shooting when the sun rose.[68]

Nonetheless, the lead brigades of the 3rd Division marched into the Canal du Nord bridgehead in the cold rain and gathering darkness on 27 September. The RCR arrived in the shattered remains of Bourlon Wood at three the next morning and linked up with 4th Division troops who had conquered and held it during the intense fight the day before. Among the soggy, splintered forest ruins, the RCR prepared to follow Currie's assignment to keep the pressure on and prevent "the enemy from setting up a new defence line west of" Cambrai.[69] The men "rested" in wet craters while their officers made plans and reconnoitered forward through what Milton Gregg described as "that horrible wood," where "trees lay scattered in every direction." The tangle was made worse by deliberately strung German barbed wire.[70] Pausing to clear obstacles or to wait for the ground to dry was inconceivable in those late September days, when the whole Allied force struck the German front from the American and French sectors around the Meuse-Argonne and Aisne to Third and Fourth British Armies south of Cambrai and even in the Belgian and British Second Army front at Ypres, as part of French marshal Ferdinand Foch's great offensive to end the war in 1918. The entire German line inside occupied France and Belgium came under pressure that week, after many German units were already immersed in the Cambrai cauldron.[71]

Most accounts report that the 3rd and 5th Divisional Artilleries opened their barrage in front of and on the German Marcoing Line at 6:00 a.m. on 28 September. The Royal Canadian Regiment led the 7th Canadian Infantry Brigade's attack, and the remaining battalions were stacked behind it in support and in readiness to press deep if the opportunity presented itself. Some forty-five eighteen-pounders and 4.5-inch field howitzers opened fire a thousand yards across their front. A supply of 300 rounds was stacked by each field gun and 250 for each field howitzer, enough for two hours of continuous firing.[72] Still, though invaluable, this was not the firepower of Vimy or the Canal du Nord.

The RCR leaned into the barrage as it crept eastward, "shooting" it down the long slope of Bourlon Heights at a familiar rate of a hundred yards every four minutes. Four tanks from the 7th British Tank Battalion clanked along behind. Lieutenant Gregg's D Company formed the right wing of the battalion's attack, accompanied by two tanks. The early morning fog mixed with shell smoke to conceal their movement from searching German eyes.[73] The lead companies smartly overwhelmed the Marcoing outpost zone, captured a pair of field guns, and prevented the fifty or more Germans who manned the outpost zone from falling back to their main line. In his diary, Gregg wrote that "some well-directed Lewis gun fire from each flank of the company" convinced the retiring outpost garrison to surrender.[74] Then the situation turned ugly. When the assault companies reached the bottom of Bourlon Heights and ascended the slight crest that lay beyond it, they finally laid eyes on the Marcoing Line. As the regimental history records, "The men realized the grim nature of the task before them. Defended by great belts of wire and many strong points, each with a garrison of trained machine-gunners and two or more guns, the German position constituted a barrier which, obviously, could only be stormed by an effort of supreme valour and determination."[75]

Canadian troops had overcome this kind of defence before but only after massive and prolonged artillery preparation, including the use of heavy guns to blast down the wire, obliterate at least some machine-gun strong points, and neutralize enemy artillery. This time, the RCR infantrymen encountered a wide belt of intact barbed wire running across their path as far as the eye could see, and "the German barrage crashed along their front and the [Marcoing] Line itself crackled with the fire of machine-guns."[76] Milton Gregg remembered that "it seemed as though the Germans let everything loose in the twinkle of an eye ... With the air reeking of metal, it would have been impossible for a man to stand upright and live."[77] The Canadian barrage lifted to the east side of the imposing wire barrier, and all three RCR assault companies took whatever cover they could find at its edge. Without radios to coordinate activity, three of the supporting tanks veered too far to the flanks to support the RCR directly. British crews fought their own personal battle against machine-gun strong points and one field gun firing over open sites until three were put out of action.[78] The RCR infantrymen were on their own.

A Company became pinned down in the centre. Most of Lieutenant William Wurtele's C Company was likewise pinned to the north of it, near the Arras-Cambrai highway at Raillencourt, although in Wurtele's words "I found a fold of ground and led No. 12 platoon through the wire."[79] To the south, Milton Gregg ordered D Company to take cover in front of the wire belt. The regimental history and the RCR war dairy contain fragments of the dramatic but chaotic story that now unfolded. The richest source of information for the plight of D Company and Roy Duplissie's last hours is the detailed personal diary of Milton Gregg. He ordered his men to stay behind cover in holes and partial trenches in front of the Marcoing Line after realizing that "none of them can possibly get as far as five yards through the wire. Then you'll [Gregg] have no company and you will be decorating the wire yourself." He then crawled forward, trying to find a way through the obstacle. "After a prolonged and dangerous search," he discovered a zigzag gap "through which one man at a time might pass into the German position."[80] By lucky chance, Gregg had stumbled on a path used by German work parties, patrols, and the outpost garrison to cross the wire belt. Nearby, he found Roy Duplissie and six other men from the company. Duplissie was the only other officer who was close enough to influence events. Lieutenant Millett was wounded and down, whereas Lieutenant Porter was somewhere in the rear. The venerable Charles Pope lay dead in front of the wire.[81]

Gregg recorded that he

> talked the whole thing over with Duplissie ... I was going to try to go through the gap in the wire and get into the German trench, as many men as possible would follow me, one by one at intervals. In the meantime, he, Duplissie, would gradually draw more men from the line and he, with them would gradually work their way through the gap and into the trench to our assistance.

Many members of D Company had already been hit by enemy fire and were lying up in shell holes, dressing their wounds. Inspiring the survivors to break from cover and resume their attack would require spirited leadership. Gregg set off with a revolver and a stash of grenades, dashing and crawling unscathed through the gap until he reached a shallow communications trench between two machine-gun strong points. He watched in horror as the first four or five men who followed him were struck down one by one. The last was an NCO who made it into the communication trench despite a bullet or fragment through his knee.[82] Though injured, the NCO used his rifle to cover northward along the trench while Gregg headed south until he reached the first strong point. Upon stepping inside, Gregg encountered two machine-gunners who were standing on the firing step and manning their guns to cover the wire belt. Before they could grab their rifles and turn to face him, Gregg shot them both at close range with his revolver. He then accepted the surrender of eighteen others who were sheltered in a dugout beneath the strong point.[83]

But one man could do only so much. Indeed, a few of his new prisoners realized that their captor was alone and bolted south toward the next intact strong point. Gregg "picked up a German rifle and shot them before they could get to that post." Afterward, he dashed back to the zigzag gap, "where I found my musketeer busy making the Germans keep their heads down in the hole on the left." By then, Duplissie had directed two more men through the gap, doubling the size of the tiny assault group to four. Gregg left one man with his wounded NCO to continue shielding the northern flank and took the other man and more grenades back down the trench to tackle the next strong point. Duplissie joined them with another handful of D Company soldiers sometime around mid-morning. Gregg assigned several of the new arrivals to reinforce the NCO and the man who were holding the defensive block to the north and took Duplissie, two other troops, and "a considerable supply of our own and German bombs" south to carry on attacking and cleaning out the chain of seven German strong points in their company sector. By the time they reached the last one, three German officers and forty-five men had surrendered on D Company's front.[84]

The remaining Germans in D Company's area retreated south, moving down the trench to the last powerful strong point commanding a road that crossed the Marcoing Line. There, they massed in strength, blocked D Company's path, and prepared to counterattack, along with reinforcements coming from Cambrai. Around that time, the fourth British tank rolled near the wire but then pointed itself westward toward home. After Gregg and Duplissie shouted at it unsuccessfully, Gregg ran as close to it at the edge of the wire and talked to the driver, who told him that machine-gun fire had killed or wounded every crewman inside. The driver then used his vehicle as an ambulance to get his mates to safety.[85] Meanwhile, Gregg, Duplissie, and their two soldiers prepared to meet the counterattack as best they could. The regimental history records that D Company's Lewis machine-gun crew set up inside the breach and opened fire on a German counterattack force that was charging west toward the Marcoing Line, running over the open ground between it and the Marcoing Support Line.[86]

At the south end of the RCR breach, Gregg, Duplissie, and their band assembled all the bombs they could to meet the counterattack that was boiling up the communication trench. Gregg wrote, "we sat tight until the bunch of Germans got to about 20 yards in front of us; then we threw bombs for all we were worth." The Germans who were not killed or wounded in the grenade volley turned and ran out of throwing range. Gregg's diary vividly describes what followed:

> Duplissie, who was a wonderful boy, suddenly exclaimed – "I know all about German machine guns, let's give them some of their own." There were plenty about so we picked one up, got it on top and began firing, Duplissie doing the work, and I, with my tin hat touching his, feeding in the belt. It was effective

shooting and there was no want of targets. Suddenly, I heard a terrible crash in my ear and, looking round, saw Duplissie's tin hat spinning in the air with a large hole in the back. He was hit through the face and just sighed as he went out.[87]

Gregg took over the German MG-08 after watching how Duplissie worked it but was soon blown backwards in the bottom of the trench when a bullet "drilled a hole" through his helmet, grazed his skull, and knocked him out cold for about nine to ten seconds.[88]

Roy Duplissie's time as a small-arms instructor and the 7th Brigade's special course on German machine guns just before the operation had paid off. The Germans in the strong point at the road crossing lost many of their comrades to D Company's volley of grenades and the fire of their own gun turned against them. After he came to, Gregg went back up the line, gathered a few more men, and mounted one final assault to clear and capture that southernmost German machine-gun position in their sector. Then he redistributed his tiny force to defend its foothold against counterattacks. With the German weapons silenced across their front, more D Company soldiers could get through the gap in the wire to reinforce the RCR cracks in the Marcoing Line. Some twenty-five men made it altogether. They held their "bridgehead" through the wire against all counterattacks from both flanks, thanks in part to Gregg, who returned through the wire gap to collect more grenades and ammunition, despite the painful injury to his head.[89]

Aftermath

The fight to win control of the Marcoing Line raged for the rest of the day. The action of D Company helped to open the breach. Gregg and Duplissie fixed enemy attention on the RCR and the 7th Brigade's southern sector while the rest of the unit swung northward through a widening gap opened by Lieutenant William Wurtele near Raillencourt on the Arras-Cambrai road. The RCR fight unfolded mostly under the direction of lieutenants. The battalion command post and signals section moved up to a captured German dugout, only to take a direct hit in the doorway from a heavy shell, which killed Captain Francis McCrea and badly wounded Lieutenant Colonel C.R.E. Willets and several of his signallers. The 3rd Divisional Artillery observation post on the Bourlon Heights, equipped with a wireless station, could not see what was happening but could relay information supplied by runners. At 8:45, it informed 3rd Division Headquarters that "our troops were advancing fast, meeting little opposition" and that German artillery retaliation was only "slight," but this information was two hours old. Only two hours later, at 10:40, a wireless message alerted headquarters that the RCR had in fact been heavily engaged along the Marcoing Line at 8:50 a.m. This clear message came from the 7th Brigade at 9:30 after being received by a runner. No messages were sent to adjust the barrage to the circumstances or to call for more fire. In any event, there was no more ammunition to fire until the gun line was replenished later in the day. The heavy artillery did provide some defensive fire, mainly counter-battery in nature.[90]

The message traffic reveals the limits of the 1918 infantry-artillery-tank team, which had not yet been equipped with radios that could operate beyond the limits of their line telephone communications system. Unable to call directly for artillery or tank fire support, junior leaders did their best, coordinating the use of light machine guns and grenades to win the day but at great cost. Between the first RCR attack on the Marcoing Line until it was relieved at the northern edge of Cambrai on 30 September 1918, the battalion lost 273 men killed, wounded, and missing. Four officers died, including Roy Duplissie, and 16 were wounded, among them Gregg and C.R.E. Willets.[91] The losses compare closely to those of all other RCR major actions since the Somme, except in the high proportion of officers. During those three days, all forward RCR officers were hit. Reserve officers from the transport lines came up afterward to take over the remnants. Others came from the Nova Scotia Regiment Depot to replace at least some of the Cambrai losses.

Mercifully, the end of the war was close at hand; the German Army on the Western Front broke in October under the converging Entente blows. It is difficult to imagine how the Canadian Corps and its officer replacement system would have kept up had the Hundred Days offensive lasted much longer, even with the arrival of more conscripts for the ranks. Perhaps it did not matter, because the Canadian Corps system worked long enough to win the war. The deeds of some of the officers and NCOs on 28 September 1918 were acknowledged. Among those recognized was Lieutenant Gregg, who earned the Victoria Cross at the right of the line. His counterpart on the left of the line, Lieutenant Wurtele, earned a Military Cross. The evidence suggests that those awards were well deserved, but many others helped Gregg and Wurtele carry the battle. Of course, officers were not the only ones who led during the fight for the Marcoing Line. Over a dozen lance corporals, corporals, and sergeants, and nearly two dozen privates were recognized for their service before Cambrai "in the regimental records."[92] Decades after the war, Wurtele wrote about those events in the regimental newsletter *Pro Patria,* lamenting that "many worthy officers had been passed over [for valour decorations], including Lt. Duplissie who had ably supported Lt. Gregg ... before being killed."[93]

General Currie felt that the sacrifice west of Cambrai was worth it. On 1 October 1918, he wrote,

The five days' fighting had yielded practical gains of a very valuable nature, as well as 7,059 prisoners and 205 guns. We had gone through the last organized system of defences on our front, and our advance constituted a direct threat on the rear of the troops immediately to the north of our left flank, and their withdrawal had now begun.[94]

The officer development and replacement system of the Canadian Army, which helped to win that victory, is worthy of deeper investigation. It is part of the wider question of how the young dominion managed to raise such a large field army that was as capable as those of the most advanced modern industrialized nations with more extensive pre-war military institutions. The key ingredient in the Canadian response was the merit-based system that identified, cultivated, and redistributed men who stood out among their peers because they demonstrated the qualities that make good leaders. Their individual stories fill in the gaps in our understanding of how political patronage and social standing gave way as officer selection determinants.

The post-war consequences of building such a system are also worthy of inquiry. Not every veteran soldier and officer soldier returned home a broken man, even if each of them had to negotiate a journey back to peacetime life. Nor were all finished with military service. Canadian historical writing has yet to fully investigate the role played by the "graduates" of the Canadian Corps leadership development system in the nation's post-war social, economic, political, or military history. Anecdotal evidence suggests that this group is worth studying. Surviving combat leaders such as C.R.E. Willets and Milton Gregg contributed a great deal after the war ended, Willets as a Permanent Force officer and Gregg as an influential infantry leadership instructor, university administrator, parliamentarian, and diplomat. Their examples are mirrored in every Canadian Corps unit.[95]

Roy Duplissie's case offers a solemn reminder of how much human potential was lost to Canada in the fields of France and Belgium. After the war, the cenotaphs erected by grieving communities would stand as a testament to their collective grief and act as a place to mourn for those who could never travel overseas to find closure in one of the countless Commonwealth War Graves cemeteries or memorials scattered along the Western Front. Roy Duplissie is buried within sight of where he fell, in the small Crest Commonwealth War Graves Cemetery, near Fontaine-Notre Dame, alongside eighty-five Canadians who were killed on the same day. The cemetery lies on the embankment above the sunken road that connects Raillencourt with Fontaine-Notre-Dame and that features in RCR accounts of 28 September. Roy's name is also emblazoned on the town cenotaph at Windsor, Nova Scotia.

Heartbreaking though the loss of Roy Duplissie and so many other fine young men was, the experience of the Canadian Expeditionary Force (CEF) during the Hundred Days was not without hope. As demonstrated by the Battles of Amiens, the D-Q Line, the Canal du Nord, and the Marcoing Line (all but the last among the ten costliest Canadian engagements of the war), the replacement of fallen officers was a daunting task but one for which the military leadership devised an effective plan. Roy Duplissie embodied both the resilience of the Canadian soldier and the resourcefulness of the CEF leadership.

Notes

1 Library and Archives Canada (LAC), RG 150, Accession 1992-93/166, Box 2763-43, Military Personnel File, Lieutenant Roy Duplissie, Record of Service, 1918.
2 LAC, RG 9-III-D-2, vol. 4911, War Diary, Royal Canadian Regiment, 28 September 1918; R.C. Fetherstonaugh, *The Royal Canadian Regiment: 1883–1933* (Fredericton: Centennial Print and Litho, 1981), 350–63.
3 Bill Rawling, *Surviving Trench Warfare: Technology and the Canadian Corps, 1914–1918* (Toronto: University of Toronto Press, 1992), 114–20, 167–70; Shane B. Schreiber, *Shock Army of the British Empire: The Canadian Corps in the Last Hundred Days of the War* (Westport: Praeger, 1997); see also Mark Osborne Humphries, "The Myth of the Learning Curve," *Canadian Military History* 14, 4 (2005): Article 3.
4 G.W.L. Nicholson, *Canadian Expeditionary Force, 1914–1919: Official History of the Canadian Army in the First World War* (Ottawa: Department of National Defence, 1962), 422–59.
5 For more on the role of Canadian conscript soldiers during the last months of the war, see Patrick Dennis, *Reluctant Warriors: Canadian Conscripts and the Great War* (Vancouver: UBC Press, 2017).
6 See especially page XX, where Broad tackles the various legends and myths regarding inadequate training and short life expectancy in the Royal Flying Corps.
7 *Report of the Ministry, Overseas Military Forces of Canada, 1918* (London: His Majesty's Stationery Office, 1918), 11–28, https://www.canada.ca/en/department-national-defence/ services/military-history/history-heritage/official-military-history-lineages/official -histories/book-1918-overseas.html.
8 Fetherstonaugh, *The Royal Canadian Regiment,* 366.
9 LAC, Duplissie, Record of Service, 1915–18.
10 LAC, RG 9-III-D-2, vol. 4911, War Diary, Royal Canadian Regiment, 28 April 1917.
11 J.L. Granatstein, *The Greatest Victory: Canada's One Hundred Days, 1918* (Don Mills: Oxford University Press, 2014), 88.
12 Ibid., 89.
13 Sharpe also used this graph in "Enlistment in the Canadian Expeditionary Force, 1914–1918: A Re-evaluation," *Canadian Military History* 24, 1 (2015): 17–60. He added a footnote that doesn't appear in the encyclopedia article, to the effect that "the enlistment data in this table are based on Appendix C of Nicholson (1962: 546). They correct what must be a typographical error in Nicholson's table, which gives a total of 24,506 'other rank' enlistments in October, 1918 – an impossible number." In a 14 January 2020 email to the editors of this anthology Sharpe noted that "This typographical error has, unfortunately, found its way into some subsequent work." Email to the editors, 14 January 2020.
14 Quoted in Granatstein, *The Greatest Victory,* 95.

15 LAC, Duplissie, Record of Service, 1917–18.
16 LAC, War Diary and Appendices, Royal Canadian Regiment, 26–29 September 1918.
17 Robert Engen, *Strangers in Arms: Combat Motivation in the Canadian Army, 1943–45* (Montreal and Kingston: McGill-Queen's University Press, 2016), 28.
18 *Report of the Ministry, 1918*, 11–28.
19 Desmond Morton, *When Your Number's Up: The Canadian Soldier in the First World War* (Toronto: Random House, 1993), 95–103.
20 Geoffrey Hayes, *Crerar's Lieutenants: Inventing the Canadian Junior Army Officer, 1939–45* (Vancouver: UBC Press, 2017), 17–18, 80.
21 *Report of the Ministry, 1918*, 15, 29.
22 Ibid., 28–30.
23 Nova Scotia Archives, "Men in the Mines: A History of Mining Activity in Nova Scotia, 1720–1992: Gypsum," https://novascotia.ca/archives/meninmines/gypsum.asp.
24 LAC, Duplissie, RCR Attestation Paper and "Particulars of Family" form.
25 Department of National Defence, Directorate of History and Heritage, "Official Lineages, vol. 3, part 2: Infantry Regiments: The Nova Scotia Highlanders," http://www.cmp-cpm.forces.gc.ca/dhh-dhp/his/ol-lo/vol-tom-3/par2/nsh-eng.asp.
26 James Wood, *Militia Myths: Ideas of the Canadian Citizen Soldier, 1896–1921* (Vancouver: UBC Press, 2010), 171–209.
27 Nicholson, *Canadian Expeditionary Force*, 215.
28 LAC, Guide to Sources Relating to Units of the Canadian Expeditionary Force, "Infantry Battalions: 112th Battalion," 10, https://www.bac-lac.gc.ca/eng/discover/military-heritage/first-world-war/Documents/infantry%20battalions.pdf.
29 Nicholson, *Canadian Expeditionary Force*, 214.
30 LAC, RG 24-C-1-a, vol. 1661, 112th Battalion, Canadian Expeditionary Force, Nominal Roll of Officers, Non-Commissioned Officers, and Men.
31 Nicholson, *Canadian Expeditionary Force*, 214.
32 LAC, RG 9-III-D-2, Duplissie, 112th Battalion Record of Service.
33 LAC, RG 9-III-D-2, Duplissie, Overseas Record of Service.
34 LAC, RG 9-III-D-2, Duplissie, Casualty Form & Attestation Paper; Photograph in Fetherstonaugh, *The Royal Canadian Regiment*, 353.
35 Nicholson, *Canadian Expeditionary Force*, 215–23. See also Figure 9.2.
36 Nicholson, *Canadian Expeditionary Force*, 220–26.
37 Fetherstonaugh, *The Royal Canadian Regiment*, 286–91.
38 LAC, War Diary, Royal Canadian Regiment, 9–12 April 1917.
39 Fetherstonaugh, *The Royal Canadian Regiment*, 286–91.
40 LAC, Duplissie, Record of Service, 16 April 1917.
41 LAC, War Diary, Royal Canadian Regiment, May 1917; Fetherstonaugh, *The Royal Canadian Regiment*, 287–88.
42 LAC, War Diary, Royal Canadian Regiment, May 1917.
43 Ibid., 8–11 June, App 4, 1917; Fetherstonaugh, *The Royal Canadian Regiment*, 288–91.
44 Fetherstonaugh, *The Royal Canadian Regiment*, 292–97.
45 Ibid., 300–11.
46 LAC, War Diary, Royal Canadian Regiment, October–November 1917.
47 *Report of the Ministry, 1918*, 101–4.
48 LAC, Duplissie, Record of Service; LAC, War Diary, Royal Canadian Regiment, December 1917–January 1918.
49 Kandace Bogaert, "Patient Experience and the Treatment of Venereal Disease in Toronto's Military Base Hospital during the First World War," *Canadian Military History* 26, 2 (2017): Article 1.

50   LAC, Duplissie, Record of Service, Casualty Form, January–August 1918.
51   LAC, RG 9-III-D-4, vol. 5078, Major G.R. Collins, "Official Textbooks and Trench Warfare," 7–9. *Chevrons to Stars: The Official Organ of the Canadian Training School,* April 1917.
52   LAC, Duplissie, Record of Service, Casualty Form, August–September 1918.
53   LAC, War Diary, Royal Canadian Regiment, August–September 1918.
54   Nicholson, *Canadian Expeditionary Force,* 430–41.
55   LAC, War Diary, Royal Canadian Regiment, 19–24 September 1918.
56   LAC, RG 24-C-1-a, vol. 1661, 112th Battalion, CEF, Nominal roll, 1916.
57   Public Archives of New Brunswick (PANB), Brigadier Milton F. Gregg Papers, MGH-II, box 3, Personal Diary, September 1918, 2.
58   Michael O'Leary, "Lt. John Stanley Millett," The First World War Officers of the Royal Canadian Regiment, Regimental Rogue, http://regimentalrogue.com/rcr_great_war_ officers/rcr_offr_millett_js.html; Michael O'Leary, "Lieut. David Arthur Porter, M.C.," The First World War Officers of the Royal Canadian Regiment, Regimental Rogue, http:// regimentalrogue.com/rcr_great_war_officers/rcr_offr_porter_da.html.
59   Nicholson, *Canadian Expeditionary Force,* 425.
60   Fetherstonaugh, *The Royal Canadian Regiment,* 348–49.
61   PANB, Gregg, Personal Diary, September 1918, 2.
62   See Granatstein, *The Greatest Victory;* and Lee Windsor, Marc Milner, Roger Sarty, *Loyal Gunners: The History of 3rd Field Artillery Regiment, Royal Canadian Artillery and New Brunswick's Artillery, 1893–2012* (Waterloo: Wilfrid Laurier University Press, 2016).
63   LAC, RG 9-III-D-3, vol. 4892, War Diary, 7th Canadian Infantry Brigade, "3rd Canadian Division Report on Cambrai Battle, September 27th to October 10th 1918."
64   LAC, RG 9-III-D-3, vol. 4974, War Diary, Canadian Corps Heavy Artillery, Order 142, Addenda 2.
65   LAC, "3rd Canadian Division Report on Cambrai Battle, September 27th to October 10th 1918."
66   LAC, RG 9-III-D-3, vol. 4970, War Diary, 9th Canadian Field Brigade, 27–28 September 1918.
67   LAC, War Diary, Canadian Corps Heavy Artillery, 20–27 September 1918.
68   LAC, RG 9-III-D-3, vol. 4974, War Diary, 2nd Canadian Garrison Brigade, 27–28 September 1918; LAC, RG 9-III-D-3, vol. 4962, War Diary, 3rd Canadian Divisional Artillery, 25–29 September 1918.
69   Nicholson, *Canadian Expeditionary Force,* 448.
70   PANB, Gregg, Personal Diary, September 1918, 3.
71   Nicholson, *Canadian Expeditionary Force,* 454–56.
72   LAC, War Diary, 3rd Canadian Divisional Artillery, 27–28 September 1918.
73   LAC, War Diary, Royal Canadian Regiment, September 1918, "Appendix: Narrative of Operations, 28–30 September 1918"; Fetherstonaugh, *The Royal Canadian Regiment,* 353–55; PANB, Gregg, Personal Diary, September 1918, 4.
74   PANB, Gregg, Personal Diary, September 1918, 4.
75   Fetherstonaugh, *The Royal Canadian Regiment,* 354.
76   Ibid.
77   PANB, Gregg, Personal Diary, September 1918, 5.
78   LAC, War Diary, Royal Canadian Regiment, "Appendix: Narrative."
79   W.G. Wurtele, "Cambrai 1918," *Pro Patria,* July 1979, Regimental Rogue, http://regimental rogue.com/rcr_history/1914-1919/cambrai_1918_wurtele.htm.
80   PANB, Gregg, Personal Diary, September 1918, 6; Fetherstonaugh, *The Royal Canadian Regiment,* 355–56.

81 LAC, War Diary, Royal Canadian Regiment, "Appendix: Narrative"; Fetherstonaugh, *The Royal Canadian Regiment,* 355–56.

82 Gregg had only just taken over D Company when Duplissie arrived in late September 1918, after long service with C Company. PANB, Gregg, Personal Diary, September 1918, 1–2.

83 Ibid., 7; Fetherstonaugh, *The Royal Canadian Regiment,* 355–56.

84 Fetherstonaugh, *The Royal Canadian Regiment,* 355–56.

85 PANB, Gregg, Personal Diary, September 1918, 8; LAC, War Diary, Royal Canadian Regiment, "Appendix: Narrative"; Fetherstonaugh, *The Royal Canadian Regiment,* 355–56.

86 Fetherstonaugh, *The Royal Canadian Regiment,* 355–57.

87 PANB, Gregg, Personal Diary, September 1918, 8–9.

88 Ibid.; Fetherstonaugh, *The Royal Canadian Regiment,* 356–57.

89 LAC, War Diary, Royal Canadian Regiment, "Appendix: Narrative"; Appendix "Topp Letter": Letter from Lieutenant Colonel C.B. Topp, 1936.

90 LAC, War Diary, 7th Canadian Infantry Brigade, September 1918, Appendix "3rd Division Log of Cambrai," 2.

91 LAC, War Diary, Royal Canadian Regiment, 27–30 September 1918.

92 Fetherstonaugh, *The Royal Canadian Regiment,* 365–66.

93 Wurtele, "Cambrai 1918."

94 *Report of the Ministry, 1918,* 162.

95 Joel Watson, "The Life and Times of Milton F. Gregg, VC" (presentation for the University of New Brunswick Remembers ceremony, Fredericton, November 2017); "Colonel C.R. Willets Dies at Age 51, A.A. & Q.M.G. of Military District No. 3 Was a Distinguished Soldier," *Montreal Gazette,* 2 September 1931, cited in the Regimental Rogue. http://www.regimentalrogue.com/rcr_great_war_officers/rcr_offr_willets_cre.html.

10

"Scars upon My Heart": Arnold and Clarence Westcott, Brothers and Soldiers

Cynthia Comacchio

> *Your battle-wounds are scars upon my heart,*
> *Received when in that grand and tragic "show"*
> *You played your part.*

IN 1918, BEFORE SHE BECAME the famous chronicler of the Great War generation, Vera Brittain wrote the simple poem "To My Brother," which is excerpted above. Its spare words stand in contrast to the weight of her emotional anguish. Even as she put her fears on paper, her brother Edward was taking part in the "grand and tragic show" of the First World War. He was killed on the Italian front in June 1918, only two days after she wrote the poem.[1]

On an undated blank page in his official war diary for 1918, Private Clarence Westcott, fighting with the 161st Huron Battalion in France, recorded a few lines of unattributed poetry: "I know not where tomorrow's path may wend / Nor what the future holds / But this I know / Whichever way my feet are forced to go / I shall be given courage to the end."[2] It is the only such quotation in a diary whose entries are otherwise sparse and unemotive. Perhaps he found the words comforting as he, too, performed in the war's closing acts. Like Edward Brittain and scores of other young men, he did not survive to see the curtain descend on the final scene.

There are innumerable pieces of literature, memoir, music, art, and historical analysis about a war that, as never before in recorded history, cast so many into bereavement. An unfathomable number of deaths, brought about by strategized acts of violence, profoundly reshaped the culture of grief in the Western world.[3] My purpose here is to consider how the loss of so many men at the front affected "those who wait and wonder" by offering a biographical sketch of two young soldiers – Arnold and Clarence Westcott – identical twins who enlisted together.[4] They were born in the rural hamlet of Seaforth, in Huron County, Ontario. In

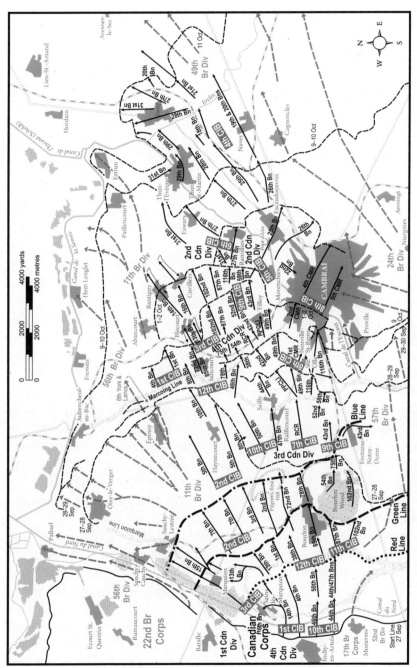

Figure 10.1 Canal du Nord, 27 September 1918. | Map by Mike Bechthold.

December 1915, at the age of twenty, they joined the newly established 161st Battalion. Arnold Westcott was seriously injured fighting near Amiens in April 1918, sustaining shrapnel wounds to his head and arm. He spent the war's final months hospitalized in Surrey, England, returning to Seaforth in January 1919. Clarence Westcott was killed in action at Bourlon Wood in late September 1918, during the Canal du Nord offensive. Hostilities ended scarcely six weeks later.

The war's greatest impact on Canadian families is simply rendered. Enlistment meant immediate separation from loved ones. This sudden absence – the first such departure from family for many soldiers, given their youth – might well apply to more than one male family member. Approximately 20 percent of the roughly 424,589 Canadian Expeditionary Force volunteers who fought overseas were married; the majority of them left behind at least one child, or expectant wives. For the many working-class and farm families that relied on male labour and wages, this dispersal of breadwinners had a considerable impact, as witnessed in the quick establishment of the Canadian Patriotic Fund to provide allowances for soldiers' wives and dependents.[5] Family farms and businesses found it increasingly difficult to replace the sons and brothers who went overseas; farmers' groups, in particular, lobbied the government to exempt their male family members.[6] Male-predominant factories and public services turned increasingly to women and older boys, and eventually to older girls, as in the case of the "farmerettes" who volunteered to help with agricultural labour.[7] At the war's end, the shocking toll of sixty thousand dead had enormous economic and demographic repercussions, both immediate and long term. It is no wonder, then, that the public lament about the "costs" of the war – in lost men, lost production, and lost future children – was a constant refrain in government and media throughout the 1920s.[8]

Far more difficult to assess are the unquestionable emotional costs of all these deaths. Although every soldier designated an official "next of kin," the many others who mourned each individual were left unrecorded and uncounted. They produced no personal accounts of their experience. Memory suspends the moment of learning the terrible news: although H. Gordon Skilling was only five when his brother was killed, decades later he "vividly" recalled the day in May 1917 "when my father came up the staircase from the store below, bearing the telegram with the news that my brother, Pte Edward Donald Skilling, had died of wounds ... As my mother wept at the head of the stairs I crept into the kitchen to cry against the wall."[9]

Even where apprehension, impact, and sorrow are documented, how well can language capture the range, depth, and breadth of grief? To what extent are recorded expressions of grief reflective of contemporary expectations as to how grief should properly be managed and expressed? Public commemoration was one way for bereavement, individual and collective, to be acknowledged and at least in some small measure expressed and acted on. Dedication to "remembrance" no doubt helped to assuage what is now classified as survivor guilt. Religious faith also comforted many and provided an accepted vocabulary of bereavement.[10] In the end, however, we can't be satisfied that any language, act, ritual, ceremony, in private or as a public event, can typify bereavement in any given moment – perhaps least of all when the cause of this mass emotional convulsion is an unprecedented global cataclysm.

Although the Westcott twins are central to this chapter, it is not a traditional biographical sketch so much as an exploration of the ways in which historians might approach the nebulous, complex, and intensely subjective matter of private grief. With only fragmentary personal testimony and little that documents the myriad and shifting private experiences of grief – if it is even possible to record *how it feels* to lose a loved one – how do we approach grief as a historical subject? Letters, diaries, reminiscences, and family lore recounted across generations permit some sense of how loss affected individuals and individual families. But unlike the public, collective, organized ritual that is commemoration, personal bereavement allows little in the way of generalization. Tolstoy's famous observation that "each unhappy family is unhappy in its own way" precisely captures the nature and experience of loss: grieving individuals chart their own course, despite the circumstances shared by so many.[11]

The only viable history of grief is one that traces changes and continuities in the practices and representations of mourning, that takes into account how socialization, acculturation, and the contexts and conditions of death shape certain conventions for grieving. Recent developments in cultural history, specifically the history of emotions, and in the psychology of grief and attachment theory, help to make meaning of the Great War's tremendous emotional consequences. Although this framework acknowledges that emotions are largely private, personal, and unique, it conceptualizes them with reference to culturally and historically specific constructs of gender, class, race, religion, age, and generation. The protocols of grief, as created by the dominant class, are intended to shape the nature, form, and extent of appropriate mourning – actually, ideal mourning – in any time and society. Consequently, even the individual impact of loss is expressed within certain socially defined parameters.[12]

The Victorian era was the apex of private loss as public performance, establishing a litany of rituals for both private and public grieving. Social status was measured by the lavishness of ceremony; the pauper's burial in an unmarked grave, grudgingly paid for with scant public funds, was a much dreaded final indignity for the poor. The fraternal associations of tradesmen and other helping societies generally included an insurance fund to ensure a "respectable" funeral.[13]

The Great War's unrelenting death count quickly pre-empted some of the public signifiers of loss. By 1916, such Victorian customs as dressing in black for specified periods and draping black crepe on doors and mirrors were becoming so pervasive as to spark discussion about their negative impact on national morale. Women, the largest sector of the war-bereaved and the traditional directors of family mourning, were admonished to dress normally, perhaps wearing a white armband to honour a loved one's memory. In a 1917 homily to the "next of kin," Nellie McClung urged the stalwart women of Canada to "hold tight to every shred of comfort," as, in her view, "we have to." She elaborated, "That's why we wear bright-colored clothes: there is a buoyancy, an assurance about them, that we sorely need! We try to economize on our emotions, too, never shedding a useless or idle tear!"[14] McClung directly associated comfort – meaning courage and endurance – with women's self-mastery and even concealment of their worry and grief, an "economizing" of emotions for the public good. The mounting death toll also made the traditional funeral, even in a modest form, increasingly impossible. The bodies of the dead could not be repatriated, even if they were intact and identified. What remained of many soldiers was interred overseas with little ceremony, occasionally in mass graves, far from the customary Christian rites and burial among family members.[15]

The war's cruel realities could not help but alter the culture of grief. Much of the Victorian code of emotional expression was nonetheless retained, confining grief within the bounds of the prevailing gendered, middle-class, Christian notion of respectability that underpinned the British value system and its standards for behaviour.[16] The ideal was a restrained, self-controlled, polite version of grief, in keeping with the expectations that were assumed to be universal among the better sort. Biological definitions of gender depicted women as fundamentally emotional creatures. Respectable women might reasonably weep without constraint, but doing so might quickly classify them as sufferers of the resolutely feminized disorder known as hysteria.[17] Also according to evolutionary science, but really in keeping with common prejudice, working-class and racialized women were thought to be predisposed to express their grief in unseemly, unwomanly, histrionic, and even animalistic fashion.[18]

As the most evolved of the species, white middle-class men were required to be rational, reserved, and stoic – manly men, who permitted themselves no visible display of anguish. If women walked a fine line in terms of what public grief was acceptable and what was medically and socially defined as abnormal, men were in many ways even more convention-bound. As Geoffrey Hayes demonstrates through the personal correspondence of the well-born Talbot Papineau, displaying emotional weakness damaged their personal honour and respectability.[19] The greater the loss, the more the public admiration for manly self-restraint. These are certainly prescriptions and not descriptions of actual behaviour, ideals simply presented as established norms. But early socialization in these principles of emotional self-control, achieved by such means as firm discouragement, shaming, and even punishment when children (boys in particular) cried – especially by calling them crybabies or sissy boys – fostered internalization of the code.[20] Although we cannot accurately measure the extent to which such standards shaped grief and its expression, it can be understood that only rare individuals could defy all the regulations of behaviour, reinforced as they were at home, at school, at church, and in the community.

The acceptance of death as a pathway to the soul's redemption and resurrection was also a Christian teaching with which children were familiarized from an early age, so much so that poignant deathbed scenes frequently appeared in children's books and periodicals.[21] They were urged to accept God's will in the loss of parents, siblings, and loved ones and to be prepared always to "go home to God." Given the high maternal and child mortality rates of the period, such teachings were also a practical response to a relatively common situation. Children could not be protected from the deaths that took place among family and friends. Both religion and reality thus encouraged their participation in the rituals associated with death, most of which occurred in the home. They were often involved in the visitation, the wake, and the service, even acting as pallbearers or otherwise taking part in funeral processions for siblings and playmates.[22]

By the time the Armistice was announced, Canadians had an established bereavement code to follow, at least those of British heritage who remained under the influence of British social practices. Because the code was firmly based on the Christian conceptualization of death, now reinforced by constant public reference to duty and sacrifice for nation and empire, it provided an important model for the many Ontario communities that remained loyal to the British middle-class Protestant value system. Certainly, this imperial attachment applied in the hamlet of Seaforth, home of the Westcott family. As a local poet declared in the town newspaper, "We are all British, and fight for the Red, White and Blue." This line ended each of her seven stanzas on the importance of supporting the war effort through to Allied victory.[23]

Much of the Westcott brothers' story had to be pieced together from the sparse details in official sources, including the censuses, birth, marriage, and death certificates, and attestation papers and other military documents.[24] James Arnold St. Clair Westcott, known as Arnold, and Charles Clarence Victor Westcott, known as Clarence or Clare, were born on 30 July 1895 at the family home on John Street.[25] Their grandparents on both sides emigrated to Huron County from Exeter, England, in 1842 to take up homesteading in the Upper

Canadian bush made famous by Susanna Moodie. They were among the first European settlers in what is now Huron East.[26] Arnold and Clarence's parents, Annie Copp and William Westcott, were both born near Seaforth. Unlike his father, William Westcott did not become a farmer; the 1901 census classifies him as a "mason." The twins were the last of the children born to their mother and father, who were then thirty-four and thirty-seven, respectively. Their four older siblings (two boys and two girls) were close in age, but an eight-year gap separated the youngest of these (Annie) from the twins, suggesting that they might have been a surprise. The eldest son, William, a "mason's apprentice" in 1901, was seventeen when the twins arrived. He probably worked alongside his father, whose major source of employment was bricklaying.[27] William Westcott Senior died in 1906, at the age of forty-eight. His death certificate succinctly records the cause of his demise: he "drank Paris Green while insane."[28] The 1911 census indicates that only the fifteen-year-old twins and their youngest sister, twenty-three-year-old Annie, remained at John Street with their mother.[29]

The twins next appear in the historical record on the occasion of their enlistment in the newly established 161st Huron Battalion. Clarence joined up on 8 December 1915, whereas Arnold waited an entire week to enlist on the fifteenth. Was he persuaded by his brother's example? This is highly likely, given their closeness. But his precise reason for enlisting is lost to us: was he moved by Clarence's patriotism and bravado, his own sense that he and his twin were a unit, separation anxiety, or feelings of responsibility and protectiveness toward Clarence? Or was the week's delay a self-assertion on Arnold's part? Given what is known of their relationship, all of these motives are plausible, and they are borne out in current findings on the psychology of twins.[30] Their attestation papers indicate that the twenty-year-old brothers had no previous militia or other military experience and that they were both unmarried. As was the case for Jonathan Vance's Rob Buchan, military culture had played virtually no role in their pre-war lives; like Buchan, the twins possessed the qualities of the "archetypal citizen-soldier" (page 46). At slightly more than five foot two and roughly 125 pounds, they were small men, but this did not disqualify them from volunteering at a time when the average height for men was about five foot seven, and the need for enlistments was already critical.[31] Sent to England for training, they were deployed to the front lines early in the new year.

But such details, though significant and relatively easy to uncover, are not what we most need or want to know in this instance. They reveal nothing about how Clarence Westcott's family – his widowed mother, his siblings, and especially his surviving twin and fellow soldier, Arnold – *felt* his loss. Their story might have remained only a scant factual outline, like the stories of most ordinary soldiers in the Great War. I was fortunate, however, to find a number of

Figure 10.2 Arnold (right) and Clarence Westcott, 1915. |
Used with permission of Clare Westcott.

newspaper columns written by a direct descendant, who was a well-known
journalist and civil servant some thirty years ago: Clare Westcott, son of Arnold,
nephew and namesake of Clarence, whom he has memorialized as "the hero I
never knew." Those writings helped to fill in much of the otherwise unknowable
detail about the twins' childhood, their relationship, their war experiences, and
how Arnold was affected by Clarence's death in battle. Even more fortuitously,
I then found Clare Westcott, who generously shared his memories of growing
up in the shadow of his father's sorrow for his lost twin.[32] Notwithstanding the
usual caveats about the uses of oral history and memory as evidence, Clare
Westcott's recollections about his father's grief, even more so than the family
lore passed along about Clarence himself, opened a small gateway into the
private emotions that exemplify a lifelong bereavement.[33]

Westcott family history depicts the young twins as healthy, rambunctious,
adventurous lads. Growing up in Seaforth and attending Central School, they
were each other's closest companions. They were reportedly inseparable, and it

was understood that anyone who attacked one of them on or off school grounds automatically took on the other. Like many country boys of that time, they were allowed considerable freedom to amuse themselves, unsupervised, when they were not in school. They enjoyed long summer days of fishing and rough-and-tumble games of shinny on frozen ponds in the winter. They played such pranks as attempting to ride hogs at the town stockyards. They loved horses. Arnold Westcott's war diary entry for 17 October 1917 recorded that "14 years ago today I received a kick from Biggins horse on the head and it nearly finished me."[34] He was eight when the accident occurred, making a physical impact and imprinting his permanent memories. Less than a year after he wrote about the incident, a severe shrapnel wound to the head while fighting at the Somme near Amiens landed him in hospital for the war's final months.[35]

Like most adolescents of their day, the twins finished their formal schooling at the age of fourteen, the province's legal age of school leaving. Their education surpassed that of most of their generation, giving them a route into the lower rungs of the middle class. Arnold apprenticed to a Seaforth jeweller, and Clare worked as a bookkeeper at a local business. They were so physically alike that they were frequently mistaken for each other. At least one of their youthful adventures exploited this close resemblance. To avoid a date that did not appeal to him, Arnold apparently persuaded Clarence, who seems to have been the more outgoing of the two, to stand in for him – naturally, without revealing the hoax to the young woman. She did not suspect the truth until she noticed the tobacco stains on Clarence's hands. Since Arnold was known to be an avowed non-smoker, the jig was up. Neither twin was permitted a second date.[36] No one who knew the young Westcotts could have been surprised by their decision to enlist together.

Ultimately, Arnold and Clarence did not relate to each other solely as siblings and twins, integral though that connection was to their lives. They were also fellow soldiers, enlisted in the same battalion, departing for training in January 1916, fighting in France for two years before Arnold was seriously wounded in the spring of the war's final year and Arnold met his death that deadly autumn. From the late nineteenth century, and ever more so after 1914, the modern army, in which each rank below the officer class was formed largely of men defined by their shared age and generation rather than their social status, increasingly emphasized the language of brotherhood.[37] The fraternal depiction of soldiering – of "brothers in arms" – reflects an intensity of shared experiences in training and in battle beyond camaraderie. Like individual survival, victory was contingent on the soldiers' mutuality, interdependence, and obedience.

Fraternal relations operated beyond the level of metaphor, however, as brothers throughout the empire enlisted together or in quick sequence. The number of brothers in the Canadian Expeditionary Force (CEF) was not recorded, but historical case studies for various Allied troops suggest that it was relatively high.[38] These men were, by and large, born in the 1890s. Because Canadian family size was already declining by the end of the nineteenth century, the pre-war years constitute the last before the post–Second World War baby boom that the average family still counted about five children. A significant number, especially in rural areas, had several more. Since births were usually spaced closely together, often barely two years apart, families could often have three or more brothers of enlistment age. Brothers of about the same age might enlist together in hopes of being able to watch out for each other at the front; this is certainly likely in the case of the Westcott twins. Their hometown of Seaforth furnished an exemplary model of such enlistments in the Hinchcliffe family, in that both sons and their father signed on with the 161st Huron Battalion. Multiple enlistments frequently meant multiple losses within one family. The Memorial (Silver) Cross, instigated in 1919, paid tribute to all mothers who had lost sons; those who had lost more than one were singled out for special honours.[39] The first Silver Cross mother, Charlotte Susan Wood, saw eleven sons off to fight; five did not return.[40]

Losing a sibling in childhood was a relatively familiar occurrence in a time of high infant and child mortality: the Westcotts had buried a seven-month-old-boy before Arnold and Clarence were born. But loss in young adulthood – considered the most robust and healthy of life stages – became steadily more common as the war progressed. This point was underlined by the gendered nature of war deaths. Young women continued to face the threat of death in childbirth, as high maternal mortality rates also continued unabated through the 1920s, but now young men in their prime were dying in unprecedented numbers. Contemporaries frequently lamented that the deaths of so many "future fathers of the nation" undermined a young and underpopulated country, at once destabilizing its present and challenging its ambitions for the future.[41]

Numerous writings, literary and personal, published and unpublished, before, during, and since the war, testify to the profound emotional impact of the death of adult siblings. Does losing a twin in adulthood, especially one who faced the same risks to life as the survivor, produce a deeper set of "scars upon the heart"? Recent psychological studies on twinship and attachment confirm the long-standing popular view that twins have a more intense interpersonal relationship than do regular siblings. Moreover, identical twins are often closer than fraternal ones: each tends to make the other integral to the self. Their co-identification is characterized from infancy by the desire to stay physically close, by separation distress if this does not occur, and by turning to each other for assurance of safety and security.[42] The twins, like many others who signed up with brothers and friends in community battalions, enlisted with hopes of remaining together at the front. As the war pressed on, casualties mounted, and recruitment lagged, men were dispersed to fill the most pressing needs. The Hurons were absorbed into the 4th Reserve Battalion on 15 February 1918.[43] Clarence was sent to the 47th Battalion of the 4th Division, which would play a monumental role in the Canal du Nord operation as the Hundred Days campaign brought the war to its end. It appears that the twins were separated at some point in late 1917, if only allocated to different camps. The brief, methodical jottings in Arnold Westcott's war diaries for the years 1917 and 1918 indicate that he and Clarence met as often as they could arrange it, frequently spending their scant free time enjoying events together. On 17 October 1917, Arnold took the train to Guildford to meet with Clarence at the YMCA, and the brothers then "went to the Methodist Sunday School room to a lecture."[44] Their individual letters home also appear to have followed the conventional script. Like most soldiers, they spoke less of fear and fighting than of everyday life in the trenches: mud, lice, rats, even the awful strawberry-rhubarb jam that undoubtedly made their mother's all the more longingly remembered.[45]

On 29 April 1918, Arnold Westcott was seriously injured at the Somme during the German spring offensive. Despite his wounds, he managed to write a diary entry that very day, recording that he "went into F line tonight. Was wounded about 430 this morning in head and arm by shrapnel. *Left Clarence never to see him again*" (emphasis added). That final phrase suggests that, in shock and in pain, Arnold did not expect to recover. His first (or last) thought was for Clarence. These few words convey a visceral torment that even his injury could not override. For those who know the sad ending of the twins' story, the words are uncannily prophetic. On the first of May, Arnold had surgery at No. 7 Casualty Clearing Station and, again remarkably, wrote to Clarence and his mother that same day. The next day, he reported that he was being "sent to Blighty." He was recovering slowly in a Surrey hospital, continually anxious about Clarence, as the final decisive battles of the war were being fought.[46]

Now fighting with the 4th Division, Clarence Westcott took part in the Canal du Nord operation planned for late September 1918. From beginning to end, despite its tactical success, the operation was fraught. Commanded by General Arthur Currie, the 1st and 4th Divisions were to cross the dry canal. The 4th Division, led by Major-General David Watson, was charged with the enormous task of seizing Bourlon Wood. Capturing Bourlon, where German forces were positioned on high ground, thus subjecting the Canadian Corps to continual artillery fire, was essential to the larger objective: to push northeast to Cambrai with reinforcements from the 2nd and 3rd Divisions.[47] Among the wounded was Canon Frederick George Scott, senior Protestant chaplain of the

1st Division, by this time a three-year veteran. Privy to the intensive month-long planning that preceded the offensive, Scott crossed the canal with the men. As he later wrote, "Probably never in the war had we experienced a moment of deeper anxiety. The men would have to climb down one side of the canal, rush across it, and climb up the other. It seemed inevitable that the slaughter would be frightful." And frightful it was. The "stupendous" attack began just before daybreak, when "the savage roar burst forth" as "field guns, heavy guns, and siege batteries sent forth their fury, and machine guns poured millions of rounds into the country beyond the Canal."[48] Military correspondent Fred James called the canal crossing and the taking of Bourlon Wood "Canada's Triumph," his eye-witness account also leaving no question about its ferocity:

> At 5:20, of the morning of September 27th, sharp on the minute, one of our 18-pounder guns barked twice. Then the length and depth of our front broke into red and orange and violet flashes; our whole line gave tongue in a crashing roar of innumerable explosions, all blending into one terrific tide of sound, wrenching the waiting earth and quiet air from peace to furious tumult in an instant of time.[49]

Also with the Canadian Corp, veteran reporter and war correspondent J.F.B. Livesay recounted in the *Globe* that the Canadians had "had a hard battle for the Canal du Nord" but they had nonetheless managed its "brilliant" capture. Livesay pronounced the engagement at Bourlon Wood "a great and impressive victory, and with relatively few casualties."[50]

The CEF's official historian concludes that "the fighting on this Sunday (29 September) had been exceedingly bitter, costing 2,089 Canadian casualties."[51] Notwithstanding its efficacy, the human cost was some 13,600 Canadian casualties – almost half the toll of the entire 30,000 lost during the Hundred Days campaign.[52] Private Clarence Westcott, from Seaforth, Ontario, enlisted with the 161st Huron Battalion, was among the fallen.

On 27 September, Clarence Westcott made one last succinct entry in his diary: "Sent to F lines." In standard fashion, his official death record declares only that he was "killed in action" two days later. His designated next of kin was his mother; the document indicates that notice was dispatched to her on 1 October. Meanwhile, in his Surrey hospital bed, Arnold was hearing rumours about the war's imminent end and recording his hope of reunion with Clarence and their return to Seaforth together. His 1917–18 diaries usually logged the day's most important events briefly and without elaboration. He rarely mentioned his feelings. Just before learning of Clarence's fate, on 3 October, he wrote, simply and without elaborating, that he was "not feeling well." This is the most that he ever articulated about a grave head wound that kept him hospitalized for the better

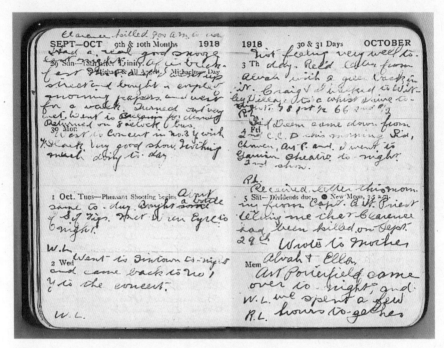

Figure 10.3 Arnold Westcott's war diary for the week of 29 September 1918; the later addition noting his brother's death is at the top left. | Courtesy of Clare Westcott and used with his permission.

part of five months. Two days later, a terse entry, perhaps all the more telling because of its brevity, stated that he had "received letter this morning from Captain A.H. Riest telling me that Clarence had been killed on Sept 29th. Wrote to Mother, Alvah and Ellen [an older brother and his wife]." It is possible that his letters to them arrived before the official notification. Arnold's only other comment on that day was a reference to a condolence visit by a fellow soldier, who "came over tonight and we spent a few hours together." Although various diary entries indicate that the twins held to their faith, participating in Methodist services and Bible readings while overseas, Arnold's diary does not mention that he turned to religion for comfort. None of this, of course, proves that he did not. It is simply evidence that he chose not to "speak" his grief aloud, even in his personal diary.[53] At some later point, Arnold added a line of text to the diary page for 29 September. In the uppermost margin, above the date and his earlier perfunctory notes about the day's events, he pencilled in "Clarence killed 9 AM today." There could have been little consolation for a sorrow that left him alone for the first time since he and his twin had entered the world together barely twenty-three years before. His life was definitively altered; his twin would remain a phantom presence for the rest of his days. Nearly ninety years later, his nephew Clare Westcott sensed precisely the meaning of his father's experience in losing his twin brother at the front: "In any ranking of emotion, the fear of being so desperately alone comes ahead of the fear of battle."[54]

Although Arnold Westcott maintained his diary at least until he disembarked in Halifax on 25 January 1919, to make his way by train to Seaforth, there is no further mention of Clarence. This sort of "numbing and suppression of emotion" was a typical response of soldiers to the deaths of their comrades, an emotional self-defence necessary to master fears about their own mortality and to avoid the anguish of witnessing deaths without end.[55] Yet the loss of a brother who was also his identical twin was probably an even greater blow for him than for their mother, not only because of the documented specialness of the twin relationship, but also because Arnold knew the battlefield, its dangers and its horrors, first-hand. The manner of his twin's death was only too familiar, too real, for someone who had also fought at the front. Given this, it is doubtful that he could have found comfort in imagining a "good death" for Clarence.

The county newspaper, the *Huron Expositor,* said little about Clarence's demise beyond acknowledging it and extending condolences to the Westcott family. Its notice was replicated in the *Globe* on 11 October. The weekly community newspaper, the *Seaforth News,* commented that Clarence was "a fine young man," that his twin had recently been wounded in battle, and that his mother deserved every sympathy for what the war had wrought: "the heart-felt sorrow of all are with them in their grief."[56] By this time, after four years of war, the tremendous casualties, and the sense of horror that the conflict would take even more young lives, there was little heart for eulogizing fallen individuals. The numbers were sobering enough, without drawing more attention to the splendid hometown boys they represented. There are no details about any memorial service for Clarence, private or public.

Studies show that the emotional impact of separation or loss is far greater for twins than for other siblings, and greater still for identical twins. It has been equated to the grief experienced for a parent or spouse.[57] Keeping the dead twin alive in memory is especially important for the survivor, through regular acts of commemoration and by ensuring that remembrance is maintained across generations.[58] Arnold's first-born son, who arrived only six years after Clarence died, was named for him, in effect embodying his memories and becoming a living tribute to him. Nonetheless, Arnold must have felt a certain pang in calling his son by the name of his beloved twin.

The same was very possibly true for Annie Westcott. Clare Westcott remembers her as an affectionate grandmother, who regularly took part in Arnold's family life and treasured her grandchildren. She also filled the traditional female role as keeper of family history, often recounting the twins' youthful exploits in Seaforth. She probably wanted to stay close to the twin who remained – also a common parental grieving strategy – and to foster a special closeness with his first-born son, her own boy's namesake.

Clare Westcott recalls hearing his father's stories about his uncle from his earliest childhood years. There were funny tales about the twins' joint and individual adventures, and serious stories about Clarence's heroism as a young soldier who perished in one of the battles that helped to end the war. The family religiously attended the annual Remembrance Day ceremony in Seaforth, where Arnold marched with his veteran friends to the war memorial, which was inscribed with his brother's name and those of friends from their childhood and youth.[59] Most of all, Clare recalls with astonishing clarity his own fear and confusion on first witnessing his father's quiet tears during Remembrance Day:

> When I was a small boy, I remember being confused and frightened when I saw my father cry. It was cold and damp and big flakes of snow were falling. I was standing by my dad at the war memorial in the town park. Heads were bowed and except for the wind in the trees there was no sound. It was November 11, 1928. I was too young to know that my name was cut into the granite base beneath the tall stone statue of the soldier. Along with the names of fathers, sons and brothers from our small Ontario town. At two minutes after 11, a sound echoed through the wet and foggy morning. It was the sad wail of "The Last Post" from a bugler in the distance. The memory of that sound on that day was forever etched in the mind of a 4-year-old boy. When I looked up at my dad, there were tears running down his cheeks. It was 10 years since Clarence Westcott was killed.[60]

Never having seen his father cry, the young Clare was shaken by the emotion that broke through his usual self-control. In the intuitive manner of children, he understood that Clarence was more than the subject of the stories his father told to keep his memory alive. He was ever-present in his absence, an unabated, inconsolable sorrow that haunted Arnold until his own passing.[61] Clarence Westcott was interred at the Anneux British Cemetery west of Cambrai, plot 4, row F, grave 86, about three miles from where shrapnel tore open his chest.[62] Like many others, his mother never saw her son's final resting place, although his namesake nephew did undertake the journey more than a half-century after he was felled at Bourlon Wood.[63]

For parents, the pain of losing a child is amplified by the death of several born close together, as many soldier-brothers were, especially if the war destroyed all the second-generation men in the family. It is understandable that losing a twin son would cause acute suffering. While trying to come to terms with the death, parents of a twin are constantly reminded, perhaps even shaken off-balance, by their regular contact with a survivor of strikingly similar appearance. Such a reminder can be a source of comfort or pain; not infrequently, it is both.[64] The blow was unquestionably hard for Annie Westcott, as for the many mothers across the land and around the world who lost their sons at the front. Arnold and Clarence were the youngest of her children by eight years, the only ones still living with her at the time of their enlistment, and she had raised them on her own during the decade between her husband's death and their departure overseas. In 1918, she had not seen them for more than two years. Their few remaining personal writings suggest that they had a warm rapport with her. Arnold noted "mother's 39th anniversary" in his war diary on 16 April 1918, despite being positioned at the front at the time and undoubtedly having more pressing concerns.

Clarence's surviving postcards echo this thoughtfulness with a teasing affection. A postcard of 6 May 1917 featured a photograph of himself, which he explained had been taken "at the camp studio" in Surrey, where he and Arnold had trained before front-line duty. In his view, it was "better" than an earlier one he had sent her. Although brief and perhaps deliberately unsentimental, the message exposes his longing for home and family with wistful references to his homecoming, meant to reassure his mother (and probably himself) that things would soon return to normal: "You will soon be getting enough of this mug won't you. I just wish I could jump off the card when it gets home." Later that year, he sent his mother a portrait card of George V and Queen Mary, urging her "don't work too hard" and closing with "Wish you were here to see some of the sights."[65] Annie Westcott was no stranger to tragedy: she endured the loss of an infant son in 1888, the shocking death of her husband in 1906, and the passing of her elder daughter, Lovica, in 1914. At age thirty-two, the mother of young children, Lovica had succumbed to the common scourge of tuberculosis. Her sister, also named Annie, herself a young mother of five – including twins – perished in the Spanish influenza pandemic.[66]

When the news of the Armistice reached Canada, Seaforth "was given over to rejoicing." Bells rang, whistles "went loose," automobiles paraded with horns honking, "bunting and flags hung everywhere," and the mayor declared a holiday.[67] The *Globe* also reported that, in Seaforth, "large crowds filled the [main] street at night, where towering bonfires lit up the town." The celebration, however, "was mixed with sadness owing to the large casualty list in the 161st Huron Battalion."[68] Because the men of Huron County enlisted in various towns throughout the war, their total number is difficult to pin down; it seems to have been around 800. The 1917 nominal roll of the 161st listed 28 officers and a total of 749 other ranks.[69] The casualties were disproportionately enormous in a rural area such as Huron County, which comprised only about ten thousand residents.[70] It must well have seemed that the entire community was in mourning.

Early in 1919, Annie Westcott received a letter from Belgium, written by John M. Graham of the 12th Canadian Field Ambulance. Graham's battalion had followed the 47th, with which Clarence had been fighting when he was killed. After expressing his "deepest sympathy," Graham added, "While advancing over the shell-torn area N. West of Cambrai with my own Brigade which was relieving, I picked up this diary. Noticing that the Regimental No. in it was one of the 161st from my own home Co., I picked it up hoping that one day it would be restored to its rightful owner."

Graham was able to shine some light on what happened at the Canal du Nord, clearly attempting to reassure Annie that her son's death confirmed his bravery and dedication to the cause:

Evidently this portion of the field had been stormed by a platoon of the 47th Battalion consisting mostly of the 161st Huron's Own Boys, who carried ever forward by that indomitable spirit, pushed back, crushing underfoot the accursed Hun who for more than three years had threatened the Civilized World. This was the courage which completely routed the Huns and resulted in one of the greatest victories ever attained. A victory which will go down in the annals of history as the grandest and most glorious achievement of the Canadian Corps.

He enclosed Clarence's diary and signed his letter with the standard Christian blessing: "May the Almighty sustain and comfort you at this sad hour."[71]

Arnold Westcott spent the rest of his days in Seaforth. He completed his apprenticeship with the watchmaker and jeweller with whom he had worked before enlisting. He married Alva Howard in 1922, and their first son was born two years later. Shortly after Clare's birth, Arnold bought the jewellery business on the owner's retirement, and the Westcotts together ran the store on Main Street for over forty years. He took care of his mother, Annie, until her death in 1946.[72] As well as the irremediable pain of losing Clarence, he continued to suffer terrible headaches and partial deafness from his injuries. Minuscule pieces of shrapnel remained in his head and arm, the ghastly mementoes of war that many veterans brought home with them, so he needed regular treatments at the veterans' hospital in London, fifty miles away, through the 1920s and 1930s. His son remembers "the many times [during those years] when mother took my baby sister and me to mind our store." Arnold Westcott died in 1961, in Toronto, at what was then known as Sunnybrook Veterans' Hospital. According to Clare, the brain tumour that ended his life was in the exact spot where he was hit in 1918.[73]

Much of this consideration of the grief experience of the next of kin is uncomfortably speculative for historians, who are essentially empirical in their methodology. In and of itself, however, traditional documentary evidence does not typically disclose much about private emotions. At best, a sense of how the subject may have felt in confronting a terrible loss can be carefully teased out of these documents. Consequently, a close reading of such personal papers as I was fortunate to find in the case of the Westcott twins, along with invaluable recollections from a direct descendent, brought me as close to the feeling of grief as I could venture. Some of this, as noted, can be contextualized and historicized with what we know of other individual and collective responses in similar situations. A judicious application of conceptual frameworks borrowed from the history of emotions and psychology also helps to fill out a story that, ultimately, cannot be recovered so much as reimagined through, and despite, the clouds of time. Above all, as historian Leonore Davidoff points out, these approaches necessarily "remind us that 'a sibling's death ends only a life, it does not end a relationship.'"[74] What can be known of Arnold Westcott's emotional experience supports the view that, for his generation of men, even the life-shattering impact of losing a twin brother to violent death was met with an intensely interiorized grief, largely kept from others, perhaps too painful to capture in words, even in private writings. Social expectations and cultural codes of expression and their related behaviour fundamentally shape even the most personal of sorrows.

The Great War veterans and fallen heroes were supposed to have fought, suffered, and died for the righteous cause of King and Empire, of democracy and Christianity, of the triumph of civilization over barbarity. Open and unrestrained sorrow on the part of veterans and next of kin might appear to challenge those core beliefs, imprinted on them since childhood. Endurance of such enormous losses, personal and collective, was aided by the belief that suffering on such a scale had to have been worthwhile. The bereavement of all who mourned the sixty-six thousand dead, in a country of barely 8 million, cast a pall over every community across the nation. For all the horror that the death count signified, however, almost 90 percent of Canadian soldiers survived the war. As was true for Arnold Westcott, their suffering must have been exacerbated by their intimacy with those who had died and with the conditions of their deaths.[75] But this sorrow is rarely discernible in tangible historical evidence except perhaps of the most private, and consequently often inaccessible, kind. Emotional codes are also historical, at once culturally defined and shaped by gender and class. Trained to stoicism and self-control since childhood, traits that were both "manly" and "soldierly," enlisted men were especially unlikely to record their innermost thoughts in diaries and correspondence that might be subject to military scrutiny. Moreover, grief cannot be simply charted, any more than the bereft can ever know what forms it might take or how long it might last. For some, like Arnold Westcott, the loss was so wrenching that they simply learned to cope as they got on with their lives. But the suffering never truly went away. The mourning that beset the world in the wake of the Great War encompassed more than the millions of deaths. As poets, writers, and musicians of that time, and a great many since, remind us, it was a requiem for a generation lost and a value system shattered.[76]

Acknowledgments

This chapter is dedicated, fondly and respectfully, to Clare Westcott, nephew and namesake of Clarence Westcott, whose various newspaper articles led me to him personally, and also in memory of his beloved daughter, Genevieve Westcott, who was very supportive of my project. Sadly, she passed away on 10 July 2020 in Auckland, New Zealand. This story very much belongs to Clare and the Westcott family, in tribute to young Clarence who lost his life in the final days of the Great War.

Notes

1 Vera Brittain, "To My Brother," First World War Poetry Digital Archive, http://ww1lit. nsms.ox.ac.uk/ww1lit/collections/item/1747. This poem was in Brittain's first poetry collection, *Verses of a V.A.D.*, published in August 1919. Her famous chronicle of the war years, *Testament of Youth*, was published in 1933. Jonathan F. Vance, *Death So Noble: Memory, Meaning, and the First World War* (Vancouver: UBC Press, 1997), considers the widespread poetic output that the Great War occasioned among Canadian soldiers and civilians alike. In Chapter 6 of this volume, Geoffrey Hayes quotes the poem "Carmina," a tribute to Talbot Papineau (page 146).

2 Although Clarence Westcott didn't cite the author, I have traced the words to Ella Wheeler Wilcox, an American poet, "New Thought" ideologue, and pacifist. The poem was published in 1908, in her *New Thought: Common Sense and What Life Means to Me*, which was reprinted and edited by Reverend Lux Newman and Phineas Parkhurst Quimby Philosophical Society, 2008. Wheeler Wilcox made a well-received appearance in France in 1918, reciting her poems at a US Army camp of nine thousand stevedores. See Newman and Parkhurst, "Introduction," in *New Thought*, 5. Is it possible that Clarence Westcott also heard Wheeler Wilcox's recitations at some point that year? He and his brother Arnold enjoyed public lectures, according to several brief entries in Arnold's diary.

3 Pat Jalland, *Death in War and Peace: A History of Loss and Grief in England, 1914–1970* (Oxford: Oxford University Press, 2010), 15; see also Carol Acton, *Grief in Wartime: Private Pain, Public Discourse* (New York: Palgrave Macmillan, 2007); and Jay Winter, *Sites of Memory, Sites of Mourning: The Great War in European Cultural History*, 2nd ed. (Cambridge: Cambridge University Press, 2014).

4 Nellie McClung, *The Next of Kin: Those Who Wait and Wonder* (Toronto: Thomas Allen, 1917).

5 The Canadian Patriotic Fund depended on public donations to supplement the family budgets of mothers and children of enlisted men who met the rather stringent financial and "moral" regulations. The classic on this subject is Desmond Morton, *Fight or Pay: Soldiers' Families in the Great War* (Vancouver: UBC Press, 2004).

6   Mourad Djebabla, "'Fight or Farm': Canadian Farmers and the Dilemma of the War Effort in World War I (1914–1918)," *Canadian Military Journal* 13, 2 (2013), http://www.journal. forces.gc.ca/vol13/no2/page57-eng.asp; John Herd Thompson, *The Harvests of War: The Prairie West, 1914–1918* (Toronto: McClelland and Stewart, 1978), 133.

7   George C. Creelman, "Impressions of a Farmerette," *OAC Review* 30 (June 1918): 448–49.

8   See Cynthia Comacchio, *Nations Are Built of Babies: Saving Ontario's Mothers and Children* (Montreal and Kingston: McGill-Queen's University Press, 1993), especially "Chapter 2: The Infant Soldier."

9   H. Gordon Skilling, *The Education of a Canadian: My Life as a Scholar and Activist* (Montreal and Kingston: McGill-Queen's University Press, 2000), 20.

10 For more on the role of religion, see Chapter 8 in this volume.

11 Leo Tolstoy, *Anna Karenina* (New Haven: Yale University Press. 2014), 3. Originally published in 1877. As Tolstoy put it, "All happy families resemble each other; each unhappy family is unhappy in its own way."

12 See André Loez, "Tears in the Trenches: A History of Emotions and the Experience of War," in *Uncovered Fields: Perspectives in First World War Studies,* ed. Jenny Macleod and Pierre Purseigle (Leiden: Brill Academic, 2004), 211–26; Jan Plamper, *The History of Emotions: An Introduction,* trans. Keith Tribe (Oxford: Oxford University Press, 2015); and Susan Matt, "Recovering the Invisible: Methods for the Study of the Emotions," in *Doing Emotions History,* ed. Peter Stearns and Susan Matt (Urbana: Chicago University Press, 2014), 41–56.

13 Fraternal associations are discussed in George Emery and J.C. Herbert Emery, *A Young Man's Benefit: The Independent Order of Odd Fellows and Sickness Insurance in the United States and Canada, 1860–1929* (Montreal and Kingston: McGill-Queen's University Press, 1999); Bryan D. Palmer, "Mutuality and the Masking/Making of Difference: Mutual Benefit Societies in Canada, 1850–1950," in *Social Security Mutualism: The Comparative History of Mutual Benefit Societies,* ed. Marcel van der Linden (Berne, Switzerland: Peter Lang, 1996), 114–16; also Todd Stubbs, "Patriotic Masculinity and Mutual Benefit Fraternalism in Urban English Canada: The Sons of England, 1874–1900," *Histoire sociale/Social History* 45, 89 (2012): 25–50.

14 McClung, *The Next of Kin,* 248; Suzanne Evans, "Marks of Grief: Black Attire, Medals, and Service Flags," in *A Sisterhood of Suffering and Service: Women and Girls of Canada and Newfoundland during the First World War,* ed. Sarah Glassford and Amy Shaw (Vancouver: UBC Press, 2012), 219–40.

15 Ross Wilson, "The Burial of the Dead: The British Army on the Western Front, 1914–18," *War and Society* 31, 1 (2012): 22–41; Joanna Bourke, *Dismembering the Male: Men's Bodies, Britain, and the Great War* (Chicago: University of Chicago Press, 1996). Even a privileged figure such as Talbot Papineau could not escape the realities of death in the Great War. As mentioned in Chapter 6 of this volume, his body was never recovered, and so he was memorialized on the Menin Gate in Ypres, along with the other Canadians who had no known grave.

16 Wilson, "The Burial of the Dead," 27.

17 See Wendy Mitchinson, *The Nature of Their Bodies: Women and Their Doctors in Victorian Canada* (Montreal and Kingston: McGill-Queen's University Press, 1990).

18 Julie-Marie Strange, "'She Cried a Very Little': Death, Grief and Mourning in Working-Class Culture, 1880–1914," *Social History* 27, 2 (May 2002): 143–61. Novelist Rebecca West captures the upper-class contempt for working-class displays of emotion in her *The Return of the Soldier* (New York: George H. Duran, 1918), especially in the first chapter, in which

the decidedly working-class Mrs. Grey arrives unannounced (and unwelcome) at the upper-class residence of soldier Christopher Baldry to notify his wife and cousin that he is injured. They treat her disdainfully and are much disturbed that she claims to have been a childhood friend of his.

19 The Canadian material on masculinity, especially in military contexts, remains thin, though Chapters 2 and 6 of this volume do address the subject. See also Geoffrey Hayes, "Exploring Masculinity in the Canadian Army Officer Corps, 1939–45," *Journal of Canadian Studies* 48, 2 (2014): 40–69; Mark Osborne Humphries, "War's Long Shadow: Masculinity, Medicine, and the Gendered Politics of Trauma, 1914–1939," *Canadian Historical Review* 91, 3 (2010): 503–31; Mark Moss, *Manliness and Militarism: Educating Young Boys in Ontario for War* (Don Mills: Oxford University Press, 2001); Anthony Fletcher, *Life, Death and Growing Up on the Western Front* (New Haven: Yale University Press, 2013), especially Chapter 4; Jessica Meyer, *Men of War: Masculinity and the First World War in Britain* (London: Palgrave Macmillan, 2009), 27–29; Michael Roper, *The Secret Battle: Emotional Survival in the Great War* (Manchester: Manchester University Press, 2009); and J.A. Mangan, *Manufactured Masculinity: Making Imperial Manliness, Morality and Militarism* (New York: Routledge, 2012).

20 Julia Grant, "A 'Real Boy' and Not a Sissy: Gender, Childhood, and Masculinity, 1890–1940," *Journal of Social History* 37, 4 (2004): 829–51.

21 Leonore Davidoff, *Thicker Than Water: Siblings and Their Relations, 1780–1920* (Oxford: Oxford University Press, 2012), 324–26.

22 Neil Sutherland, *Children in English-Canadian Society: Framing the Twentieth-Century Consensus*, 2nd ed. (Waterloo: Wilfrid Laurier University Press, 2000), 56–58.

23 Margaret G. Campbell, "All British," *Seaforth News*, 3 January 1918, 7. In 2017, fully 80 percent of Seaforth residents were of British heritage.

24 Although there are allusions to the brothers' letters home, few remain, unlike the notably "rich wartime correspondence" of Talbot Papineau, as explored by Geoffrey Hayes in Chapter 6 of this volume. Nor were their letters published in the local newspaper, as Jonathan Vance drew upon in Chapter 2, for his discussion of Rob Buchan.

25 There is some confusion about Clarence's first name, which is recorded as "Charlie" on his birth registration but listed as "Charles" on his attestation papers; the family gravestone in Maitlandbank Cemetery, Seaforth, gives his name as "Clarence Charles." He was evidently called "Clare," but Arnold Westcott's diary always refers to him as "Clarence."

26 Susanna Moodie (1803–85) had arrived a decade earlier, in 1832, as chronicled in her famous *Roughing It in the Bush* (New York: G.P. Putnam, 1852); see also James Weber Scott, *Seaforth* (Goderich: Huron County Historical Committee, 1954).

27 *Fourth Census of Canada, 1901* (Ottawa: S.E. Dawson, n.d.). The Westcotts lost a seven-month-old son, Harold, in 1888.

28 Paris Green is an extremely toxic emerald-green arsenic compound that was invented in the eighteenth century to tint paint and wallpaper, thereby accidentally killing people; it was later used to exterminate mice and other vermin and was a very common household product in the early twentieth century, especially on farms. Its ingestion brought about a prolonged and agonizing death. William Senior's death certificate indicates that the poison took twelve hours to kill him. His grandson, Clare Westcott, filled in the context during an interview: William Westcott had spent hours in the hot sun, working on a roof, and was probably overtaken by sunstroke and dehydration, which brought on mental disorientation. Author interview with Clare Westcott, Campbellford, Ontario, 13 July 2017.

29 *Census of Canada, 1911* (Ottawa: Dominion Bureau of Statistics, n.d.).

30 See, for example, Nancy L. Segal, *Entwined Lives: Twins and What They Tell Us about Human Behavior* (New York: Dutton, 1999); and Nancy L. Segal, "Twins: The Finest Natural Experiment," *Personality and Individual Differences* 49 (2010): 317–23. For an important earlier study, see R.C. Ainslie, *The Psychology of Twinship* (Northvale, NJ: Jason Aronson, 1997).

31 The twins' attestation papers do not record their height or weight; these are found on the "identification page" at the front of their individual war diaries for 1918. At that time, Arnold recorded his weight as 125 pounds, and Clarence seems to have been somewhat heavier at 135 pounds, as given in his own diary. Clarence Westcott and Arnold Westcott, War Diaries, in the possession of Clare Westcott and used here with his permission. As Tim Cook points out, the initial height requirement for enlistment was "at least 5 feet 3 inches tall," whereas gunners, because of their heavy work, had to be a minimum of five foot seven. The pressing need for recruits meant that the height requirements were quickly overlooked. See Tim Cook, "The Canadian Great War Soldier," 7 August 2014, *Canadian Encyclopedia*, http://www.thecanadianencyclopedia.ca/en/article/the-canadian-great-war -soldier/. See also Roy Bailey, Timothy Hatton, and Kris Inwood, "Health, Height and the Household at the Turn of the 20th Century," IDEAS Discussion Paper 8128, 2014, Institute of Labor Economics, http://ideas.repec.org/p/iza/izadps/dp8128.html.

32 Born in Seaforth in 1924, Clare Westcott wrote for the now defunct *Toronto Telegram* during the 1960s and then served for many years as an assistant to Conservative minister of education Bill Davis (who was also the eighteenth premier of Ontario, 1971–85). Westcott is credited with having done the groundwork to create the province's system of community colleges. During the 1990s, he was commissioner of the Toronto Police Department. He completed his public career as a citizenship judge in the early 1990s. He currently resides in Campbellford, Ontario. Author interview with Clare Westcott, 13 July 2017. The Clare Westcott fonds, mostly covering his years in public office, are held at the Archives of Ontario. I am enormously grateful to Mr. Westcott for sharing his memories, the war diaries of his father and uncle, and his wonderful photographs, used here with permission. Thanks are due also to his son, Chris Westcott, for facilitating our interactions.

33 Oral history and memory studies have flourished in the past decade. For recent Canadian examples of note, see the chapters in Nolan Reilly, Alexander Freund, and Kristina R. Llewellyn, eds., *The Canadian Oral History Reader* (Montreal and Kingston: McGill-Queen's University Press, 2015). On memory and the Great War, see James Wood, "History and Memory of the Great War: A Review Essay," *BC Studies* 191 (Autumn 2016): 123–32; and Tim Cook, "Battles of the Imagined Past: Canada's Great War and Memory," *Canadian Historical Review* 95, 3 (September 2014): 417–26.

34 Arnold Westcott, War Diary, 17 October 1917.

35 Arnold Westcott, War Diary, 19 April 1918; see also Clare Westcott, "The Hero I Never Knew," *Toronto Star*, 11 November 1994.

36 As recounted by Clare Westcott, who heard the story from his father, Arnold. Author interview with Clare Westcott, Campbellford, Ontario, 5 July 2017.

37 Fletcher, *Life, Death and Growing Up*, especially Chapter 4; Josephine Hoegaerts, "Benevolent Fathers and Virile Brothers: Metaphors of Kinship and the Construction of Masculinity and Age in the Nineteenth Century Belgian Army," *BMGN-Low Countries Historical Review* 127, 1 (2012): 72–100. See also the contemporary pamphlet urging Americans to join the war effort by American war correspondent Edward Alexander Powell, *Brothers in Arms* (New York: Houghton Mifflin, 1917).

38 I have not been able to locate specific numbers for brother-soldiers in the Canadian Expeditionary Force.

39 Suzanne Evans, *Mother of Heroes, Mother of Martyrs* (Montreal and Kingston: McGill-Queen's University Press, 2007), discusses the Silver Cross and its meanings.

40 Sarah Glassford and Amy Shaw, "Introduction," in Glassford and Shaw, *A Sisterhood of Suffering*, 13, point out that women were urged to take pride in sacrificing their sons. Because of her unenviable position as the mother who had lost the most sons in the war, Charlotte Wood was selected to place a wreath at the Vimy Memorial during its official unveiling in 1935; as her husband had previously married, some of the eleven were stepsons.

41 Comacchio, *Nations Are Built*, 54–59.

42 C.M. Tancredy and R.C. Fraley, "The Nature of Adult Twin Relationships: An Attachment-Theoretical Perspective," *Journal of Personality and Social Psychology* 90, 1 (2006): 78.

43 In January 1917, soldiers with Canadian battalions in England were placed in twenty-six new reserve battalions with men from the same military districts in Canada, and deployed to reinforce infantry battalions in France. LAC, *Guide to Sources Relating to Units of the Canadian Expeditionary Force Reserve Battalions*, https://www.bac-lac.gc.ca/eng/discover/military-heritage/first-world-war/Documents/reserve%20battalions.pdf.

44 Arnold Westcott, War Diary, 17 October 1917.

45 Westcott, "The Hero I Never Knew." Westcott is citing the twins' individual diaries here.

46 Arnold Westcott, War Diary, April to October 1918. Arnold's diary notes that he sent letters to Clarence and his mother on 3 May 1918, but the correspondence has not survived. The casualty clearing stations were meant for quick treatment, including emergency surgery, but the wounded could not remain there for recuperation. The stations were located behind the front lines and were constantly in danger, so they were moved often. The information I have found about No. 7 Casualty Clearing Station places it at Ligny St. Flochel, a few kilometres west of Arras, from 18 April to 18 December 1918. For contemporary views, see J. George Adami, *War Story of the Canadian Army Medical Corps* (Toronto: Musson, 1918); and the first-hand accounts by Nova Scotia-born nurse Clare Gass of her time with the No. 3 Canadian Casualty Clearing Station reprinted in *The War Diary of Clare Gass, 1915–1918*, Susan Mann, ed. (Montreal and Kingston: McGill-Queen's University Press, 2000). See Mann's introduction, xxvii–xxix, in which she briefly recounts the "obstacle course" that wounded soldiers were obliged to endure before being admitted to hospital. They were usually first transported to a field ambulance unit to be assessed and stabilized, then to a C.C.S., then to a base hospital in France, and finally to a hospital in England.

47 The engagement at the Canal du Nord was one of a series of linked clashes during the Battle of Cambrai, which took place from 27 September to 11 October 1918. Fred James, *Canada's Triumph* (London: Charles and Son, 1918), 42–44, 46. Canada's Hundred Days, so-called because the Canadian Corps played a substantial role in attaining Allied victory, began on 8 August 1918 with the Battle of Amiens and carried through to the Battle of Mons on the date of the Armistice, 11 November 1918. The Canadian Corps sustained over forty-five thousand casualties in a mere three months of fighting, which was not only its highest casualty rate of the entire war, but in the subsequent history of the Canadian military for a similar period of time. See G.W.L. Nicholson, *Canadian Expeditionary Force, 1914–1919: Official History of the Canadian Army in the First World War* (Ottawa: Department of National Defence, 1962), 445–53; and Ryan Goldsworthy, "Measuring the Success of Canada's Wars: The Hundred Days Offensive as a Case Study," *Canadian Military Journal* 13, 2 (Spring 2003): 46–56. http://www.journal.forces.gc.ca/vol13/no2/page46-eng.asp.

48 Canon Frederick George Scott, *The Great War as I Saw It* (Vancouver: Clarke and Stuart Co., 1934), 306, 309. Frederick George Scott (1861–1944) was a Canadian poet and author,

known as the Poet of the Laurentians. An ordained Anglican minister, Scott published thirteen books of Christian and patriotic poetry, as well as many hymns to the British Empire and Canada's roles in the South African War and the Great War. One of his sons was killed at the Somme; he was also the father of Frederick Reginald (F.R.) Scott (1899–1985). In contrast to his father, the younger Scott was a member of the Montreal Group of modernist poets and a founding member of the social-democratic League for Social Reconstruction, as well as the CCF (later NDP). See Keith Richardson, "Frank Scott," 5 March 2015, *Canadian Encyclopedia*, http://www.thecanadianencyclopedia.ca/en/article/frank-scott/.

49 James, *Canada's Triumph*, 42–44, 46.

50 J.F.B. Livesay, "Canadian Troops Take Bourlon Wood," the *Globe*, 28 September 1918. This article appeared under the front-page headline, "British Triumph in Cambrai Area: Most Important Defences Are Carried Out by Canadian Troops." Also "Canadians Take Bourlon Wood," *Seaforth News*, 10 October 1918.

51 Nicholson, *Canadian Expeditionary Force*, 125. See also David Borys, "Crossing the Canal: Combined Arms Operations at the Canal du Nord, Sept–Oct 1918," *Canadian Military History* 20, 4 (Autumn 2011): 23–38.

52 N.M. Christie, *The Canadians at Cambrai and the Canal du Nord, September–October 1918: A Social and Battlefield Tour* (Nepean: CEF Books, 1997), 14, 19–20. I initially came across the Westcott twins through Christie's book, which features their portrait in uniform on its back cover.

53 Discussions of "ways of grieving" in times of war include David Cannadine, "War and Death, Grief and Mourning in Modern Britain," in *Mirrors of Mortality: Studies in the Social History of Death*, ed. Joachim Whaley (New York: St. Martin's Press, 1981), 187–242; and Alan Wilkinson, "Changing English Attitudes to Death in the Two World Wars," in *The Changing Face of Death: Historical Accounts of Death and Disposal*, ed. Peter C. Jupp and Glennys Howarth (London: Macmillan, 1997), 149–63.

54 Clare Westcott, "No Medal for My Father," 4 November 2007, Canada Free Press, http://canadafreepress.com/article/no-medal-for-my-father.

55 On page 60 of this volume, Jonathan Vance points to Rob Buchan's stoic re-entry into community life after his discharge in 1919 as suggesting that "... in his mind, the war's impact on him had been limited ..." See also Alex Watson, "Self-Deception and Survival: Mental Coping Strategies on the Western Front, 1914–18," *Journal of Contemporary History* 41, 2 (2006): 247–68; and Roper, *The Secret Battle*.

56 "Killed in Action," *Huron Expositor*, 11 October 1918; "At Canadian Ports," the *Globe*, 11 October 1918; "Town Topics," *Seaforth News*, 17 October 1918.

57 A pioneering study on the loss of a twin, using a grief-intensity scale, found that the level of grief is comparable to that of losing a spouse, especially for identical twins. See Nancy L. Segal and T.J. Bouchard, "Grief Intensity Following the Loss of a Twin and Other Close Relatives: Test of Kinship-Genetic Hypothesis," *Human Biology* 65 (1993): 87–105; and Nancy L. Segal et al., "Comparative Grief Experiences of Bereaved Twins and Other Bereaved Relatives," *Personality and Individual Differences* 18, 4 (1995): 511–24. Nancy Segal is a psychologist and the founder and head of the Twin Studies Center at California State University.

58 Davidoff, *Thicker Than Water*, 309–13.

59 Westcott, "No Medal for My Father."

60 Westcott, "The Hero I Never Knew"; see Katrina Srigley and Stacey Zembrzycki, eds., "Remembering Family, Analyzing Home: Oral History and the Family," special issue, *Oral History Forum* 29 (2009).

61 This sense of living with a family ghost is not uncommon. Davidoff, *Thicker Than Water,* 308–9, discusses the phenomenon. See also the recent memoir by Diana Bishop, *Living Up to a Legend: My Adventures with Billy Bishop's Ghost* (Toronto: Dundurn, 2017), 12. A granddaughter of Billy Bishop, who has no personal memory of the famous flying ace, Diana Bishop nonetheless felt that because he was very much a public hero and because his memory dominated her family life, "even if I couldn't see him, Grandpa Billy was always around ... like a ghost hiding in the house."

62 Clare Westcott reports this detail in "'The Hero I Never Knew.'" It was passed on by Arnold Westcott, but how he learned of it is unknown.

63 Clarence is remembered on the family gravestone in the Methodist Maitlandbank Cemetery in Seaforth.

64 Davidoff, *Thicker Than Water,* 310.

65 Clarence Westcott, Postcards, dated 6 May and 13 November 1917, in the possession of Clare Westcott.

66 Westcott family lore states that Arnold was still in the Surrey hospital when he received word that Lovica and Annie had died in the Spanish flu pandemic. However, the death records for Lovica (1914), who died of tuberculosis prior to the pandemic, and Annie (1920), as well as their cemetery headstones, do not support this.

67 "Victory," *Seaforth News,* 12 November 1918.

68 "Hilarity When the News Came," the *Globe,* 12 November 1918.

69 See Nominal Roll, 161st Battalion, Ottawa, Canadian Expeditionary Force, 1917, http://www.canadiana.ca/view/oocihm.9_08774/1?r=0&s=1.

70 In 1875, Seaforth was incorporated as a town of about 2,060 people, a figure that has barely fluctuated since that time. According to the 2016 census, 2,680 of Huron County's 59,297 residents lived in Seaforth. See Census Profile, 2016 Census, Statistics Canada, https://www12.statcan.gc.ca/census-recensement/2016/dp-pd/prof/details/page.cfm?Lang= E&Geo1=CD&Code1=3540&Geo2=PR&Code2=35&SearchText.

71 John M. Graham, 12th Canadian Field Ambulance, Belgium, to Mrs. Annie Westcott, Seaforth, Ontario, 12 February 1919, in the possession of Clare Westcott. Clarence Westcott's diary is currently inaccessible, so that I was able to see only a few photocopied pages.

72 "Completes 40 Years as Jeweler," *Seaforth News,* undated clipping; and "Obituary," typescript draft written by Alva Howard Westcott for publication, announcing Arnold Westcott's passing on 3 July 1961, both in the possession of Clare Westcott.

73 Westcott, "No Medal for My Father."

74 Davidoff, *Thicker Than Water,* 333. Davidoff is quoting Stephen P. Bank and Michael D. Kahn, *The Sibling Bond* (New York: Basic Books, 1982), 271.

75 Alexander Watson and Patrick Porter, "Bereaved and Aggrieved: Combat Motivation and the Ideology of Sacrifice in the First World War," *Historical Research* 83, 219 (February 2010): 146–64; Tim Cook and Natascha Morrison, "Longing and Loss from Canada's Great War," *Canadian Military History* 16, 1 (2007): 60.

76 The classic work on the generational impact of the Great War is Robert Wohl, *The Generation of 1914* (Cambridge, MA: Harvard University Press, 1979).

11
The CEF during the Hundred Days:
Desertion and Punishment

Teresa Iacobelli

IN THE FALL OF 1918, as the First World War reached its final days, the soldiers of the Canadian Expeditionary Force (CEF) were an eclectic mix. Some were tired and battle-weary veterans who had endured the long stalemate of trench warfare. Others were new recruits who were undertrained and sometimes unenthusiastic, conscripted to see this war through to its end. Some had the

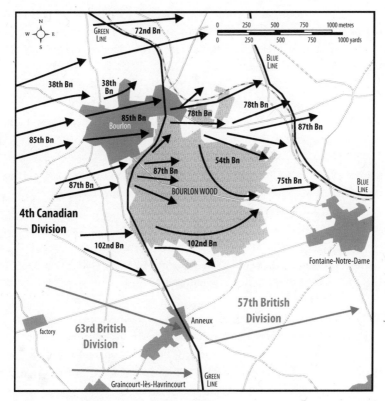

Figure 11.1 Bourlon Wood, 28 September 1918. | Map by Mike Bechthold.

fortitude to endure; but others, suffering from psychological distress or simply exhausted, were unable to continue fighting.[1] Given what troops on all sides had experienced since 1914, this should not be surprising. Yet most men stopped short of absenting themselves.[2]

This chapter concentrates on three Canadian soldiers who did take the fateful step of deserting, deciding late in the war to remove themselves from the firing line. They did so in the context of the Battle of Bourlon Wood, an engagement that was part of the larger Canal du Nord offensive during the autumn of 1918. I have chosen to discuss three men instead of one because, though these soldiers chose to desert together, their testimonies and defences at their courts martial reveal that each had unique reasons for deserting. Presenting this one crime from three perspectives provides insight into the attitudes and motivations of soldiers who abandoned their duties and gives a glimpse into the variety of soldiers' backgrounds and experiences.

The Canal du Nord offensive took place over five days, from 27 September to 1 October 1918. The main objective was to smash German defences at the Hindenburg Line and to capture the city of Cambrai, which operated as a centre for German communications and supplies. The British Army, including Canadian soldiers, was tasked with the capture of Cambrai while other Allied forces concentrated their efforts on attacking three additional German positions along the Western Front.[3]

The Canadian Corps prepared for the imminent attack by sending combat engineers ahead to construct roads and bridges across the flooded, partially excavated canal. As Patrick Dennis has recently pointed out, General Arthur Currie's plan was both ambitious and risky:

> Currie proposed to begin by funnelling lead elements of two divisions through a narrow gap, about 2.5 kms wide, opposite the village of Inchy-en-Artois, where the unfinished portion of the canal was relatively dry. These and follow-on forces (about 30,000 men) would then fan out north and east in a broad arc 10 kms wide. A very risky plan, it required the assembly of all attacking forces in front of a heavily congested chokepoint, one well known to the enemy and therefore extremely vulnerable to artillery bombardment.[4]

Given the circumstances of the moment, Currie's daring stroke was understandable. The Allies felt that they had now achieved momentum and that a bold move like this could accelerate their enemy's retreat. However, the cost in lives lost (and men wounded) was likely to be great. Certainly, after the war, military leaders were accused of callousness in making their risk/reward calculations. Currie even faced allegations of having been indifferent to the suffering of his troops during the Hundred Days.[5]

Speculating about the thoughts of those who are preparing for the next major assault is always à dangerous exercise. It is highly likely, however, that the spirits of the Canadians in the line would have been buoyed by the fact that the days of stalemate were over and because the Allies were clearly gaining ground. At the same time, casualty rates were high, and this would not have been lost on the men. The war diary for the 102nd Battalion (one of the units assigned to the assault on the Canal du Nord) may shed some light on the state of morale. In a typically low-key way, covering the days from 3 to 7 October 1918, immediately after the Battle of Bourlon Wood, noted, "During the five days spent in this location the usual routine consequent on a strenuous tour in the Front Line was carried out. A Muster Parade was held and every effort made to bring the Battalion records up to date ... A cinema show was established near by in Queant. Baths, of a kind, were available."[6] The fact that a pause was ordered, and creature comforts were laid on, demonstrates that commanders were aware of the threat of exhaustion, even if the men themselves were only moderately impressed by the accommodations.

Describing the attack on the Canal du Nord, the 102nd's war diary remarked,

> The failure of the Imperials on our right to make good their advance had left our flank exposed and been the cause of heavy casualties, and though we had gained our objective and successfully linked up with the 54th Battalion on the Southern edge of the wood and had formed a defensive flank, it was known that elements of the enemy, especially machine gunners, still existed in the wood ... Our casualties for the day were heavy ... But the success was great and in addition to the strategically important ground taken, we captured 257 prisoners, 15 guns and 18 machine guns and inflicted heavy casualties.[7]

After clearing the Canal du Nord, the Canadians advanced on Bourlon itself. This necessitated another risky manoeuvre; the Allied forces immediately fanned out on the east side of the canal in an effort to widen the front against the Germans.[8]

The intensity of the fighting during the forty-eight-hour period beginning on 27 September was suggested by William G. Wurtele, who was then a lieutenant in the Royal Canadian Regiment, which participated in the attack. Writing years later in *Pro Patria*, the regiment's journal, Wurtele remembered,

We moved up during the night which my Company spent in a culvert. This is the only time I had the misfortune to have to chase an officer, at pistol point, to the rear. He had been sent up during the night and was mumbling how we would all be dead the next day, with devastating results on the morale of the troops.[9]

As this incident reveals, the rapid succession of tough battles during the Hundred Days – despite the gathering momentum of the Allies – was having a negative effect on morale. In this context, acts of indiscipline such as desertion were bound to be more common.

Leadership may also have contributed to the decision taken by the three soldiers whose fates I follow in this chapter. On 12 September 1918, John Arthur Clark, the highly decorated former commander of the 72nd Seaforth Highlanders, was named brigadier general in charge of the 7th Canadian Infantry Brigade (CIB), replacing Hugh Dyer. Clark had an impeccable record, but he was only thirty-two, much younger than the usual age for a brigadier general. As one observer puts it,

Whether it was the best decision for 7th CIB "to change horses in midstream" is another matter. As will be seen, the battles of the last 100 days became more chaotic and unpredictable, making demands upon those in command and control to have well-tested and smooth operating procedures in place, and the knowledge to execute them effectively. Dyer's replacement, the younger 32-year-old Clark ... had won the DSO three times but would appear from the outset to have been uncomfortable as a brigade commander.[10]

News that a new man was being put in place in the short pause between the Battle of Arras and the Battle of Cambrai may well have dented morale at this crucial moment.

By the end of 28 September, the Canadian Corps had taken Bourlon Wood, allowing the Allied advance to move forward and clear the road toward Cambrai.[11] As Tim Cook notes, the capture of Bourlon Wood was considered one of the most difficult battles of the First World War.[12] It won the Canadian Corps the admiration of British Expeditionary Force (BEF) leaders, who saw the Canadians as the "backbone" of First Army. Nevertheless, Cook points out,

For the veterans of the infantry, it was heartbreaking to look around and see comrades, men who had survived Ypres, the Somme, Vimy, Hill 70, Passchendaele – even Amiens and Arras – killed or maimed in the final stretch of the war. As they were forced to attack again and again, the troops began to listen to and spread rumours that their corps commander was sacrificing them to appease his British masters. Such false reports were unfair, as Currie always tried to ration men's lives, and had stood up to the British in the name of his corps time and time again, but more than 42,000 casualties since Amiens seemed too many even for the battle-hardened Dominion troops. Unlike past similar instances, this simmering anger was not quelled after some rest and rum, as many Canadians continued to feel that they had been pushed too hard.[13]

Continued high expectations for success combined with dwindling resources to sow discontent and disillusionment within the ranks. Though not determinative, such conditions could only encourage indiscipline of various kinds, including desertion.

FLAGGING MORALE, POOR discipline, absences, and desertions have been part of the narrative of warfare since ancient times, and both the Central Powers and the Allies were forced to deal with these issues to varying degrees during the First World War. The difference between military collapse and effectiveness often hinged on how weakening morale and rising indiscipline were addressed. Historian J.G. Fuller argues that, among the British and dominion armies, entertainments that mirrored the institutions of civilian life were useful in sustaining morale and strengthening the bonds among soldiers. Activities such as playing sports, keeping a trench journal, and attending concert parties were especially important during periods away from the front lines, when the opportunities for desertion were greatest.[14]

For a contrasting example, historians have pointed to the armies of the Austro-Hungarian Empire, suggesting that they contained far too many disparate nationalities to achieve the level of morale that cohesion and shared identity can produce. Nationalist movements, bolstered by promises of self-determination, proved far more attractive than fighting on behalf of a distant and out-of-touch monarchy.[15] Additionally, soldiers were subject to low morale brought on by deprivation caused in part by a successful British naval blockade that strangled the delivery of basic supplies. This affected, not only the men in the trenches but also their families; news of suffering at home reached the fathers, sons, and brothers at war, resulting in protests and desertions. By October 1918, the final collapse of the Habsburg army had begun.[16] Although the German Army was not forced to address the atomizing influence of nationalism, Germany was plagued by similar shortages in food and other supplies. As conditions worsened, an increasing number of troops refused to fight, deserting their posts and heading homeward.[17]

Among the Allies, the low morale of the Italian troops manifested itself in their stunning defeat at Caporetto in November 1917. That same year, on the

Eastern Front, soldiers in the Russian Army deserted en masse, motivated by Bolshevik propaganda, the events of the October Revolution, and battle exhaustion worsened by the lack of adequate food, clothing, and weapons.[18] In 1917, what General Robert Nivelle promised would be an offensive breakthrough proved instead to be a costly endeavour for the French Army that gained four miles at the expense of 130,000 casualties, including 29,000 killed, before it was halted.[19] This abject failure prompted a series of mutinies across French units that threatened Allied efforts on the Western Front.

As historian Leonard V. Smith cautions, it is crucial to remember that the mutinies were about far more than frustration over one failed offensive. Instead, there were political causes, mirroring civilian strikes on the home front; the mutinies were an expression of citizen-soldiers' dissatisfaction with their situation and their leadership.[20] French mutineers were largely non-violent toward their officers, who often sympathized with their troops' demands for better food, more leave, and more carefully planned offensives. Although these soldiers remained willing to fight and to defend their homeland, they insisted that the risks be better calculated. In response to the mutinies, Marshal Philippe Pétain replaced General Nivelle and satisfied many of the soldiers' demands, including granting additional leave and promising to assume a more defensive posture for a while. Pétain also imposed renewed discipline: there were 3,427 courts martial, resulting in 554 death sentences. Although most of these were commuted, 49 soldiers were shot for their roles in the mutinies, and these men have continued to exert a powerful influence on French memory to this day.[21]

Although discipline remained relatively intact among British troops, a mutiny at the British base, training, and transit camp at Étaples in September 1917 resulted in three hundred arrests and the execution of one member of the BEF. The troubles had begun a month earlier, when an Australian soldier was arrested for verbally assaulting an officer and for resisting arrest. Relations between soldiers, officers, and the military police continued to deteriorate, culminating in the uprising, which lasted for several days.[22] Certainly, outbreaks of indiscipline late in the war (or after its end) have garnered much attention. However, earlier examples of insubordination were not absent from the British forces. Between 1914 and 1918, there were some three hundred executions in the BEF alone.[23]

In comparison to other forces, the CEF was relatively stable. Indiscipline became an issue among Canadian troops only after the war, when soldiers became increasingly frustrated with the slow pace of demobilization caused by the sheer number of troops returning home. The most serious incident occurred at a camp in Kinmel Park, Wales, where soldiers endured poor living conditions and limited pay as they waited to sail to Canada. In March 1919, their impatience boiled over, resulting in a two-day riot that left five men dead, twenty-three wounded, seventy-eight arrested, and twenty-five convicted of mutiny.[24] In this instance, the critical factor was one of the most powerful emotional pulls on men in the field: the desire to go home. The prospect of returning home could cover a multitude of trials, and conversely, seemingly unjustified delays in being released could stoke the fires of resentment. The only other factor that approached the promise of home in terms of its influence on the troops was the provision of creature comforts. Suitable billets and good food in adequate supply were critical to maintaining morale.[25]

That the Canadians had not succumbed to indiscipline long before the demobilization crisis is all the more remarkable, given the toll exacted on them in the final stages of the war, when they were "at the sharp end" and were frequently called upon to lead the Allied advance to ensure victory.[26] Not surprisingly, fear of advancing towards the enemy was a major cause of desertion. Records show that a large proportion of soldiers deserted immediately before major military engagements.[27] Above and beyond ordinary fear, shell shock, or neurasthenia, also affected many soldiers. Initial studies suggested that 2–4 percent of First World War combatants suffered from this affliction, but more recent estimates by historian Jay Winter put the figure as high as 20 percent.[28] And even those who were not incapacitated as a result of their condition faced a tough time reintegrating upon their return home.[29] None of this was helped by the fact that the military authorities were struggling to identify, understand, and respond to what is now known as post-traumatic stress disorder. Persistent stigma and patchy record keeping have ensured the virtual impossibility of producing accurate estimates for the numbers of men who suffered from shell shock.[30]

In addition to the mental stress brought on by war, soldiers also deserted for more commonplace reasons. Some simply failed to return from leave at their appointed date. Some got drunk, lost track of time, and panicked and stayed away, instead of returning to face the consequences of their actions. Others were confronted by personal issues and responsibilities at home, such as a sick or dying parent or worries about the fidelity of a spouse. Reasons for desertion were plentiful, and each court martial record reveals a unique story.

CASES OF INDISCIPLINE ARE best understood through the personal narratives of the soldiers themselves and the multiple records that were produced for each case. When a CEF member was officially tried for desertion, he faced a field general court martial. Conducted in the field, this included the defendant as well as three officers from any corps or unit in the CEF. The selected officers were not necessarily trained to sit on courts martial; indeed, many were equipped only with their limited knowledge of the *Manual of Military Law,* the legal guidebook used by British and dominion forces from 1914 to 1918.[31]

Courts martial proceeded much like civilian trials, with evidence presented by both the prosecution and the defence. An accused soldier could be defended by a "prisoner's friend," often chosen by the defendant on the basis of a close personal relationship rather than legal expertise. This was hardly a recipe for stout legal defence. Still, as with any trial, evidence was presented and weighed, and witnesses were called and cross-examined.[32] The testimonies given at each field general court martial were recorded by hand, and the transcripts became part of the official court martial records now at Library and Archives Canada.[33] Unfortunately, the full court martial proceedings for the twenty-three Canadian soldiers who were executed for desertion and cowardice in the Great War no longer survive; they were destroyed under the authority of the Department of Defence in 1926, after being held for the prescribed period of seven years. Commuted cases were retained since they potentially might prove relevant in later applications for pensions.

In addition to the transcripts of the courts martial, files contain supporting documents, such as the list of charges and follow-up letters from commanding officers, which commented on whether a convicted soldier should be executed or returned to the ranks. Every soldier who served in the CEF also had a personnel file, which mapped his journey throughout the war. Such files contain the attestation papers that he completed when he enlisted, as well as documents outlining his health and any disciplinary actions undertaken during his time in service.[34] Depending on the author, war diaries could also include valuable details such as the day's weather, the nature of particular engagements, the conditions of battle, and losses sustained by the unit.[35]

Combined, court martial and personnel files help to illuminate the individual accounts of soldiers who took the momentous step of abandoning the front lines, men such as John Wellman Campbell, Edward Dean, and George Murree, three members of the 3rd Battalion, Canadian Machine Gun Corps, who deserted together in the days immediately preceding the Battle of Bourlon Wood. They left their unit on 25 September 1918 and were arrested by military police just one day later while on a leave train in Calais, France.[36] Each man's story, as presented at his own trial, was unique.

John Wellman Campbell was the first to be tried for desertion. He had enlisted at the Niagara Camp in August 1915, at which time he was a labourer living in Cochrane, Ontario. He was twenty-two. First assigned to the 76th Canadian Infantry Battalion, he later transferred to the 58th Battalion in France. In September 1916, while at the Somme, Campbell received gunshot wounds to his left arm and right leg. These flesh wounds left no permanent disability. Campbell recovered in Leeds, England, throughout the autumn of 1916 and was then sent back into service. Prior to his 1918 court martial, his disciplinary record was not immaculate. He had been charged for drunkenness and nuisance, as well as for disobedience and absence without leave (AWL). The latter two charges had resulted in punishments of fourteen days of detention and twenty-one days of Field Punishment No. 1 (FP No. 1), respectively.[37] The field punishment entailed both labour and some form of physical restraint.

Edward Charles Dean served alongside Campbell in the 3rd Battalion, Canadian Machine Gun Corps. Originally from Port Dover, Ontario, he was working as a machinist in Detroit when he enlisted for service in Windsor, Ontario, in 1916. Aged twenty when he joined up, he was assigned to the Canadian Mounted Rifles.[38] Prior to deserting, Dean had been AWL once, from 4 August to 18 August 1918, earning twenty-one days of FP No. 1.[39]

The final member of the three deserters was George Murree. Born in Tusket, Nova Scotia, he worked as a fireman before going to Halifax to enlist in 1917 at age twenty-eight. His personnel records show that he had enlisted under the name George Muise, but a note on his casualty form, dated 23 September 1918, declared his true name to be Murree and stated that all documents would be altered accordingly. The reason behind this name change is unknown, but the Tusket census records for 1911 do list several Muises and no Murrees.[40] Murree was initially assigned to the Canadian Medical Corps but was subsequently transferred to the 3rd Battalion, Canadian Machine Gun Corps in March 1918. Prior to deserting, he had a clean disciplinary record.[41]

On 4 August 1918, a little more than a month before the offensive at Bourlon Wood, the three men made their first attempt at desertion, staying away for two nights before they returned to their unit. Despite the differences in their disciplinary records, all three received the same punishment for this short absence – twenty-one days of FP No. 1.[42] This was not unusual; research has shown that disciplinary records actually had very little impact on sentencing.[43] A few weeks later, on 25 September 1918, as the 3rd Battalion, Canadian Machine Corps moved up the line in preparation for the attack on Bourlon Wood, Campbell, Dean, and Murree again fled, probably aware of the upcoming action and determined to avoid it. On the night of 26 September, as troops moved into their assembly areas under the cover of darkness, struggling through slippery and uncertain conditions caused by a fresh rain, the trio was arrested in Calais.[44]

In cases of desertion that did not involve the military police, courts martial did not necessarily occur. There were many reasons why a commanding officer at platoon, company, or battalion level would choose to treat a desertion simply as an absence if he felt that it did not warrant a court martial. Avoiding official channels of punishment was an easier option than initiating formal proceedings and all that entailed, including gathering witnesses and a panel of three officers. Dealing with infractions within the unit also helped to support a bond of trust between the officers and their troops. Leniency was especially useful if the deserter presented no real threat to unit morale or discipline. Unfortunately for them, Campbell, Dean, and Murree were apprehended by military police; thus, their offence was reported to headquarters, which triggered the formal proceedings for court martial.

Campbell and Murree offered very different justifications for their actions. Unfortunately, the incomplete records from Dean's court martial file do not include details of his defence. Campbell stated that he was motivated by the death of his mother: he had received a letter from home, informing him that she had died. Propelled by grief, he had absconded, perhaps hoping to find a way back to Canada. Campbell also made a point of citing his service record, emphasizing at his trial that "I have been about 15 months in France. I was wounded on the Somme in 1916."[45] He hoped that his grief, his service, and his injury would compel his superior officers toward mercy.

Murree's defence relied on technicalities. Though acknowledging that his actions constituted absence without leave, he did not admit to desertion. As he stated at his court martial, "I am guilty of AWL, but not guilty of desertion. I was told by the Major on the 23rd September that we might be going in the line at any time. I did not take this as a warrant for the line. I got on a leave train not knowing where it was going."[46] Murree's focus on the order to go into the line probably stemmed from his understanding that absenting himself while under a direct order could prove decisive in determining the verdict. According to the *Manual of Military Law,* what distinguished desertion from absence without leave was the *intention* of the soldier. Intention could be proven in a number of ways. A man wearing civilian dress tended to be seen as a deserter; in addition, those whose absences were longer, or who disappeared following an order to proceed to the front or to carry out a specific duty were most likely to be charged with desertion.[47] Among the 197 Canadian soldiers who were found guilty of desertion or cowardice and who had their sentences commuted, six, including Murree, stated in their defence that they either did not hear or did not understand orders from their superiors to proceed up the line.[48]

Since Campbell, Dean, and Murree deserted together, they were tried at the same time, on 20 October 1918.[49] All were found guilty of desertion and sentenced to death. Following a guilty verdict, their superiors were asked to comment on whether the sentence should be confirmed or commuted. As in all cases resulting in a death sentence, the officers did so in light of several criteria, such as

- the state of discipline in the battalion;
- the soldier's character, including record of service;
- the reasons a death sentence should or should not be carried out;
- whether the crime was committed deliberately.[50]

A survey of letters of commutation reveals that many commanding officers also took the opportunity to write about extenuating circumstances that should be considered in a particular case, including issues of physical or mental health. The letters were collated, with the lowest-ranking officer, typically a battalion commander, writing first, and superiors following up the chain of command until the division or corps commander had provided his assessment. The letters were then forwarded to the commander-in-chief, who made the final decision on whether to confirm or commute the death sentence.[51]

In the case of Campbell, Dean, and Murree, the same officers wrote on behalf of each man, recommending that the sentence be confirmed. Major General Frederick Loomis of the 3rd Canadian Division described the behaviour of the accused as "indifferent" and stated that their intention was to avoid their duty.[52] General Commander Henry Horne of First Army wrote, "There is no doubt in my mind that their action was deliberate and that they acted with a view of avoiding duty in the front line." He added that "there is no difference in the degree of guilt in either of the three men."[53] Despite these recommendations, the sentences were ultimately commuted. Each man received a forfeiture in pay for his absence and fifteen years of penal servitude at a military prison, which, according to the *Manual of Military Law*, could be served in Great Britain or a British colony.[54]

During the Great War, death sentences for desertion were commonly commuted; in the CEF, this occurred in approximately 90 percent of all death sentences,[55] often for reasons that went far beyond the preservation of manpower. After 1915, each conviction or commutation had to be confirmed by the commander-in-chief, Sir Douglas Haig. However, when signing off on sentences, Haig did not typically include an explanation for his decisions. The best evidence for the rationale behind commutations comes from the letters of recommendation written by the soldiers' commanders, which show a remarkable degree of flexibility within the military legal system, as well as a great capacity for mercy. Commanders regularly took into account issues of health or previous good service. However, the most significant factors influencing recommendations for commutation remained the timing of the offence and the overall discipline of a battalion. During the First World War, soldiers of the CEF were most likely to have a death sentence commuted if their battalion had shown good discipline or if their infraction occurred when no major offensive was looming. Under such circumstances, the boost to morale provided by an execution was likely to be deemed unnecessary.[56] Still, though Campbell, Dean, and Murree had deserted during a major push and had all been the subject of unfavourable letters, they were fortunate enough to receive commutation.

John Wellman Campbell had his prison sentence suspended on 1 February 1919 and was demobilized from the 58th Battalion in September 1919. Left with physical scars on his right leg and left arm from gunshot wounds sustained in September 1916, he probably carried emotional scars as well.[57] His date of death is unknown. Interestingly, his personnel file includes a note announcing that his medals had been sent – probably to a proud descendant, eager to have a material reminder of his military service – in May 1990.[58] Edward Charles Dean was struck off strength as a deserter from military prison in December 1918 but was found and sent back to prison in April 1919 and sent to England to serve the remainder of his term. His sentence was ultimately remitted and he was demobilized in September 1919. As a result of his misconduct, he was denied a war service gratuity upon his discharge. He wrote to the military, requesting payment in 1956 and was again denied.[59] George Murree was released from his sentence in February 1919 and was demobilized in September of that year. At that point, his conduct was described as good, and he received the British War and Victory Medals. He died on 30 October 1950.[60]

The cases of Campbell, Dean, and Murree follow some familiar patterns related to crime and punishment during the First World War. Like most deserters, they did not abandon their posts while in the heat of battle, in contrast to the usual trope of war movies.[61] Instead, they left the front lines when the opportunity presented itself. Like many other deserters, they also attempted to flee on more than one occasion. Perhaps such men felt emboldened to reoffend once they realized that, should they be caught, discipline would often be handled within the battalion itself and that even if court martial proceedings did pronounce them guilty, they were far more likely to be returned to service than to be executed. Given that only 10 percent of death sentences were confirmed, they may have felt confident in taking a calculated risk to escape the front lines, particularly if a major assault were looming.

The treatment of Campbell, Dean, and Murree mirrored that of other soldiers who deserted and were captured and tried during the Great War. As with most cases, their disciplinary records meant very little in determining their punishment. Some soldiers whose records were far worse had their death sentences commuted, whereas others who had committed no previous offence were executed. Punishments seemed arbitrary in that they had very little to do with the individual soldier and far more to do with the timing of the offence and overall strategies for maintaining discipline. Most men had their death sentences commuted to terms of prison or penal servitude. In this sense, Campbell, Dean, and Murree were not unique. The pattern that applied to them was established early in the war, and it remained evident until its final days.

Though we cannot say with certainty what prompted these three men to desert on that September day, it is very likely that orders to move forward and fears of the upcoming battle played a major role. Rumours and plans surrounding major offensives often prompted an increase in desertions and disciplinary responses throughout the Great War, and the intensity of battle during the Hundred Days simply exacerbated these tensions. Of course, the men themselves may have been only dimly aware of the full range of their motives. The experience of the front challenged the self-image and the sense of agency of these citizen-soldiers. Campbell, Dean, and Murree sought to strike a blow in the name of their own agency by deserting amidst the confusion and carnage of the Hundred Days. But their attempt to escape the machinery of war was a failure, and the repercussions of their act simply confirmed that they were not masters of their own fate.

Notes

1 A useful overview of the situation in the Allied armies is provided by Ashley Ekins, who remarks that, "after four long years of war, the armies of many nations were fighting at the limits of their endurance." Ashley Ekins, "Fighting to Exhaustion: Morale, Discipline and Combat Effectiveness in the Armies of 1918," in *1918 Year of Victory: The End of the Great War and the Shaping of History,* ed. Ashley Ekins (Auckland, NZ: Exisle, 2010), 111.

2 For a description of the ways in which morale was maintained in the Canadian Expeditionary Force, see Chapter 3 in this volume.

3 See G.W.L. Nicholson, *Canadian Expeditionary Force, 1914–1919: Official History of the Canadian Army in the First World War* (Ottawa: Department of National Defence, 1962), 442–44. Nicholson is careful to position the Canal du Nord attack in the broader context of the Hundred Days. As he puts it, "No longer were the Allied leaders seeking to knock out the enemy by battering him at his strongest point while absorbing tremendous punishment in the attempt. The great dull blows rained on the enemy from 1915 to 1917 by the lethargic heavyweight, 'leading with his chin' now became the subtle crippling punches of a skilled boxer, elusive and wary, but crowding his opponent towards defeat." Ibid., 442.

4 Patrick Dennis, *Reluctant Warriors: Canadian Conscripts and the Great War* (Vancouver: UBC Press, 2017), 124.

5 See Tim Cook, *The Madman and the Butcher: The Sensational Wars of Sam Hughes and General Arthur Currie* (Toronto: Allen Lane, 2010).

6 Library and Archives Canada (LAC), RG 9-D-III-3, War Diary, 102nd Canadian Infantry Battalion, 3–7 October 1918. http://data2.collectionscanada.ca/e/e045/e001123538.jpg.

7 LAC, War Diary, 102nd Battalion, 27 September 1918. Canadian Great War Project, http://www.canadiangreatwarproject.com/WarDiaries/diaryDetail.asp?ID=3305.

8 The official history notes that this transition from narrow funnel to widened front posed a difficulty for the Canadians. Nicholson, *Canadian Expeditionary Force,* 443.

9   W.G. Wurtele, "The Royal Canadian Regiment and the First World War – 1914–1919: Cambrai 1918," *Pro Patria* 40 (July 1979), Regimental Rogue, http://regimentalrogue.com/rcr_great_war/rcr_great_war_1918_cambrai_wurtele.html.

10 Ian McCulloch, "Crisis in Leadership: The Seventh Brigade and the Nivelles 'Mutiny,' 1918" in *The Apathetic and the Defiant: Case Studies of Canadian Mutiny and Disobedience, 1812 to 1919*, ed. Craig Leslie Mantle (Kingston: Canadian Defence Academy Press, 2007), 375–76. One officer in the Royal Canadian Regiment claimed that after the war, Clark had admitted "how uncomfortable it was for a new brigadier to ask so much from well-known regiments, to be under such pressure himself and scarcely more than a name to the brigade." See Robert England, *Recollections of a Nonagenarian of Service in the Royal Canadian Regiment, 1916–1919* (Robert England, 1983).

11 David Borys, "Crossing the Canal: Combined Arms Operations at the Canal du Nord, Sep–Oct 1918," *Canadian Military History* 20, 4 (2011): 28.

12 Tim Cook, *Shock Troops: Canadians Fighting the Great War, 1917–1918* (Toronto: Viking, 2008), 548.

13 Ibid., 549.

14 J.G. Fuller, *Troop Morale and Popular Culture in the British and Dominion Armies, 1914–1918* (Oxford: Clarendon Press, 1990). For a recent examination of morale from a Canadian perspective, see Tim Cook, *The Secret History of Soldiers: How Canadians Survived the Great War* (Toronto: Allen Lane, 2018). In Chapter 3 of this volume, Kyle Falcon emphasizes the ways in which the CEF brought a little bit of home to the front.

15 Graydon A. Tunstall, "The Military Collapse of the Central Powers," 30 April 2015, International Encyclopedia of the First World War, https://encyclopedia.1914-1918-online.net/article/the_military_collapse_of_the_central_powers.

16 Ibid.

17 Ibid.

18 Teresa Iacobelli, *Death and Deliverance: Canadian Courts Martial in the Great War* (Vancouver: UBC Press, 2013), 57.

19 John Keegan, *The First World War* (Toronto: Key Porter Books, 1998), 329.

20 Leonard V. Smith, *Between Mutiny and Obedience: The Case of the French Fifth Infantry Division during World War I* (Princeton: Princeton University Press, 1994).

21 Keegan, *The First World War*, 329–31. For the classic interpretation of the French mutinies, see Guy Pedroncini, *Les Mutineries de 1917* (Paris: Presses universitaires de France, 1967). Evidence of the emotion elicited by the mutinies was provided in 1998, when French prime minister Lionel Jospin decided to pardon the soldiers who were punished for their role in the revolt, thereby setting off a political firestorm. French society was divided on this issue. BBC World Service, "French Row over Rehabilitating WWI Mutineers," *BBC News*, 9 November 1998, http://news.bbc.co.uk/2/hi/europe/210983.stm.

22 D. Gill and G. Dallas, "Mutiny at Étaples Base in 1917," *Past and Present* 69, 1 (1972): 88–112.

23 The exact number of BEF executions remains disputed. In 1999, the *Guardian* claimed that 306 men had been executed. See John Sweeney, "Lest We Forget: The 306 'Cowards' We Executed in the First World War," *The* Guardian, 14 November 1999. Two years later, reporting on the inauguration of a monument to the men who were shot for desertion, the BBC gave the figure of 309. "Tribute to WWI 'Cowards,'" *BBC News*, 21 June 2001, http://news.bbc.co.uk/2/hi/uk_news/1399983.stm. For figures concerning the BEF and empire forces, see Gerard Oram, *Death Sentences Passed by Military Courts of the British Army, 1914–1924*, ed. Julian Putkowski (London: Francis Boutle, 1998), 13–14. Oram sets the total at 361.

24 Desmond Morton, "Kicking and Complaining: Demobilization Riots in the Canadian Expeditionary Force, 1918–1919," *Canadian Historical Review* 61, 3 (1980): 334–60. See also Howard G. Coombs, "Dimensions of Military Leadership: The Kinmel Park Mutiny of 4–5 March 1919," in *The Apathetic and the Defiant: Case Studies of Canadian Mutiny and Disobedience, 1812–1919,* ed. Craig Leslie Mantle (Kingston: Canadian Defence Academy Press, 2007), 405–38.

25 Craig Leslie Mantle, "Loyal Mutineers: An Examination of the Connection between Leadership and Disobedience in the Canadian Army since 1885," in *The Unwilling and the Reluctant: Theoretical Perspectives on Disobedience in the Military,* ed. Craig Leslie Mantle (Kingston: Canadian Defence Academy Press, 2006), 58.

26 In addition to Cook, *Shock Troops,* see J.L. Granatstein, *The Greatest Victory: Canada's One Hundred Days, 1918* (Don Mills: Oxford University Press, 2014).

27 Oram, *Death Sentences,* 14. For a detailed discussion of the role of fear in indiscipline, see Bernd Horn, "'But ... It's Not My Fault!' – Disobedience as a Function of Fear," in Mantle, *The Unwilling and the Reluctant,* 169–92.

28 Jay Winter, "Shell Shock," in *The Cambridge History of the First World War* (Cambridge: Cambridge University Press, 2014), 3:310–33.

29 Philip Gibbs, an official British reporter during the Great War, noted that returning veterans did not "come back the same men. They were subject to queer moods and tempers. Fits of depression alternated with a restless desire for pleasure." Quoted in Denis Winter, *Death's Men: Soldiers of the Great War* (London: Penguin Books, 1979), 243. Desmond Morton underlines the ways that veterans could feel left behind or unappreciated. Something as simple as the number of automobiles on the road after the war could drive this feeling home. See Desmond Morton, *When Your Number's Up: The Canadian Soldier in the First World War* (Toronto: Random House, 1993), 268. For a fuller treatment of the predicament of returning troops, see Desmond Morton and Glenn Wright, *Winning the Second Battle: Canadian Veterans and the Return to Civilian Life, 1915–1930* (Toronto: University of Toronto Press, 1987).

30 For evolving attitudes to shell shock, see Edgar Jones and Simon Wessely, *Shell Shock to PTSD: Military Psychiatry from 1900 to the Gulf War* (New York: Psychology Press, 2005); and Anthony Babington, *Shell-Shock: A History of the Changing Attitudes to War Neurosis* (London: Leo Cooper, 1997).

31 War Office, *Manual of Military Law* (London: His Majesty's Stationery Office, 1914).

32 Iacobelli, *Death or Deliverance,* 28–31.

33 For court martial records of the First World War, see (LAC, RG 150, Ministry of the Overseas Military Forces of Canada, Series 8, reel numbers T-8651–T8696).

34 For personnel records of the First World War, see LAC, RG 150, Ministry of the Overseas Military Forces of Canada, Accession 1992-93/166.

35 For war diaries of the First World War, see LAC, RG 9-D-III-3.

36 LAC, RG 150, Ministry of the Overseas Military Forces of Canada, Series -8, File 649-C-5522, Microfilm Reel Number 8653, Finding Aid Number 150-5, Court martial of J.W. Campbell, E.C. Dean, and G. Murree.

37 LAC, RG 150, Accession 1992-93/166, Box 1455, File 47, Personnel File of John Wellman Campbell. In Field Punishment No. 1, a soldier was assigned to additional labour duties and spent some time handcuffed or fettered to a fixed object, typically a wheel or a post. FP No. 1 could last for up to twenty-one days, but the period of restraint could occur only up to two hours a day for three consecutive days. The punishment was intended to humiliate the offender and to deter others. See S.T. Banning, *Military Law Made Easy,* 11th ed. (London: Gale and Polden, 1917), 16.

38 For more on the history of the Canadian Mounted Rifles, see Chapter 4 in this volume.

39 LAC, RG 150, Accession 1992-93/166, Box 2390, File 9, Personnel File of Edward Charles Dean.

40 See "Search Results: Census of Canada, 1911," LAC, https://www.bac-lac.gc.ca/eng/census/1911/Pages/results.aspx?k=cnsSurname%3a%22muise%22+AND+cnsGivenName%3a%22George%22+AND+cnsProvinceCode%3a%22NS%22. The census listed numerous George Muises in the Yarmouth area, including three in Tusket, but none match the age of the man who joined the CEF in June 1917.

41 LAC, RG 150, Accession 1992-93/166, Box 6543, File 41, Personnel File of George Murree.

42 LAC, Personnel Files of John Wellman Campbell, Edward Charles Dean, and George Murree.

43 Iacobelli, *Death or Deliverance*, 88.

44 LAC, Court martial record of J.W. Campbell, E.C. Dean, and G. Murree.

45 LAC, Court martial record of J.W. Campbell, E.C. Dean, and G. Murree.

46 Ibid.

47 War Office, *Manual of Military Law*, 454.

48 Iacobelli, *Death or Deliverance*, 50.

49 LAC, Court martial record of J.W. Campbell, E.C. Dean, and G. Murree.

50 S.S. 412, "Circular Memorandum on Courts-Martial for Use on Active Service," Issued by the Adjutant's General Branch of the Staff, General Headquarters, cited in Christopher Pugsley, *On the Fringe of Hell: New Zealanders and Military Discipline in the First World War* (Toronto: Hodder and Stoughton, 1991), 107.

51 Iacobelli, *Death or Deliverance*, 84.

52 LAC, Court martial record of J.W. Campbell, E.C. Dean, and G. Murree.

53 Ibid.

54 War Office, *Manual of Military Law*, 444–45.

55 Iacobelli, *Death or Deliverance*, 111.

56 Ibid., 136–41.

57 LAC, Personnel File of John Wellman Campbell.

58 Ibid.

59 LAC, Personnel File of Edward Charles Dean.

60 LAC, Personnel File of George Murree.

61 For more on the tension between popular images of the First World War and the historical reality, see Chapter 4 in this volume.

Conclusion

Peter Farrugia

The Panoramic Shot versus the Close-Up

There is a famous Great War photograph in the collections of the Imperial War Museum in London. Used in many publications, it adorns the cover of Malcolm Brown's study of the war's final year.[1] It depicts a brigadier general standing on a damaged bridge, speaking to the men of his brigade, who are gathered along the bank of the river they have just traversed. As a metaphor for the standard

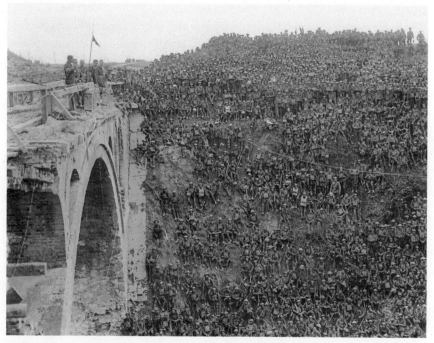

Figure C.1 Brigadier General John Vaughan Campbell addresses men of the 137th Brigade (46th Division) on the Riqueval Bridge over the St. Quentin Canal, 2 October 1918 | Imperial War Museum, Q9535.

approach to the Great War, it is apt. We speak of the 10 million killed in all combatant states, the sixty-one thousand Canadian dead, or the twenty thousand who perished on 1 July 1916, the single bloodiest day in the history of the British Army.[2] But do we necessarily feel the weight of those numbers? Can we distinguish any of the faces looking up at their commanding officer in that famous photograph? Can we discern any of the emotions – relief, cynicism, grief, anger – that were probably playing in men's minds at that moment? This volume is an attempt to zoom in, however fleetingly, on some of the faces of those who served in the Canadian Expeditionary Force (CEF) in the Great War, to flesh out their reactions to the circumstances in which they found themselves and to suggest how their experiences might reinforce or challenge some of the more deeply held attitudes regarding the war among both professional historians and the public. As we shall see shortly, the close-up shot that is provided by this volume offers a number of intriguing overlaps and juxtapositions, some of which seriously challenge current orthodoxy about the First World War.

In this sense, the full title of the collection – *Portraits of Battle: Courage, Grief, and Strength in Canada's Great War* – is significant. It implies that the historiographical debates that we revisit here are battles of a kind themselves. They feature active and quiet fronts, shifting tactics, and territorial gains and losses. This battle metaphor is not just a rhetorical flourish. Others, with far greater experience in these matters, have characterized history as a battle. The former director of the Imperial War Museum, Noble Frankland, entitled his autobiography *History at War* and maintained,

> I was fortunate to escape with my life from the glimpses of history being made that the Second World War afforded me, and I was also fortunate to emerge from writing my part of the official history of the war with a career ahead of me. In that career, I had to struggle for years with the powers that be to achieve a base from which I could seek worthwhile historical results.[3]

Frankland, a decorated RAF pilot in WWII and co-author of a study of Bomber Commands tactics against Nazi Germany that drew considerable fire, suggests that history and memory are intertwined, siblings locked in an often contentious relationship over how we make sense of the past.[4]

Lest We Forget

Lest we forget.[5] Three simple words that, in the aftermath of the Great War, became freighted with the hopes and fears of a generation traumatized by the bloodshed of 1914–18. But the seductive simplicity of the phrase overlooks a critical feature of remembering: the act of remembrance *necessarily* entails inaccuracies, conflations, elisions, and outright fabrications.[6] And having lived through a historical moment is no guarantee of accuracy. Any law enforcement officer will gladly tell of the fragility of eyewitness testimony; seven witnesses will give seven different descriptions of the perpetrator of a crime and of how the situation unfolded.

The inadvertent distortions occasioned by the limitations of human memory are difficult enough. In the case of a conflict such as the Great War, it is the deliberate distortions – the silences in the face of propaganda, atrocity, dissidence, and profiteering – that add layers of complexity to the task of understanding the past. After suggesting the military metaphor for the relationship between history and memory, Noble Frankland named some of the individuals against whom he had to do battle in his own efforts to make sense of the role of Bomber Command in the Second World War and underlined the powerful ideas that they propagated. He then stated, "In addition to these, or perhaps even deriving from them, there are also group and national misconceptions, which, because they represent more than personal views and sometimes amount to public opinion, are far more powerful in democratic terms than the thoughts of individuals."[7] The influence of powerful individual interests and public myth was particularly difficult to dislodge in the case of the First World War. To cite but one example, within a few years of the conclusion of the war, the Treaty of Versailles was an orphaned peace. People began to doubt its fairness and validity.[8] The assessment of Versailles affected contemporary attitudes to the outbreak of the war, as well as interwar international relations, and had a direct impact on the revival of hostilities in 1939. Without the view of Versailles as *diktat*, the Nazi Party might never have won power in Germany. This is a graphic instance in support of the assertion that history matters and that battles can be historiographical as much as physical.

During the preparations for this volume, the editors asked themselves where some of the most hotly contested salients in Great War historiography might be. Readers who are familiar with the debates over the experiences of Canadians in the Great War era will probably recognize many of the themes in this collection: the quality of leadership in the war, the impact of the conflict on gender roles, and the experience of First Nations soldiers among them. However, the perspectives offered on individual questions and the links between the men and women who are featured in this book will hopefully be fresh and thought provoking. Certainly, the creation of this collection was a learning process for all involved. The very nature of the task that we set ourselves as editors could foster an absence of the kind that we were trying to avoid. For example, given the gendered expectations of 1914 – particularly concerning the appropriate, non-combatant role of women in the conflict – it was prima facie more difficult to find women than men who could be counted among the lost in the costliest battles of the Great War. As Sarah Glassford remarks, "roughly 2 percent of all nursing sisters died as a result of their military service, as compared to 10 percent of CEF soldiers who died during the war from illness or injury" (page 154). These figures do not suggest that the nurses were any less invested in the outcome of the war, worked less diligently, or suffered fewer consequences as a result of their service.

First Nations people were also long absent from the dominant narrative surrounding Canada and the war. It has only been since the 1990s that attention has focused more squarely on the subject.[9] Even so, some confusion remains as to the relative strength of the First Nations response to calls for enlistment.[10] Still, a growing body of work discusses the important contribution of First Nations to the CEF. A healthy academic literature has been built up, central institutions such as the Canadian War Museum and Veterans Affairs shine light on their role,[11] and politicians are careful to underline the sacrifices of men and women from across Indigenous communities.

Even so, the notion of a collaborative effort that was fully recompensed by a grateful nation is not entirely accurate. As Evan J. Habkirk points out in his chapter on Wilfred Lickers, First Nations soldiers were seen as capable enough to risk their lives in battle but not as competent enough to make their own financial and political decisions in post-war Canada. Habkirk concludes, "Due to their legal status as wards, Lickers and other First Nations veterans had to rely on the [Department of Indian Affairs] and the paternalistic federal government, who monitored and documented their every move, to make their decisions for them" (page 122). This could only have had a profound effect on young men who had risked life and limb in the hope that their sacrifice would earn them equal status.

Interplay of Past, Present, and Future

Another theme that runs through this collection is the interconnection between past, present, and future. Even a cursory glance at the events of the First World War and the ways in which that conflict has been remembered over time reveals that we should be wary of too rigid a delineation between the three.[12] Many of the military engagements that proved costly for the CEF underline the prudence of taking a more nuanced approach.

Chief among these is the Battle of Vimy Ridge. The fact alone that the 100th anniversary of this iconic battle prompted some of Canada's best-known historians to write about the attack is worth noting. Add to this their widely divergent conclusions, and the significance of Vimy becomes all the more apparent. For Tim Cook, the battle remains vitally important to understanding our past, even if it is not the source of our nationhood, as is often claimed. He concludes his study of the meaning of the battle by declaring, "The memorial is for the dead, but it is remade generation after generation by the living. Canada was forever changed by the war, but Vimy did not make the nation. It was the nation that made Vimy."[13] For Ian McKay and Jamie Swift, something more sinister is at play in the cult of Vimy. They reject the mythologizing that has enshrouded the battle and conclude that "from Varley and Kollwitz to Prost and Thomson, post-patriotic commemorations take us beyond the narrow nationalisms that have for so long claimed to speak authoritatively about the meanings of state orchestrated mass death from 1914 to 1918."[14] In this reading of the past, war is always wrong, always a failure. And as long as nationalism is not eradicated, the possibility of future senseless bloodshed looms on the horizon.

Interestingly, despite their ultimate disagreement over Vimy's centrality to the Great War and to Canadian identity, these authors do share common ground. They acknowledge that the meaning of Vimy Ridge – as interpreted by successive generations of Canadians – has shifted dramatically. In 1918, the American critic Van Wyck Brooks asked, "What, out of all the multifarious achievements and impulses and desires of the American literary mind, ought we to elect to remember?"[15] He was essentially making the case for selective remembering to suit contemporary purposes. If ever there were a worthy case study for the tenacity of this approach, it would be the assault on Vimy Ridge, which has morphed from example of the cost of war to symbol of Canadian fortitude and even to icon, marking the birth of a nation.

Is it enough simply to note the quicksilver nature of memory when it comes to significant military engagements such as Vimy? It is probably best practice to strive to see a past event as objectively as possible – not overly confident that we can ever distill out present challenges, fashions, or exigencies but working diligently to prevent these from obscuring how the event was viewed in its own time. Vimy was a surprising victory, achieved under difficult circumstances that understandably stimulated national pride. It was neither the turning point of the Great War nor the moment when Canada became a nation. Attempts to cast Vimy as a blueprint for Canadian (primarily military) engagement with the world or as a shining example of Canada's devotion to immigration and recognition of First Nations are equally misguided.[16]

If Vimy has suffered from overexposure – particularly in its centenary – another battle, fought shortly afterward, has endured neglect in the public consciousness. The Battle of Hill 70 is largely unknown among Canadians. One of the co-editors of the excellent recent study *Capturing Hill 70* began his introduction by writing,

Just for fun, I conducted my own very unscientific survey of about twenty friends and family members. I asked them to name any battle of the First World War, the first one that popped into mind. That all but one or two of them answered "Vimy Ridge" was no surprise ... When pressed to name a second battle, a few who had taken history courses in high school or university, or even if they were just History Channel aficionados, blurted out "the Somme" or "Passchendaele," two battles that have come to symbolize the slaughterhouse of the First World War. A couple who were familiar with Jack Granatstein's recent book, *The Greatest Victory,* even mentioned the "Hundred Days," which was actually a series of battles between August and November 1918. Only one referred to the Second Battle of Ypres in 1915. No one mentioned the Battle of Hill 70.[17]

This obscurity is all the more puzzling, given the achievement that Hill 70 represented. As General Arthur Currie himself remarked, "It was altogether the hardest battle in which the Corps has participated," and despite the difficulty of the operation, senior officers in the British Army regarded it "as one of the finest performances of the war."[18]

It was not simply the result that added lustre to the Battle of Hill 70. Its significance also lay in the fact that it was part of an ongoing debate among British military experts over best practice. Hill 70 lent credence to those who contended that focusing on more limited objectives was preferable to remaining preoccupied with a breakout.[19] Meanwhile, emphasis on integration of various units proved critical in the wake of this battle. As one observer puts it,

Attacks would now be characterized by a remarkably tight integration of infantry and artillery. Objectives were limited so as not to outrun fire support, and every effort was made to bring firepower forward as quickly as possible to the new front. This approach was both more sophisticated and effective than the German practice, and, incidentally, was ideally suited to handle the central element of all German defensive systems – the immediate counterattack on an assault force before it could solidify its new defensive position.[20]

Although any fully orbed examination of the reasons for Allied success in 1918 must take into account slipping German industrial output and morale given the length of the conflict, the integration of infantry and artillery clearly played an important role in the victories of that year.

Like Vimy, the Battle of Flers-Courcelette, another costly day for the CEF, has been overwhelmed by myth. Because it was part of the massive Somme campaign, popular understanding has submerged it in the wider offensive. And that offensive has come to be identified with its first catastrophic day, 1 July 1916, when the British Army suffered the highest single-day losses in its illustrious history. As William Philpott correctly points out, the fortunes of attacking units varied on 1 July. Where German defenders could not get to their guns in time, the attackers penetrated the line. However, where the wire was not broken, or the defenders had enough time to ready themselves, little progress was made at the highest possible cost. In these sectors, Philpott explains,

> the attack was shot to pieces by concentrated machine gun fire and horrifying casualties were inflicted. Gommecourt, Serre, Beaumont Hamel, Thiepval, La Boiselle and Ovillers, where battalions, sometimes whole brigades were mown down, are names inscribed in Britain's collective memory. This is the Somme of popular myth, of poems, plays and novels; the graveyard of locally raised "pals" battalions, "Two years in the making. Ten minutes in the destroying," in author John Harris' memorable and oft-cited conclusion to his novel about the destruction of the Sheffield City Battalion at Serre.[21]

Still, despite recognition of the great cost of 1 July, it was not until the 1960s that the image of the Somme offensive as pernicious slaughter began to take hold, largely in the wake of Alan Clark's *The Donkeys* and the West End play (and later film) *Oh! What a Lovely War.*[22]

In academic circles at least, a steady re-evaluation of the Somme began during the 1980s. On the simplest of levels, attention was brought to bear on the *full* campaign, which lasted until 18 November, some four and a half months after the first day of the operation. Most people would be shocked to learn this. The determination not to allow a single day to overshadow the larger picture was evident in a 1991 exhibition on the battle organized by the Imperial War Museum, which included the following timeline:

1　The Battlefield
2　The Bloodiest Day: 1 July 1916
3　The Next Ten Days
4　The Attack on the German Second Position
5　The Summer of Attrition
6　The Debut of the Tank
7　The Autumn Fighting
8　The Final Phase: The Battle of the Ancre[23]

Clearly, the inference was that the first day, no matter how devastating, remained a brief moment in a long battle of attrition. Peter Simkins, who played a critical role in planning the 1991 exhibition, subsequently published *From the Somme to Victory.* In asserting that "the Somme battle was an undeniable Allied victory," he quoted military historian John Terraine, who stated that it "laid the essential foundation for the final defeat of the Germans in the field."[24] So, not only was the first day of the Somme a tiny element in a more complex event, but it was also part of what ultimately proved to be a victory, one that contributed significantly to the defeat of the German Army.

The battle over the meaning of the Somme has not been confined to Britain either. For the people of Newfoundland – a separate dominion at the time of the war – 1 July has an entirely different meaning. This is because the Newfoundland Regiment, which went over the top in the *third* wave of Allied attackers, when it was already obvious that the assault was doomed, suffered 90 percent casualties, with more than six hundred killed or wounded. Even a Canadian government publication describing the Somme is unable to maintain detachment:

> The losses sustained by the 1st Newfoundland Regiment at Beaumont-Hamel on July 1, 1916, were staggering. Of the 801 Newfoundlanders who went into battle that morning, only 68 were able to answer the roll call the next day, with 255 dead, 386 wounded and 91 missing. The dead included 14 sets of brothers, including four lieutenants from the Ayers family of St. John's.[25]

Many who saw the Blue Puttees go into battle on that day were stunned by their courage. As one observer remarked, their progress was orderly and deliberate. They made virtually no allowance for the storm of steel, but "instinctively they tucked their chins into an advancing shoulder, as they had so often done when fighting their way home against a blizzard in some little outport in far-off Newfoundland."[26]

One final point is worth making about the damage done in Newfoundland by the Somme offensive. The scar was an indelible one, marking a shattering change. That change

> was an absence. It was marked eventually with war memorials and parades which, by their very existence, contradicted what they were supposed to represent. July 1 is Memorial Day in Newfoundland – the first services were held one year after Beaumont Hamel, on July 1, 1917 – and what the cenotaphs and marches really commemorate is nothing. They substantiate not what had been before the war, and not what happened during it, but what never was to be, after the war was over.[27]

There was another, more prosaic if no less powerful reason for the continued influence of 1 July. Of the 5,482 men that Newfoundland sent to Europe, some

67 percent were killed or wounded, which represented the worst casualty rate of any imperial force. And the resulting obligation to the survivors – wounded and "unscathed" alike – amounted to $40 million, a doubling of the island's debt and a burden that ultimately made independence impractical. Is it any wonder that Newfoundlanders remain conflicted about the national holiday that coincides with their historic tragedy?[28]

If Vimy and the Somme have attracted considerable attention in the historiography of the Great War, the Hundred Days, much like the attack on Hill 70, has languished in obscurity in public consciousness. As Jack Granatstein puts it,

> Today, Canadians know little of their Corps' history except for the victory at Vimy Ridge ... Vimy was important in giving Canadian soldiers the confidence that they could do anything. However, the greatest victories of the Canadian Corps took place in the critical period from August 8, 1918, to the Armistice of November 11 ... In a succession of battles planned and directed by Canadian Lieutenant-General Sir Arthur Currie, the Corps' commander since June 1917, these soldiers played a huge role in the Allied victory over Germany in the First World War.[29]

Granatstein goes on to claim that the CEF's work in late 1918 represented "Canada's greatest contribution to the Allied victory. In fact, Canada's Hundred Days was the most important Canadian role in battle ever."[30] Such a pronouncement might arouse indignation among Second World War specialists, who might cite D-Day as Canada's greatest contribution in battle. Still, whether or not one believes that Granatstein was indulging in hyperbole in his assessment of Canada's contribution to the Hundred Days, there is no question that the CEF's role was very important. The series of attacks saw the Allies stem the tide of German advances and push the Wehrmacht back to the borders of Belgium and France, so that, in a strange symmetry, Mons featured as the site of the war's first and last great battles. However, the cost on both sides was high. The 760,000 German casualties (and an even more significant number of German desertions) were matched by some 700,000 Allied casualties.[31] Of the ten bloodiest days for the Canadians in the war, four took place during the Hundred Days.[32]

The Shadow of the Centenary

Some of the controversies mentioned above remain the preserve of academic historians and rarely attract public attention. However, general interest in the Great War has been stoked by the recent centenary. Given the human tendency to look to round-figure anniversaries for added significance, it is perhaps not surprising that so much effort was devoted to commemorating the 100th anniversary of a war that remains, in many minds, the fulcrum of the twentieth century.[33] And yet these commemorations have not been without acrimony.

One case in point involves Dr. David Stephens, secretary of the Honest History Coalition and convenor of its Honest History website. Stephens has expressed concern at the expenditures associated with Australian commemorations.[34] He emphasizes that Australia led all combatants in spending on the anniversary, allocating $552 million (Australian dollars) to remembrance initiatives, $470 million of which came from taxpayers. Ian McPhedran, another concerned observer, further points out that the "Australian outlay is roughly five times more than the UK Government and some 17 times higher than our Anzac brethren across the Tasman."[35] A closer look at the expenditures is fascinating (see Table C.1). Discomfort regarding spending was not confined to Australia. In Canada, a debate raged about how best to mark the 100th anniversary. However, its tone differed greatly from that in Australia. A significant portion of interested observers believed that Canada was not spending *enough*. Historian Jack Granatstein, writing in the *Globe and Mail* in 2014, noted the significant spending in Britain and elsewhere, though he added, "The government has a long list of events and commemorations, to be sure. But there is no new money behind this string of events – government departments, agencies and Crown corporations have been ordered to finance the commemoration costs out of existing budgets."[36]

Whatever we may think of Granatstein's wider position on the centrality of military history in the teaching of Canadian history, he does raise many points that are worth contemplating. When it comes to government-sponsored commemorative events, a number of non-historical factors may exert considerable influence on decisions made. Looming elections, mounting casualties in and protest over contemporary wars, and responses to previous attempts at commemoration all probably shaped the environment with respect to Great War memorialization. It is also impossible to understand the centenary celebrations

Table C.1

Spending on Great War centenary commemorations

Combatant state	War deaths	Cash outlay
Australia	62,000	$552 million or $8,889 per death
New Zealand	18,100	$31 million or $1,713 per death
Canada	66,000	$31 million or $465 per death
United Kingdom	1.012 million	$110 million or $109 per death
France	1.737 million	$90 million or $52 per death
Germany	2.8 million	$6 million or $2 per death

without reference to the federal election of 19 October 2015, which ushered in Justin Trudeau's Liberals, or the Canadian withdrawal from Afghanistan on 15 March 2014. It is still too soon to expect a cogent analysis of the impact of the Great War centenary on interpretations of the conflict. Few forays have been made to date,[37] and nothing has been written from the Canadian perspective. However, it is safe to say that one fact remains indisputable: "Memory is always about the future. When political conditions change, so do narratives about the past."[38]

Complexity over Simplicity

It would seem that one obvious lesson to be drawn from the First World War is that it defies easy summation. Neat and tidy narratives do not do justice to the variety of developments – both positive and negative – that emerged from the conflict. Even a cursory glance at the war's impacts proves breathtaking in its scope. Regimes crumbled. The Ottoman and Austro-Hungarian Empires disappeared; the monarchy in Germany dissolved; and the Russian Revolution ushered in an entirely new form of government. European borders were re-drawn and colonies around the globe changed hands. The League of Nations – a recognition of the immense cost of the failure of diplomacy – was created. It is hard not to agree with Wade Davis, who, in his fascinating contribution to a volume dedicated to John McCrae's "In Flanders Fields," declared, "Everything you know of your life, every sense you have of being modern, every existential doubt, each burst of confusion, every neurotic affirmation or affliction was born of the mud and blood of Flanders."[39]

Complexity is a watchword throughout this collection. Graham Broad provides nuance in two important ways in his exploration of Eddie McKay and the Battle of Flers-Courcelette. He acknowledges that technology – as epitomized, in this instance, by the airplane – was both a blessing and a curse. He rightfully points out that the Royal Flying Corps was a dangerous place, with high casualty rates (though not as outrageously high as subsequently claimed). At the same time, the flyers were admired and, themselves, embraced the image of being knights of the air.[40] Additionally, though the myth of courageous men betrayed by callous and inept leaders remains hardy, the reality in the flying corps at the time of Courcelette was that commanders were experiencing their own version of the "learning curve" in which continuous adjustments to new weap-onry and fresh tactical and operational circumstances prompted innovative thinking about how to fight the war.

Jonathan Vance similarly eschews an overly simplistic conception of the Great War. Examining Rob Buchan and his role in the Battle of Thiepval Ridge, Vance contends that Buchan, like so many of his colleagues in the CEF, was a citizen-soldier who had little background in matters martial. For him, the defining elements of his identity remained his small-town Ontario roots and his close circles of family and friends, even in the face of the mounting violence of the Great War.[41] The proponents of the war culture thesis tend to see the First World War as a process of gradual accommodation to brutality. As Leonard Smith puts it, "The homogeneity of war culture was both cause and effect, as the protagonists fought the stalemated war with ever-greater ferocity. Commitment on both sides of the conflict deepened with adversity."[42] Vance argues against the notion of a blanket war culture, insisting that men like Buchan did what they had to do and retained the values that had motivated them initially, despite the horrors they witnessed.

The notion of individual agency – which sometimes gets lost in the debate over the existence of an all-dominating war culture – lies at the heart of several chapters in this collection. Sarah Glassford paints a moving portrait of three Canadian nursing sisters who, despite the gender norms of the day, served at the front and ultimately gave their lives. She points out that their thoughts and actions contravene the constructed narrative of nurses as angels of mercy. At the same time, she admits that the women themselves could be moved to remember their wartime work differently from one another as they sought to make sense of their service and to educate popular audiences in the post-war period.[43]

The struggle surrounding agency is also tellingly highlighted in the contributions of Evan J. Habkirk and Geoffrey Hayes. One can hardly imagine two more disparate individuals than their chosen soldiers. Wilfred Lickers was a resident of Six Nations who lost his wife during the war. He survived the conflict but nearly lost the land he had been given by the government as a result of the economic downturn. He died in 1960. Talbot Papineau, the scion of one of Quebec's best-known families, engaged in a public controversy with his nationalist cousin, Henri Bourassa, over whether the war was just. He died in 1917. Lickers was subjected to constant surveillance by the federal authorities, and even basic decisions – most notably, how to allocate his pay so as to support his daughter – were contravened by government operatives. Papineau, who had clear political ambitions, spent part of the war in the relatively safe role of staff officer. However, in the final analysis, Papineau may well have been just as constrained as Lickers. He was haunted by the dead and ashamed of his comfort and security behind the lines. He wrote, "More friends have gone. By what strange law am I still here? What right have I to selfish pleasure any longer? Should my living life not be consecrated just as their dead lives have been?"[44] He made a fateful decision to return to the front lines, where he was killed on 30 October 1917.

Complexity is further revealed in the story of the spiritual dimensions of the Great War. Another common myth is that the war undermined the faith of the soldiers who fought it. Kyle Falcon calls this generalization into question in his exploration of how soldiers coped with their experiences. In examining the various ways in which soldiers kept themselves sane at the front, Falcon touches not only on the well-known elements of trench journals, sports, and concert parties but also on the less commonly discussed areas of faith and the supernatural. He discusses the syncretism of men in the trenches, who unabashedly combined traditional Christian tenets with good luck charms and rituals based in superstition.

Finally, even in connection with dereliction of duty, the story has all too often been painted in broad strokes. During the Great War and in its immediate aftermath, those who proved unwilling or unable to carry out their duties were often portrayed as villains. Typical of this response was the statement of one medical officer in the 2nd Royal Welch Fusiliers in 1917, on the eve of Passchendaele. He remarked, "two or three score mean fellows are encouraged to slip away every time there is a risk to their skins, so more and more average men learn to shirk with impunity, attacks fail, and losses run into untold thousands."[45]

Teresa Iacobelli rightly points out that there was no single wartime narrative regarding those who deserted. She presents the cases of John Wellman Campbell, Edward Dean, and George Murree, who abandoned their unit just before the attack on Bourlon Wood. The men had experienced varying degrees of difficulty in accommodating to military discipline and did not defend their decision to desert in identical terms. For example, Campbell blamed the sudden death of his mother for his actions; he also leaned on his previous record, pointing out that "I have been about 15 months in France. I was wounded on the Somme in 1916." In contrast, Murree's defence emphasized the legal distinction between desertion and being absent without leave (page 258). In the same way that these men used differing strategies to plead their cases, the deliberations of courts martial were far from uniform, proving once again that simple, monochromatic interpretations of delicate issues such as desertion do not capture the full breadth and depth of the phenomenon.

The Pity of War

Given the variety of experiences that the soldiers, flyers, and nurses went through, given the uniqueness of their individual qualities and circumstances, what, if anything, can we claim as common ground? In his poem "Strange Meeting," Wilfred Owen famously spoke of "the truth untold, / The pity of war, the pity war distilled."[46] This seems a fitting place to begin.

The central fact of the Great War is that it marked the passing of 10,057,600 souls.[47] The disappearance of so many men and women prompted a tidal wave of grief, as millions of families sought to cope with the loss they had suffered. Cynthia Comacchio beautifully captures the essence of this process in her exploration of twin brothers Arnold and Clarence Westcott. She opens her contribution by quoting Vera Brittain's simple poem to her brother: "Your battle-wounds are scars upon my heart" (page 224). She goes on to declare that, as staggering as the casualty figures were, "Far more difficult to assess are the unquestionable emotional costs of all these deaths. Although every soldier designated an official 'next of kin', the many others who mourned each individual were left unrecorded and unaccounted" (page 226). Sarah Glassford also touches on the theme of mourning. She notes that grieving practices were challenged and sometimes revolutionized by the unprecedented mass death occasioned by the war.[48] And, as I point out in my own reflection on Samuel Bothwell and the assault on Vimy Ridge, when the pain becomes too much to bear, we shave its rough edges, we flatten it, trim it, and seek to contain it in fine boxes. For Bothwell, there was no triumphant return home, no presence at the birth of a new nation. Instead, his family was torn apart, his wife remarrying and returning to Britain and his eldest child remaining in Canada.

Still, even this rendering of the Great War does not fully do it justice. Its myriad faces defy easy characterization.[49] Major Guy Chapman, recipient of the Military Cross and an OBE for his service with the Royal Fusiliers between 1914 and 1920 underlines this:

At the halts they lay in the long wet grass and gossiped, enormously at ease. The whistle blew. They jumped for their equipment. The little grey figure of the colonel far ahead waved its stick. Hump your pack and get a move on. The next hour, man, will bring you three miles nearer to your death. Your life and your death are nothing to these fields – nothing, no more than it is to the man planning the next attack at G.H.Q. You are not even a pawn. Your death will not prevent future wars, will not make the world safe for your children. Your death means no more than if you had died in your bed, full of years and respectability, having begotten a tribe of young. Yet by your courage and tribulation, by your cheerfulness before the dirty devices of the world, you have won the love of those who have watched you. All we remember is your living face, and that we loved you for being of our clay and our spirit.[50]

This excerpt underlines the protean nature of those who served in the Great War. The same man who shirked sentry duty or complained about his commanding officer in the most colourful language could demonstrate incredible courage, loyalty, and self-sacrifice in the heat of battle. This respect for the individuals who gave so much is what undergirds our approach in this collection.

Young and old, Indigenous and recent immigrant, farmer, and aspiring politician, they shared precious little save the knowledge of the ugliness of war and, at least in the majority of cases, a paradoxical resolve not to let that deter them from doing their duty.

One of the most astounding things about the Great War is the simple, humble determination of those who fought it. The perseverance in the face of unimaginable desolation proved a buoy that prevented many from sinking beneath the waves. As Kyle Falcon points out, sport, humour, and organized concert parties all helped to maintain the spirits of the men in the British Army. J.G. Fuller, meanwhile, notes that the British Expeditionary Force did not suffer indiscipline on anything near the scale of what took place in the French, German, Italian, or Russian Armies; instead, even at the peak of the casualties, "British and Dominion forces kept going, withstood the mightiest blows and took the leading part in the great war-winning offensives [of 1918] ... At no time did discipline collapse."[51] Fuller concludes – much as Jonathan Vance does in his analysis of Rob Buchan – that "the evidence ... suggests that the British and Dominion troops in the First World War carried over from civilian life many institutions and attitudes which heled them to adjust to, and to humanize, the new world in which they found themselves."[52]

Citizen-Soldiers

This leads to the final common element that links the individuals whose stories are told in *Portraits of Battle*. All were citizen-soldiers. Of the sixteen men and women studied in this collection, four were labourers, three were nurses, and two were accountants/bookkeepers; the others were a carpenter, farmer, gardener, jeweller, lawyer, machinist, and recently graduated student. Not a single person was a career soldier.[53]

But what were the implications of the fact that so many of the men and women in the CEF were citizen-soldiers? Perhaps most obviously, they were subject to the potent forces demonstrating that equality was still a distant dream. Some, especially if they served in branches of the forces where prejudice was strong, encountered class bias. For example, as Graham Broad points out, Eddie McKay had to work hard to assure those in the Royal Flying Corps that he was worthy of inclusion in a service where a recruiter could boast of having averted disaster by screening out a "farm labourer" and someone who "ran a newspaper stand in Regina" (page 24).

Gender also remained a powerful restrictive force. Two of the nurses studied in this book felt compelled to include the word "graduate" or "professional" on their attestation papers.[54] The simple word "nurse" seemed to be inadequate. Once in the field, they were still challenged by gendered expectations regarding how they were to behave in the operating theatre or recovery area, as well as during their moments of free time. In the end, though there was, of course, no single typical experience for women in the war, they made a significant contribution. The workers in munitions factories as well as the nurses in the front lines come to mind immediately. However, the impact of their voluntary unpaid labour should not be overlooked either. Most importantly, "aside from its economic value, women's wartime work also served as an emotional resource. Their support for the war helped to create the impression of unity in sacrifice that was critical to how ordinary people tried to make sense of the conflict."[55]

Interestingly, the same impetus for change that was reshaping gender expectations for women was also affecting notions of masculinity. In her novel *Regeneration*, Pat Barker writes, "One of the paradoxes of the war – one of the many – was that this most brutal of conflicts should set up a relationship between officers and men that was ... domestic. Caring."[56] The various effects of the conflict on images of manliness are manifest in the life of Talbot Papineau, from the homo-erotic undertones of his relationships with brother officers through to his struggle with the temptations of the flesh to his final decision to rejoin his unit at the front in order to live up to the manly ideal that drove him, as Geoffrey Hayes ably demonstrates.

Despite the forces that often worked against individual agency, the Great War did provide numerous examples of people who seized the opportunities that presented themselves and, as a result, widened the scope of their involvement in the war. Roy Duplissie was a shining example of how the emerging system of officer replacement could function to good effect. As Lee Windsor asserts,

> The officer development and replacement system of the Canadian Army, which helped to win that victory, is worthy of deeper investigation. It is part of the wider question of how the young dominion managed to raise such a large field army that was as capable as those of the most advanced modern industrialized nations with more extensive pre-war military institutions. (page 219)

Examples like Duplissie's aside, the promise of advancement proved illusory for many soldiers. More than four thousand First Nations troops fought in the CEF during the Great War, but their service would not mean that they were treated as equals once they returned home, a fact that generated considerable frustration. For some, the war proved a turning point. It convinced Lieutenant Frederick Loft of the Six Nations that emancipation would be possible only if a mass movement of Indigenous people could be formed in Canada. The League of Indians of Canada, founded by Loft in 1919, was just such an organization, and its struggle "represents an early attempt at structured, non-violent opposition to the Canadian State, and can be seen as a predecessor to the national Native political organizations that currently exist."[57] Ultimately, the league was thwarted. The implacable opposition of the Canadian government, coupled with Loft's advanced age during the period of his greatest political action, meant that he could not accomplish the Herculean task he had set himself.[58] Nevertheless, his work to advance the cause of fairer treatment for First Nations marked an important step on the path to improved Indigenous-settler relations, and the League of Indians was a direct precursor of the Assembly of First Nations, which is so active in Canadian politics today.

The post-war activism of Levi General, or Deskaheh, also demonstrated that Indigenous peoples in Canada continued to face inequities. Like Loft, he was inspired to some degree by the creation of the League of Nations at the end of the Great War. General was confident that, once apprised of the treaty relationship the Six Nations had with the British Crown, the League would pressure the federal government to recognize the Six Nations as a separate nation. In 1923, he went to Geneva, hoping to address the League regarding autonomy for Indigenous peoples. However, the Canadian government alerted London, and the British delegation in Geneva ensured that General was not permitted to speak.

Costly Battles

This collection begins with the costliest engagements fought by the CEF in the First World War. If nothing else, these battles reveal the Sisyphean nature of the historian's task. We are engaged in an ongoing struggle – against our own predilections, powerful schools of thought, the influence of potent guardians of memory, and contemporary exigencies – to better understand this highly significant event in history. And given the ferocity with which some outdated views of the war are defended, or the ease with which novels, television programs, and websites can communicate a more accessible version of the conflict, we do not always stay the course. We begin to doubt that a vision of the war that is firmly rooted in evidence but free of jargon, nuanced without being obscurantist, can ever win the day. Perhaps this is only natural. Like the Blue Puttees of Newfoundland on 1 July 1916, we advance deliberately across the field, tucking in our chins and hoping to inch through the shrapnel. But our campaign has a worthy objective – to situate the Great War somewhere between abattoir and field of honour. Our efforts on this front are grounded in the richly varied experiences of individuals, not that different from us, who worked, played, lived, and died amidst this most terrible of wars.

Notes

1 Malcolm Brown, *The Imperial War Museum Book of 1918: Year of Victory* (London: Pan Books, 1998).

2 Antoine Prost, writing in the online International Encyclopedia of the First World War, arrives at a grand total of 10,057,600 for all combatants but prefaces his estimates with a lengthy and compelling discussion of the various factors that make reaching an accurate number extremely difficult. See Antoine Prost, "War Losses," 8 October 2014, International Encyclopedia of the First World War, https://encyclopedia.1914-1918-online.net/article/war_losses. Interestingly, though the Canadian War Museum suggests that "close to 61,000 Canadians were killed during the war," it further clarifies that 59,544 of them were members of the Canadian Expeditionary Force. See "The Cost of Canada's War," Canadian War Museum, https://www.warmuseum.ca/firstworldwar/history/after-the-war/legacy/the-cost-of-canadas-war/. The first day of the Somme offensive – 1 July 1916 – remains etched on the minds of many in Britain and continues to attract the attention of historians. See, for example, Peter Hart, *The Somme: The Darkest Hour on the Western Front* (New York: Pegasus Books, 2008).

3 Noble Frankland, *History at War: The Campaigns of an Historian* (London: Giles de la Mare, 1998), 2.

4 For a classic encapsulation of this complicated relationship, see Jay Winter, *Remembering War: The Great War between Memory and History in the Twentieth Century* (New Haven: Yale University Press, 2006), 5–13.

5 The phrase comes from Rudyard Kipling's 1897 poem "Recessional," which begins "GOD of our fathers, known of old – / Lord of our far-flung battle-line – / Beneath whose awful Hand we hold / Dominion over palm and pine – / Lord God of Hosts, be with us yet, / Lest we forget, lest we forget!" "Recessional," *London Times,* 17 July 1897. For the history of the Imperial (later Commonwealth) War Graves Commission, see David Crane, *Empire of the Dead* (London: William Collins, 2013).

6 The classic text on the theme of memory and forgetting is Paul Ricoeur, *Memory, History, Forgetting,* trans. Kathleen Blamey and David Pellauer (Chicago: University of Chicago Press, 2004).

7 Frankland, *History at War,* 5.

8 The most significant assessment of the treaty in the immediate post-war period was John Maynard Keynes, *Economic Consequences of the Peace* (New York: Harcourt, Brace and Howe, 1920).

9 See L. James Dempsey, *Warriors of the King: Prairie Indians in World War I* (Regina: Canadian Plains Research Centre, 1999); P. Whitney Lackenbauer, R. Scott Sheffield, and Craig Leslie Mantle, eds., *Aboriginal People and the Canadian Military: Historical Perspectives* (Kingston: Canadian Defence Academy Press, 2007); and Timothy C. Winegard, *For King and Kanata: Canadian Indians and the First World War* (Winnipeg: University of Manitoba Press, 2012).

10 It is true that First Nations communities opposed conscription when it was introduced. Viewing their nations as sovereign and loyal allies of the Crown, Indigenous leaders felt it was unnecessary and insulting to be coerced into serving, particularly because participation rates among First Nations people were strong and because promises were made during the signing of the numbered treaties in western Canada that they would not be forced into military service in times of war. See, for example, Robert Talbot, "'It Would Be Best to Leave Us Alone': First Nations Responses to the Canadian War Effort, 1914–18," *Journal of Canadian Studies* 45, 1 (Winter 2011): 90–120; and Noah Riseman and Timothy C. Winegard, "Indigenous Experience of War (British Dominions)," International En-

cyclopedia of the First World War, https://encyclopedia.1914-1918-online.net/article/indigenous_experience_of_war_british_dominions.

11 See "First Nations Soldiers," Canadian War Museum, https://www.warmuseum.ca/first worldwar/history/people/in-uniform/first-nations-soldiers/; and "Thousands Volunteer: The First World War," Veterans Affairs Canada, https://www.veterans.gc.ca/eng/remembrance/those-who-served/indigenous-veterans/native-soldiers/first_response.

12 The ancient Greek philosopher Heraclitus is credited with declaring that "no man can cross the same river twice." However, a more literal translation of the Greek reveals that he actually stated, "On those stepping into rivers staying the same other and other waters flow." See "Heraclitus," 3 September 2019, Stanford Encyclopedia of Philosophy, https://plato.stanford.edu/entries/heraclitus/. For a fuller discussion of the implications of this for the study of history, see Peter Farrugia "Introduction," in *The River of History: Trans-National and Trans-Disciplinary Perspectives on the Immanence of the Past,* ed. Peter Farrugia (Calgary: University of Calgary Press, 2005), 2–3.

13 Tim Cook, *Vimy: The Battle and the Legend* (Toronto: Allen Lane, 2017), 84.

14 Ian McKay and Jamie Swift, *The Vimy Trap: Or, How We Learned to Stop Worrying and Love the Great War* (Toronto: Between the Lines, 2016), 269.

15 Van Wyck Brooks, "On Creating a Usable Past," in *The Dial,* 11 April 1918, 340.

16 In speeches made during public remembrance ceremonies, Prime Ministers Stephen Harper and Justin Trudeau bent the battle to these uses. For details, see Chapter 4 of this volume.

17 Douglas E. Delaney, "Introduction," in *Capturing Hill 70: Canada's Forgotten Battle of the First World War,* ed. Douglas E. Delaney and Serge Marc Durflinger (Vancouver: UBC Press, 2016), 3.

18 Arthur Currie, "Combined Diary Entries, 15–18 August," in Mark Osborne Humphries, ed., *The Selected Papers of Sir Arthur Currie: Diaries, Letters, and Report to the Ministry, 1917–1933* (Waterloo: LCMSDS Press of Wilfrid Laurier University, 2008), 48–49.

19 See Paddy Griffith, *Battle Tactics of the Western Front: The British Army's Art of Attack, 1916–18* (New Haven: Yale University Press, 1994), 32–33, for a discussion of the merits of both breakthrough operations and bite and hold attacks.

20 Ian M. Brown, "Not Glamorous, But Effective: The Canadian Corps and the Set-Piece Attack, 1917–1918," *Journal of Military History* 58, 3 (July 1994): 426.

21 William Philpott, *Bloody Victory: The Sacrifice on the Somme* (London: Abacus, 2016), 341.

22 For the period of balance in the historiography of the Somme offensive, see Dan Todman, *The Great War: Myth and Memory* (London: Continuum, 2005), 112–13, 193–94. Todman discusses the subsequent influence of *The Donkeys* and *Oh! What a Lovely War* on pages 99–108.

23 Imperial War Museum Archives, EXTA 0275, "Chronology," in Folder: conversion to travelling exhibition, Somme exhibition 1991 general.

24 Peter Simkins, *From the Somme to Victory: The British Army's Experience on the Western Front, 1916–1918* (Barnsley, UK: Praetorian Press, 2014), 27.

25 Veterans Affairs Canada, *Canada Remembers: The 1st Newfoundland Regiment and the Battle of the Somme* (Ottawa: Minister of Veterans Affairs, 2006), 2.

26 Quoted in Robert Everett-Green, "July 1, Memorial Day," *Globe and Mail,* 30 June 2016. The regiment was known as the Blue Puttees due to the colour of the men's leggings.

27 David Macfarlane, *The Danger Tree* (Toronto: HarperCollins, 1991), 197.

28 Ibid., 200–1.

29 J.L. Granatstein, *The Greatest Victory: Canada's One Hundred Days, 1918* (Don Mills: Oxford University Press, 2014), xi.

30 Ibid.
31 Nicholas Lloyd, "Hundred Days Offensive," 8 October 2014, International Encyclopedia of the First World War, https://encyclopedia.1914-1918-online.net/article/hundred_days_offensive.
32 See Table I.1: The costliest days for the CEF in the Great War, on page 6 of this volume.
33 In 1996, the BBC in the United Kingdom and PBS in the United States collaborated with Jay Winter to produce the documentary series *The Great War and the Shaping of the Twentieth Century*. For discussion of the making of the documentary, see Jay Winter, "Producing the Television Series *The Great War and the Shaping of the Twentieth Century*," *Profession* (1999): 15–26. For the debate on the merits of the series – which was characterized as too focused on suffering in the United Kingdom – see Todman, *The Great War*, 147–51.
34 See Honest History, "Budget 2015: Honest History Factsheet: centenary spending $551.8 million," at http://honesthistory.net.au/wp/budget-2015-honest-history-factsheet-centenary-spending-551-8-million/.
35 Ian McPhedran, "Government Spending More Than $8800 for Every Digger Killed during WW1," News.com.au, 3 September 2015, https://www.news.com.au/national/anzac-day/government-spending-more-than-8800-for-every-digger-killed-during-ww1/news-story/34808367386af87773c8e4326d2a46e8.
36 J.L. Granatstein, "Why Is Canada Botching the Great War Centenary?" *Globe and Mail*, 21 April 2014. Granatstein's concerns mirror his anxiety about the future of history more generally, as articulated in his bestseller, *Who Killed Canadian History?* (Toronto: HarperCollins, 1998), especially 63–68.
37 For an exception see Helen B. McCartney and David G. Morgan-Owen, eds., "Commemorating the Centenary of the First World War: National and Trans-national Perspectives," special issue, *War and Society* 36, 4 (October 2017).
38 Jay Winter, "Commemorating Catastrophe: 100 Years On," *War and Society* 36, 4 (2017): 239.
39 Wade Davis, "Of War and Remembrance," in *In Flanders Fields: 100 Years of Writing on War, Loss and Remembrance*, ed. Amanda Betts (Toronto: Alfred A. Knopf, 2015), 141.
40 Eric Leed sees the myth of the chivalric contest in the skies as largely compensatory. See Eric Leed, *No Man's Land: Combat and Identity in World War I* (New York: Cambridge University Press, 1979), 134–35.
41 As the list of bloodiest days for the CEF reveals, all of them come after 1 July 1916, with three occurring in 1916, three in 1917, and four in 1918. See Table I.1: The costliest days for the CEF in the Great War, on page 6 of this volume.
42 Leonard V. Smith, "The 'Culture de guerre' and French Historiography of the Great War of 1914–1918," *History Compass* 5, 6 (2007): 1969.
43 In this, nurses faced similar challenges to combat veterans. See Todman, *The Great War*, 204–7.
44 Papineau to Beatrice Fox, quoted in Sandra Gwyn, *Tapestry of War: A Private View of Canadians in the Great War* (Toronto: HarperCollins, 1992), 338.
45 Quoted in John Keegan, *The Face of Battle: A Study of Agincourt, Waterloo and the Somme* (London: Pimlico, 1991), 271.
46 Wilfred Owen, "Strange Meeting," in Jon Stallworthy, ed., *The War Poems of Wilfred Owen* (London: Chatto and Windus, 1994), 35.
47 Again, the figure is Antoine Prost's best estimate. See Prost, "War Losses."
48 The extent to which time-tested rituals were discarded as a result of their dubious utility lies at the heart of a debate between Paul Fussell and Jay Winter. See Paul Fussell, *The*

Great War and Modern Memory (New York: Oxford University Press, 1975); and Jay Winter, *Sites of Memory, Sites of Mourning: The Great War in European Cultural History* (Cambridge: Cambridge University Press, 1995).

49 "Myriad faces" is from Trevor Wilson, *The Myriad Faces of War: Britain and the Great War, 1914–1918* (Polity Press, 1986).

50 Guy Chapman, *A Passionate Prodigality: Fragments of Autobiography* (New York: Holt, Rinehart and Winston, 1933), 122.

51 J.G. Fuller, *Troop Morale and Popular Culture in the British and Dominion Armies, 1914–1918* (Oxford: Clarendon Press, 1990), 1–2.

52 Ibid., 175.

53 It is true that Edward Dean listed his occupation as soldier on his officer's declaration paper, but he was working as a machinist in Detroit when he joined up.

54 Gladys Wake and Margaret Lowe respectively. See Library and Archives Canada (LAC), Canadian Expeditionary Force (CEF), RG 150, accession 1992-93/166, box 9989-48, file Wake, Gladys Maude Mary; and LAC, CEF, RG 150, accession 1992-93/166, box 5768-43, file Lowe, M., NS.

55 Sarah Glassford and Amy Shaw, "Conclusion," in *A Sisterhood of Suffering and Service: Women and Girls of Canada and Newfoundland during the First World War*, ed. Sarah Glassford and Amy Shaw (Vancouver: UBC Press, 2012), 317.

56 Pat Barker, *Regeneration* (New York: Plume, 1991), 107.

57 Peter Kulchyski, "'A Considerable Unrest': F.O. Loft and the League of Indians," *Native Studies Review* 4, 1–2 (1988): 96.

58 John Leonard Taylor, *Canadian Indian Policy during the Inter-War Years, 1918–1939* (Ottawa: Indian and Northern Affairs Canada, 1984), 167–85; Kulchyski, "'A Considerable Unrest,'" 99.

Selected Bibliography

Acton, Carol. *Grief in Wartime: Private Pain, Public Discourse*. New York: Palgrave Macmillan, 2007.

Airhart, Phyllis D. "Ordering a Nation and Reordering Protestantism, 1867–1914." In *The Canadian Protestant Experience, 1760–1990*, ed. George Rawlyk, 98–138. Burlington: Welch, 1990.

Allen, Richard. *The Social Passion: Religion and Social Reform in Canada, 1914–28*. Toronto: University of Toronto Press, 1973.

Angus, Murray E. "King Jesus and King George: The Manly Christian Patriot and the Great War, 1914–1918." *Papers of the Canadian Methodist Historical Society* 12 (1997–98): 124–32.

Ashton, E.J. "Soldier Land Settlement in Canada." *Quarterly Journal of Economics* 39, 3 (May 1925): 488–98.

Ashworth, Tony. *Trench Warfare: The Live and Let Live System*. London: Macmillan, 1980.

Audoin-Rouzeau, Stéphane. *Men at War, 1914–1918: National Sentiment and Trench Journalism in France during the First World War*. Washington, DC: Berg, 1995.

Audoin-Rouzeau, Stéphane, and Annette Becker. *14–18: Understanding the Great War*. Trans. C. Temerson. New York: Hill and Wang, 2002.

Auger, Martin F. "On the Brink of Civil War: The Canadian Government and the Suppression of the 1918 Quebec Easter Riots." *Canadian Historical Review* 89, 4 (1 December 2008): 503–40.

Babington, Anthony. *For the Sake of Example: Capital Courts-Martial, 1914–1920*. New York: St. Martin's Press, 1983.

–. *Shell-Shock: A History of the Changing Attitudes to War Neurosis*. London: Leo Cooper, 1997.

Bailey, Roy, Timothy Hatton, and Kris Inwood. "Health, Height and the Household at the Turn of the 20th Century." IDEAS Discussion Paper 8128, 2014. Institute of Labor Economics. http://ideas.repec.org/p/iza/izadps/dp8128.html.

Bank, Stephen P., and Michael D. Kahn. *The Sibling Bond*. New York: Basic Books, 1982.

Banning, S.T. *Military Law Made Easy*. 11th ed. London: Gale and Polden, 1917.

Barker, Pat. *Regeneration*. New York: Plume, 1991.

Barker, Ralph. *A Brief History of the Royal Flying Corps in World War I*. London: Robinson, 2002.

Barnes, Deward. *It Made You Think of Home: The Haunting Journal of Deward Barnes, Canadian Expeditionary Force: 1916–1919*. Ed. Bruce Crane. Toronto: Dundurn Group, 2004.

BBC World Service. "French Row over Rehabilitating WWI Mutineers." *BBC News*, 9 November 1998. http://news.bbc.co.uk/2/hi/europe/210983.stm.

Beattie, Kim. *48th Highlanders of Canada, 1891–1928*. Toronto: 48th Highlanders, 1932.

Bedal, Penny, and Ross Bartlett. "'The Women Do Not Speak: The Methodist Ladies' Aid Societies and World War I." *Canadian Methodist Historical Society Papers* 10 (1993–94): 63–86.

Bell, Steven A. "The 107th 'Timber Wolf' Battalion at Hill 70." *Canadian Military History* 5, 1 (1996): 73–78.

Bercuson, David Jay. *The Patricias: The Proud History of a Fighting Regiment.* Toronto: Stoddart, 2001.

Berthiaume, Lee. "Thousands of Canadians Gather in France to Mark 100th Anniversary of Vimy Ridge." *Toronto Star,* 9 April 2017.

Berton, Pierre. *Vimy.* Toronto: Anchor Canada, 1986.

Bird, Will R. *And We Go On: A Memoir of the Great War.* Montreal and Kingston: McGill-Queen's University Press, 2014.

Blanchard, Jim. *Winnipeg 1912.* Winnipeg: University of Manitoba Press, 2005.

Bliss, J.M. "The Methodist Church and World War I." *Canadian Historical Review* 49, 3 (September 1968): 213–33.

Bogaert, Kandace. "Patient Experience and the Treatment of Venereal Disease in Toronto's Military Base Hospital during the First World War." *Canadian Military History* 26, 2 (2017): Article 1.

Boire, Michael. "The Battlefield before the Canadians, 1914–1916." In *Vimy Ridge: A Canadian Reassessment,* ed. Geoffrey Hayes, Andrew Iarocci, and Mike Bechthold, 51–61. Waterloo: Wilfrid Laurier University Press, 2007.

Borden, Robert Laird. *The Diaries of Sir Robert Borden, 1912–1918.* Ottawa: Library and Archives Canada. Ottawa: Library and Archives Canada, unpublished, transcribed by Dr. Kathryn Rose entry for 25 May 1916, ttps://research.library.mun.ca/2428/5/1916.pdf.

Borys, David. "Crossing the Canal: Combined Arms Operations at the Canal du Nord, Sep–Oct 1918." *Canadian Military History* 20, 4 (2011): 23–38.

Bourke, Joanna. *Dismembering the Male: Men's Bodies, Britain, and the Great War.* Chicago: University of Chicago Press, 1996.

Brandon, Laura. "The Sculptures on the Vimy Memorial." Canadian War Museum. https://www.warmuseum.ca/the-battle-of-vimy-ridge/the-sculptures-on-the-vimy-memorial/#tabs.

Broad, Graham. *One in a Thousand: The Life and Death of Captain Eddie McKay, Royal Flying Corps.* Toronto: University of Toronto Press, 2017.

Brookfield, Tarah, and Sarah Glassford. "Home Fronts and Frontlines: A Gendered History of War and Peace." In *A Companion to Women's and Gender History in Canada,* ed. Carmen Nielsen and Nancy Janovicek, 151–70. Toronto: University of Toronto Press, 2019.

Brooks, Van Wyck. "On Creating a Usable Past." *The Dial,* 11 April 1918, 337–41.

Brown, Eric, and Tim Cook. "The 1936 Vimy Pilgrimage." *Canadian Military History* 20, 2 (2011): 37–54.

Brown, Ian M. "Not Glamorous, But Effective: The Canadian Corps and the Set-Piece Attack, 1917–1918." *Journal of Military History* 58, 3 (July 1994): 421–44.

Brown, Malcolm. *The Imperial War Museum Book of 1918: Year of Victory.* London: Pan Books, 1998.

Brown, Robert Craig, and Donald Loveridge. "Unrequited Faith: Recruiting the CEF 1914–1918." *Canadian Military History* 24, 1 (2015): 61–87.

Brownlie, Robin. *A Fatherly Eye: Indian Agents, Government Power, and Aboriginal Resistance in Ontario, 1918–1939.* Toronto: University of Toronto Press, 2003.

Buitenhuis, Peter. *The Great War of Words: British, American, and Canadian Propaganda and Fiction, 1914–1933.* Vancouver: UBC Press, 1987.

Bujak, Edward. *Reckless Fellows: The Gentlemen of the Royal Flying Corps.* London: I.B. Tauris, 2015.

Campbell, Lara. "'We Who Have Wallowed in the Mud of Flanders': First World War Veterans, Unemployment, and the Development of Social Welfare in Canada, 1929–1939." *Journal of the Canadian Historical Association* 11 (2000): 125–49.

Cannadine, David. "War and Death, Grief and Mourning in Modern Britain." In *Mirrors of Mortality: Studies in the Social History of Death*, ed. Joachim Whaley, 187–242. New York: St. Martin's Press, 1981.

Carter, Sarah. *Lost Harvests: Prairie Indian Reserve Farmers and Government Policy.* Montreal and Kingston: McGill-Queen's University Press, 1990.

Catholic War League. *The Facts of the Raid on the Jesuit Novitiate.* Toronto: Catholic Truth Society of Canada, 1918.

Chadwick, E.M. *People of the Longhouse.* Toronto: Church of England, 1897.

Chaiton, Alf, and Neil McDonald, eds. *Canadian Schools and Canadian Identity.* Toronto: Gage, 1977.

Chapman, Guy. *A Passionate Prodigality: Fragments of Autobiography.* New York: Holt, Rinehart and Winston, 1933.

Chasseaud, Peter. *Rats Alley: Trench Names of the Western Front, 1914–1918.* Extended 2nd ed./Kindle ed. Stroud, UK: History Press, 2017.

Christie, N.M. *The Canadians at Cambrai and the Canal du Nord, September–October 1918: A Social and Battlefield Tour.* Nepean: CEF Books, 1997.

Clark, Alan. *The Donkeys.* London: Hutchinson, 1961.

Comacchio, Cynthia. *Nations Are Built of Babies: Saving Ontario's Mothers and Children.* Montreal and Kingston: McGill-Queen's University Press, 1993.

Conrad, Margaret, Jocelyn Létourneau, and David Northrup. "Canadians and Their Pasts: An Exploration in Historical Consciousness." *Public Historian* 31, 1 (Winter 2009): 15–34.

Cook, Ramsay, and Wendy Mitchinson, eds. *The Proper Sphere: Woman's Place in Canadian Society.* Toronto: Oxford University Press, 1976.

Cook, Tim. *At the Sharp End: Canadians Fighting the Great War, 1914–1916.* Toronto: Viking, 2007.

–. "Battles of the Imagined Past: Canada's Great War and Memory." *Canadian Historical Review* 95, 3 (September 2014): 417–26.

–. "The Gunners at Vimy: 'We Are Hammering Fritz to Pieces.'" In *Vimy Ridge: A Canadian Reassessment,* ed. Geoffrey Hayes, Andrew Iarocci, and Mike Bechthold, 105–24. Waterloo: Wilfrid Laurier University Press, 2007.

–. "'I Will Meet the World with a Smile and a Joke': Canadian Soldiers' Humour in the Great War." *Canadian Military History* 22, 2 (2013): 48–62.

–. *The Madman and the Butcher: The Sensational Wars of Sam Hughes and General Arthur Currie.* Toronto: Allen Lane, 2010.

–. "'More a Medicine than a Beverage': 'Demon Rum' and the Canadian Trench Soldier of the First World War." *Canadian Military History* 9, 1 (2000): 6–22.

–. *Shock Troops: Canadians Fighting the Great War, 1917–1918.* Toronto: Viking, 2008.

–. "The Singing War: Canadian Soldiers' Songs of the Great War." *American Review of Canadian Studies* 39, 3 (2009): 224–41.

–. *Vimy: The Battle and the Legend.* Toronto: Allen Lane, 2017.

Cook, Tim, and Natascha Morrison. "Longing and Loss from Canada's Great War." *Canadian Military History* 16, 1 (2007): 53–60.

Coombs, Howard G. "Dimensions of Military Leadership: The Kinmel Park Mutiny of 4–5 March 1919." In *The Apathetic and the Defiant: Case Studies of Canadian Mutiny and Disobedience, 1812–1919,* ed. Craig Leslie Mantle, 405–38. Kingston: Canadian Defence Academy Press, 2007.

Crane, David. *Empire of the Dead*. London: William Collins, 2013.

Creelman, George C. "Impressions of a Farmerette." *OAC Review* 30 (June 1918): 448–49.

Crerar, Duff. *Padres in No Man's Land: Canadian Chaplains and the Great War*. Montreal and Kingston: McGill-Queen's University Press, 1995.

Dadrian, Vahakn N. *The History of the Armenia Genocide: Ethnic Conflict from the Balkans to Anatolia to the Caucasus*. New York: Berghahn Books, 2003.

Davidoff, Leonore. *Thicker Than Water: Siblings and Their Relations, 1780–1920*. Oxford: Oxford University Press, 2012.

Davis, Wade. "Of War and Remembrance." In *In Flanders Fields: 100 Years of Writing on War, Loss and Remembrance*, ed. Amanda Betts, 141–70. Toronto: Alfred A. Knopf, 2015.

Delaney, Douglas E., and Serge Marc Durflinger, eds. *Capturing Hill 70: Canada's Forgotten Battle of the First World War*. Vancouver: UBC Press, 2016.

Dempsey, L. James. "The Indians and World War One." *Alberta History* 31, 3 (1983).

–. *Warriors of the King: Prairie Indians in World War I*. Regina: Canadian Plains Research Centre, 1999.

Dennis, Patrick. *Reluctant Warriors: Canadian Conscripts and the Great War*. Vancouver: UBC Press, 2017.

Denton-Borhaug, Kelly. "US War Culture and the *Star Wars* Juggernaut." *Theology and Science* 14, 4 (2016): 393–97.

Department of National Defence, Directorate of History and Heritage. "Official Lineages, Vol. 3, Part 2, Infantry Regiments: The Nova Scotia Highlanders." http://www.cmp-cpm. forces.gc.ca/dhh-dhp/his/ol-lo/vol-tom-3/par2/nsh-eng.asp.

Dewar, Katherine. *Those Splendid Girls: The Heroic Service of Prince Edward Island Nurses in the Great War, 1914–1918*. Charlottetown: Island Studies Press, 2014.

Djebabla, Mourad. "'Fight or Farm': Canadian Farmers and the Dilemma of the War Effort in World War I (1914–1918)." *Canadian Military Journal* 13, 2 (2013). http://www.journal. forces.gc.ca/vol13/no2/page57-eng.asp.

Dobson, Chris. *Airmen Died in the Great War, 1914–1918*. Suffolk: J.B. Hayward and Son, 1995.

Dodd, Dianne. "Commemorating Canadian Military Nurse Casualties during and after the First World War: Nurses' Perspectives." In *Routledge Handbook on the Global History of Nursing*, ed. Patricia D'Antonio, Julie A. Fairman, and Jean C. Whelan, 55–75. New York: Routledge, 2013.

Durflinger, Serge. "Safeguarding Sanctity: Canada and the Vimy Memorial during the Second World War." In *Vimy Ridge: A Canadian Reassessment*, ed. Geoffrey Hayes, Andrew Iarocci, and Mike Bechthold, 291–305. Waterloo: Wilfrid Laurier University Press, 2007.

Durocher, René. "Henri Bourassa, les évêques et la guerre de 1914–1918." *Canadian Historical Association Papers* 6, 1 (1971): 254–69.

Dye, Peter. *The Bridge to Airpower: Logistics Support for Royal Flying Corps Operations on the Western Front, 1914–1918*. Annapolis: Naval Institute Press, 2015.

Ekins, Ashley. "Fighting to Exhaustion: Morale, Discipline and Combat Effectiveness in the Armies of 1918." In *1918 Year of Victory: The End of the Great War and the Shaping of History*, ed. Ashley Ekins, 111–29. Auckland, NZ: Exisle, 2010.

Emery, George, and J.C. Herbert Emery. *A Young Man's Benefit: The Independent Order of Odd Fellows and Sickness Insurance in the United States and Canada, 1860–1929*. Montreal and Kingston: McGill-Queen's University Press, 1999.

Engen, Robert. *Strangers in Arms: Combat Motivation in the Canadian Army, 1943–45*. Montreal and Kingston: McGill-Queen's University Press, 2016.

Evans, Suzanne. "Marks of Grief: Black Attire, Medals, and Service Flags." In *A Sisterhood of Suffering and Service: Women and Girls of Canada and Newfoundland during the First World War*, ed. Sarah Glassford and Amy Shaw, 219–40. Vancouver: UBC Press, 2012.

–. *Mother of Heroes, Mother of Martyrs*. Montreal and Kingston: McGill-Queen's University Press, 2007.

Everett-Green, Robert. "Mélanie Joly to Reset 'Symbols of Progressiveness' as Heritage Minister." *Globe and Mail*, 6 November 2015.

Farrugia, Peter. "Introduction." In *The River of History: Trans-National and Trans-Disciplinary Perspectives on the Immanence of the Past*, ed. Peter Farrugia, 1–31. Calgary: University of Calgary Press, 2005.

Ferris, John. "Seeing over the Hill: The Canadian Corps, Intelligence, and the Battle of Hill 70 July–August 1917." *Intelligence and National Security* 23, 3 (2007): 351–64.

Fetherstonaugh, R.C. *The Royal Canadian Regiment: 1883–1933*. Fredericton: Centennial Print and Litho, 1981.

Fletcher, Anthony. *Life, Death and Growing Up on the Western Front*. New Haven: Yale University Press, 2013.

Fogg, Ally. "Sainsbury's Christmas Ad Is a Dangerous and Disrespectful Masterpiece." *The Guardian*, 13 November 2014.

Foster, Kenneth Walter. "The Memoir of Kenneth Walter Foster." Canadian Letters and Images Project. http://canadianletters.ca/content/document-4021.

Frankland, Noble. *History at War: The Campaigns of an Historian*. London: Giles de la Mare, 1998.

Fuller, J.G. *Troop Morale and Popular Culture in the British and Dominion Armies, 1914–1918*. Oxford: Clarendon Press, 1990.

Fussell, Paul. *The Great War and Modern Memory*. New York: Oxford University Press, 1975.

Gaffen, Fred. *Forgotten Soldiers*. Penticton, BC: Theytus Books, 1985.

Gamble, Richard M. *The War for Righteousness: Progressive Christianity, the Great War, and the Rise of the Messianic Nation*. Wilmington: ISI, 2003.

Gilbert, Martin. *The Battle of the Somme: The Heroism and Horror of War*. Toronto: McClelland and Stewart, 2006.

Gill, D., and G. Dallas. "Mutiny at Étaples Base in 1917." *Past and Present* 69, 1 (1972): 88–112.

Glassford, Sarah. "'The Greatest Mother in the World': Carework and the Discourse of Mothering in the Canadian Red Cross Society during the First World War." *Journal of the Association for Research on Mothering* 10, 1 (2008): 219–33.

–. *Mobilizing Mercy: A History of the Canadian Red Cross*. Montreal and Kingston: McGill-Queen's University Press, 2017.

Glassford, Sarah, and Amy Shaw. "Conclusion." In *A Sisterhood of Suffering and Service: Women and Girls of Canada and Newfoundland during the First World War*, ed. Sarah Glassford and Amy Shaw, 315–22. Vancouver: UBC Press, 2012.

Goldstein, Joshua. *War and Gender: How Gender Shapes the War System and Vice Versa*. Cambridge: Cambridge University Press, 2001.

Goldsworthy, Ryan. "Measuring the Success of Canada's Wars: The Hundred Days Offensive as a Case Study." *Canadian Military Journal* 13, 2 (Spring 2013). http://www.journal.forces.gc.ca/vol13/no2/page46-eng.asp.

Goodman, Lee-Anne. "Justin Trudeau Makes Acting Debut in CBC Docudrama." *Toronto Star*, 4 April 2007. https://www.thestar.com/entertainment/2007/04/04/justin_trudeau_makes_acting_debut_in_cbc_docudrama.html.

Gordon, Charles W., ed. *Postscript to Adventure: The Autobiography of Ralph Connor*. New York: Farrar and Rinehart, 1938.

Gough, Paul. "Sites in the Imagination: The Beaumont Hamel Newfoundland Memorial on the Somme." *Cultural Geographies* 11, 3 (July 2004): 235–58.

Gould Lee, Arthur. *No Parachute*. London: Jarrolds, 1968.

Granatstein, J.L. *The Greatest Victory: Canada's One Hundred Days, 1918*. Don Mills: Oxford University Press, 2014.

–. *Who Killed Canadian History?* Toronto: HarperCollins, 1998.

–. "Why Is Canada Botching the Great War Centenary?" *Globe and Mail*, 21 April 2014.

Grant, John Webster. *The Church in the Canadian Era*. Burlington, ON: Welch, 1988.

Grant, Julia. "A 'Real Boy' and Not a Sissy: Gender, Childhood, and Masculinity, 1890–1940." *Journal of Social History* 37, 4 (2004): 829–51.

Great War Centenary Association, Brantford, Brant County, Six Nations. "About the GWCA." http://doingourbit.ca/node/4854.

Guttman, Jon. *Pusher Aces of World War 1*. Oxford: Osprey, 2009.

Gwyn, Sandra. "Papineau, Talbot Mercer." Dictionary of Canadian Biography. http://www.biographi.ca/en/bio/papineau_talbot_mercer_14E.html.

–. *Tapestry of War: A Private View of Canadians in the Great War*. Toronto: HarperCollins, 1992.

Habkirk, Evan J. "Militarism, Sovereignty, and Nationalism: Six Nations and the First World War." Master's thesis, Trent University, 2010.

Hamilton-Paterson, James. *Marked for Death: The First War in the Air*. London: Pegasus, 2016.

Hart, Peter. *Bloody April*. London: Cassell, 2007.

–. *The Somme: The Darkest Hour on the Western Front*. New York: Pegasus Books, 2008.

Hayes, Geoffrey. *Crerar's Lieutenants: Inventing the Canadian Junior Army Officer, 1939–45*. Vancouver: UBC Press, 2017.

–. "Exploring Masculinity in the Canadian Army Officer Corps, 1939–45." *Journal of Canadian Studies* 48, 2 (2014): 40–69.

Hayes, Geoffrey, Andrew Iarocci, and Mike Bechthold, eds. *Vimy Ridge: A Canadian Reassessment*. Waterloo: Wilfrid Laurier University Press, 2007.

Head, R.G. *Oswald Boelcke: Germany's First Fighter Ace and the Father of Air Combat*. London: Grub Street, 2016.

Heath, Gordon L., ed. *Canadian Churches and the First World War*. Eugene: Pickwick, 2014.

–. "The Canadian Protestant Press and the Conscription Crisis, 1917–1918." *Historical Studies* 78 (2012): 27–46.

– "'Thor and Allah in a Hideous, Unholy Confederacy': The Armenian Genocide in the Canadian Protestant Press." In *The Globalization of Christianity: Implications for Christian Ministry and Theology*, ed. Steve Studebaker and Gordon L. Heath, 105–28. Eugene: Pickwick, 2014.

–. "'We Are through with War': The Rise and Fall of Pacifism among Canadian Baptists between the Two World Wars." *Baptistic Theologies* 9, 2 (2017): 37–53.

Heath, Gordon L., and Michael A.G. Haykin, eds. *Baptists and War: Essays on Baptists and Military Conflict, 1640s–1990s*. Eugene: Pickwick, 2014.

Heath, Gordon L., and Paul Wilson, eds. *Baptists and Public Life in Canada*. Eugene: Pickwick, 2012.

Heick, W.H. "The Lutherans of Waterloo County during World War I." *Waterloo Historical Society* 50 (1962): 23–32.

Hodder-Williams, Ralph. *Princess Patricia's Canadian Light Infantry, 1914–1919*. 2 vols. Toronto: Hodder and Stoughton, 1923.

Hogan, Brian F. "The Guelph Novitiate Raid: Conscription, Censorship and Bigotry during the Great War." *Canadian Catholic Historical Association, Study Sessions* 45 (1978): 57–80.

Holmes, Richard. *Tommy: The British Soldier on the Western Front, 1914–1918*. London: HarperCollins, 2004.

Holt, Richard. *Filling the Ranks: Manpower in the Canadian Expeditionary Force, 1914–1918*. Montreal and Kingston: McGill-Queen's University Press, 2017.

Horrall, Andrew. "'Keep-A-Fightin! Play the Game!' Baseball and the Canadian Forces during the First World War." *Canadian Military History* 10, 2 (2001): 27–40.

Hryniuk, Stella. "Pioneer Bishop, Pioneer Times: Nykyta Budka in Canada." *Canadian Catholic Historical Association Historical Studies* 55 (1988): 21–41.

Humphries, Mark Osborne. "The Myth of the Learning Curve." *Canadian Military History* 14, 4 (2005): Article 3.

–, ed. *The Selected Papers of Sir Arthur Currie: Diaries, Letters, and Report to the Ministry, 1917–1933*. Waterloo: LCMSDS Press of Wilfrid Laurier University, 2008.

–. "War's Long Shadow: Masculinity, Medicine, and the Gendered Politics of Trauma, 1914–1939." *Canadian Historical Review* 91, 3 (2010): 503–31.

Iacobelli, Teresa. *Death or Deliverance: Canadian Courts Martial in the Great War*. Vancouver: UBC Press, 2013.

Inglis, K.S. *Sacred Places: War Memorials in the Australian Landscape*. Melbourne: Melbourne University Press, 2001.

Jalland, Pat. *Death in War and Peace: A History of Loss and Grief in England, 1914–1970*. Oxford: Oxford University Press, 2010.

Jenkins, Dan. "Fight for Hill 70, 15 August 1917." *Esprit de Corps* 7, 9 (2000): 21–24.

Jenkins, Philip. *The Great and Holy War: How World War I Became a Religious Crusade*. New York: Harper One, 2014.

Jones, Edgar, and Simon Wessely. *Shell Shock to PTSD: Military Psychiatry from 1900 to the Gulf War*. New York: Psychology Press, 2005.

Jukes, Geoffrey, Peter Simkins, and Michael Hickey. *The First World War*. New York: Routledge, 2003.

Keegan, John. *The Face of Battle: A Study of Agincourt, Waterloo and the Somme*. London: Pimlico, 1991.

Keelan, Geoff. "Canada's Cultural Mobilization during the First World War and a Case for Canadian War Culture." *Canadian Historical Review* 97, 3 (2016): 377–403.

Keshen, Jeffrey. *Propaganda and Censorship during Canada's Great War*. Edmonton: University of Alberta Press, 1996.

Kulchyski, Peter. "'A Considerable Unrest': F.O. Loft and the League of Indians." *Native Studies Review* 4, 1–2 (1988): 95–117.

Lackenbauer, P. Whitney. "Soldiers Behaving Badly: CEF Soldier 'Rioting' in Canada during the First World War." In *The Apathetic and the Defiant: Case Studies of Canadian Mutiny and Disobedience, 1812–1919*, ed. Craig Leslie Mantle, 195–260. Kingston: Canadian Defence Academy Press, 2007.

Lackenbauer, P. Whitney, R. Scott Sheffield, and Craig Leslie Mantle, eds. *Aboriginal People and the Canadian Military: Historical Perspectives*. Kingston: Canadian Defence Academy Press, 2007.

LaPointe, Arthur. *Soldier of Quebec (1916–1919)*. Trans. R.C. Fetherstonhaugh. Montreal: Editions Edouard Garand, 1931.

Leed, Eric. *No Man's Land: Combat and Identity in World War I*. New York: Cambridge University Press, 1979.

Lloyd, Nicholas. "Hundred Days Offensive." 8 October 2014. International Encyclopedia of the First World War. https://encyclopedia.1914-1918-online.net/article/hundred_days_offensive.

Loez, André. "Tears in the Trenches: A History of Emotions and the Experience of War." In *Uncovered Fields: Perspectives in First World War Studies*, ed. Jenny Macleod and Pierre Purseigle, 211–26. Leiden: Brill Academic, 2004.

Luciuk, Lubomyr. *Searching for Place: Ukrainian Displaced Persons, Canada, and the Migration of Memory*. Toronto: University of Toronto Press, 2000.

Mackersey, Ian. *No Empty Chairs*. London: Phoenix, 2013.

Mann, Susan. *Margaret Macdonald: Imperial Daughter*. Montreal and Kingston: McGill-Queen's University Press, 2005.

–, ed. *The War Diary of Clare Gass*. Montreal and Kingston: McGill-Queen's University Press, 2000.

Mantle, Craig Leslie. "Loyal Mutineers: An Examination of the Connection between Leadership and Disobedience in the Canadian Army since 1885." In *The Unwilling and the Reluctant: Theoretical Perspectives on Disobedience in the Military*, ed. Craig Leslie Mantle, 43–85. Kingston: Canadian Defence Academy Press, 2006.

Marshall, David. "Methodism Embattled: A Reconsideration of the Methodist Church and World War I." *Canadian Historical Review* 66 (March 1985): 48–64.

–. *Secularizing the Faith: Canadian Protestant Clergy and the Crisis of Belief, 1850–1940*. Toronto: University of Toronto Press, 1992.

Masse, Martin. "Vimy Ridge: Can a War Massacre Give Birth to a Nation?" *Le Québécois libre* 102 (13 April 2002). http://www.quebecoislibre.org/020413-2.htm.

Matt, Susan. "Recovering the Invisible: Methods for the Study of the Emotions." In *Doing Emotions History*, ed. Peter Stearns and Susan Matt, 41–54. Urbana: Chicago University Press, 2014.

McClung, Nellie. *The Next of Kin: Those Who Wait and Wonder*. Toronto: Thomas Allen, 1917.

McDonald, George. "Preface." In Talbot Papineau, *The War and Its Influences upon Canada: Address Delivered by the Late Major Talbot Papineau, M.C., to the Canadian Corps School at Pernes in February 1917: Read to the Members of the Canadian Club of Montreal, on Monday, January 26th, 1920, by Mr. E. Languedoc, K.C.*, 1920, 1–2. http://archive.org/details/McGillLibrary-128705-4858.

McGowan, Mark G. "Harvesting the 'Red Vineyard': Catholic Religious Culture in the Canadian Expeditionary Force, 1914–1919." *Historical Studies* 64 (1998): 47–70.

–. *The Imperial Irish: Canada's Irish Catholics Fight the Great War, 1914–1918*. Montreal and Kingston: McGill-Queen's University Press, 2017.

–. "Rendering unto Caesar: Catholics, the State, and the Idea of a Christian Canada." *Canadian Society of Church History Historical Papers* (2011): 65–85.

McKay, Ian, and Jamie Swift. *The Vimy Trap: Or, How We Learned to Stop Worrying and Love the Great War*. Toronto: Between the Lines, 2016.

McPhedran, Ian. "Government Spending More Than $8800 for Every Digger Killed during WW1." News.com.au, 3 September 2015. https://www.news.com.au/national/anzac-day/government-spending-more-than-8800-for-every-digger-killed-during-ww1/news-story/34808367386af87773c8e4326d2a46e8.

McPherson, Kathryn. *Bedside Matters: The Transformation of Canadian Nursing, 1900–1990*. Toronto: University of Toronto Press, 2003.

–. "Carving Out a Past: The Canadian Nurses' Association War Memorial." *Histoire sociale/ Social History* 29, 58 (1996): 417–29.

Meyer, Jessica. *Men of War: Masculinity and the First World War in Britain.* Basingstoke, UK: Palgrave Macmillan, 2009.

Milburn, Geoffrey, and John Herbert, eds. *National Consciousness and the Curriculum: The Canadian Case.* Toronto: Ontario Institute for Studies in Education, 1974.

Millman, Brock. *Polarity, Patriotism, and Dissent in Great War Canada, 1914–1919.* Toronto: University of Toronto Press, 2016.

Minenko, Mark. "Without Just Cause: Canada's First National Internment Operations." In *Canada's Ukrainians: Negotiating an Identity,* ed. Lubomyr Luciuk and Stella Hryniuk, 288–303. Toronto: University of Toronto Press, 1991.

Mitchell, T.J., and G.M. Smith, eds. *History of the Great War Based on Official Documents. Medical Services. Casualties and Medical Statistics of the Great War.* London: His Majesty's Stationery Office, 1931.

Moorehead, Caroline. *Dunant's Dream: War, Switzerland and the History of the Red Cross.* New York: Carroll and Graf, 1998.

Morin-Pelletier, Mélanie. *Briser les ailes de l'ange: Les infirmières militaires canadiennes, 1914–1918.* Outremont: Athéna, 2006.

–. "Héritières de la Grande Guerre: Les infirmières militaires canadiennes durant l'entre-deux-guerres." PhD diss., University of Ottawa, 2010.

Morton, Desmond. "A Canadian Soldier in the Great War: The Experiences of Frank Maheux." *Canadian Military History* 1, 1 (1992): 79–89.

–. *Fight or Pay: Soldiers' Families in the Great War.* Vancouver: UBC Press, 2004.

–. "Kicking and Complaining: Demobilization Riots in the Canadian Expeditionary Force, 1918–1919." *Canadian Historical Review* 61, 3 (1980): 334–60.

–. *When Your Number's Up: The Canadian Soldier in the First World War.* Toronto: Random House, 1993.

Morton, Desmond, and Glenn Wright. *Winning the Second Battle: Canadian Veterans and the Return to Civilian Life, 1915–1930.* Toronto: University of Toronto Press, 1987.

Moss, Mark. *Manliness and Militarism: Educating Young Boys in Ontario for War.* Don Mills: Oxford University Press, 2001.

Nicholson, G.W.L. *Canadian Expeditionary Force, 1914–1919: Official History of the Canadian Army in the First World War.* Ottawa: Department of National Defence, 1962.

Nicholson, Virginia. *Singled Out: How Two Million Women Survived without Men after the First World War.* London: Penguin, 2008.

Niezen, Ronald. "Recognizing Indigenism: Canadian Unity and the International Movement of Indigenous Peoples." *Comparative Studies in Society and History* 42, 1 (2000): 119–48.

Norman, Alison. "'In Defense of the Empire': The Six Nations of the Grand River and the Great War." In *Sisterhood of Suffering and Service: Women and Girls of Canada and Newfoundland during the First World War,* ed. Sarah Glassford and Amy Shaw, 29–50. Vancouver: UBC Press, 2012.

O'Leary, Michael. "Lieut. David Arthur Porter, M.C." The First World War Officers of the Royal Canadian Regiment. Regimental Rogue. http://regimentalrogue.com/rcr_great_war_officers/rcr_offr_porter_da.html.

–. "Lieutenant John Stanley Millett." The First World War Officers of the Royal Canadian Regiment. Regimental Rogue. http://regimentalrogue.com/rcr_great_war_officers/rcr_offr_millett_js.html.

Ontario, Department of Education. *Report of the Minister of Education, Ontario, 1896.* Toronto: Warwick Bros. and Rutter, 1897.

Oram, Gerard. *Death Sentences Passed by Military Courts of the British Army, 1914–1924.* Ed. Julian Putkowski. London: Francis Boutle, 1998.

Osborne, Ken. "Who Killed Canadian History?" *Canadian Historical Review* 80, 1 (March 1999): 114–18.

Parliament of Canada. "Papineau, Louis-Joseph, K.C., B.C.L." https://lop.parl.ca/sites/ParlInfo/default/en_CA/People/Profile?personId=1673.

Pedroncini, Guy. *Les Mutineries de 1917.* Paris: Presses universitaires de France, 1967.

Philpott, William. "Beyond the 'Learning Curve': The British Army's Military Transformation in the First World War." *Commentary,* 10 November 2009. Royal United Services Institute. https://rusi.org/commentary/beyond-learning-curve-british-armys-military-transformation-first-world-war.

–. *Bloody Victory: The Sacrifice on the Somme.* London: Abacus, 2016.

–. *Three Armies on the Somme: The First Battle of the Twentieth Century.* New York: Alfred A. Knopf, 2010.

Pickles, Katie. *Transnational Outrage: The Death and Commemoration of Edith Cavell.* Basingstoke, UK: Palgrave Macmillan, 2007.

Pierce, John. "Constructing Memory: The Vimy Memorial." *Canadian Military History* 1, 1 (1992): 5–8.

Plamper, Jan. *The History of Emotions: An Introduction.* Trans. Keith Tribe. Oxford: Oxford University Press, 2015.

Pollins, Harold. "Jews in the Canadian Armed Forces in the First World War: A Statistical Research Note." *Jewish Journal of Sociology* 46 (2004): 44–58.

Prior, Robin, and Trevor Wilson. *The Somme.* New Haven: Yale University Press, 2005.

Prost, Antoine. "War Losses." 8 October 2014. International Encyclopedia of the First World War. https://encyclopedia.1914-1918-online.net/article/war_losses.

Pugh, James. *The Royal Flying Corps, the Western Front, and Control of the Air, 1914–1918.* Abingdon, UK: Routledge, 2017.

Pugsley, Christopher. *On the Fringe of Hell: New Zealanders and Military Discipline in the First World War.* Toronto: Hodder and Stoughton, 1991.

Purseigle, Pierre, ed. *Warfare and Belligerence: Perspectives in First World War Studies.* Boston: Brill, 2005.

Quiney, Linda J. "Gendering Patriotism: Canadian Volunteer Nurses as the Female 'Soldiers' of the Great War." In *Sisterhood of Suffering and Service: Women and Girls of Canada and Newfoundland during the First World War,* ed. Sarah Glassford and Amy Shaw, 103–25. Vancouver: UBC Press, 2012.

Raleigh, Walter. *The War in the Air.* Vol. 1. Oxford: Clarendon Press, 1922.

Rawling, Bill. *Surviving Trench Warfare: Technology and the Canadian Corps, 1914–1918.* Toronto: University of Toronto Press, 1992.

Report of the Ministry, Overseas Military Forces of Canada, 1918. London: His Majesty's Stationery Office, 1918. https://www.canada.ca/en/department-national-defence/services/military-history/history-heritage/official-military-history-lineages/official-histories/book-1918-overseas.html.

Reynolds, Mark. "The Guelph Raid: When Police Routed Alleged World War I Draft Dodgers – Including a Cabinet Minister's Son – In a Catholic Seminary in the Heart of Orange Ontario, a National Scandal Erupted." *The Beaver* 82, 1 (February–March 2002): 25–30.

Richards, Samuel J. "Ministry of Propaganda: Canadian Methodists, Empire, and Loyalty in World War I." Master's thesis, Salisbury University, 2007.

Ricoeur, Paul. *Memory, History, Forgetting.* Trans. Kathleen Blamey and David Pellauer. Chicago: University of Chicago Press, 2004.

Riseman, Noah, and Timothy C. Winegard. "Indigenous Experience of War (British Dominions)." *International Encyclopedia of the First World War*. https://encyclopedia.1914-1918-online.net/article/indigenous_experience_of_war_british_dominions.

Roper, Michael. *The Secret Battle: Emotional Survival in the Great War*. Manchester: Manchester University Press, 2009.

Rosenzweig, Roy, and David Thelen. *The Presence of the Past: Popular Uses of History in American Life*. New York: Columbia University Press, 1998.

Rutherdale, Robert. *Hometown Horizons: Local Responses to Canada's Great War*. Vancouver: UBC Press, 2004.

Samuel, Raphael. *Theatres of Memory: Past and Present in Contemporary Culture*. New York: Verso, 1994.

Sawell, Steven, ed. *Into the Cauldron: Experiences of a CEF Infantry Officer during the Great War*. Privately printed, 2009.

Scates, Bruce S. "Manufacturing Memory at Gallipoli." In *War Memory and Popular Culture: Essays on Modes of Remembrance and Commemoration*, ed. Michael Keren and Holger H. Herwig, 57–76. Jefferson, NC: McFarland, 2009.

Schreiber, Shane B. *Shock Army of the British Empire: The Canadian Corps in the Last Hundred Days of the War*. Westport: Praeger, 1997.

Schweitzer, Jason. *The Cross and the Trenches: Religious Faith and Doubt amongst the British and American Great War Soldiers*. London: Praeger, 2003.

Scott, Frederick George. *The Great War as I Saw It*. Toronto: F.D. Goodchild, 1922.

Seal, Graham. *The Soldiers' Press: Trench Journals in the First World War*. London: Palgrave Macmillan, 2013.

Segal, Nancy L. *Entwined Lives: Twins and What They Tell Us about Human Behavior*. New York: Dutton, 1999.

–. "Twins: The Finest Natural Experiment." *Personality and Individual Differences* 49 (2010): 317–23.

Segal, Nancy L., and T.J. Bouchard. "Grief Intensity Following the Loss of a Twin and Other Close Relatives: Test of Kinship-Genetic Hypothesis." *Human Biology* 65 (1993): 87–105.

Segal, Nancy L., T.J. Bouchard, S.M. Wilson, and D.G. Gitlin. "Comparative Grief Experiences of Bereaved Twins and Other Bereaved Relatives." *Personality and Individual Differences* 18, 4 (1995): 511–24.

Sharpe, Chris. "Enlistment in the Canadian Expeditionary Force, 1914–1918: A Reevaluation." *Canadian Military History* 24, 1 (2015): 17–60.

Shaw, Amy J. *Crisis of Conscience: Conscientious Objection in Canada during the First World War*. Vancouver: UBC Press, 2009.

Sheffield, G.D. *Leadership in the Trenches: Officer-Man Relations, Morale, and Discipline in the British Army in the Era of the First World War*. London: Macmillan, 2000.

Sheffield, Gary. *Forgotten Victory – The First World War: Myths and Realities*. London: Review, 2002.

–. "Vimy Ridge and the Battle of Arras: A British Perspective." In *Vimy Ridge: A Canadian Reassessment*, ed. Geoffrey Hayes, Andrew Iarocci, and Mike Bechthold, 15–29. Waterloo: Wilfrid Laurier University Press, 2007.

Sheffield, R. Scott. "Indifference, Difference and Assimilation: Aboriginal People in Canadian Military Practice." In *Aboriginal Peoples and the Canadian Military: Historical Perspectives*, ed. P. Whitney Lackenbauer and Craig Leslie Mantle, 57–71. Kingston: Canadian Defence Academy Press, 2007.

Simkins, Peter. *From the Somme to Victory: The British Army's Experience on the Western Front, 1916–1918.* Barnsley, UK: Praetorian Press, 2014.

Simons, Jon, and John Louis Lucaites. *In/Visible War: The Culture of War in Twenty-First-Century America.* New Brunswick, NJ: Rutgers University Press, 2017.

Smith, Keith D. *Liberalism, Surveillance, and Resistance: Indigenous Communities in Western Canada, 1887–1927.* Edmonton: University of Athabasca Press, 2009.

Smith, Leonard V. *Between Mutiny and Obedience: The Case of the French Fifth Infantry Division during World War I.* Princeton: Princeton University Press, 1994.

–. "The 'Culture de guerre' and French Historiography of the Great War of 1914–1918." *History Compass* 5, 6 (2007): 1967–79.

Snape, Michael. *God and the British Soldier: Religion and the British Army in the First and Second World Wars.* New York: Routledge, 2005.

Socknat, Thomas. *Witness against War: Pacifism in Canada, 1900–1945.* Toronto: University of Toronto Press, 1987.

Special Joint Committee of the Senate and the House of Commons Appointed to Examine and Consider the Indian Act. *Minutes of Proceedings and Evidence.* Ottawa: King's Printer, 1946.

–. *Minutes of Proceedings and Evidence.* Ottawa: King's Printer, 1947.

Spears, Tom. "'Shame Shame on You!' Hundreds Complain to Veterans Affairs about Disorganized Vimy Ridge Ceremony." *National Post*, 11 December 2017.

Srigley, Katrina, and Stacey Zembrzycki. "Remembering Family, Analyzing Home: Oral History and the Family." In "Remembering Family, Analyzing Home: Oral History and the Family." Special issue, *Oral History Forum* 29 (2009): 1–19.

"Statement by the Prime Minister of Canada on the 100th Anniversary of the Battle of Vimy Ridge." 9 April 2017. http://pm.gc.ca/eng/news/2017/04/09/statement-prime-minister-canada-100th-anniversary-battle-vimy-ridge.

Stewart, William. "The Barrier and the Damage Done Converting the Canadian Mounted Rifles to Infantry, December 1915." *Canadian Military History* 24, 1 (2015): 285–319.

–. *Canadians on the Somme, 1916.* London: Helion, 2017.

Story, Eric. "'The Awakening Has Come': Canadian First Nations in the Great War Era, 1914–1932." *Canadian Military History* 24, 2 (2015): 11–35.

Strange, Julie-Marie. "'She Cried a Very Little': Death, Grief and Mourning in Working-Class Culture, 1880–1914." *Social History* 27, 2 (May 2002): 143–61.

Street, Kori. "Patriotic, Not Permanent: Attitudes about Women's Making Bombs and Being Bankers." In *Sisterhood of Suffering and Service: Women and Girls of Canada and Newfoundland during the First World War,* ed. Sarah Glassford and Amy Shaw, 148–70. Vancouver: UBC Press, 2012.

Strickland, Tod. "Creating Combat Leaders in the Canadian Corps: The Experiences of Lieutenant-Colonel Agar Adamson." In *Great War Commands: Historical Perspectives on Canadian Army Leadership, 1914–1918,* ed. Andrew Godefroy, 201–38. Kingston: Canadian Defence Academy Press, 2010.

Strong-Boag, Veronica. "Who Killed Canadian History?" *Historical Studies in Education* 11, 2 (October 1999): 283–85.

Summerby, Janice. *Native Soldiers – Foreign Battlefields.* Ottawa: Veterans Affairs Canada, 2005.

Sutherland, Neil. *Children in English-Canadian Society: Framing the Twentieth-Century Consensus.* 2nd ed. Waterloo: Wilfrid Laurier University Press, 2000.

Swyripa, Frances, and John Herd Thompson, eds. *Loyalties in Conflict: Ukrainians in Canada during the Great War.* Edmonton: Canadian Institute of Ukrainian Studies, 1983.

Talbot, Robert. "'It Would Be Best to Leave Us Alone': First Nations Responses to the Canadian War Effort, 1914–18." *Journal of Canadian Studies* 45, 1 (Winter 2011): 90–120.

Tancredy, C.M., and R.C. Fraley. "The Nature of Adult Twin Relationships: An Attachment-Theoretical Perspective." *Journal of Personality and Social Psychology* 90, 1 (2006): 78–93.

Taylor, John Leonard. *Canadian Indian Policy during the Inter-War Years, 1918–1939.* Ottawa: Indian and Northern Affairs Canada, 1984.

Teichroew, Allen. "World War I and the Mennonite Migration to Canada to Avoid the Draft." *Mennonite Quarterly Review* 45 (July 1971): 219–49.

"Text of Prime Minister Stephen Harper's Speech." *CTV News*, 9 April 2007. http://www.ctvnews.ca/text-of-prime-minister-stephen-harper-s-speech-1.236701.

Thompson, John Herd. *The Harvests of War: The Prairie West, 1914–1918.* Toronto: McClelland and Stewart, 1978.

Thomson, W. Stewart. "The Late Major Papineau." *The Globe*, 7 November 1917, 6.

Titley, E. Brian. *The Indian Commissioners: Agents of the State and Indian Policy in Canada's Prairie West.* Edmonton: University of Alberta Press, 2009.

–. *A Narrow Vision: Duncan Campbell Scott and the Administration of Indian Affairs in Canada.* Vancouver: UBC Press, 1986.

Todman, Dan. *The Great War: Myth and Memory.* London: Continuum, 2005.

Toman, Cynthia. "'Help Us, Serve England': First World War Military Nursing and National Identities." *Canadian Bulletin of Medical History* 3, 1 (2013): 143–66.

–. "'My Chance Has Come at Last!' The Weston Hospital, the Women's Christian Temperance Union, and Indian Nurses in Canada, 1917–1929." *Native Studies Review* 19, 2 (2010): 95–119.

–. *Sister Soldiers of the Great War: The Nurses of the Canadian Army Medical Corps.* Vancouver: UBC Press, 2016.

Tosh, John. "What Should Historians Do with Masculinity? Reflections on Nineteenth-Century Britain." *History Workshop* 38 (1 January 1994): 179–202.

Tunstall, Graydon A. "The Military Collapse of the Central Powers." 30 April 2015. International Encyclopedia of the First World War. https://encyclopedia.1914-1918-online.net/article/the_military_collapse_of_the_central_powers.

Van Die, Marguerite, ed. *Religion and Public Life in Canada: Historical and Comparative Perspectives.* Toronto: University of Toronto Press, 2001.

Vance, Jonathan F. *Death So Noble: Memory, Meaning, and the First World War.* Vancouver: UBC Press, 1997.

–. *A Township at War.* Waterloo: Wilfrid Laurier University Press, 2018.

VanWyngarden, Greg. *Jagdstaffel 2 'Boelcke.'* Oxford: Osprey, 2007.

Veterans Affairs Canada. *Canada Remembers: The 1st Newfoundland Regiment and the Battle of the Somme.* Ottawa: Minister of Veterans Affairs, 2006.

Walker, James W. St. G. "Race and Recruitment in World War I: Enlistment of Visible Minorities in the Canadian Expeditionary Force." *Canadian Historical Review* 70 (March 1989): 1–26.

War Office. *Manual of Military Law.* London: His Majesty's Stationery Office, 1914.

Watson, Alexander. *Enduring the Great War: Combat, Morale and Collapse in the German and British Armies, 1914–1918.* Cambridge: Cambridge University Press, 2008.

–. "Self-Deception and Survival: Mental Coping Strategies on the Western Front, 1914–18." *Journal of Contemporary History* 41, 2 (2006): 247–68.

Watson, Alexander, and Patrick Porter. "Bereaved and Aggrieved: Combat Motivation and the Ideology of Sacrifice in the First World War." *Historical Research* 83, 219 (February 2010): 146–64.

Wellington, Jennifer. *Exhibiting War: The Great War, Museums, and Memory in Britain, Canada, and Australia.* Cambridge: Cambridge University Press, 2017.

Westcott, Clare. "The Hero I Never Knew." *Toronto Star,* 11 November 1994.

–. "No Medal for My Father." 4 November 2007. Canada Free Press. http://canadafreepress.com/article/no-medal-for-my-father.

Whitaker, Reg. "Harper's History: Does the Right Hand Know What the Other Right Hand Is Doing?" *Labour* 73 (Spring 2014): 218–21.

Wilkinson, Alan. "Changing English Attitudes to Death in the Two World Wars." In *The Changing Face of Death: Historical Accounts of Death and Disposal,* ed. Peter C. Jupp and Glennys Howarth, 149–63. London: Macmillan, 1997.

Wilson, Fay. "Booze, Temperance, and Soldiers on the Home Front: The Unraveling of the Image of the Idealised Soldier in Canada." *Canadian Military History* 25, 1 (2016). http://scholars.wlu.ca/cmh/vol25/iss1/16.

Wilson, Jason. *Soldiers of Song: The Dumbells and Other Canadian Concert Parties of the First World War.* Waterloo: Wilfrid Laurier University Press, 2012.

Wilson, Ross. "The Burial of the Dead: The British Army on the Western Front, 1914–18." *War and Society* 31, 1 (2012): 22–41.

Wilson, Trevor. *The Myriad Faces of War: Britain and the Great War.1914–1918,* London: Polity Press, 1986.

Windsor, Lee, Marc Milner, and Roger Sarty. *Loyal Gunners: The History of 3rd Field Artillery Regiment, Royal Canadian Artillery and New Brunswick's Artillery, 1893–2012.* Waterloo: Wilfrid Laurier University Press, 2016.

Winegard, Timothy C. *For King and Kanata: Canadian Indians and the First World War.* Winnipeg: University of Manitoba Press, 2012.

Winter, Denis. *Death's Men: Soldiers of the Great War.* London: Penguin Books, 1979.

–. *The First of the Few: Fighter Pilots of the First World War.* London: Allen Lane, 1982.

Winter, Jay. "Commemorating Catastrophe: 100 Years On." *War and Society* 36, 4 (2017): 239–55.

–. "Museums and the Representation of War." *Museum and Society* 10, 3 (November 2012): 150–63.

–. "Producing the Television Series *The Great War and the Shaping of the Twentieth Century.*" *Profession* (1999): 15–26.

–. *Remembering War: The Great War between Memory and History in the Twentieth Century.* New Haven: Yale University Press, 2006.

–. "Shell Shock." In *The Cambridge History of the First World War,* Vol. 3, 310–33. Cambridge: Cambridge University Press, 2014.

–. *Sites of Memory, Sites of Mourning: The Great War in European Cultural History.* 2nd ed. Cambridge: Cambridge University Press, 2014.

Wohl, Robert. *The Generation of 1914.* Cambridge, MA: Harvard University Press, 1979.

Wood, James. "History and Memory of the Great War: A Review Essay." *BC Studies* 191 (Autumn 2016): 123–32.

–. *Militia Myths: Ideas of the Canadian Citizen Soldier, 1896–1921.* Vancouver: UBC Press, 2010.

Wurtele, W.G. "Cambrai 1918." *Pro Patria,* July 1979. Regimental Rogue. http://regimental rogue.com/rcr_history/1914-1919/cambrai_1918_wurtele.htm.

Yeats, V.M. *Winged Victory.* New York: H. Smith and H. Hass, 1934.

Contributors

Graham Broad is an associate professor of history in King's University College at Western University.

Cynthia Comacchio is a professor in the Department of History at Wilfrid Laurier University.

Kyle Falcon has a PhD in History from the Wilfrid Laurier University and works at the Laurier Centre for Military, Strategic and Disarmament Studies.

Peter Farrugia is an associate professor in the History program and is co-ordinator of the Humanities with Leadership Foundations program at Wilfrid Laurier University.

Sarah Glassford is a social historian and an archivist in the Leddy Library at the University of Windsor.

Evan J. Habkirk is a historian and lecturer in the Indigenous Studies program at the University of British Columbia, Okanagan Campus.

Geoffrey Hayes is a professor in the Department of History at the University of Waterloo.

Gordon L. Heath, FRHistS, is a professor of Christian history at McMaster Divinity College in Hamilton, Ontario. He is also Centenary Chair in World Christianity and director of the Canadian Baptist Archives.

Teresa Iacobelli is an independent scholar from Ottawa, Ontario.

Jonathan F. Vance is the J.B. Smallman Chair in the Department of History, Western University.

Lee Windsor is Fredrik Eaton Chair in Canadian Army Studies and an associate professor of history at the Gregg Centre for the Study of War and Society, University of New Brunswick.

Index

Studies in Canadian Military History

Wendy Cuthbertson, *Labour Goes to War: The CIO and the Construction of a New Social Order, 1939–45*

P. Whitney Lackenbauer, *The Canadian Rangers: A Living History*

Teresa Iacobelli, *Death or Deliverance: Canadian Courts Martial in the Great War*

Graham Broad, *A Small Price to Pay: Consumer Culture on the Canadian Home Front, 1939–45*

Peter Kasurak, *A National Force: The Evolution of Canada's Army, 1950–2000*

Isabel Campbell, *Unlikely Diplomats: The Canadian Brigade in Germany, 1951–64*

Richard M. Reid, *African Canadians in Union Blue: Volunteering for the Cause in the Civil War*

Andrew B. Godefroy, *In Peace Prepared: Innovation and Adaptation in Canada's Cold War Army*

Nic Clarke, *Unwanted Warriors: The Rejected Volunteers of the Canadian Expeditionary Force*

David Zimmerman, *Maritime Command Pacific: The Royal Canadian Navy's West Coast Fleet in the Early Cold War*

Cynthia Toman, *Sister Soldiers of the Great War: The Nurses of the Canadian Army Medical Corps*

Daniel Byers, *Zombie Army: The Canadian Army and Conscription in the Second World War*

J.L. Granatstein, *The Weight of Command: Voices of Canada's Second World War Generals and Those Who Knew Them*

Colin McCullough, *Creating Canada's Peacekeeping Past*

Douglas E. Delaney and Serge Marc Durflinger, eds., *Capturing Hill 70: Canada's Forgotten Battle of the First World War*

Brandon R. Dimmel, *Engaging the Line: How the Great War Shaped the Canada–US Border*

Meghan Fitzpatrick, *Invisible Scars: Mental Trauma and the Korean War*

Patrick M. Dennis, *Reluctant Warriors: Canadian Conscripts and the Great War*

Frank Maas, *The Price of Alliance: The Politics and Procurement of Leopard Tanks for Canada's NATO Brigade*

Geoffrey Hayes, *Crerar's Lieutenants: Inventing the Canadian Junior Army Officer, 1939–45*

Richard Goette, *Sovereignty and Command in Canada–US Continental Air Defence, 1940–57*

Geoff Jackson, *The Empire on the Western Front: The British 62nd and Canadian 4th Divisions in Battle*

Steve Marti and William John Pratt, eds., *Fighting with the Empire: Canada, Britain, and Global Conflict, 1867–1947*

Steve Marti, *For Home and Empire: Voluntary Mobilization in Australia, Canada, and New Zealand during the First World War*

Peter Kasurak, *Canada's Mechanized Infantry: The Evolution of a Combat Arm, 1920–2012*

Sarah Glassford and Amy Shaw, eds., *Making the Best of It: Women and Girls of Canada and Newfoundland During the Second World War*

Alex Souchen, *War Junk: Munitions Disposal and Postwar Reconstruction in Canada*

Tim Cook and Jack Granatstein, eds., *Canada 1919: A Nation Shaped by War*

Arthur W. Gullachsen, *An Army of Never-Ending Strength: Reinforcing the Canadians in Northwest Europe, 1944–45*

STUDIES IN CANADIAN MILITARY HISTORY
Published by UBC Press in association with the Canadian War Museum